The Wild Black Region

The Wild Black Region

Badenoch 1750–1800

David Taylor

John Donald

First published in Great Britain in 2016 by
John Donald, an imprint of Birlinn Ltd

West Newington House
10 Newington Road
Edinburgh
EH9 1QS

www.birlinn.co.uk

ISBN: 978 1 906566 98 2

The publishers gratefully acknowledge the
support of the Scotland Inheritance Fund
towards the publication of this book.

British Library Cataloguing-in-Publication Data
A catalogue record for this book is available
on request from the British Library.

Typeset by Mark Blackadder

Printed and bound in Britain by TJ International Ltd, Padstow, Cornwall

For Ailsa

'But the view from the Corryarrick was neither great, beautiful, nor picturesque. On the south it looked into the wild black region of Badenoch'

John Leyden,
Journal of a Tour in the Highlands and Western Islands of Scotland in 1800

Contents

List of Illustrations and Tables

Figures

Black and white plate section

Colour plate section

Tables

Foreword

All around the world, during the eighteenth and nineteenth centuries, older modes of social and economic organisation were displaced by the beginnings of the highly commercialised global order we continue to live with today. What happened in the Highlands of Scotland during the fifty or so years following the Battle of Culloden was one aspect of this general process. Where lives had been lived (for ages as it seemed) within the kin-based frameworks bound up with clans and clanship, new influences – having to do, in particular, with opportunities to make and spend money – were more and more at play. As a result, everyday fundamentals of all sorts were revolutionised – among them the way that land was thought about, made use of and laid out.

Partly because of their being written mostly from perspectives external to the localities where 'modernisation' of this type occurred, accounts of it often downplay the role of local actors in the wider drama. Hence the tendency for indigenous populations like Africans, Native Americans, or (for that matter) Highlanders to be relegated to bit players in the story of how their homelands came to enter into trading and other relationships with faraway centres of industry and empire. Described for ages as 'backward', even 'savage', most such populations, even when those earlier terms became unacceptable, were thought widely to have had little meaningful say in what happened to them. They were, it was said or implied, the essentially passive victims of forces beyond their control – people whose outlook and circumstances, or so it was assumed, precluded the possibility of their evolving their own distinctive accommodations with an aggressively emergent capitalism.

David Taylor has no truck with that approach. Here he shows, and shows convincingly, that eighteenth-century Highlanders, certainly those central to his narrative, were every bit as capable as any south country farmer or businessman of taking advantage of the openings created by an expanding national economy and by the United Kingdom's imperial ambitions. The Highland communities David describes and analyses – and no other set of post-Culloden communities has been subjected to such searching scrutiny – were in no way lacking in initiative, enterprise and innovation. Particularly to the fore in this regard were tacksmen. Constituting, in effect, clanship's gentry or officer class, this group has over the years been dismissed – whether by contemporary commentators or historians – as so hopelessly conservative and so wedded to outmoded ways of doing things as to be, by definition, surplus to a commercial civilisation's requirements. Taylor, however, shows that this is drastically to over-simplify. His pages are replete with tacksmen who, instead of opposing change and rejecting modernity, turn themselves into buccaneering entrepreneurs of exactly the sort the Gaelic-speaking Highlands are still sometimes said to have always lacked. Where there was a guinea to be earned from marketing cattle or raising troops for service in late eighteenth-century Britain's numerous wars, there were tacksmen, David Taylor demonstrates, practically falling over themselves in their eagerness to make and to pocket it.

Or so it was at any rate in Badenoch, the district examined in this book. Despite its being traversed today by the main rail and road routes into the Highlands from the south, Badenoch, in essence a couple of straths or river valleys bounded by the Cairngorms on one side and the Monadhliath on the other, has attracted far less attention from historians than, for instance, the West Highlands, Skye, the Outer Isles and Sutherland. In David Taylor, however, Badenoch has found someone ideally equipped to make good this deficiency – not least because of his deep understanding of the place's natural environment.

Historians, Simon Schama comments at the start of *Landscape and Memory*, his pathbreaking study of how people have responded aesthetically to their physical surroundings, mostly think themselves 'supposed to reach the past always through texts, occasionally through images; things that are safely caught in the bell jar of academic convention'. But influenced by one of his own teachers, whom he describes as 'an intellectual hell-raiser . . . [who] had always insisted on directly experiencing "a sense of place" [and] of using "the archive of the feet"',[1] Schama embarked on first-hand explorations of the landscapes he then wrote about. David Taylor has done the same. During more than thirty years spent teaching history and modern studies at Kingussie High School, in the heart of Badenoch, he acquainted himself – and, by way of school fieldtrips, his students too – with the painstakingly cultivated inbye ground, the river embankments, the homestead sites and the now deserted hill shielings that feature to such striking effect on ensuing pages.

In order to repopulate (as it were) Badenoch's landscapes with the folk who lived among them some 250 years ago, David has more recently conducted extensive research in the National Records of Scotland, Scotland's National Library, and other (both public and private) repositories. The archival collections he found there have allowed him to construct all manner of intricate – and highly revealing – analyses of farm rents, cattle prices, weather patterns and much else. Equally impressive, however, is the remarkable extent to which David has been able to restore to life – the phrase is not too strong – memorable characters of the kind who, in a great deal of history writing, are lost to view in overarching generalities. Reorganising landholdings in the vicinity of Loch Laggan we find a hard-bitten army chaplain whose daily pint of port wine, he insists, is downed 'to cure [his] Stomach of Flatulency'. The many surviving letters of two of eighteenth-century Badenoch's leading factors reveal them to have taken – in a way factors are not usually believed to have done – a close and compassionate interest in the people in their charge. A widow managing an inn at Ruthven asks for a rent rebate because the Jacobite army's destruction of the barracks in 1746 has caused a 'decay of consumption' of liquor. A man in his late eighties recalls how, many years before, he had walked the Drumochter march or boundary between two estates and how his companion, whose business it was to know precisely where that boundary lay, had given the then younger man 'a Blow on the side of the head at different parts of the March, that he might remember the March more particularly'. And here, there and everywhere in eighteenth-century Badenoch (or so it sometimes appears) is the key figure of John Dow (*Iain Dubh*) Macpherson, otherwise 'the Black Officer'; tacksman, soldier, recruiting officer, farmer and drover; a man whose dizzying speculations and risk-taking give the lie to any lingering notion that his was a society sunk in sloth, conformity and caution.

Supplying John Dow with the cattle he exported south across Drumochter were farming families who, David Taylor shows, knew exactly how to extract maximum value from the territory they occupied. Today, when the greater part of Badenoch is inside the Cairngorm National Park, much of the district is considered to be – and sometimes imagined to have always been – 'wild land'. There was next to no 'wild' land in the Badenoch this book investigates. Then, David establishes, virtually every acre between the River Spey and high-altitude mountain corries was subjected to an intricate grazing regime which his sources have enabled him to describe and explain more illuminatingly than has ever been done before. As in most of the rest of the eighteenth-century world, farming in Badenoch was – thanks to flood, frost and snow as well as occasional price collapses – a precarious business. But it was in no way primitive or haphazard. In their careful utilisation of the Badenoch high country, indeed, John Dow Macpherson and his contemporaries were arguably better and more efficient land managers than lots of their more recent successors.

The ground-breaking insights this book offers into Highland history make it important. It is also a good and entertaining read. All this, and more besides, became evident to us during the period when, following his retirement, David Taylor was a postgraduate student in the Centre for History at the University of the Highlands and Islands. There we were the supervisors of the research that resulted first in David gaining a PhD and then in his turning his doctoral thesis into the narrative that follows. During our time together, we learned more from David than he learned from us. But it was our pleasure as well our privilege to have been associated with his researches – just as it is equally our pleasure and privilege to commend David's findings to the wider audience they well deserve.

James Hunter
Marjory Harper
Elizabeth Ritchie

1 S. Schama, *Landscape and Memory* (New York: Knopf, 1995), 24.

Acknowledgements

I must firstly thank the University of the Highlands and Islands for enabling me to undertake a PhD on my home territory – there is nowhere I would rather have pursued my studies and nowhere that I could have been in better hands. I am particularly indebted to my supervisory team, Jim Hunter, Marjory Harper, Elizabeth Ritchie, and in the early days, Karen Cullen, for their unstinting enthusiasm, encouragement and perceptive criticism. Thanks are also due to David Worthington, Director of the Centre for History, for his help over administrative issues, and to Alison MacWilliam and all the other department members for their friendship and support.

Particular thanks are also due to the Gaelic Society of Inverness for financial assistance during my studies. Many institutions have contributed to this book, and my appreciation goes to all the staff who have assisted my research in the National Records of Scotland, the National Library of Scotland, Inverness Public Library, the Highland Archive Centre in Inverness, Aberdeen Art Gallery and Museums, the Sir Duncan Rice Library in Aberdeen and West Sussex Records Office. Certain individuals merit particular mention: Pete Finlayson and Tessa Spencer for their patience and unstinting help in the old West Register House; Mary Robertson at the Huntington Library in California for tracing documents in the Loudoun collection; Rachel Chisholm for access to the Highland Folk Museum archives and library; Angus Macpherson for access to the Sir Thomas Macpherson archive; Jane Anderson for her help in the Blair Castle archives; the Russells in Ballindalloch Castle for allowing me unrestricted use of their invaluable records; Eve Boyle of the Royal Commission on the Ancient and Historical Monuments of Scotland for much helpful advice and information during fieldwork sessions; and not least my local Kingussie librarians, Kathryn Main and Andrea Newbery, not only for coping with innumerable obscure requests, but for facilitating access arrangements to reference texts.

This book owes much to the support and help of many local people. Local genealogist Mary Mackenzie has been invaluable not just in identifying innumerable Macphersons and Mackintoshes, but in correcting many misunderstandings. Ross Noble, former curator of the Highland Folk Museum, has always been ready to help with advice on local issues, explaining the intricacies of old settlements and landscapes during our many field visits, while also offering perceptive comments on the entire manuscript. Richard and Sally Spencer produced a wonderful old estate map that proved invaluable to my research, while Graham Grant, Iain McGillivray, Campbell Slimon and Jamie Williamson have given freely of their expertise on land use and on sites of local interest, as indeed have many others too numerous to mention. Very special thanks are due to Nicki Gow and Dave Stewart for their patience and assistance with more technical issues.

On the broader historical front I owe a huge debt of gratitude, going back more than forty years, to Bill Ferguson in the Scottish History Department in Edinburgh University who not only inspired my love of research and writing but shaped my understanding of historical process. More recently I have benefited greatly from the research and advice of other local and Highland historians: George Dixon who has generously shared his extensive knowledge of the Gordon papers with me; Alan G Macpherson, the clan historian, whose own PhD thesis provided the starting point for my own research and who has helped with queries from afar; Maureen Hammond for sharing her research into Badenoch textiles; and particularly Matthew Dziennik and Malcolm Bangor-Jones who have helped explain many of the more obscure issues of Highland history. While all of the above have helped shape the ideas in this book, any errors, misunderstandings and controversial conclusions are entirely my own responsibility.

Because my research was heavily based in Edinburgh, this book owes a huge debt to the generosity of old friends in providing accommodation, food and the occasional beverage to recharge the research batteries – many thanks to Hamish, Chris and Stewart, Agnes and Bruce, Sarah and Matthew. Thanks are also due to my family: my daughters and grandsons for reminding me there is life beyond history, but most particularly to my wife, Ailsa, not just for her tremendous support and encouragement throughout the last five years, but for reading and re-reading every chapter, helping to iron out all the little errors while clarifying my thoughts by asking awkward questions. I would finally like to thank all those former pupils, parents, colleagues and friends in Badenoch who have so enthusiastically encouraged my endeavours and shared their knowledge and love of the area with me.

The process of converting my PhD thesis into this book would not have been possible without the very generous financial support of the Scotland Inheritance Fund to whom I owe an immense debt of gratitude. Sincere thanks are also due to all the staff at Birlinn, particularly Mairi Sutherland, and Jackie Henrie, for steering me through the intricacies of publication. Thanks are also due to all those who supplied illustrations for reproduction, who are acknowledged in individual captions, and to Jim Lewis for preparation of the maps.

David Taylor

Explanatory Notes

Quotations from documents have been left with their original spelling and punctuation. Because eighteenth-century spelling and punctuation were totally random and inconsistent, the use of [sic] for every 'error' seems superfluous, especially as in most cases the meaning is perfectly intelligible. Where meanings are not clear, explanations have been included in square brackets. Words like farm were often spelt as ffarm, and the double ff has been preserved in quotations. Though the summer pastures were in earlier times spelt as sheilings or shealings, the more modern form shielings has been preferred unless within a quotation. Italics within quotations are original unless otherwise specified.

Place-names have been standardised to the Ordnance Survey map spellings, but names within quotations or not to be found on modern maps have been left in their original form. The only exception is the use of Benchar (pronounced Benachar) for the modern Banchor because this was the form used consistently through the eighteenth century when referring to either farm or family. Significantly, the neighbouring glen was always differentiated, being written in its current form, Glen Banchor (Banachor). The name Glen Banchor refers to the whole geographical glen; the form Glenbanchor is used for the specific half-davoch/farm of that name within the glen. Similarly, Loch Laggan refers to the loch and surrounding area, while Lochlaggan is used for the estate. Though the terms Lowlands or Low Country generally mean the area south of the Highland line, they also broadly include the eastern lowlands of the Moray Firth hinterland. The latter is specifically designated as such where appropriate.

Highland surnames (Mc/Mac) in the eighteenth century were completely random, and these have generally been standardised into the form Macpherson or Mackintosh, unless there was a clear reason for not doing so. Because of the inevitable risk of confusion over the many similar clan names, particularly Macphersons, they are usually identified in a specific way as in John Dow, or Captain John, or by the name of their farm.

Money is given in pre-decimalisation pounds sterling (£ s d) unless otherwise stated. For those not familiar with this currency, there were 20s (shillings) to £1, and 12d (pennies) to 1s. Decimal equivalents are given only where it helps to explain the relationship between monetary sums. Scots money occasionally appears in the primary sources: £1 Scots was one-twelfth £1 sterling; one merk was two-thirds of £1 Scots. It is impossible to convert eighteenth-century sterling sums into exact modern values, but a multiplication factor of around sixty is required to achieve a rough equivalent.

Principal Characters

The Gordons
    Cosmo: 3rd Duke; died 1752.
    Katherine: 3rd Duchess; ran estate after Cosmo's death until 1764.
    Alexander: 4th Duke, born 1743; took over estate 1764; died 1827.
    Lady Jane Maxwell: 4th Duchess; married Alexander 1767; estranged during 1790s; died 1812.

    Gordon estate officials
        Charles Gordon: Duke's Edinburgh lawyer.
        James Ross: chamberlain/treasurer/manager of Gordon estates at Fochabers 1769–82.
        William Tod: factor in Badenoch and Lochaber 1769–82; farmed at Gordon Hall; overall factor at Fochabers after Ross's death.

    Land surveyors for Duke of Gordon
        George Brown.
        Alexander Taylor.
        George Taylor.
        John Williams: mineralogist.

Grant
    Mrs Ann Grant of Laggan: author of *Letters from the Mountains*; minister's wife; farmer.
    Elizabeth Grant of Rothiemurchus: daughter of John Peter Grant, an Edinburgh lawyer who became laird of Rothiemurchus; author of *Memoirs of a Highland Lady*, relating to early nineteenth century though written much later.

General James Grant: laird of Ballindalloch; governor of Florida; important figure in British military establishment; slave and plantation owner; sister Grace married George Macpherson of Invereshie.
Patrick Grant: laird of Rothiemurchus estate.
Sir James Grant of Grant: chief of Clan Grant; improving landowner in neighbouring Strathspey.

Macdonell/Macdonald

These name variants were completely interchangeable in the eighteenth century. The form Macdonell has generally been used for the Aberarder family.
Ranald: tacksman of Aberarder on Loch Laggan's northern shore; evicted 1770; then tacksman of Moy at west end of the loch.
Alexander: tacksman of Tullochroam adjoining Aberarder; brother of Ranald; evicted 1770; moved to Garvamore and then Garvabeg.
Alexander: son of the above Alexander; tacksman of Garvabeg until death 1808; an important drover.

McHardy

John: father was Laggan schoolmaster, mother from Skye; brought in as tacksman of Crathiecroy 1770; improver; later established lint mill and bleachfield at Kingussie; bankrupt 1790s.

Mackintosh

Balnespick

William: pre-1748, laird of Balnespick; sold his estate to Invereshie 1748; became tacksman of Dunachton; the 'Old Balnespick' of I.F. Grant's *Every-day Life on an Old Highland Farm*.
Captain Lachlan: son of 'Old Balnespick'; tacksman of various farms in Laggan, and then Kincraig and Dunachton.
William: Lachlan's son; tacksman of Dunachton till end of century.

Raitts

Brigadier William Mackintosh of Borlum: laird of Raitts; early agricultural improver; Jacobite leader 1715, imprisoned in Edinburgh Castle; author of *An Essay on Ways and Means for Inclosing, Fallowing, Planting, etc.*
Shaw Mackintosh: the Brigadier's son; laird of Raitts.

Edward Mackintosh: Shaw's son; bankrupted the estate; notorious highway robber; fled Britain 1773.

Kincraig

Helen (Nelly) Mackintosh: tacksman of Kincraig farm – the only female to be tacksman in her own right; possibly sister of Captain Lachlan.

Maclean

John: tacksman and innkeeper at Pitmain; originally from Dalwhinnie; worked for the Gordons at Huntly before taking lease of Pitmain 1751; tacksman at Cluny after falling out with Duke 1788; tacksman at Benchar from 1796 till death 1808.

Macpherson

Ballachroan

John Dow Macpherson: originally from Phones; tacksman of Ballachroan 1770; lieutenant in Seven Years' War, captain in American War of Independence; recruiting officer; improving farmer; drover; 'The Black Officer' of legend.

Belleville

James Macpherson: of Ossian fame, known as 'Fingal' locally; born Invertromie; government propaganda agent; huge influence in India; MP for Camelford; became laird of Raitts estate, renaming it Belleville 1788; also purchased Phones, Etteridge, Invernahavon and Benchar.

James: illegitimate son; officer in India; inherited Belleville 1796.

Benchar

Andrew Macpherson: tacksman; later laird of Benchar and Clune.

Captain John: Andrew's son; inherited estate 1788; died 1791.

Captain Evan: John's brother; inherited estate 1791; sold it 1795; died at Seringapatam in India 1799.

Parson Robert: Andrew's half-brother; chaplain to Fraser's 78th Highlanders 1757–63; tacksman of Aberarder 1771; later tacksman of Dalchully; died in Perth 1791.

Breakachy

Donald Macpherson: tacksman of Breakachy; Duke's forester for Drumochter; brother-in-law of Ewen of the '45; leader of clan post-'45; lost Breakachy 1773.

Colonel Duncan: Donald's son; managed Breakachy for father; tacksman of Catlag (Catlodge) in his own right; later owned two estates in Perthshire; appears as captain, major and colonel at various points as he rose through the ranks; later known as Colonel Duncan of Bleaton.

Cluny

Ewen: son of Lachlan, the clan chief; officer in Loudoun's Regiment; joined Jacobite army; exiled after '45; escaped to France 1755, dying there 1764.

Duncan of the Kiln: Ewen's son; British military officer, reaching rank of colonel; estates restored to him 1784.

Invereshie

George Macpherson: laird of Invereshie c.1730–95; married Grace Grant of Ballindalloch (sister of General James Grant).

William: eldest son; laird 1795–1812; absentee for much of his life.

Captain John: British army officer seriously wounded 1777; returned to run estate from 1780 till death 1799.

Ralia

Lachlan Macpherson: tacksman of Ralia, then Breakachy 1773; successful cattle drover for fifty years.

Shanvall

Allan Macpherson: highly successful drover.

Strathmashie

Lachlan Macpherson: Gaelic poet and musician.

Uvie
Hugh Macpherson: brother of Donald of Breakachy; lost Uvie 1773.
Evan 'Uvie': son of Hugh; triggered the droving crash of 1793; became a major in the army.
Ann: daughter of Hugh; widow of John Macpherson of Inverhall; then married John Dow.

Mitchell
Andrew: sheep farmer from Ayrshire; took lease of Aberarder sheep walk 1779; first southern sheep farmer in Badenoch.
William: son; ran Tullochroam sheep farm (part of Aberarder); became one of the key farmers and officials on the Gordon estates.

Shaw
Lieutenant Shaw: tacksman of Uvie 1773.

Ministers
John Anderson: Kingussie, appointed 1782; improving farmer at Dell of Killiehuntly; factor for Belleville (including Phones, Etteridge, Invernahavon), for Benchar, for Duchess at Kinrara, before becoming factor for Duke in Badenoch; eventually overall estate factor in Fochabers 1809.
John Gordon: Alvie.
James Grant: Laggan; husband of Mrs Grant of Laggan.

Annexed Estate Officials
William Ramsay: 1749–53, factor.
James Small: 1754–66, factor.
Henry Butter: 1766–84, factor.
William Tennoch: land surveyor.

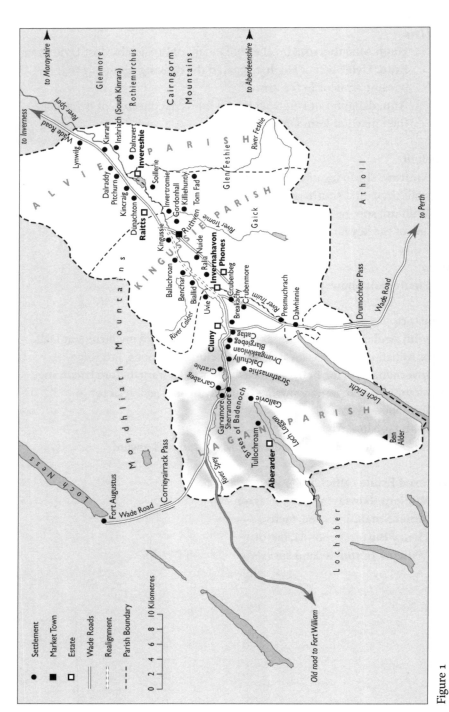

Figure 1

Boundaries, parishes and settlements in mid eighteenth-century Badenoch.

Introduction

It was just eight days since Prince Charles Edward Stuart had raised the Jacobite standard at Glenfinnan. General Cope's small army of English and Lowland Scots soldiers – hastily dispatched by the British government to snuff out this new Highland threat – had already reached Badenoch. On the morning of 27 August 1745 they set off from the bleak environs of Dalwhinnie, heading northwards along General Wade's recently constructed military road towards the steep mountain pass of Corrieyairrack. Aware that the Prince already held the north end of the pass, the local Macpherson clansmen must have followed the movements of the Hanoverian army with mounting interest – amongst them, no doubt, Iain Dubh mac Alasdair, son of a tacksman from the small Macpherson estate of Phones. A swarthy young Highlander of just twenty years, he would have seen Cope's men swing westwards at Catlag, halting at the small farm of Blargiebeg on the south side of the River Spey. There – probably much to his surprise – they wheeled round (the spot still known locally as 'Cope's Turn') and retraced their steps to Catlag, thus avoiding a potentially disastrous ambush. From there Cope headed eastwards along another of General Wade's roads towards Ruthven Barracks and Inverness. By chance, this road passed right through the estate of Phones, and later that day the Redcoat army filed wearily through Iain Dubh's ancestral domain.[1]

The young man would have been well aware of the contempt in which his people were held by these southern troops, for he belonged to a clan system where both society and culture differed radically from the rest of Britain. His Gaelic heritage, his place in the clan hierarchy, and the primacy of his chief, Cluny Macpherson, had been instilled into him both by his father, a Macpherson, and his mother, a Catholic Macdonell from Aberarder on Loch Laggan-side – one of the Keppoch Macdonalds. Yet Iain Dubh was no stranger to southern ways: indeed, contact with the British military was nothing new. Six years before he was born the Hanoverians had built and garrisoned Ruthven Barracks, just 5 miles from his home; as a child, he had witnessed Wade's soldiers construct the military road past his house; in adolescence, he would regularly have encountered them on patrols and at the Ruthven markets. Moreover, he had acquired fluent English at the grammar school in the burgh of Ruthven, while his early droving ventures had already brought him into contact with southern dealers.[2]

But he was well aware that his clan also was looking southwards – the Cluny family had, after all, built a fashionable eighteen-room mansion just the previous year. Two of Cluny's younger sons already had professional military careers: John with the Scots Dutch Brigade fighting against Catholic France, and Lachlan with the British army, firstly at the siege of Cartagena and now in India. Ewen, the oldest son and heir, had also just become a British officer under the Earl of Loudoun. Yet the Macphersons had long-standing Jacobite sympathies, and old Cluny's son-in-law, Donald Macpherson of Breakachy, had already made contact with the Prince. The young Highlander watching Cope's soldiers that day was perhaps himself experiencing rather uncertain loyalties.[3]

Had Iain Dubh pondered beyond his own immediate future, he could scarcely have conceived the turmoil and hardship that his native Badenoch would suffer from Cope's decision that fateful August day. Far less could he have foreseen the dramatic transformation that would consume the region by the time of his death in 1800 – nor, indeed, his own role as catalyst in that process. As such, his story is woven into the fabric of this book, but not as Iain Dubh, for that was his name in oral Gaelic culture. In correspondence he signed himself John Macpherson, to the army he was Lieutenant, then Captain John Macpherson, to the Gordon estates and his friends he was known by the Anglicised corruption John Dow (Dubh), tacksman of Ballachroan farm. To posterity, however, he is simply *An t-Othaichear Dubh* – the legendary Black Officer of Badenoch.[4]

•   •   •

Walking over Phones today the extent of change is only too apparent. Low turf outlines of long-ruined dwellings testify to the once thriving community of John Dow's lifetime – sufficient in 1757 to supply twenty-five men to the British army. The landscape now is dominated by a shooting lodge – sheep inhabit the low ground, grouse the moors and deer the hills to the south. Such scenes, of course, are replicated across the Highlands, but it was the deserted settlements of Badenoch, like Lynallan in Phones (Colour plate 1), discovered literally through the soles of the feet, that provided the inspiration for this study – those many unknown, unremembered ruins, their names lost through time, their inhabitants long vanished. The search for Badenoch's lost population, however, has uncovered the much deeper and more complex story of how this historically neglected region reacted to the traumatic economic and social upheaval that was sweeping the Highlands in the eighteenth century – an upheaval born paradoxically of both Jacobitism and Britishness.[5]

Even aside from dynastic confrontation, the world in which John Dow and his contemporaries grew up was already gripped by the forces of change. The social fabric of clanship had been suffering steady erosion since at least the early seventeenth century, a process accelerated when the 1707 Treaty of Union opened the door to the vast commercial potential of both British and world markets. Further stimulus arose from the onset of the Agricultural and Industrial Revolutions – 'commercial forces . . . so powerful that social change in Gaeldom became irresistible.'[6] It was, moreover, an era of unprecedented global expansion, with opportunities for imperial and military service that would impinge on every sector of society. The ideological movement known as the Enlightenment – a rational framework for notions of 'civilisation' and 'improvement' – was already permeating the Highlands, relentlessly driven forward by the post-Culloden impetus for assimilation to British ideals, not least the all-consuming concept of 'progress'. It was a fusion of political, economic and cultural forces that would impact dramatically on the region's fortunes.

Though situated right in the heart of the Highlands, with Laggan 'the highest and most inland parish in Scotland', Badenoch had a distinct historical identity dating back to the creation of the Lordship of Badenoch in the thirteenth century, though reaching its political apogee in the late fourteenth under Alexander Stewart, the notorious 'Wolf of Badenoch'.[7] The Lordship acquired a new political significance in 1451 when awarded by James II to the 1st Earl of Huntly to help impose royal authority in the Highlands – and for the next 380 years the region's fate was inexorably bound to the House of Gordon.[8] That political significance was further enhanced in the eighteenth century as its strategic centrality made Badenoch the natural hub of government militarisation in the Highlands. Even into the next century, the region retained its status as the Lordship, though by this time more for administrative convenience than political significance.

But Badenoch also had a distinct geographic identity that defies the normal broad division into the northern and western Highlands, and the eastern and southern Highlands – alternatively categorised as 'the crofting Highlands' and 'the farming Highlands' respectively.[9] Michael Lynch has indeed warned against such 'sweeping generalisations', suggesting that it is more instructive to consider Highland history as 'a collection of intensely local societies', and eighteenth-century Badenoch was undoubtedly one such society.[10] The region simply does not sit comfortably within either the above geographic zones or economic models, rather belonging to its own sub-category of central Highlands. Though naturally sharing characteristics with the broader divisions above, and inevitably sharing much of the general Highland experience, it was shaped by its own distinctive characteristics, displaying areas of divergence, sometimes subtle but often radical, from the general narrative of Highland history where the more dramatic events of the northern and western peripheries are often presented as the universal regional norm.

While Badenoch geographically falls into the broad definition of southern Highlands, its landlocked nature – hemmed in by the mountain ranges of Cairngorm, Drumochter, Benalder, Meagaidh and Monadhliath – deprived it of the principal benefit of that area, ease of access to the Lowlands. Indeed, the region experienced a degree of isolation that is hard to appreciate today, while the mountain landscape bequeathed its own distinctive identity in terms of climate, altitude and environment – an identity well recognised, generally unfavourably, by those few who ventured thither (Figure 2).

It was John Leyden, the Scottish linguist, who as late as 1800 curtly dismissed it as 'the wild black region of Badenoch' when first looking into it from the summit of the Corrieyairrack Pass – before promptly turning his back on it.[11] Its distinctiveness was more quaintly recognised by the writer James Hogg, observing that 'the country of Badenoch is . . . almost peculiar to itself'.[12] To others it was simply 'bleak and dreary', or 'wild and barbarous'.[13] The main approach over Drumochter was 'one of the most frightful that can be conceived', the pass through the Corrieyairrack comparable to 'the wildest and most dreary solitude of Siberia', the route by Aviemore 'more calculated for the abode of Moor Fowl than of Men', while there was simply no road at all westwards to Fort William by Loch Laggan – and being cut off for much of the winter did little to make the region more welcoming.[14]

Regional distinctiveness, however, is not the sole rationale for studying Badenoch, for it was in itself subdivided into 'a collection of intensely local societies'. While the aristocratic Gordons dominated the area, other proprietors

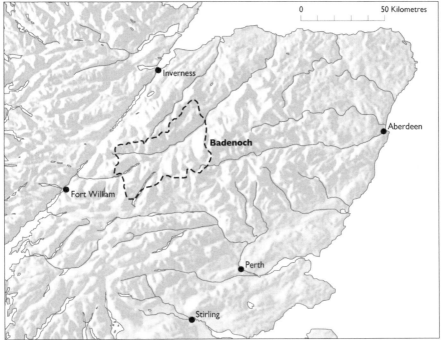

Figure 2
Badenoch in the Central Highlands, landlocked and mountainous, with the narrow strath of the River Spey providing the main settlement zone.

were forging very different paths to the future based on their own concept of estate management; the remnants of three once-powerful clans were struggling to retain some vestige of former glories; the lesser 'movers and shakers' – wadsetters, tacksmen and estate officials – were all jockeying for position, power and economic gain; below them, the various ranks of peasantry also sought an escape from the perpetual struggle for survival. Yet, while all faced the same general problems of geographical and environmental constraints, and all were equally enmeshed by the broader forces shaping eighteenth-century Britain, there was a remarkable divergence in individual response which highlights the significance of human agency in shaping Highland history.

This interplay between background or impersonal forces and human agency lies at the heart of this study. Indeed, there is a danger in seeing Highland history as 'the consequence of seemingly inexorable demographic and economic forces': not only does it remove the human factor from an

5

intensely human situation, but, as Charles Withers points out, it implies that Highlanders were 'passive respondents to outside influence without pausing to consider their role as participants and active agents'.[15] The unfortunate cumulative impression of this view is of a doom-laden society – Highlanders trapped in their own slough of despond – with no prospect of ever improving their material condition, thus justifying the Clearances as both inevitable and beneficial.[16] Tom Devine significantly criticises this overly negative approach, suggesting that Highland history has been too focused 'not on the reasons for success but on the causes of failure'; similarly, Matthew Dziennik observes that earlier obsessions with conquest, defeat and victimhood have 'blinded historians . . . to agency', and argues the need for 'a positive articulation of Highland identity'.[17]

This book tries to explore that 'positive articulation' not just by placing the Badenoch community, to paraphrase James Hunter, at the 'centre of its own history', but also by placing it within the wider Highland, British and global dimensions.[18] Furthermore, it analyses that community within the multi-faceted context of political, social, economic, cultural and ideological developments. The narrative is, wherever possible, shaped by the words of the principal players in an intimate study – warts and all – of a society forging its destiny in a rapidly changing world. It is, in essence, a portrait of life across the entire social spectrum within this one regional community, with the inevitable paradoxes and contradictions that create the fabric of human existence. Above all, however, it charts the fortunes and fates of a community living through a period of profound transition.

In spite of the earlier reservations concerning negative interpretations, this study of Badenoch from 1750 to 1800 cannot but begin with the disastrous events of 1745–6. Modern scholarship rightly downplays the significance of Culloden in the collapse of the clan system and the subsequent destruction of Gaeldom, instead tracing this decline back to at least the early seventeenth century – a process both externally imposed by the monarchy to assert state control on the lawless Highlands, and internally driven by ambitious clan chiefs seeking to enhance their commercial and personal status in line with their southern peers.[19] But that does not, of course, mean that the '45 and its aftermath should be ignored, and Allan Macinnes and Tom Devine have both reasserted the argument that post-Culloden policies undoubtedly accelerated the pace of change.[20] Moreover, academic debate of long-term trends cannot be allowed to obscure the brutal reality faced by Badenoch's citizens in the immediate aftermath of the '45.

Repression and Collaboration

The uncertainties which faced John Dow in August 1745 were reflected across the community. The Macphersons and Laggan Macdonells had supported the Stewart cause in 1689 and 1715, and Brigadier Mackintosh of Borlum, laird of the local estate of Raitts, had been a prominent Jacobite commander in 1715. Monarchical fears brought forth the barracks at Ruthven in 1719, and ten years later Badenoch became pivotal to the whole military communication network as General Wade constructed the Dunkeld to Inverness road through the region, followed by the remarkable Dalwhinnie to Fort Augustus road through the Corrieyairrack Pass. The local populace must have felt at times as if they inhabited a militarised zone.

Yet Badenoch, like most Highland regions, was not universally Jacobite: nor indeed was the Macpherson clan itself. The Macphersons of Invereshie and Killiehuntly were loyal Hanoverians. The fore-mentioned involvement of Cluny Macpherson's sons in the military establishment in itself sent mixed messages. Even the very presence of the Hanoverian troops was divisive, providing lucrative opportunities for enterprising locals such as John Macpherson of Knappach, the Barrack-master. James Stewart capitalised on the situation by building 'a Publick House at Ruthven of Badenoch' in 1732, admittedly not just because of the soldiers, but also 'for the Conveniency and entertainment of Strangers whereof the town is very much destitute to the great discouragement of travellers and loss of the place & Country' – for Ruthven was no mere village, but a Burgh of Regality with weekly markets and six annual fairs.[21]

Tension was inevitable. The army imposed a 400-yard exclusion zone round the barracks, showing little sympathy for those like Malcolm Clark whose house lay within the prohibited area: 'I dare not so much as offer to Lay on a Diffat or feall to repair it But ame yearly threatened by General Wade & the officers Commanding here to level it to the Ground'.[22] For those moral guardians, the kirk session, there were other concerns:

A great many dissolute and unmarried women from different parts of the kingdom, commonly follow the soldiers at the barracks of Ruthven, and are sheltered in some houses in the parish, where they and the soldiers have frequent meetings, and very often upon the Lord's Day, to the great scandal of religion.[23]

More seriously, the governor of the barracks had 'destroyed the whole Corns of Invertromy for two years by troops of Horse', even commandeering some land for 'the English horses' – perhaps explaining why Invertromie himself had been outlawed 'for killing some of the English who garison'd the Castle of Ruthven'.[24]

Further divisions resulted from the '45 itself. Ewen Macpherson, heir to Cluny, had just accepted a Hanoverian commission in Loudoun's regiment, and was soon boasting of 'my Success in Recruiting'. Just two weeks before Prince Charles Edward Stuart raised his standard at Glenfinnan, young Cluny asked Loudoun for command of Ruthven Barracks, 'the only quarters proper for my Company is Ruthven in Badenoch, So that I beg of your Lordship to appoint it for me'.[25] His subsequent decision to join the Prince had serious repercussions. His defence – that he was captured in his bed by the Jacobite army – defies credibility, and is best dismissed as a pre-emptive bid to avoid the obvious fate awaiting him as rebel, traitor and deserter. His kinsman, James Macpherson of Killiehuntly, writing immediately thereafter, had no doubt that the young chief was a 'rebell' who had 'deserted the King's Service'.[26]

At least eighteen Macpherson tacksmen, including John Dow, followed Cluny as clan officers, raising well over 300 clansmen – though not always voluntarily: 'William Robertson in Badenoch declares Young Cluny came to his house and ordered 20 cows and six horses to be taken from him and otherwise threatened him and upon consenting to go they were restored except one cow which had been killed'.[27] The Reverend John Gordon of Alvie, undoubtedly protecting his flock from retribution, confirmed that most 'were carried of[f] by the most arbitrary & violent method: such as burning their houses, carrying of their Cattle, & breaking their heads'.[28] Apart from the Macpherson regiment, at least twenty-nine of the Loch Laggan Macdonells also followed the Prince under their chief, Keppoch, as did those Mackintoshes who followed Colonel Anne, the chief's wife, who established her own regiment in defiance of her husband. While participation brought death or imprisonment for some, the Macphersons' absence from the Battle of Culloden in 1746 meant they escaped relatively lightly, though others like John and James Shaw of Kinrara died there fighting with the Mackintosh regiment.[29] The real hardship, however, began subsequently.

Allan Macinnes has aptly castigated the government's post-Culloden strategy as 'punitive civilising . . . systematic state terrorism, characterised by a genocidal intent'.[30] Fears for national security in a volatile Europe undoubtedly forced the government to lock the back door, but its response went far beyond the simple pacification of a disaffected area: revenge for the humiliation inflicted by a supposedly inferior army, the use of brutality as a means to civilising the Highland savage, and an ideological and cultural antipathy to Scots in general and Highlanders in particular, all underlay government policy.

Badenoch became the immediate focus, for, as Sir Archibald Grant warned the Hanoverian Ludovick Grant of Grant, 'Badenoch was the Chief place of Dispersion, that Many Arms, Horses etc may be found there, If soon sought for.'[31] Rumours that fugitive Jacobite leaders, Cluny, Lochiel, John Roy Stewart and the Prince himself were skulking in the Badenoch mountains heightened the military presence. A month after Culloden, Cumberland justified the brutality: 'Lord Loudoun is now gone into Badenoch for two or three days to burn and destroy that Country, which has not yet laid down their Arms, but I believe they immediately will.'[32] In February 1747, Loudoun was still scouring the area 'with 300 men, in quest of Cluny & Jo: roy Stuart.'[33] This threat loomed over Badenoch for a whole decade owing to the continued presence of Cluny – according to General Bland, Commander-in Chief for Scotland, 'the person of all the attainted rebels the most obnoxious to the Government', with the Macpherson clan described as an 'Artfull Cunning set of People.'[34] With troops stationed at Garvamore, Sherramore, Glen Banchor, Dalwhinnie, Lynaberrack, Glen Feshie and Ruthven, and with weekly patrols scouring the mountains, Badenoch was effectively under an army of occupation.[35]

Hanoverian policy is well illustrated in a letter of 1752 from James Wolfe, then a young officer, expressing the desire to march into Macpherson territory *'ou j'aurais fait main basse, sans misericorde* [where I would have attacked without mercy]'. Further comments, 'It was my real intention . . . to keep the Highlands in awe', 'a people better governed by fear than favour', plus an order 'to massacre the whole clan if they show the least symptom of rebellion', support Macinnes's claim of 'genocidal intent.'[36] Nine years after Culloden, Bland still maintained the pressure, quartering a party of 'three officers and 100 men upon eighteen of the principal Macphersons most devoted to Cluny's interests' – a deliberate tactic to break the clan gentry who had to carry the costs of quartering.[37] He even considered punishing Cluny's brother, the half-pay British army officer Captain Lachlan, for not divulging the chief's whereabouts, by restoring him to a full commission and dispatching him to the West Indies![38] Unsurprisingly, resentment was growing in the community, and Bland requested that the officers of the quartering party be chosen carefully so that the local people could not 'raise a clamour of military government & oppression.'[39] After escaping to France in 1755, Cluny complained that 'twenty-four garrisons still lie in that country [Badenoch] in the houses of gentlemen of his blood and name, where they use all the heinous liberties of a vengefull enemy and command as masters.'[40] John Macpherson of Strathmashie ratcheted up the rhetoric:

> Murders, burnings, ravishings, plunderings! Ane army of fiends let loose from Hell, with Lucifer himself at their head! Barbarities unheard of – no distinction of sex or age – cruelties never as much named among any people who made profession of or pretend to Christianity, and all not only with impunity, but by command.[41]

Equally devastating were the economic consequences. In the weeks after Culloden, Major Lockhart drove off 243 cattle, 84 horses and over 1,500 sheep and goats from the poor hill farms in the Braes of Badenoch, totalling £768 sterling in value.[42] The five families of the township of Garvabeg at the foot of the Corrieyairrack lost stock to the value of £131, equivalent to twenty-two years' rent. The seven tenants of neighbouring Sherrabeg lost £101 worth of stock, including fifty-three cattle – fourteen years' rent. Eighteen townships (eighty-one families) in this corner of Laggan suffered similarly. Though no similar record exists for Cluny estate, there is a contemporary account of losses in Benalder Forest: 'he [Cluny] keeps a harass [breeding herd] of some hundred mares, all of which after the fatal day of Culloden became the pray of his enemies.'[43] A Hanoverian medical officer confirmed that such claims were not exaggerated:

> We had twenty thousand head of cattle brought in [to Fort Augustus], such as oxen, horses, sheep and goats, taken from the rebels (whose houses we also frequently plundered and burnt) . . . so that great numbers of our men grew rich by their shares in the spoil.[44]

Things might have been worse, but the minister of Duthil reported that Cluny's men, 'when they heard that their country was to be burnt have sent up their Cattle & Effects to the Glens and keep themselves in a Bothy.'[45]

Property also suffered. Loudoun, camped at nearby Sherramore, razed Cluny's new mansion house, 'a most pretty, regular, well-contrived house as any be-north the river of Tay', along with 'such office-houses as were near it, [and] all the houses that they apprehended belonged to it at a good distance from it.'[46] For the common people it was far worse as Cluny himself noted: 'many poor Families who groan'd in want by haveing their houses burn'd to the ground their cattle and goods carried off, were at the point of perishing in Miserie'.[47] The Drumochter farms also suffered as Brigadier John Mordaunt raided and burnt the townships, specific reference being made to five tenants in Dalannach, five in Phones, and eleven in Presmuchrach.[48] William Ramsay, the annexed estates' factor, confirmed the general hardship: 'numbers of these little possessions having been laid waste by the Calamities of the Country', with rents unpaid because of farms 'laid intirely waste and desolate as the Tenants were then lurking until the General Indemnity in June 1747' – a reminder that many farms were seriously neglected, if not abandoned, for at least two years.[49] The fore-mentioned medical officer even described the wanton destruction of people's homes – 'We were obliged to pull down many houses for firing' – simply to provide fuel for the soldiers.[50]

The legacy of devastation haunted Badenoch. In 1752, the Duke of Gordon forgave William Mackintosh of Crathiemore half of his rent arrears because he 'was extremely poor and unable to pay, his Effects having been carried away by Major Lockhart . . . in the year 1746 and at same time he was not in Rebellion, but that he was always an honest good Payer of his Rents until then'.[51] Donald Macpherson of Cullinlean, one of the clan elite, argued in 1768 that 'by a universal Calamity occasioned by the late Rebellion none of the Tenants in the Lordship of Badenoch were able to pay their rents in the Year 1745, consequently they are all in Arrears . . . down to this very time'.[52] The Duke's accountant agreed, explaining in 1769 (twenty-three years after Culloden) that 'a considerable part of these arrears took rise from the distress which the tenants suffered in 1745 and 1746'.[53] Even in 1790 the estate acknowledged, referring retrospectively to the rising, that 'The Poor Tenants who had their all taken ffrom them were Proper Objects of Commiseration'.[54] Inevitably, the economic consequences of the '45 fell most heavily on the shoulders of the poor.

With their men fugitives, women bore the brunt of post-war hardship, watching helplessly as their homes and stock were plundered and burnt, and testifying to the devastation in the Duke's Regality Court. A distraught mother pleaded for help to free her 'unluckie son' because the cost of his maintenance in prison 'will soon exhaust my Smal Substance'.[55] Women themselves were sometimes on the run. Soldiers searching the remote glens reported finding such dangerous munitions as '6 Balls of Worsted Yarn, and about ten yards of Coarse Worsted Stuff'. In 1749, Ann Macpherson of Garvamore appealed for help because the 'whole bigging and Contents were Demolished by his Majesties Troops in the year 1746 and she being a poor widow was obliged to Run out therefrom Untill Lord Albemarle gave her protection'.[56] Mary Fraser,

whose husband was in hiding, even refused to go to the shielings, 'being alone
. . . and afraid of being chased by the Soldiers'.[57]

Civil war inevitably divided society across the whole spectrum. Support
for the Prince across Badenoch was, in fact, limited. The vast majority of the
Alvie tacksmen, Macphersons included, remained neutral, and the Reverend
John Gordon compiled a list of 144 men there who had not joined. In Laggan,
at least eighty remained home.[58] Indeed, only in that parish – Cluny's home –
did more than half the men of fighting age (55 per cent) follow their chief; in
Kingussie, fewer than 40 per cent; in Alvie, 20 per cent.[59] Even within the
townships of Laggan the menfolk divided fairly evenly: at Crathie at least six
men joined while five remained, at Strathmashie, seven and five respectively,
and at Gaskbeg four and seven, though whether those remaining were unfit,
left as a skeleton workforce, or were not Jacobite enthusiasts is impossible to
say.[60] There was also clear Hanoverian support. James Macpherson of
Killiehuntly (Cluny's cousin) was a serving officer with Loudoun, Donald
Macpherson from Ruthven was reporting Jacobite army positions to Ludovick
Grant in February 1746, and John Macpherson, the Barrack-master, continued
to supply Hanoverian needs during and after the '45.[61] Such internal divisions
are symptomatic of how far clan power and chiefly authority had already
declined even before Culloden.

George Macpherson of Invereshie, as substantial a laird as Cluny,
maintained his Hanoverian loyalty, informing Ludovick Grant about Jacobite
movements in Badenoch only two days after Culloden – sensibly trying to
guarantee his own safety from any blanket retribution by requesting Grant to
do 'what else youll judge proper for my Safety in Case the Innocent should
Suffer with the Guilty'.[62] Furthermore, Invereshie, along with his neighbour
Mackintosh of Balnespick, collaborated with Loudoun. Submitting a proposal
for 'the Proper Scheme for Securing this, and the Neighbouring Countries',
they requested more troops: 'a less Number will not Effectuate the Design, the
Quota for the Wester End of Loch Errach [Ericht], is thought rather too few'.[63]
They suggested eleven different local stations for troops, 'in order', they
claimed, 'to prevent thieves, lodging with, or without, Cattle'. It was a blatant
manipulation of government forces to protect their own economic interests
by replicating Cluny's own pre-'45 'watch' established to prevent large-scale
cattle raiding, but it encouraged the long-term presence of soldiers in
Badenoch. These two lairds also provided Loudoun with '150 plaids for the
use of the Troops lying at Inverness', adding, somewhat cringingly, 'the people
will give them cheerfully for the troops under your Command'.

These same gentlemen exploited the military presence to purge the community of undesirables. In 1752, Lieutenant Hartley was presented with a document containing an unequivocal instruction:

> They also made a list of thieves, and chuse out a number of the most notorious, a list of whom they have given me in order to apprehend . . . and have undertaken to find evidence sufficient against them, at least to transport if not to hang them.[64]

Lesser troublemakers were also targeted in a separate list 'of second degree of villain, to whom they have agreed and promised . . . not to give any place of settlement under them', while a third group was forced 'to give security for their good behaviour for three years to come'. With clan powers severely curtailed, the local gentry were again exploiting the central power of the state for their own ends.

Already in terminal decline, clanship was effectively destroyed. While defeat and persecution seriously wounded the clan as a physical entity, the state exploited its victory by abolishing heritable jurisdictions. The gradual imposition of centralised authority over the previous two centuries was finally realised in post-Culloden legislation: already weakened as an economic and social unit, the clan ceased to exist as an independent legal and political entity. But the damage ran deeper. The Macphersons were not just divided, but leaderless. Cluny spent nine fugitive years in Badenoch, eventually dying in exile in France, while his heir, 'Duncan of the Kiln', was but a child, born in 1748 in the shelter of a corn kiln. Furthermore, the ravaged clan lands were under government administration. The Macdonells of Loch Laggan were also leaderless, having lost Keppoch, their chief, at Culloden, while the Mackintoshes had been torn apart by a pro-Hanoverian chief whose wife had raised a Jacobite regiment.

Beyond the immediate persecution lay a wider drive towards cultural assimilation. Not only had the initial success of the Jacobites caused panic, it had dramatically highlighted the social and cultural gulf between the Highlands and the rest of Britain. A report in 1749 presented the establishment view:

> the Disaffected and Savage Highlanders need to be Bridled and kept in awe by Garrisons and Standing Forces, till the present Generation wears out . . . [and] those unhappy and infatuated People will still

Continue Savages if nothing else is done to recover them from their
Ignorance and Barbarity. . . [65]

The post-Culloden legislative and cultural assault on the Highland way of life
– such as imprisoning Grigor Macpherson from Glen Banchor simply for
'wearing the philibeg' – was merely the first course in the 'civilising' of the
Highlands, not for altruistic reasons, but to ensure the political security of the
state.[66]

The immediate impact of the '45 should not be dismissed lightly, for, as
George Macpherson had feared, its consequences were visited on Jacobite and
Hanoverian alike. The brutality, the pillaging, the sustained cultural attack and
the permanent presence of the military could not but be etched on the psyche
of the community over the next decade. Yet, paradoxically, there is no evidence
that in the longer term the Badenoch peasantry wallowed in despair and bitter-
ness over this assault on their Gaelic world. Political grievances were simply an
unaffordable luxury in the daily struggle for survival, besides which, clanship's
demise perhaps brought a degree of liberation for the lower orders. Furthermore, the military interests of the British state – Macpherson clansmen ironically fighting under General James Wolfe in Canada only five years after he had
plotted their extermination – ushered in a new era of opportunity outwith the
narrow confines of Badenoch society. For whatever reasons, the common
people emerged from Culloden's legacy more proactive in seeking their own
destinies than had ever been the case in the first half of the century.

For those local gentry who had been Jacobite officers – powerful, well-
educated community and clan leaders – the paradox was less striking, for they
escaped the vengeance visited upon their chief, and apart from short-term loss
of rents, suffered little hardship. For them personally Culloden was also a
watershed, for it marked a decisive break with lingering traditions, and, more
than for the peasantry, liberation from clan and chiefly authority.[67] Their future
lay not so much in atonement for past deeds – for there is not the slightest
hint of guilt over Jacobite loyalties – but in cultivating a new, more positive
persona as Highland, or rather British, gentry, to facilitate their acceptance
into the wider economic and social sphere of the rapidly developing British
state. In so doing, they themselves would become part of this drive to civilise
and improve their 'barbarous' Highland heartland from within, making
themselves more acceptable, even indispensable, to estate, nation and empire.
To facilitate this new identity they would, with a certain irony, re-invent the
clan to further their own, and the nation's, imperial ambitions.

The Highlands were, of course, already in the sway of major change long before Culloden, but the 'Year of the Prince', by hastening the demise of clanship and highlighting the cultural divide, undoubtedly accelerated the pace and degree of change. The ensuing narrative of Badenoch, however, dwells not on the notion of a defeated and oppressed people: on the contrary, it depicts a society engaging with wider British ideals even before the '45, and thereafter proactively integrating into and exploiting the potential arising from the economic and imperial expansion of the British state. Thus, though intensely localised, this narrative is not constrained by regional perspectives for it places people and events firmly within a national and international context. The lowliest cottars were linked to their townships, their tacksmen and their landlords through land, rent and services: they were also tied into Lowland society through seasonal labour, to London through cattle sales, and to Europe and the Empire through military service.

Chapter 1
The Social Hierarchy

Though the Hanoverian presence still loomed over northern Scotland, new windows of opportunity were opening for such as had an eye on the wider world. Caught between the conflicting interests of clanship and commercialism, the Highlands had long been in a state of flux. Increasing contact with the Lowlands and England over the previous two centuries had undoubtedly raised the social and economic aspirations of the clan gentry, but individual desires to emulate the lifestyles of the south did not sit comfortably with older notions of a more communally oriented clan society.

Economy and society were indeed an intricately woven web, subtle shifts in one inevitably rippling through the other. Like the rest of the Highlands, Badenoch itself was in the throes of economic and social change well before 1745 – a transformation that would increase in intensity in the post-Culloden decades. Change within the region would, however, be driven and moulded by a hierarchy whose traditional structure was in the process of disintegration. The evolution of this change is best understood through analysing the three main social cohorts: landowners, tacksmen and peasantry – not just their status within the tenurial pyramid but also the longstanding social and cultural relationships that had bound them into a coherent community.

The Proprietorial Classes

When the Duke of Gordon proposed selling the feudal superiorities of his Badenoch lands in 1792 to raise much-needed cash, his commissioners warned that 'retaining those superiorities keeps up . . . the Ancient Connection Between the Duke and his Vassals, which to one of his Grace's Rank, may appear an Object, particularly in the Highlands'.[1] That maintaining feudal

16

relationships was still at this late date regarded as sufficiently important to forego a vital income boost was remarkable: even more so the geographical emphasis, for in spite of all the post-Culloden 'civilising', Highland society was clearly still considered more feudal than Lowland Britain. Furthermore, these 'vassals' were not the lower classes, but proprietors who had bought estates from the Duke. It was a strange paradox, a testimony to the residual power of clanship: since the 1750s, Highland gentry had become vital players in Britain's military, empire and commerce – yet they were still considered more psychologically bound to an antiquated patriarchal society than their southern peers.

The complexity of the feudal relationship is demonstrated in this tenurial 'pyramid' of 1752. The Duke of Gordon had sold the feu of Invereshie estate to George Macpherson, the laird; he in turn leased the davoch of Killiehuntly to James Macpherson, the principal tacksman; James then leased the township of Lynaberrack to Malcolm Clerk, tacksman thereof; Malcolm then leased one-quarter of it to his tenant, Alexander Grant; the latter, being a reasonably substantial tenant, probably sublet some of his land to a cottar.[2] Thus society was bound together in a framework of charter and lease, reinforced by feu duties, rents and labour services. Power inevitably rested with those who topped the pyramid, the landowning classes. But landownership was no universal concept: it was, rather, a highly subjective force driven by the personality, ideology, ambition – even whim – of the individual. Indeed, Badenoch possessed three completely different proprietorial models, all shaping the destiny of their lands in their own distinctive ways.

At the pinnacle stood the Gordons, by far the predominant landowning family. Cosmo, the third duke, died in 1752, leaving the estate in the capable hands of the dowager Duchess, Katherine, followed by their son, Alexander, the 4th Duke, from 1764 until 1827. The Gordons epitomised absentee landlordism. Admittedly, theirs was a complex world where conflicting interests required dextrous juggling, but since the Union of 1707, their political ambitions had been centred on London, with Cosmo entering the House of Lords in 1747. Influence in Westminster was crucial, and Lady Katherine successfully convinced both the king and the current government, the Pelham administration, of the loyalty and importance of the Gordon interest after the '45. Alexander's southern priorities were also revealed when, in 1784, he claimed a seat in the Lords as Earl of Norwich, while already holding that right as a Scottish peer.

This increasingly southern orientation did not bode well for Badenoch's future. When in Scotland, the family's time was primarily spent at Gordon

Castle in Fochabers: Cosmo and Lady Katherine paid scant attention to their Highland estates, while Alexander's occasional visits owed more to his passion for hunting than business. James Robertson, the agricultural writer, observed that the Duke was too remote from Badenoch 'to engage in carrying on, in this district, such improvements as might require the eye of the owner of the land'.[3] The absence of that eye would have serious repercussions. Political ambition brought added pressures. Residences were required in Edinburgh and London, matched by a lifestyle commensurate to a British peer, while fortunes were spent on acquiring political influence.[4] Inevitably, estate policy became increasingly driven by financial difficulties.

Absenteeism, ambition and extravagance proved a fatal triumvirate that would, as for many Scottish landowners of the time, light a smouldering fuse of self-destruction. But, though primarily a Lowland landowner with estates in Aberdeenshire and Morayshire, Alexander still harboured clannish notions of aristocratic paternalism towards his poorer Highland tenantry. Balancing the conflicting interests of family, estate and tenantry was a feat that would have taxed even the most assiduous of landlords – and assiduity was not one of the 4th Duke's virtues. For him, a simple life of rural pastimes was more attractive than the daily grind of estate business – something that would impact on the Badenoch community until his death in 1827. Indeed, the observation that the Gordons had in the seventeenth century been 'a conservative, old-fashioned household' who had failed 'to diversify and expand operations beyond the limits of traditional landownership', remained equally true throughout the eighteenth.[5]

The model of landownership at Invereshie could hardly have been more different. Throughout his long lairdship, George Macpherson, 'a very plain, respectable, elderly gentleman', displayed no pretensions to political ambition or extravagance: more significantly, he was a resident proprietor.[6] His support for the Hanoverian establishment and his close family ties with the influential General James Grant of Ballindalloch allowed him to steer a moderate and successful path through the middle years of the century. The keys to his success, according to his son William, were his 'horrors at contracting debt', and 'the preservation of our Family'.[7] That financial prudence coupled to his personal residence distinguished him from the archetypal Highland proprietor. Though but a small estate compared to the Gordon empire, Invereshie survived and prospered under George's canny management.

The third model was the forfeited estate of Cluny. After Culloden the lands of Jacobite clans had been confiscated by the government and initially placed under the administration of the Barons of Exchequer and later of the Commissioners for the Annexed Estates. These bodies were not just absentees: they knew nothing of the estate and its people, had no expertise in the Highland economy, nor indeed, any paternalistic interest. Their remit was blunt: 'applying the Rents and Profits [of the estates] for the better civilising and improving of the Highlands', neatly paraphrased by Allan Macinnes as 'exemplary civilising' – part of the government's post-Culloden policy of integrating the Highlands into the British state through education and improvement schemes.[8] With an annual rental of just £133 to invest, a major transformation of Cluny estate was unlikely, but at least the desire for improvement was genuine, for the last thing the government wanted was the burden of a starving tenantry.[9]

Other local landowners included Mackintosh of Mackintosh who held some scattered Badenoch lands, the Mackintoshes of Borlum who occupied Raitts estate, and a few petty lairds possessing small feus like Phones, Invernahavon and Invertromie. Though all these estates, large and small, faced the same general problems, their individual responses over the next five decades took them down different roads, often with markedly different policies and markedly different outcomes.

Tacksmen and Wadsetters

Proprietors might head the social hierarchy, but they had no monopoly of power, for below them came the tacksmen and wadsetters, the military officers and managerial class of the old clan system. Though not landowners, they were undoubtedly gentry, sometimes wealthier and more powerful than the lairds.[10] Across the Highlands, their status was already causing tensions with commercially driven chiefs and landowners, and as early as the 1730s the Duke of Argyll had tried removing the tacksmen to maximise both his authority and rentals.[11] The Gordons, however, had not adopted such policies, and in the post-Culloden years the Badenoch tacksmen appeared almost untouchable. Indeed, the power struggle between Duke and tacksmen would dominate estate policy for the rest of the century, exacerbated by a lingering allegiance to the Macpherson clan – a conflict of loyalty between economic and cultural interests.

Further tension surfaced over tenurial rights. The feudal hierarchy outlined above, though clearly enshrined in law, was not so clear within the cultural context of the *Gàidhealtachd* where the ancient landholding concept of *duthchas* still survived in clan consciousness. Essentially *duthchas* was a traditional right, or heritage, to land based on continuous occupation over at least three generations – not difficult for most Highland gentry to substantiate.[12] Estate and tacksman both recognised the cultural power of this right, and though not legal currency, it was a card to be played when expedient. In 1744, John Macpherson of Crubenmore took the tack of Uvie even though rack-rented, 'looking upon Ovie as part of the Duchus of his family'.[13] Duncan Macpherson of Breakachy, as late as 1784, tried to regain lost family lands in order 'to recover & possess the Duchas of our Predecessors'.[14] The estate also accepted the concept, allowing William Mackintosh, in spite of substantial arrears, to remain on his farm, 'for which he has a great Passion as his Duchass', while on another occasion using 'the possession of his Duthchas' as a bargaining counter with a difficult tenant.[15] Personal association with land also indicates the strength of *duthchas* – though William Mackintosh had sold the farm of Balnespick in 1748, over fifty years later his grandson was still known as Balnespick. Once again, a cultural clash between legalised tenure and traditional rights made confrontation inevitable between the Duke and the clan elite in whom those rights were enshrined.

The significance attached to *duthchas* was evident when Hugh Macpherson, tacksman of Uvie, gave up the farm in 1773. Captain Shaw (of the Mackintosh clan) took the lease, intending to keep on the existing subtenants. Whether through personal dislike, clan loyalty, or intimidation, the sitting Macpherson subtenants refused to serve under his tacksmanship. Shaw complained that he was 'universally hated for no other crime than for taking the ffarm of Uvie . . . [my] character torn to pieces and the few subtenants I got, threatened for taking Land from me'.[16] Without the labour and rent of subtenants, Shaw's tacksmanship was doomed. His rueful comment that 'he ventured to take Ovie when nobody else . . . dared to meddle with it', indicates the political sensitivity of *duthchas*.[17] While suggesting a certain degree of leverage for the peasantry, it could equally be that they were being manipulated by the Macpherson hierarchy to regain lost clan territory.

But it was not just tenurial issues that threatened the status of the clan gentry. Tacksmen had traditionally been an integral part of the clan elite as military leaders with authority over clan lands. That military function had long been obsolete, with the '45 perhaps seized on as a last chance to play out the old role so integral to their status. For those Macpherson tacksmen who joined Cluny's regiment, leading their men on this impossible venture, was it merely clan loyalty, or was there a wistful longing for glory, perhaps a legacy enshrined in the annals of clan heritage? John Dow's eulogy, composed in the early 1800s, did indeed glorify his deeds in battle more than half a century earlier:

Choisinn thu 'm blàr a bha 'm Pìoraid
A leag an trùp Gallda gu h-ìseal.

You won the battle at Penrith
That laid low the foreign troop.[18]

The loss of that military role had undoubtedly undermined the tacksmen's status, leaving them technically as principal tenants, commercial farmers whose role, according to Macinnes, had become 'primarily managerial', acting as 'intermediaries' between landlord and peasant.[19]

The Badenoch tacksman certainly fulfilled this dual role as farmer and manager. John Macpherson of Pitchurn, for instance, kept one-third of the davoch arable for himself, about 25 acres, subletting the remainder among eight subtenants, while Angus Macpherson in neighbouring Pitowrie farmed half himself, about 27 acres, dividing the other half among three subtenants.[20] Additionally, John and Angus could keep as much livestock as they wanted on the common hill grazings for their own commercial benefit. Their wider managerial roles included such tasks as controlling land allocation, managing multi-tenant farms, supervising farm work, allocating soumings (the livestock allowed to each farmer), collecting rents and liaising with estate officials.

However, classifying tacksmen like these as mere intermediaries denies their true standing, for they retained that most crucial of clan roles – the right to sublet. The tenants were essentially *theirs*, not those of their chief or landlord, not just giving them power and authority over the common people, but greatly enhancing their economic status. By making the subtenants pay them the same as (or more than) what they paid the Duke, these tacksmen in reality held their lands free. Moreover, they were able to extort from their subtenants the free labour services due not just to themselves but also to the Duke. Hence, the more land and subtenants they controlled, the greater their power and influence.

While in some districts the tacksman seems to have had responsibility for one township or *baile*, in Badenoch most held the larger unit of the davoch, and sometimes considerably more.[21] Each davoch comprised several multiple-tenant townships along with individual small farms and crofts. Strathmashie contained four townships, likewise Gaskinloan, though others like Easter Lynwilg had only two.[22] Killiehuntly, a typical davoch, contained twenty-eight tenant farmers in 1752, a population of over 100 people, all under one tacksman.[23] Acreages were also impressive. Donald Macpherson of Breakachy boasted 95 acres arable, 108 acres grass pasture, 21 acres woodland, and 2,441 acres of hill and moor, not counting a further 6,000 acres in the Forest of Drumochter.[24] It was similar with personal wealth: Donald Macpherson of Cullinlean was described at the time of the '45 as 'a gentleman of opulence'.[25] These tacksmen, even by mid century, were clearly (and successfully) developing their managerial role into the realm of commercialism. Badenoch had perhaps bestowed on them particular advantages, including substantial hill grazings for the cattle trade and large numbers of subtenants for rent and labour. But equally significant was the freedom to operate largely unseen in the remote wilderness of their *duthchas* – a freedom reinforced by the absenteeism of their landlord. It was, thus, neither landlords nor chiefs who were the *de facto* leaders of the Badenoch community in 1750: it was the tacksmen.

Substantial tacksmen were not unique to the Gordon estates. William Mackintosh of Balnespick, tacksman of Dunachton, and the Shaws of Dalnavert, both holding from the Mackintosh chiefs, were just as powerful as their Macpherson counterparts, while on the shores of Loch Laggan, a group of Macdonell tacksmen operated with almost unchecked power. The common factor for all was the absence of a strong resident proprietor or chief.

Tacksmen, and even lairds, increased their influence further by holding multiple davochs, sometimes from more than one landowner and in more than one region. In 1771, Patrick Grant, laird of Rothiemurchus, was also tacksman of two davochs on the Gordon estates, Wester Delfour and Kinrara; Borlum, laird of Raitts, held the tacks of four neighbouring farms in Kingussie; Alexander Macdonell, heritor of the small half-davoch of Easter Delfour in Badenoch, was tacksman of six farms in Lochaber, over 50 miles away.[26] Ordinary tacksmen, too, could hold multiple tacks, sometimes with confusing and conflicting loyalties. Ranald Macdonell not only held the lands of Aberarder down Loch Lagganside as a wadset (see below) from Mackintosh of Mackintosh, but also the neighbouring farms of Torgulbin, Moy and Kylross as a tack from the Duke of Gordon – while owing his clan allegiance to Keppoch in Lochaber.[27] In Laggan, Lachlan Macpherson held the tack of three neighbouring farms, Blargiebeg, Dalchully and Turfadown, while John Dow, tacksman of Ballachroan in Badenoch, also held tacks for Fersit in Lochaber and Dalnaspidal in Perthshire.[28]

Most remarkable of all in the mid eighteenth century were the Benchar family. John Macpherson, while already holding wadsets from Borlum of two davochs, Benchar and Clune, acquired a third, Easter Lynwilg, from the Duke, some 18 miles further east.[29] In addition to these three wadsets the family held tacks for two neighbouring half-davochs, Strone and Glenbanchor, while leasing seven other farms in the Braes of Laggan, 8 miles to the west. In the early 1750s, this one family held twelve farms in three separate parishes.[30] Though no figures are available for the home davochs of Benchar and Clune, the other farms provide accurate acreages for their combined holdings (with estimated totals including Benchar and Clune in brackets): arable 498 (700), grass 337 (500), wood 391 (500), hill and moor 21,396 (25,400) – without actually owning a single acre.[31] When compared with the entire extent of Cluny estate (800 arable, 154 grass, 156 wood, 27,413 hill and moor), the lands of the Benchar Macphersons were indeed impressive.[32]

The eighteenth-century tacksman was not, however, locked into the role of mere middleman, for the tenurial system provided access to the social ladder. Some tacksmen like Invereshie and Phones had already achieved proprietorial status by purchasing small estates from the Duke as feus, paying him an annual feu duty in return – ownership of land being the ultimate goal. But there was also an intermediate rung on the ladder, the wadset. By the eighteenth century, wadsets were simply a financial expedient for landowners to raise short-term loans. Generally described as a kind of mortgage, the wadset is usually glossed over or interpreted only in relation to the landlord's financial situation. Its real significance, however, was for the tacksman. In this context it is easier to understand the wadset as a loan or investment. A tacksman who acquired wealth, perhaps through cattle, might not wish to trust his profits to the insecure eighteenth-century banking world, rather lending the money to a powerful landlord like the Duke of Gordon either for a fixed term or until the landowner had the capital to repay the loan.

The best deal legally was a 'proper wadset', where the interest due on the loan given by the tacksman exactly matched the rent he had to pay to the landlord, the two sums cancelling each other out. Thus, until the wadset was redeemed the tacksman held the land free of all rent and commitments, giving him complete autonomy, and, if of sufficient value, conferring the right to vote. The reality for the tacksman, as defined by one legal commentator, was that 'until the time of redemption come, they have the full enjoyment of the lands as much as if they were absolute proprietors'.[33] Significantly, three of the six heritors responsible for repairing the church in Kingussie in 1755 were actually wadsetters.[34] As *de facto* owner of the land the wadsetter was, of course, spared the rack-renting that other tacksmen were suffering, while being freed from the restrictive conditions and onerous services of the lease. Every pound of rent wrung from his subtenants was entirely his, and every extra pound he could make by improving and developing his lands was total profit. Moreover, his initial capital investment was still secure. The Gordon estates acknowledged this profitability when commenting that Donald Macpherson of Cullinlean 'was in opulent Circumstances' because, as well as holding a wadset of that davoch from the Duke, he also 'held a lucrative Wadsett of the lands of Noidmore & others from his Chief the Laird of Cluny'.[35]

Though enabling a quick cash fix, wadsets were disastrous for the landowner. Indeed, wadset lands, for instance Nessintully in1751, were not included in estate rentals.[36] In a time of commercial expansion, increasing land values, and a highly profitable cattle trade, the landowner could not touch the money being made by the wadsetter until he redeemed the wadset. Indeed, the question of whether a wadsetter could demand the return of his loan brought the sardonic legal response that 'wadsetters generally got too beneficial bargains to think of parting with the possession of the lands and calling back their money'.[37]

A wadset could also be a stepping stone to lairdship, either through the landowner being financially unable to redeem it, or through the wadsetter eventually purchasing it outright. The Macphersons of Benchar again provide an interesting case study. Originally tacksmen of their *duthchas*, the davochs of Clun and Benchar, they took wadsets on these lands in 1678 from Mackintosh of Borlum, laird of Raitts. As late as 1750 the Borlum family had been unable to buy back the lands, and it was legally uncertain whether wadsets could actually be redeemed after such a period. Shaw Mackintosh, the then laird of Borlum, sought legal advice, prompting John Macpherson of Benchar to complain that, 'considering the Improvements and the great expense both his father and he had laid out towards meliorating the Lands', they were now worth far more than the original wadset – adding pointedly that those improvements had 'made the lands of Benchar worth the Redeeming and raised that avaritious Spirit . . . Mr McIntosh to Reap where he has not Sown'.[38] In 1754, John managed to purchase the davoch of Clun from Borlum, thus achieving lairdship. John's son, Andrew, spent the next three decades trying to secure the other davoch, Benchar (vital for the family name), spending £1,500 on legal expenses to block Shaw's claims.[39] In a further twist, Shaw's son, Edward, fled the country in 1773 on account of his involvement with a gang of highway robbers, finally enabling Andrew to purchase Benchar outright in 1787 for £1,340 – though not before having to pay out 'a considerable sum of money' to some distant American relatives of Borlum's who suddenly registered a claim.[40] A tortuous case, indeed, but it does reveal the lengths and expense a Highland family would go to, not just to secure their *duthchas,* but to attain the highest rung – the prestige and status of lairdship itself.

The resultant irony of Badenoch's expansionist gentry was the emergence of a new phenomenon: the absentee tacksman – for these ambitious tacksmen and wadsetters could obviously neither reside in nor personally supervise their widely scattered lands. But why did tacksmen like Benchar accumulate multiple davochs, or lairds like Rothiemurchus choose to become lower-status tacksmen to a neighbouring landlord? The answer can only be wealth – the means to support increasingly lavish lifestyles.

In his survey of Kinrara, George Brown observed: 'the Principal Tacksman of this farm is Mr Grant of Rothymurchas; who occupies no part of it himself, but has the whole subset to Ten or twelve Subtennants', adding pointedly of Grant's other tack of Wester Delfour, 'Mr Grant . . . gets a very considerable additional rent from these poor body's besides the Customs and services'.[41] Indeed, one of those subtenants, Donald Grant, boatman of Kinrara, specifically asked to hold his land directly off the Duke because the land under Rothiemurchus 'has been double Rented these three years agoe'.[42] William Tod, the Duke's factor, was also well aware of such profiteering, criticising the Mackintoshes of Balnespick who kept numerous tacks 'for the sake of what they could get by subsetting'.[43] If the subtenants were paying the entire rent or more, then Rothiemurchus *et al.* basically held the lands free, so the entire produce of their multiple farms was profit. Similarly for the Benchar family: their twelve farms in 1751 comprised vast hill grazings and shielings, and, predating sheep walks, the principal justification had to be the increasingly lucrative cattle trade – aside, of course, from the accumulated rents of innumerable subtenants. Those eighteenth-century Highland gentry would probably have seen such exploitation of the commonalty as the natural order of society, a means to a lifestyle commensurate with their status. Significantly, however, their actions were condemned at the time, not only by subtenants like Donald Grant, but by those middle-class officials like Tod and Brown who witnessed the impact of such actions on the poor.

Not all tacksmen, however, fit this expansionist model, for some possessed no more than a half-davoch, while others showed little ambition: as late as

1771, Lieutenant Macpherson of Biallidmore still lived in a house no better than those of his subtenants.[44] Mrs Grant commented that, though many of her Laggan neighbours were kind, civil and well bred, they were 'not rich to be sure'.[45] On smaller estates like Raitts and Phones, or those like Invereshie, with a resident laird, there simply was no scope or need for substantial tacksmen or intermediaries. Meanwhile, on Cluny, the forfeited estates' officials deliberately prevented the emergence of a wealthy tacksman class by pegging all rents to a maximum £20 and leasing land directly to the subtenants.[46] Though there were two wealthy tacksmen on Cluny, their power derived from also holding tacks of Gordon land. Cullinlean, for example, held both Cluny's farm of Nuide on the south side of the Spey and the Duke's farm of Ballachroan on the immediate opposite side, creating a very substantial holding.

Women occasionally feature as tacksmen in the estate rentals, usually as widows maintaining the family *duthchas* until a son could take over. But single women could also achieve this status: Andrew Macpherson of Benchar's sister was given the tacksmanship of Nessintully provided he acted as guarantor for the rent.[47] The most interesting example, however, was Miss Helen (Nelly) Mackintosh who first appears in 1771 as tacksman of Crubenmore.[48] She was subsequently the most substantial farmer (probably tacksman) at Raitts before becoming tacksman of the productive Mackintosh farm of Kincraig in 1786 with a rent of £60, though Colonel Duncan Macpherson of Bleaton (formerly Breakachy) had to act as guarantor.[49] After successfully negotiating extra land for her agricultural enterprises, however, she requested a renewal of her lease in 1793, but refused to have a male guarantor. Her demand was accepted – the only known example in Badenoch of a woman holding a substantial tack entirely in her own right.[50] Miss Nelly was clearly a remarkable lady, challenging her male counterparts – including the formidable John Dow – in litigation, and sufficiently well educated to quote legal texts to her lawyer, Campbell Mackintosh, when telling him how to proceed.[51]

Badenoch's powerful tacksmen were clearly the product of large estates with absentee landlords who needed men with authority and wealth to control and develop their lands. The benefits were mutual, for absenteeism allowed these tacksmen considerable independence in their *modus operandi*, not least their traditional right to sublet. Typical of this class were characters like the 'opulent' Donald Macpherson of Cullinlean; Donald Macpherson of Breakachy, 'a gentleman of considerable estate'; Andrew Macpherson of Benchar, so astute that the Duke's factor was wary of tackling 'a man of his *abilities*'; and the Mackintoshes of Balnespick who had 'a great deal of "The High and Mighty"' about them.[52] Contrary to the Argyll experience, these semi-autonomous mid eighteenth-century tacksmen were the 'upwardly mobile' class of Badenoch, ascending the social ladder through wadsets and feus, accumulating multiple tacks for economic gain and social status.

The anti-clan legislation and exiling of their chief may even have done them a favour: freeing them from the last constraints of clanship; freeing them from any lingering nostalgia for Jacobitism; freeing them from the control of the landowner's jurisdictions – while encouraging them to embrace a future within the Hanoverian state.[53] But by the same token, the demise of clanship had undermined their traditional status. Territorial expansion and wadsets were perhaps ways to regain that position as community leaders, a social power every bit as important as the economic gains. From the Duke's stand-point, however, these powerful tacksmen and wadsetters were already a thorn in the estate's flesh – their quest for status making further confrontation inevitable.

That quest for status was underpinned by a degree of wealth that prompted the astute nineteenth-century antiquarian Charles Fraser-Mackin-tosh to pose the question, 'from whence did the surrounding Macphersons get the cash which seemed so abundant?' – clearly hinting at murky dealings in his mysterious addendum, 'I have an idea which wild horses will not drag from me.'[54] Had he perhaps discovered the following extraordinary claim from the Duke's lawyers? 'So far was the Rebellion from being a Calamity to Badenoch that it was one of the greatest Blessings which that Country ever experienced'! To substantiate the claim they produced a receipt showing that Donald Macpherson of Cullinlean's 'very first money [rent] paid after the Rebellion was in French Louisdores [gold coins].'[55] The explanation was simple: after Culloden, Cluny had been entrusted with 24,000 *Louis d'Ors*, part of the French gold sent to help the Jacobites: the infamous 'Locharkaig Treasure'.

With the chief in hiding, administration of this money devolved to his brother, Major John, and brother-in-law, Donald Macpherson of Breakachy, who distributed substantial sums among the clan elite, partly for safe-keeping, but also, in fairness, as reparations, for 'the houses of severalls of them [had been] burned and their cattle carried away.'[56] James Small, later factor to Cluny Estate, underlined its importance to the Macphersons: 'that money that is so useful to the whole name.'[57] Breakachy himself had acquired at least 'Six hundred Louis D'ors . . . for his own use out of a large sum which had been deposited in a bog sometime after the battle of Culloden' (and possibly a lot more than that), while in 1763/4 James Macpherson of Killiehuntly had received £800, 'part of the money sent over from France', which he banked in Edinburgh – before rather unwisely informing the authorities of its origin.[58] His claim that the Cluny family 'mean to make the most of the Money[s] that have been entrusted into their hands their own' only served to aggravate the situation. It is hardly surprising that the clan developed 'a general Odium against Killiehuntly', resulting in his lynching after church service in Laggan by a mob of women organised by Lady Cluny herself.[59]

Years after Cluny had escaped to France and supposedly accounted for the money to the Prince, Breakachy still had access to enough of this 'french Gold' not only to 'pay all the debts affecting the Esteat of Clunie', but also to 'purchase a better Estate'.[60] This substantial, though rather dubious, windfall undoubtedly played a significant part in helping the clan gentry: withstanding General Bland's extensive quartering of troops in the region; financing their open defiance of both the Duke of Gordon and the Barons of Exchequer; underpinning their entrepreneurial activities as cattle dealers and drovers (an economic advantage not shared by their Highland neighbours); and, ironically, perhaps using French gold to buy commissions in the British army to fight against the French. Above all, however, it provided the wherewithal to pursue those social ambitions that were the hallmark of post-Culloden Gaeldom.

The Peasantry

Far below the gentry lay the various ranks of peasantry, their status confusingly vague, their very existence in the historical record shadowy. For certain, they do not conform to any romanticised images of 'Highland clansmen', for mid century they appear trapped in their lowly status not just by the feudal hierarchy, but by the economic reality of poverty. Yet even within this class, differentials in status and wealth are discernible, for one of the empowering consequences of subinfeudation was that even the peasant farmers enjoyed some authority and material superiority over the cottar and labouring classes below them.

Most of the peasantry held their land from tacksmen, generally without written lease, though they appear bound directly to their 'master'. When John Dow became tacksman of Ballachroan in 1770, the subtenants had to renounce their farms and strike a new deal with him, or be evicted – though all, in fact, were reinstated excepting Kathryn MacDonald 'who was obstinate'.[61] When he then took a lease of Fersit in Lochaber, some 30 miles distant, at least eight of his Ballachroan subtenants transferred there under his brother's management. When later applying to extend the Fersit lease, John Dow claimed he did not want to 'see my Brother with his . . . Family & the other honest men who Came such a Distance Set adrift all at once', implying that the subtenancies ended with the lease.[62] When he lost Fersit, some of those subtenants did indeed return to Badenoch. His successor in Fersit, Alexander Macdonald, must also have brought his own subtenants because, when he was removed in 1797, ten of them left with him; the tacksman of Strathmashie, when evicting his tenants, pointed out that 'all the Tenants Cottars etc were brought to the farm by my Mother and were not on the farm when we got possession'; the Gordon estate's fear over removing the powerful tacksman of Breakachy was partly due to the 'danger of his drawing people after him'.[63] The clear impression is of subtenants tied to the tacksman rather than to the physical entity of the land which they farmed. Significantly, eviction notices to tacksmen automatically included all their subtenantry.

For the tacksman, the advantage lay in taking with him tenants he knew and trusted, or, at least, whose subservience was already guaranteed, but what about the subtenant? Without lease or security it was unlikely that any subtenant could claim a three-generation occupancy of specific land, so the only *duthchas* rights he might have would be to the wider clan lands, particularly those of his tacksman.[64] It was also a matter of security – better the devil you knew than an outsider who might replace you with his own people.

The leading Clan Macpherson historian has, however, suggested that ordinary tenants, even at the end of the eighteenth century, did possess heritable rights to land 'rooted in at least a thousand years of folk history' – a remarkable claim of *duthchas* for the clan commoner.[65] There is certainly some evidence supporting a territorial association with specific families: in 1729, seven out of eight tenants in Glenbanchor were Kennedys; seventy-five years later, there were still four, though the presence of eight other families indicates a diminishing association.[66] Such prolonged occupation is perhaps more easily explained by the insular nature of peasant communities, familiarity with locality and the existence of long-established neighbourhood networks, rather than specific heritable rights, for while the common people might retain older cultural notions of *duthchas*, their only real security was the tacksman's good will.

The lack of security is confirmed by a pattern of high tenant mobility. In Strathavon there was a remarkable turnover of tenantry in the mid eighteenth century.[67] The Badenoch evidence generally supports this: Alexander Kennedy was in his fourth farm by the age of forty; Malcolm Macpherson had been tenant in at least three local farms, Brae Ruthven, Craggan of Nuide and Strathmashie, all within 12 miles; James Macpherson had farmed in Cluny, Dalnashalg and Pittagowan, all within 2 miles, and, though lying within three different estates (Cluny, Benchar, Gordon), all were traditional Macpherson land.[68] The majority of tenants seem to have moved two, three, or occasionally more times, perhaps suffering eviction, being relocated by their tacksman, or proactively seeking a better deal elsewhere. These moves, however, were generally within a very tight radius, and primarily within the traditional clan lands.[69] This may be indicative of clan *duthchas* rights, or it may simply be that moving within the wider clan domain under the direction of known clan tacksmen would foster a greater sense of security, with the added bonus of convenience, familiarity and local networks.

•   •   •

Most of these subtenants occupied communal runrig farms of two to eight tenants, most commonly four. The origin and development of such multiple-tenant farms is complex, but Glenbanchor, a half-davoch comprising two equal townships, does suggest a farm in evolution.[70] In 1729, four Kennedys 'possess equally the whole eastertown of Glenbanchor', while three tenants occupied the other township, Westertown, including two more Kennedys (specified father and son) with the third possibly an in-law.[71] The non-Gaelic township names may actually indicate a comparatively recent partition – a single farm divided to accommodate an expanding family, for it is inconceivable that the Kennedys in this isolated glen were not closely related. The later appearance of Midtown (1749) and Newtown of Glenbanchor (1798), both tenanted by Kennedys, supports this scenario.[72]

There were also many small joint-tenancies of two and three, indicative of family holdings. Donald and Duncan Macbean held Achacha in Raitts jointly with shared rent; Biallidbeg was held by Donald, John and Murdoch Macpherson; at Glengynack, the family relationship, 'Donald Davidson Younger & Older', was specific.[73] The flexibility of the family farm is clearly evident in Lag, on Cluny estate. Whereas in 1748 there was a single tenant, John Macpherson, paying £3 rent, in 1770 there were two, John and William Macpherson, each paying £1 15s 6d – perhaps the original John with son, or two sons dividing their father's farm. By 1784, the farm had reverted to a single tenancy under William.[74] With no viable economic alternatives, farms simply had to respond to changing family situations. Estates naturally disliked the subdivision of farms into smaller uneconomic units – one landowner faced with four brothers sharing a single farm actually stipulated that 'they shall manage the farm as one & divide the produce but not the Land'.[75]

Estate rentals help to provide an understanding of the peasantry's social standing. Rents consisted of three components – cash, customs and services. Cash rents were levied in different ways. For many, like Islenuird on Strathmashie, rent, both cash and produce, was communal to the whole township rather than individual, and similarly in Kingussiemore, Donald Oliphant and Ewen Maclauchlan paid the rent 'betwixt them'.[76] Whether these farms operated as communes with shared work and produce as well as rent is not clear, though John Walker certainly observed such a system as late as the 1760s.[77] In other farms rent was divided equally: at Croft Carnoch the three tenants paid the communal rent by a 'Tripartite Division', while at Presmuchrach all four paid an equal quarter-share, as did the four Kennedys in Eastertown, even though farming jointly.[78]

Many of the townships in Badenoch by mid century were, however, moving towards proportional rents, reflecting both expansion and division. At Wester Raitts, one tenant, presumably the tacksman, held roughly half the township at a rent of £20. The remainder comprised seven small tenants, five at £3 14s each, and two at £1 17s, so this half of the farm comprised six equal shares, one of which had been subdivided.[79] The basic unit in these shares was an aughten (an eighth part of the davoch arable) used in apportioning land within the runrig farm. Midtown of Gaskinloan was a farm of two aughtens extent, probably originally divided into four equal shares (Table 1). By 1748 two of those had been subdivided, so that it now comprised two tenants with half-aughtens and four with quarter-aughtens. However, because these were runrig lands, the division probably reflected the number of rigs held rather than a precise acreage. Rents again were directly proportional to land.[80]

Such proportionality could run across a wide social spectrum, as shown in the rental of Delfour, a half-davoch of four aughtens arable, where expansion rather than subdivision is apparent (Table 2). The rents of the first six tenants (who held the four aughtens between them in runrig) were directly proportional to extent, while even the rents of the cottars and crofters were in identical ratio. The social spectrum ranged from the moderate fifty-merk holdings right down to the five-merk cottar holdings of house and garden. That the poorest runrig farmers with a quarter-aughten were rented at only double the

Table 1

Rental of Midtown of Gaskinloan.

Tenant	Aughtens	£ s d
Duncan Macdonald	½	1 12 9 (1.64)
Angus Macdonald	½	1 12 9
Katharine Macpherson	¼	0 16 4 (0.82)
Andrew Clark	¼	0 16 4
John Macdonald	¼	0 16 4
James Macpherson	¼	0 16 4

Source: NRS, E745/1/3, Cluny Rentroll, 1748.

cottar's rent for house and garden demonstrates the small size of their holdings. However, the holdings and rents of James Macdonald, John Macdonald and John Fraser imply a better class of subtenant. Even within the constraints of the communal farm, and even at these lower social levels, it was clearly possible for some farmers to expand their holdings.[81]

Delfour contained some small single-tenant farms alongside the multitenant one, and and such single tenancies were common in Badenoch. At Ballachroan in 1730, there were not only two communal townships with five and four tenants, but also five single-tenant farms, some dating back to the sixteenth century.[82] The davoch of Killiehuntly in 1750 contained three multiple-tenant townships totalling eleven tenants, but also seventeen small single-tenant farms.[83] The relationship of these small units to the larger communal farms is problematic and best considered along with that other confusing tenancy – the croft.

Crofts have become almost synonymous with the overcrowded west-coast townships associated with the nineteenth-century clearances.[84] But crofts existed long before it is possible to talk of a crofting way of life. Some Badenoch crofts were clearly historic survivals. Ballachroan contained five crofts in the 1595 rental, three of which – Croftdonachie, Croftaulddlarie and Croftgowan – still feature in the rentals of 1729 and 1730, the first two continuing well into the nineteenth century.[85] At Ruthven there were nine crofts, presumably relics of the old burgh tradesmen – including the 'Smith's Croft', the 'Miller's', the 'Turner's' – and five of them had been of a standard 10-acre size.[86] Some appear blandly: 'a field called the croft', as at Druminard in Laggan, perhaps denotes some long-forgotten past, though the term croft was sometimes used

Table 2
Rental of Delfour.

Tenant	Land	Shares	Rent (Merks)
James Macdonald	1¼ aughtens	5	50
John Macdonald	1¼ aughtens	5	50
John Fraser	¾ aughten	3	30
James Anderson	¼ aughten	1	10
James Smith	¼ aughten	1	10
Janet Anderson	¼ aughten	1	10
John Macdonald	House & Garden		5
John Wilson	House & Garden		5
Donald Macdonald	Croft		10
Peter Macdonald	Croft		5
George Anderson	Croft		5
Donald Macbain	Torness		20

Note: The original rental has 0.4 merks added to every tenant – presumably the compulsory cess, minister's stipend, etc. 1 merk was 13s 4d Scots. 50 merks was roughly £2 15s sterling.
Source: NRS, GD44/27/11/1/14x, Rental of Delfour, 1772.

to denote infield arable.[87] Many crofts, however, were still attached to essential workers who required a supplementary income or food supply like the blacksmith, as in the many Croftgowans.[88] Every miller also had his croft, and every ferryman on the Spey, for example, the Boat Croft in Kingussie.[89] Other more specialist examples included the 'Hawker's Croft' at the foot of Creag Dubh, and 'Creit [croft] Pyper' at Gaskbeg.[90] Crofts were also created as temporary 'social security' homes for the frail, as in the case of Marjory, widow of Crubenmore.[91]

Size varied: the Hawker's Croft and Croftdarroch on Easter Lynwilg were 2 acres or less (a size cultivable by spade), but most averaged 3–6 acres.[92] Rentals also indicated size. Two of the Delfour crofts were rented equally with the cottars, while the largest was only equivalent to the poorest runrig farmer; Croft Drellan's rent was less than two-thirds of the neighbouring farm of Tullichierro; Croftnalandish paid 10 shillings, well below the poorest tenants at Midtown.[93] Such examples support the traditional concept of crofts as very small holdings roughly equivalent to cottar status.

Some Badenoch crofts, however, do not correspond at all to the standard model. Croft Carnoch with its £10 rental was well beyond the means of the average subtenant, while Croft Carnal on Crathiemore with 22 acres of arable, and Croft Bain, at Gordonhall with 29 acres, were substantial farms comparable to tacksman farms like Pitchurn.[94] Nor were crofts always held directly from the landlord. In 1751, the rents of Mill Croft and Boat Croft at Ardbryllach were specifically deducted from the tacksman's rent because they were paid directly to the Duke. Every other croft in the 1751 and 1770 rentals, however, was incorporated into the tacksman's rent, suggesting that they were created or controlled directly by the tacksman.[95] Another accepted feature – that crofts were all single-tenant farms – does not hold true for Badenoch either. Croft Drellan in Glen Banchor was held by John and Angus Kennedy paying a joint rent of £4, Croft Coinneach by John and William Mackintosh, while Croft Carnoch actually had three joint tenants.[96] It is also generally believed that crofts did not have access to common grazings and shielings, but Croft Carnoch's lease specified 'an equal division of the Common Pasturage above the Military Road', while Croft Carnal had complete access to the shielings of the davoch of Crathymor.[97] As many of these Badenoch crofts also shared the same custom rents and labour services as the neighbouring farms, it begs the question of what eighteenth-century crofting tenure actually was.

There is no universal definition. Some, indeed, may simply be the lingering names of historic relics, their origin long forgotten. Others were clearly created by landlord or tacksman to fill a specific community need: for essential workers, as a social service, perhaps even as a reward for some service (for many have personal names like Croftdonachie) as would later happen with soldiers' crofts. The most significant group, the small crofts, were probably created to meet labour needs. The traditional workforce was supplied largely from the cottar population, but, as many of them were attached to the subtenants and townships, they would not constitute a dedicated workforce for the tacksman. Considering that crofter and cottar rents were often identical (as at Delfour), crofts may have been deliberately created to secure the tacksman's own labour force – perhaps to retain those subtenants displaced by his own farm improvements. All crofts, however, no matter how small, did have certain benefits: unlike the runrig farmer, the croft tenant held a consolidated unit of land to be improved as he wished, probably supported by the security of a lease.

How these smaller single-tenant farms and crofts fitted into the wider relationship of the davoch community is unclear. Alone, they could not possibly have provided the requisite equipment, plough team, or manpower, so there must have been some *quid pro quo* with the larger farms, presumably repaid with free labour – hence the croft must be seen not as an independent, free-standing agricultural unit but as an integral component of the wider economic structure of the davoch. Once again, however, the existence of the larger crofts confirms the notion of social mobility even amongst the humblest ranks on the tenurial pyramid.

At the foot of the social pyramid lay the mass of cottars and servants, 'not only insecure, but also invisible', though the agricultural economy largely rested on their shoulders.[98] Cottars, however, included not just the township labour force, but also the infirm, widows and the elderly, often provided with a cot as social security – Mrs Clark, an elderly widow, was given 'a small holding (say) a Cow's grass, or potatoes croft, which to most old Cottar wife's is sufficient'.[99] Occasionally cottars appear in rentals as in Delfour, or at Kingussie where James Gordon, a 'mealler' with house and kail yard, paid five merks and the price of a shearer, showing that they were tied into the tenurial system with land, rent and labour.[100] But because their relationship was usually with the subtenantry, most were never recorded. Whether cottars were common to the whole township or employed by an individual subtenant is unclear, though either way their freedom was curtailed. Indeed, one cottar, Lachlan Maclean, asked if he could hold his house and garden directly from the laird, because, 'by paying rent to you I will then be at liberty to go to work whenever I can get it to do, without incurring the displeasure of any person'.[101]

The cottar's lowly status was indisputable. John Macpherson of Muccoul complained, 'these indigent people are the worst of Neighbours and not able to pay even the Land Tax to his Majestie . . . far less any rent for the same'.[102] Alexander Macdonell, tacksman of Tullochroam, put it even more succinctly when threatened with eviction, protesting that he and his brother were 'not like a parcel of small Cottars who may be turned out at pleasure without altering their station in Life'! The contempt of the rich for their social inferiors could hardly have been clearer.[103]

The other substantial group of poor was the labouring class, both fee'd servants and day-labourers, many of whom came from the ranks of subtenantry – perhaps younger children surplus to family labour requirements and with no chance of a future share in the family rigs. Most were employed on the six-month feeing system common in Lowland Scotland, working as agricultural, domestic, or estate servants. Service provided opportunities to boost family income, to achieve a degree of independence, or perhaps accumulate modest savings for the future – though pay was but a pittance (women earning only 5s 7d (28p) for a six-month term), board and lodging being regarded as the principal remuneration.[104]

This servant class was generally regarded with suspicion: idleness in the poor was anathema to the rich. The local Justices of the Peace – gentry, tacksmen, employers – controlled the conditions and wages of the labouring class through the Quarter-Session court. Old vagrancy laws were invoked to prevent unemployment. Servants had to secure a new placement before they left the old, or they would be regarded as a 'Stroller vagabond and out of Service', and as such, 'attacked and pursued . . . by any person wanting a Servant'.[105] Even less secure were the day-labourers, seeking work wherever and whenever they could. Though paid more than fee'd servants, they had neither the security of board and lodging, nor of regular work.

•   •   •

While cash rentals reveal the tenurial status of the commonalty, customs and services reveal more about their lives. Customs (rents in kind) varied according to the local economy. While the Duke's Aberdeenshire lands filled the Huntly girnels with corn rents, only three Badenoch farms ever paid a corn rent – Kingussiemore, Nuidemore and Ballachroan. For the rest, customs reflected the more pastoral economy. Alex Gordon in Corriebuie paid one wedder, a 'reek-hen' and a dozen eggs; Angus Kennedy in Strone, two wedders, a quart of butter and thirty head of cheese; Malcolm Mackenzie in Presmuchrach, four pints butter, forty-six cheeses, the tenth lamb, the tenth fleece, and one merk for every milk cow – the last three items smartly taxing any increase in the tenant's stock.[106]

Custom rents were, however, being converted into cash on the Gordon estates as early as 1712, for money was becoming increasingly important in supporting aristocratic lifestyles.[107] On the farm of Breakachy, conversion rates in 1725 amounted to a 25 per cent addition to the existing cash rent, though cash conversion was optional at this point.[108] But that option soon disappeared. In 1744, the Uvie conversion rates were imposed without choice, while the 1751 Gordon rental mentioned neither customs nor conversions, suggesting they had simply been incorporated into the cash rent.[109] Cash conversions, however, did not necessarily make life easier for the poor; paying a fixed quota of produce was easier than trying to market it, especially if the selling price was less than the rent. To overcome this problem, part of the tacksman's managerial role involved converting custom rents into cash – in 1725, Malcolm Macpherson of Breakachy had 'to uplift the Custom butter and Cheise of Breakachy, Preesmuchrach, & Crubenmore and pay the Conversion thereof to my Lord Duke'.[110] Custom rents were never actually abandoned totally. Estates still called on them when cash was scarce: the subtenants 'were all poor and unable to pay Rents, except where the master is always at hand, ready to take any Effects they have in kind', while in the 1770s, James Ross, the estate chamberlain, authorised taking cattle as rent because 'it is certainly better to do so than lose it all together'.[111]

Conversions in fact brought the first public protest by the Badenoch peasantry – a 'rent-strike' caused by the rental demands of the Duke's factor, Gordon of Glenbucket. In 1725, John Warrand, tenant of Strone, renounced his holding because of a huge increase from two wedders and forty head of cheese to four wedders and sixty head of cheese. Malcolm Macpherson of Strone specifically stated he was leaving because 'he will not pay the wedders & cheese'.[112] Nine out of the ten tenants of Strone township renounced their lands, though with the caveat, 'they are yet still willing to stay in possession providing they get the wedder and ten heads of cheese of new Imposition upon every half aughten part diminished'. Furthermore, they demanded a cut in the conversion rate to 'a merk on the butter and half a merk on the cheese below the ordinary Conversion of the Country'. In nearby Pitmain another nine tenants took the same action, demanding they be freed from cash conversions on butter and cheese. It was an interesting exercise in collective action – surely calling Glenbucket's bluff as it would have proved hard for eighteen tenants simultaneously to find new possessions. By the same token, the estate would have found it difficult to replace so many tenants, thereby risking the loss of both the produce and rental of the farms. Though there is, unfortunately, no record of the outcome, it is the first glimpse of open defiance by the lower orders.[113]

Customs payments at Invereshie continued throughout the century, with the estate running a flock of 'custom wedders' in Glen Feshie from the dues of each township.[114] As late as 1800, the Reverend John Anderson, the estate factor, expressed his concern to the laird that the custom cheeses and fowls might have to be destroyed unless, 'you are coming to eat a share of these that are reserved' – another reason for converting them into cash![115] On both Invereshie and Belleville estates customs continued well into the nineteenth century, with tenants being fined for non-delivery.[116] Although generally converted by 1750 to meet the increasing demand for specie (coin money), custom rents clearly survived long after on some of the smaller estates. All landowners, however, reserved the option of reverting to payment in kind when circumstances required.

More onerous than customs were labour services – a last bastion of feudal imposition. As early as 1729, Brigadier Mackintosh of Borlum (proprietor of Raitts) had commented, 'Vassalage is so unreasonable, and the cruel Services we have over our Commons so inhuman.' He described the tenants as 'downright slaves, where they do all their Master's Work', and worse, were exploited as 'cheap rent' by landowners who practised a 'despotick tyrannick Power over the Commons'.[117] Four decades later, little had changed, as William Tod, the Duke's new factor demonstrated: 'I told the Tennants they behooved to look upon me as their Master and made them cut my Peats in consequence of my being so' – deliberately using services to establish his authority in the community.[118]

The labour service at Breakachy in the 1720s was three days at each of ploughing, harvesting, casting peats and leading peats, twelve days in total for every half-aughten of land. On one of the townships, Presmuchrach, the tenants provided among them forty-eight days of free labour on these four tasks alone, while from Breakachy as a whole the tacksman benefited from a total of 192 days of free labour, not including the time given to 'forest services' in Drumochter – patrolling the marches, protecting the grazings and driving the deer for the Duke's hunting expeditions. The benefits were significant – Mackintosh of Balnespick appears never to have paid for any labour at Dunachton in the 1770s, apart from occasional extras in an exceptional harvest, as services covered all the farm's needs.[119] Services were even a tradable commodity: in 1768, when Mackintosh's lands had been ravaged by the Spey, he requested the use of the Invereshie tenants' labour services, offering to return the favour should Invereshie ever require it.[120]

Services could be multifarious: John Macpherson in Phones, 'spreading his dunghills' for the laird; Angus Ferguson in Killiehuntly, 'to Bark [tan] three Rock [rough] hides to his Master'; Malcolm Mackenzie, 'to lead home and Cast his proportion of all the masters peatts with two Horses'; Donald Gollonach in Glen Feshie, 'to assist Repairing the Master's Bothy in the Glen'; Uvie's falconer, 'to assist at the Harrying of the Hauks of Craigow yearly', supplying peregrines for the Duke.[121] Invereshie services targeted building. Alexander Shaw in Glen Feshie had to provide 'two men with four horses for one day to lead & Cast thatch for houses, two men with four horses for one day for leading timber for houses, the like number of men & horses for one

Day leading Lime Stone, a proportion of men & horses for the Closs [court-yard] of Biggings at Invereshie'; Donald Gollonach, 'Leading earth to Bigging . . . leading Timber out of the wood for Bigging'; Alexander Gordon in Farletter, 'four Load of Heather for thatch to houses'.[122] Gordon's lease in fact detailed twelve different labour services for the estate, on top of the improvements specified for his own farm. Even Mrs Grant of Laggan, the minister's wife, had no compunction over exploiting the system – 'the tenants who do us service . . . are going to stay two days in the oak-wood, cutting timber for our new byre'.[123]

Peats were the most onerous service, for on top of their own needs, tenants provided the entire fuel supply of their 'masters', no mean task with the fashion for larger houses. Considering that a farmhouse required approximately 15,000 peats yearly, Cluny's mansion with its 'eighteen fire-rooms [rooms with fireplaces to heat them]' would have consumed vast quantities of peat.[124] In 1768, Alexander Macpherson in Raitts had to 'Cast, Win, Lead and Build, Peat . . . well shaped & oozed out of any Mosses' into a stack three feet, by twelve, by twelve, for Borlum, to be 'Cut on month of May and all led on or before the tenth of August'.[125] Nearly everyone there had to provide the laird with a similar stack, with joint-tenancies providing two or even three. Even in 1812, George Macpherson-Grant of Invereshie was demanding 'custom peats' from the estate, amounting to nearly 8,000 cubic feet.[126] Colonel Thornton, witnessing peat services at Phones in the 1780s, described them as 'a very severe tax on the poor people, sufficiently oppressed without it'.[127]

Carriages were also demanded: 'four loads of Candle ffir' (bog pine for lighting); 'carrying there masters Corn and Meall from and to the Miln'; 'bring home millstones'; 'Cutt and Carry home from the Woods of Glenfeshie Eight loads of Timber yearly'.[128] 'Long carriages' were usually the responsibility of the tacksman, though usually passed on to the subtenants – the three joint-tenants of Croft Carnoch having to perform four long carriages of up to 30 miles annually. By utilising the long carriage services, Balnespick was even able to send seven carts and thirteen pack-horses with bark to the tanners in Elgin without having to pay anyone.[129]

The Mackintosh tacks focused on flood prevention – often designated as a tacksman service. In 1765, William Shaw of Dalnavert was to 'do his outmost endeavour in fencing against any Incroachment of the waters of Spey and Fishie to prevent their cutting or destroying any ground'.[130] Though working on the riverbanks himself, Shaw's role was primarily managerial, organising the labour force from subtenants and cottars, 'for two months of the Summer

Season with a number of horses and Servants to be employed in carrying stones and making Bullworks'. He was given a reduced rent in return for organising the work, though whether he passed it on to those 'servants' is not recorded. River services were hefty, even for small tenants. Alexander Meldrum had 'to work at the Bullwarks of Feshie as usual for twenty five days of one man . . . or eight days with a horse and cart', and this was demanded for each half-aughten of land! He was further required 'to keep two horses working at the Bulwark for the space of 6 weeks', though this was an additional service paid at the daily rate of one shilling each for horse and man. There was even a flexibility clause: 'one man for three days att laying the stones . . . and in Case of Extraordinary occasion by Speats [spates] they are to provide a fourth Day'.[131]

Further labour services could be imposed outwith the immediate township. 'Ruthven services' had to be provided for the Duke's home farm, which, for the township of Crathiemore (10 miles distant) amounted to a stack of peats, the sowing of two bolls of seed, six hooks (sickles/reapers) at harvest and 'to putt up a Couple room of a bigging [building]'.[132] Laggan tenants had to perform long carriages to supply food to the workmen rebuilding Garvamore Inn.[133] At Glenmore, tenants were called in 'to Repair the Sluice' to enable the estate's forestry operations.[134] Some services had a wider community function, Benchar sacrificing his own service needs if his subtenants were required 'for any Work in the Country – such as Bulwarks'.[135] Tod was told, 'The Duke approves of your applying the services of the Country, on [the bulwark] at Cullinlean, so as to do something effectual there', while as late as 1820, the estate factor was told that 'every individual must be bound for four days' labour at the Waters – and such as have horses must work for the same number of days with them.'[136] Also in the nineteenth century, Macpherson-Grant demanded a total of 278 days labour on the Invereshie bulwarks from his fifty-eight tenants.[137]

Services were also manipulated for specific needs. When the new factor, Tod, took over Gordonhall in 1770, the Duke agreed to his 'using the Services of Brae Ruthven & Drumgellavie this Season, as you will, no doubt, have a great deal to do this first year'.[138] Even into the next century, William Mitchell, when taking over Brae Ruthven, was told that he could demand peat services from the tenants, and 'From every Mealander [cottar] in the place you may exact ten Days Work – at Hay, Harvest, or Peats'.[139] Estates could, however, be flexible: Invereshie tenants breaking in virgin land were freed from services so they could devote all their time to establishing the new farm, while essential workers like the miller, boatman and smith were exempt.[140] In addition, tenants had to carry out 'statute-labour' duties on road construction: 'The people of Killiehuntly to attend at the Bridge of Tromy with their spades, picks, axes & other necessary Tooles with their horses . . . to perform their statute Work at making the road leading from them to the Bridge of Feshie'.[141] Every davoch along the road was called out in turn – a considerable inconvenience in July.

Unsurprisingly, the subtenantry loathed services, not just because of time, inconvenience and lack of pay, but because they were open to abuse. Nelly Mackintosh of Kincraig had clearly demanded more than her entitlement at harvest time, because the Mackintosh chief forbade her to take the services of more than two shearers from each aughten part of her farm.[142] The Drumgellovie folk appealed to the factor that they were 'Grievously overburdened with Peats to Mr Mitchell' and that it was 'impossible to continue in such servitude', while the Brae Ruthven peat service was 'very vexatious and troublesome'.[143] Another complaint concerned the carriage of timber for fencing at ploughing time when it was 'inconvenient for Tenants to be called upon for their carriage'.[144] That some of these complaints come from the nineteenth century indicates their persistence in Badenoch. Subtenants failing to fulfil their services were, however, fined – 3 shillings for each day absent from river duty, triple the wage paid to the replacement labourers.[145]

Again there is evidence of rebellion. In 1732, the Ardbryllach tacksman complained that his tenants 'refuse to go the length of Strathspey to fetch me home a boll of meal'.[146] Sometimes opposition was more subtle. Invereshie Baron Court demanded that the tenants deliver their quota of custom fir 'in Peat Creells, which always used to be done', because recently they had started to 'Carry the Firr . . . in muck Creels [much smaller] by which means the master is Defrauded of the one half of the Firr they were in use to pay'.[147] Tacksmen also dodged service obligations: Donald Macpherson of Cullinlean 'refuseth to perform the four Long Carages due out of the Daugh Land of Ballachroan', because, 'upon reading his Tack [he] found that they were not expressly meant [mentioned] there' – reading the small print clearly mattered even then! However, even though no longer performing these services, Cullinlean still demanded the conversion rates for them: 'he makes his Subtenants pay them yearly to himself in money at a very high Ratte'.[148] As always, life at the bottom was tough.

Services were increasingly being converted to cash as it dawned on tacksmen like Lieutenant Macpherson of Biallidmore, when building flood-banks on the River Calder, that 'A Rabble of People without subordination,

Convin'd for a day are not the thing for an arduous work of this kind.'[149] Tod also recognised that such labour would be fine for 'leading the Stones, or in dragging the Wood from the Forrest' but not 'for the nicer parts of the Work.'[150] Again, flexibility was maintained: 'tenants perform some years more services than other years as it is in the Proprietors Option to Call upon his tenants when he has Occasion for Services.'[151] Alexander Gordon in Farletter's lease stipulated a conversion rate 'in case Invereshie does not Require the peats optional to him' – potentially costly, as the total conversion of services on Croft Carnoch increased the cash rent by 60 per cent.[152] As late as 1800, when times were harsh and cash scarce, Invereshie's factor, John Anderson, offered tenants a choice:

> I allowed your people an option, either of paying in their Custom Peats, as formerly, in kind; or paying at a Conversion of ten shillings for each Leet [stack]. In this Year of Distress, it is my opinion, they will nearly to a Man put in their Peats, but this is no Loss; as you do not require them, they can be sold to advantage afterwards.[153]

Invereshie repeated this policy in the desperate hardship of the 1830s, making the people pay custom peats even though the laird already had so much that he 'would not . . . require a single load almost for two years.'[154]

The longevity of customs and services in Badenoch might at first seem surprising, many still being demanded in the mid nineteenth century and surviving even into the 1870s.[155] Perhaps the elite were deliberately retaining these last vestiges of feudalism as a symbolic reminder to the lower orders of their subservient status. But, as Macinnes suggests, their survival may also reflect the real difficulty of replacing the traditional economic structure with a totally commercial model, as could indeed be argued for the Badenoch demands – at least as regards the gentry.[156] Because the nearest coal depot was at Inverness over 40 miles distant and the region had no rail service until 1863, access to fuel supplies became increasingly problematic. With the gentry's propensity for ever larger houses it was hardly surprising that peat services and long carriages remained in use for so long. Flood control also was a never-ending job requiring intensive labour, and the only mechanism for emergency repairs was the traditional on-the-spot labour force. As flooding constituted the most serious threat to both rich and poor, this particular service would at least have been more acceptable than the maintenance of lairdly comforts.

Whatever, the reasons, the remarkable extent and diversity of these services give a real insight into the life and work of an eighteenth-century Highland community, and though an archaic relic, it is hard to see any practical alternative for an isolated area like Badenoch. Necessary they might have been, but the onerous nature of these demands impacted heavily on the tenantry's own farming commitments. As the Reverend John Anderson of Kingussie noted in the 1790s, perhaps with a touch of hyperbole, though echoing Brigadier Mackintosh's complaint of 1729: 'personal services are so often demanded, that the tenant . . . is more at the disposal of his landlord, than the feudal vassal was of his superior in former times.'[157]

The status of the lower orders is undoubtedly clothed in confusion. For the subtenantry, large communal townships and small joint tenancies inter-mingled with single-tenant farms and crofts, and below them the cottar and labouring classes. Rentals were just as confusing – communal, equal, propor-tional, or individual, with a flexible blend of cash, produce, labour and conver-sions. Whether farm, croft or cot, however, the arable was of such small extent that all lived on the margins of subsistence. Generally without rights or security, prospects of social improvement must indeed have seemed remote in the shadow of those post-Culloden years, a society trapped in poverty and subservience by its tenurial status. Yet the situation was not devoid of hope, for there was a degree of fluidity as farms expanded and contracted according to circumstances – a society already in slow transition from the quasi-equality of runrig tenure. Subdivision of land inevitably brought greater poverty for some. But, for others, even within the pre-improvement runrig structure, opportunities for social mobility were becoming apparent, with tenants holding shares of two, three, or even five times more land than their township neighbours, while in the occasional defiance over rents and services lay the first stirrings of challenge to the existing social order.[158]

Conclusion

Mid eighteenth-century Badenoch was a highly stratified community – yet, for all the apparent rigidity of the strata, the entire social pyramid was bound together in a mutually interdependent relationship. Though each cohort embraced the desire to improve its material conditions and social standing, it could not do so alone. The Duke could not fulfil his aristocratic dreams without the managerial and commercial skills of his tacksmen, nor indeed could they improve their status without the labour and rents of those below them: likewise, both tacksman and subtenant were utterly dependent on those above them for the land from which their aspirations could be met. Aspiration, however, carried the seeds of confrontation, as self-interest increasingly turned one class against another. The dynamics of improvement did not, of course, operate in a vacuum, but within a rapidly changing national dimension: the post-Union expansion of economic markets, the cultural drive to 'civilise' the Highlands, and the broader ideological framework of Enlightenment philosophy, all impacting directly and indirectly across the social spectrum.

More immediately, whether at personal or regional level, improvement was subject to the severe constraints that accompanied life in the central Highlands – constraints that would impose limitations on the economic potential of each social class, exacerbating those underlying tensions between Duke Alexander and his powerful but troublesome tacksmen at one end of the spectrum, and between those same tacksmen and the suppressed but restless peasantry at the other end. It is with those constraints and the lives of the common people that the focus remains, for while this chapter has explored the tenurial status and obligations of the subtenantry, the next details the relationship of people and environment in the struggle for survival within the subsistence economy.

Chapter 2
The Subsistance Economy

Few people set foot in Glas-choire nowadays. Lying in the upper reaches of the Allt Fionndrigh in Glen Banchor some two and a half hours' walk across the roughest of mountain terrain, the corrie has an almost tangible sense of desolation. Yet it was not always so. Within its remote bounds lie the faint outlines of ancient shieling bothies – the very ones used by the Kennedys of Easterton and Westerton three centuries ago for the summer grazing of their cattle. With the uppermost ruin lying at a remarkable 2,525 feet, this is one of the highest shielings in the Highlands. Nothing could better illustrate the chasm separating their world from ours: nothing could better illustrate the importance of transhumance to the local community. The underlying reason for all those shielings like Glas-choire that once populated the remote mountain burns and corries of Badenoch with hundreds of families was encapsulated in a single sentence by Kingussie's minister, the Reverend John Anderson: 'This, indeed, is not a district adapted for raising grain.'[1] That simple fact had forced Badenoch, like much of the Highlands, to pursue a subsistence strategy heavily dependent on pastoralism and transhumance – 'cultural practices worked out, often over centuries, in the context of a given environmental and social setting', as Charles Withers aptly observed.[2] It was, however, a system vulnerable to criticism.

Early southern travellers, touring the Highlands with an ideological zeal for 'improvement' and confident in their cultural superiority, were contemptuous of what they saw, typically condemning the Badenoch peasant as 'poor, ignorant, unskillful [with a] Veneration for old customs which impels the Highlanders like all Savages, to oppose all innovations'.[3] It was a criticism patronisingly continued by nineteenth-century writers, referring to 'the absurd system of *run-ridge* farming', to agriculture 'in its primitive infancy', to Highland farmers having 'done their utmost to make their country waste, and

assisted nature by their stupidity to make it barren'.[4] Such negative generalisations indeed continued throughout the twentieth century: 'conditions of
penury and squalor that can fairly be compared with those of a famine area in
contemporary India'.[5]

It is all too easy to dismiss the Highlands as a domestic 'underdeveloped
country', and historical analysis has inevitably been coloured by the terrible
famines of the 1830s and 1840s.[6] These, however, were the result of a very
specific combination of circumstances, not least the imposition by landowners
of an alien crofting economy, destroying the indigenous agricultural system
that had evolved over time to meet local conditions and requirements. As
such, the nineteenth-century experience cannot be generalised back into the
previous century.[7] Negative perceptions have been further perpetuated by
unfortunate comparisons with modern society, not least I.F. Grant's reference
to living standards 'that would now be considered incompatible with a civilised
existence'.[8] To judge an eighteenth-century rural subsistence economy against
the standards of an urban consumerist society underwritten by a welfare state
is, however, utterly meaningless – far more relevant to compare the Badenoch
peasantry with their slum-dwelling urban contemporaries.

Criticism of this negative view does not, of course, imply that the Highland
peasant's life was one of abundance. For them, existence was, as Tom Devine
put it, 'delicately and precariously balanced between a meagre sufficiency and
occasional shortage'.[9] In assessing this economic balance, it is important to
understand the nature of the Badenoch economy – its isolation, its arable
limitations, the nature and importance of pastoralism, and, above all, the
significance of transhumance.

Isolation

Remoteness from markets was the most significant constraint on the regional
economy. In the absence of any waterborne transport – sea, river, or canal –
Badenoch's economy was totally dependent on the old Wade roads traversing
mountain passes like Drumochter, Slochd and Corrieyairrack – formidable
obstacles to horse-drawn vehicles, and though there were other mountain
routes suitable for foot or horse, these were impossible for wheeled traffic.

Road transport was fraught with difficulty. In 1740, even when Wade's
road was comparatively new, Lord Lovat experienced a nightmare journey
when heading southwards: 'I was not 8 miles beyond Aviemore when the axle

of the rear wheels broke in two', and after a costly repair and stay at Ruthven, 'I was not gone four miles when it broke again.'[10] Seventy years later, James Robertson still complained that, 'from Aviemore to Pitmain is the worst military road in Scotland . . . large stones are jutting up half above ground or lying loose in great numbers', while Elizabeth Grant of Rothiemurchus observed that 'it took us three days to reach home from Perth', a distance of only 85 miles.[11] General Wade's bridge at Garvamore on the upper reaches of the Spey being the only such crossing, all transport was dependent on ford and ferry, making the river impassable during spates. Winter created further obstacles. General Grant noted that it would not be until the 'End of march when the Communication by Drummochker with the rest of the world, might with a little exertion be opened', while Robertson noted how the same pass was 'often . . . fatal to the lives of the unwary in the winter season'.[12] With such roads, trade with expanding southern markets would at best be slow and costly, at worst prohibitively expensive.[13]

Lack of internal trading centres aggravated the situation. Though Ruthven had weekly markets, it inevitably suffered from transport deficiencies.[14] The destruction of the barracks in 1746 deprived it of a major trading focus, while the government's abolition of heritable jurisdictions (specifically, the Duke's right to hold courts there) further undermined its importance. The local tavern, established in earlier times when 'the better accommodation of strangers' was necessary, inevitably suffered.[15] In 1748, Widow Stewart, the innkeeper, requested a rent rebate because of 'the Regality [court] now being gone, which will occasion the Country people being seldome in Ruthven . . . Consequently there must be a Decay of Consumption from both the Country and passingers.'[16]

The last straw was the realignment of the road along the north bank of the Spey in 1763 and the construction of a new bridge at Ralia, 3 miles upstream, completed in 1765.[17] Now a bypassed community, the old burgh crumbled into oblivion. In 1773, John Clark, Baron-Baillie of Ruthven, looked back (ironically) on those 'good times' when 'the Kings Road lead [there] & a detachment of Soldiers lay in this place', lamenting that it had 'lost these publike Benefits for some time past'.[18] William Tod, the Duke's factor, agreed that the burgh was 'going fast to Ruin'.[19] In the 1790s, Kingussie's minister commented that the lack of any village market was an 'inconvenience . . . severely felt. Not only the luxuries, but even many of the common necessaries of life, must be sent for to the distance of more than forty miles.'[20] Long overland routes with slow and costly transport made it nigh impossible for the region to indulge in any substantial trade other than livestock, not only inhibiting commercial potential, but enforcing almost total self-sufficiency.

Arable

The eighteenth-century Badenoch farm was a closely integrated eco-system, generally running in a narrow strip from river to distant mountain-top (Figure 3). It was this 'vertical' alignment that provided the essentials of self-sufficiency: the riverside for hay meadows and winter pasture; the natural terraces and lower slopes for arable and grass; the woodlands for timber, bark and pasture (Colour plate 2); the moorland for grazing, peat, turf and heather; the higher mountains for shielings. Indeed, freely taking such timber and peat as

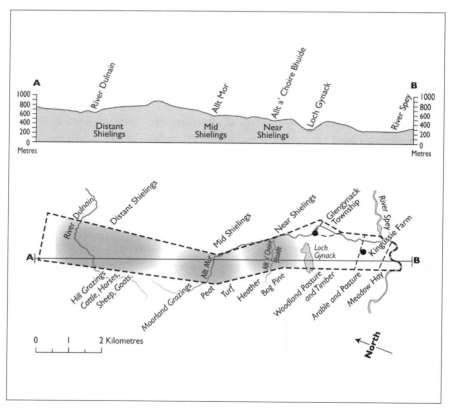

Figure 3
Kingussiemore, showing the 'vertical alignment' of a Badenoch farm or davoch that was essential for the community's survival.

was required for subsistence was a servitude or customary right. As Mrs Grant of Laggan noted, 'This farm [Gaskbeg] supplies us with everything absolutely necessary; even the wool and flax, which our handmaids manufacture to clothe the children.'[21]

The Highland landscape has often been condemned by historians for the vast extent of land that 'had always lain empty', or was 'entirely waste', in the years before commercial sheep farming was established.[22] Such arguments, however, fail to recognise that the totality of subsistence – food, clothing and shelter – was dependent on exploiting the integral nature of this vertical landscape where each zone had its relevance for survival, even if not in daily agricultural use. Indeed, any davoch lacking the total package struggled. John Dow suffered because Ballachroan had 'no hill Grass upon the Farm but a small piece above the Town fit for sheep pasture only'; the Biallidbeg tenants, when deprived of their peat grounds, complained it would 'hurt and Destroy your Petitioners & Render [the] . . . Lands Waste & without Tenants'; Cluny Macpherson exhorted Mackintosh of Mackintosh to preserve the Loch Laggan woods, for 'supplying your Tenants with such Timber as they may have occasion for', particularly the construction of their dwellings; the tenants at Balintian argued their need for a specific piece of riverside land, 'being the only place they could get their faill [turf] in'.[23] Survival thus depended, not just on the arable, but on the total environment, 'waste' or not.

Farming in the Highlands has been described as a 'complex web of opportunities and challenges' – though the Badenoch farmer would have perceived precious few 'opportunities', at least within the arable sector.[24] Indeed, the greatest challenge was simply growing sufficient corn to survive. Oats, some 94 per cent of grain production, were the staple crop, with bere (an early form of barley) the remainder.[25] But cereal self-sufficiency was rare. It is easy to blame the system, 'all those bad habits', for the shortages, but environmental factors were actually far more significant than methodological deficiencies, as the lairds of Alvie explained:

> barren mountains . . . ill fitted even for pasture; the only arable lands . . . are some small patches on the sides of the rivers . . . and by their inundations the crops are frequently destroyed. Indeed, so little is it a crop parish, that [the] crops produced are almost in no season sufficient for the maintenance of the few inhabitants who reside in it: the rent of the parish is paid entirely from the price of cattle, and the heritors receive no victual rent from the tenants.[26]

The region's arable limitations are confirmed by the Gordon rentals: out of the sixty or so Badenoch farms held by the Duke in the seventeenth century, only three had ever paid a corn rent.[27]

Arable cultivation was, in fact, subject to serious environmental constraints, not least the landscape itself. Only 2 per cent of the entire Badenoch landmass was arable, some Laggan farms falling below 1 per cent, with Garvamore only half of that.[28] Even in Assynt in Sutherland the arable percentage was four, while Loch Tayside reached six, with some regions even into double figures.[29] From that perspective, Badenoch appears disadvantaged, especially as the fertile but largely unusable floodplain of the Spey was counted as arable – 63 of Ballachroan's 158 supposedly arable acres lying on the vulnerable haughs (riverside meadows).[30] However, greater parity with other regions is revealed if acres per family are compared. Dodgshon calculated an arable acreage ranging between 3 acres and 13 acres per family across a range of Highland estates.[31] Badenoch was roughly similar: 4–10 acres on Cluny estate, 6–8 acres in Glenbanchor, 9 acres in Easter Lynwilg, and a generous 12–14 acres in Kinrara.[32] Regarding quantities sown, the Cluny tenantry averaged 6 bolls of oats per family, similar to Lochtayside, but considerably higher than west-coast Barrisdale.[33] Such figures, however, are less significant than actual yields, and Badenoch did not fare well in that respect.

The quality of arable was abject. The Spey's propensity to flood had forced cultivation onto river terraces and hillsides generally between 900 and 1,200 feet, occasionally rising to 1,300 feet as at Presmuchrach and Tomfad. The Reverend James Hall noted that 'in Badenoch, there are spots cultivated near fifteen hundred feet above the level of the sea'.[34] Though probably exaggerating, he was clearly struck by the altitude of cultivation. Such marginal land, inevitably, was 'barren . . . and sterile' according to surveyor William Tennoch, while George Brown dismissed it as 'but poor, being thin and dry with many Stones'.[35]

Inadequate fertilising further diminished fertility. Without the rich coastal manures of seaweed and shell sand, and lacking easily accessible supplies of lime or marle, the Badenoch farmer depended on 'the dung of his Cattle, the only manure of the Country', supplemented by the recycling of soot-enriched thatch and turf from the buildings.[36] The quantity of dung itself was limited by the number of animals that could be overwintered, which in turn was limited by the poor quality of land. It was a manurial dilemma: to produce more manure the farmer needed more pasture, reducing arable, and hence food; but to increase grain production meant reducing pasture, resulting in fewer cattle, less manure, and hence lower yields.[37]

Climate was, however, the greatest problem. John Anderson, farmer as well as minister, summarised the precarious relationship between subsistence and weather:

> This indeed is not a district adapted for raising grain. Storms are frequent at all seasons; frosts are uncommonly intense; and as they continue late in spring, and begin early in Autumn, with heavy falls of rain during the harvest months, crops are always rendered uncertain.[38]

The absence of the Gulf Stream, the amphitheatre of mountains (particularly the 4,000-foot Cairngorm massif), and the altitude of farmland, brought a climate much harsher than coastal regions. Late twentieth-century figures show Badenoch enjoying fewer sunshine hours than Nairn, Perth and the Western Isles, while facing substantially lower temperatures than east or west coasts through three seasons of the year, particularly, for the farmer, spring and autumn.[39] Rainfall, though less devastating than in the west, could still wreak havoc – especially Anderson's harvest rains. Tennoch also noted the 'unspeakable damage both in Seed time and Harvest' of floods, while William Tod referred to August as the 'rainy season', a point confirmed to some extent by modern statistics.[40]

Topography exacerbated the problem, for the region's mountains formed a vast amphitheatre funnelling the entire precipitation down fast-flowing tributaries like the Calder, Truim, Tromie and Feshie – 'the devastations of the uncontrolable Fische' – into the Spey.[41] John Williams, a mining engineer working in Badenoch, noted how these torrents would 'tear away . . . the greatest part of the soil of the pretty little haughs . . . & often sweeps away the greater part of their crop, to their unspeakable grief & loss'.[42] When the cumulative spates reached the Spey, results could be catastrophic: 'By an uncommonly high Flood in the River these two days past – the poor People have lost their whole Cropt of Hay – which I believe will . . . complete their Ruin.'[43] Such random floods, fuelled by rain or snowmelt, could, of course, bring devastation not just at any time of the year, but any number of times in the year – and no Spey Dam existed to divert water into hydro schemes.

Anderson's other climatic grievance was the 'intense frosts'. The only really frost-free weeks in Badenoch are from mid June to mid August, and those snap frosts of late spring and early autumn were equally destructive to seedling crops and harvests. Potatoes were, of course, particularly vulnerable, but even hay and corn might be destroyed before harvesting. Tod commented one September how the tenantry were complaining of 'the Cropts being hurt by a violent Frost we had . . . some Weeks agoe', while John Macpherson of Invereshie wrote of similar effects even in June – 'the frost has done much damage to the Bear [Bere] – and a good deal to the Oats'.[44] Weather inevitably dictated the farming calendar. The Reverend Hall commented that 'seed time . . . often does not commence till the month of May', a point also noted by historian Annette Smith, though she blamed the late sowing on the 'custom' and 'conservatism' of Highland farmers.[45] This criticism, however, fails to recognise the extent to which seasonal activities were shaped by the harsh realities of climatic experience – the cumulative wisdom of many generations.

Balnespick's account book clearly reveals that climate, not conservatism, drove the spring season. In 1779, he commenced sowing on 8 March; a year later, not until 20 April. In 1771, 'from the 13th April till Friday 19th there was no plowing, nor sowing till the 22nd, with snow and drift.' In 1778, his frustration was particularly evident. Sowing could not commence till 1 April, and was then beset with constant interruption:

> The season was very cold with frost and high winds till the first and second of April . . . The season after the 12th turned very cold with frost snow and wind till the 17th . . . [when he sowed a bit more]. The season still continuing cold tho' the snow was mostly off the rigs . . . There was no more sown till the 25th there being snow and frost with high winds. [He started sowing again on 4 May.] Then till yesterday we had most disagreeable weather. Wind snow frost and rain for 22 days past so that last week I did not sow any.[46]

Seed times were also dictated by the environment. Livestock had to be moved beyond the head dyke before sowing, but that could not happen until moor and hill experienced their spring flush, inevitably later than the township grass. Though no local dates exist, in Rannoch sheep were moved before ploughing commenced, while cattle and horses went before sowing.[47] Local farmers simply had no choice but to work within these climatic constraints though they were only too aware of the potential consequences, for late sowing entailed the risk of late harvesting. In 1787, Balnespick's grandson wrote despairingly on 9 November, that his crops were 'as yet two thirds uncut,' while two years later he noted that, on the even later date of 24 November, there were 'as yet one third of my crops rotting in the fields'.[48]

Such constraints made low yields inevitable. Balnespick, a diligent farmer with good-quality land, averaged returns of only two to threefold on his oats, and three to four on his heavily manured bere.[48] In bad years crops barely broke even. Such yields were often well below those of more favoured coastal areas. Marianne McLean has demonstrated that inland areas of Lochiel had notably lower yields than the coastal farms, while Knoydart's seafront 'added to local prosperity'.[50] Thomas Pennant, an early tourist, noted an eleven-fold return on bere in Islay in 1769, while Peter May, a highly respected surveyor and reputable source on Highland agriculture, recorded returns of twelve to sixteen at Little Gruinard, acknowledging that this was 'almost incredible to a stranger'.[51] Such yields, products of Gulf Stream and seaweed, were far beyond the dreams of any Badenoch farmer – and coastal families could further supplement the diet through sea fishing.

On top of these environmental constraints, there were also inherent problems with the farming system itself. In fairness, the large multiple-tenant runrig farm had much to commend it as a unit of collective self-sufficiency. As James Hunter has argued, it gave tenants 'a permanent stake' in the township land, 'enabling them to provide for themselves from their own resources'.[52] Though by the mid eighteenth century each tenant generally farmed his own land under the umbrella of the runrig farm, its communal structure provided access to the totality of its resources, a large pool of free labour, shared access to draught animals and equipment, a degree of mutual security over rent, and, not least, a vital support network in vulnerable times like widowhood or old age. Long-established family ties and associations further reinforced the economic and social interdependence of the township – bonds that would prove essential to community survival during difficult years.

Single-tenant farms and crofts, of course, had no need for the old system of intermingled rigs, but multiple-tenant townships were locked into it (Plate 1). Brown's survey of 1770 referred, for example, to Strone, where 'Eight or nine subtenants . . . occupy the lands in Runrigg'. Other farms, like Glenban-chor with its eight subtenants, though not specified as runrig, would almost certainly have been so. At Pitchurn, however, Brown noted an interesting variation. Here, land was held 'in Runridge and Kavells' – rigs, though still intermingled, were no longer reallocated, so that each tenant had his own land, albeit scattered throughout the farm.[53] Though there is no evidence of this happening elsewhere, it perhaps marks the first movement away from the old system.

While runrig proved adequate for the needs of self-sufficiency, it was hardly a springboard for commercialism: indeed, its very communality denied scope for individual ambition. The system inevitably gravitated towards the lowest common denominator, for constant reallocation negated individual initiative. As late as 1800, the Reverend Anderson reflected bluntly, 'Run Riggs are the Bane of every kind of Improvement', while thirty-five years later, the minister of Alvie could still condemn this 'absurd division of the land' as an 'insurmountable obstacle in the way of agricultural improvement'.[54] Not that local farmers themselves were to blame, for major tenurial reform could only be instigated by their superiors.

The difficulties were exemplified by the runrig tenants of Presmuchrach, three of whom petitioned the Duke about the fourth, Finlay MacDonald, complaining that he was 'a Clamorous & unpeaceable Nighbour'.[55] The petitioners were introducing improvements, converting some of their arable rigs to grass (presumably because of rising cattle prices), while Finlay continued to grow crops on his. Thus, when they took their cattle to the new grass rigs, Finlay, not surprisingly, drove them away from his rigs of corn, 'so as they cannot get their cattle to eat [the new grass] without Daily Demur and Struggle'. A second grievance concerned the allocation of rigs, for Finlay had received higher ground away from the River Truim, and so would 'not Contribute one days Service or any Assistance to make any ffence or Bullworks for preservation of the Town'. Thirdly, not only was he keeping 'Triple the Number of Cattle' stipulated, but, in a bit of private speculation, he 'sells their out pasture to Drovers', thereby destroying the common grazing. Irrespective of rights and wrongs, the case exposed three inherent problems of runrig: improvements were impossible unless the entire township agreed, co-operation over common interests like flood protection was essential, and individual greed could undermine the welfare of all. Though often petty in nature, such personal tensions bedevilled the runrig townships, thwarting any realistic prospect of improvement.

The nature of the fields was another limitation. Though some reached 12 acres in extent, small plots were more the norm, ranging from 3–4 acres down to one-quarter or even less. Kinrara consisted of 142 arable acres divided into forty-three separate plots, while the arable of Kyllross included seven plots beside Loch Laggan totalling only half an acre between them.[56] This multiplicity of plots made enclosure nigh impossible without considerable trouble and expense, and the Reverend James McLean acknowledged that the consolidation of farms in Badenoch would prove difficult because their lands were 'broken and disjoined by baulks, cairns, hillocks, and brushwood'.[57]

A further problem concerned the random intermingling of grass, moor, wood and arable. Gaskbeg had 14 acres of 'grass and Coarse pasture lying . . . among the Corn fields'; at Moy there were 22 acres of 'Moor ground among the Cornfields', and 11 acres of 'Moss between [fields] Nos 1 & 2 covered with Long Heath'; while in Wester Lynwilg 'The Cornfields ly interspersed in Different patches among the natural Birchwood'.[58] These small plots, carved out of moor and woodland, cannot have made cultivation any easier.

In his survey, George Brown surprisingly saw this unimproved landscape not so much a problem as an aesthetic enhancement. Describing Lynwilg's intermingled arable and woodlands, he wrote, 'The Situation and Exposure of this farm is very pleasant . . . and commands a delightfull prospect of Loch Alvie and the neighbouring Country'. Though but a surveyor producing an official report, Brown indulged frequently in such imagery. Pitchurn was 'both Beautifull and pleasant, The Cornfields hanging with an Easie Declivity', while Glengynack – its faint outlines still discernible on the sixth hole of Kingussie's golf course – had a 'fine romantic situation'.[59] Such musings, of course, bore no relation to the practicalities of estate valuation, but revealed Brown, writing in 1771, to be a 'modern man', *au fait* with the new fashion for nature and romanticism.

Romantic this landscape might have been, but Brown well knew that the arable sector rarely provided even a bare sufficiency. In fact, the tacksman farms, with their much larger arable acreages, regularly sold meal to their subtenants, Balnespick making eighty-five such transactions between 1769 and 1778, and the ruins of substantial barns on farms such as Crubenmore and Uvie (Plate 2) seem to confirm this function, reducing the need for expensive importations from the Lowlands.[60] In particularly difficult years, meal from the Gordon girnels in Huntly, or beyond, made up the deficiency. This cycle of sufficiency and dearth was, of course, common to all peasant societies, but Badenoch's environmental constraints ensured that the population, literally, could not live by bread alone. As laird and minister stated, this was not a region conducive to cereal production. Highland farming, however, cannot be condemned purely on the uncertainty of its crops, for this was but one component in the diet. To the ordinary Badenoch farmer subsistence had never been about grain alone, but about the totality of food that the farm could yield over the course of the year – and integral to that was the pastoral sector.

Pastoral

When the Reverend James Hall described the Badenoch people as 'little short of Abyssinian savageness', simply for using the blood of cattle to make black puddings, he inadvertently touched on the importance of livestock – an importance far beyond the occasional bleedings.[61] A general oversimplification of the Highland economy is to see corn as the subsistence crop with cattle being 'entirely for sale', an export commodity bringing vital cash both for rent and for the oatmeal required to supplement harvest shortfalls.[62] The Gaelic proverb *'is fearr aon sine bò no bolla dhe 'n mhin bhain'* – one teat of a cow is better than a boll of meal – suggests a rather different scenario.[63]

The interrelationship of the arable and pastoral sectors has also been viewed in terms of conflicting interests between the subsistence and commercial economies.[64] Dodgshon, for instance, sees an 'inner conflict' arising from population pressure as tenants 'relegated everything – including stock production – to the needs of arable', even arguing that livestock 'took second place' to arable.[65] But no such tensions are evident within the domestic Badenoch scene where both sectors remained equal and complementary partners, perhaps reflecting the relatively stable population. Indeed, the only evidence of prioritisation comes from those Presmuchrach tenants who were converting their rigs into pasture, sacrificing arable for livestock. James Hall confirmed that high cattle prices had resulted in local farmers having 'seldom more ground under the plough than is absolutely necessary for their subsistence'.[66]

Life depended on maintaining the arable–pastoral balance. The pre-potato diet has to be seen not as a staple corn crop with perennial shortages and hence a starving populace, but as a natural balance between cereal and dairy. From harvest to spring, oatmeal and dairy produce (from cattle, sheep and goats) were probably roughly equal in proportion, while from late spring until harvest, dairy became dominant, supplemented by meagre rations of meal. William Lorimer recorded how the old Highlanders lived largely on milk and cheese, while James Robertson observed that over the summer 'they live in great simplicity, on the produce of the dairy and some meal'.[67] Samuel Johnson referred frequently to dairy produce, noting that after dinner, 'there are always set different preparations of milk', while Boswell described a family that 'lived all the spring without meal, upon milk and curds and whey alone'.[68] In a fascinating nineteenth-century discussion of shieling life, Mary Mackellar from Lochaber described about ten different preparations of dairy produce to meet almost any culinary requirement – significantly stating that 'milk, in its different forms, was their chief sustenance'.[69] It has even been suggested more recently that the low-calorie, milk-based summer diet coincided with a low-energy period in the farming cycle, 'an energy-conservation policy that was not in itself seen as a hardship'.[70]

Rather than an annual round of starvation following scanty harvests, there was a variably balanced cereal–pastoral diet, with local tacksmen topping up corn supplies from their own barns as necessary. When crops failed completely, cattle provided an additional cash lifeline: 'The meal here is quite done', wrote Ranald Macdonell of Aberarder, 'Ready money cannot be had just now till people sell some cattle'.[71] In such times, the local economy had its advantages. After one dreadful harvest, Robert Grant of Elchies feared that the cereal farmers of Morayshire faced utter starvation, but significantly added, 'It will be no great hardship to the highland Countries, as they have plenty of Milk'.[72] It was a rare endorsement of the oft-criticised Highland economy, but one that would ring true for all pastoral societies. In Moy and Dalrossie, the parish immediately north of Kingussie, the minister acknowledged the importance of livestock in reducing the dependence on grain, while commenting on the health and longevity of his flock.[73] Local consumption was boosted by poultry, eggs, kale, and occasional mutton and goat flesh, while the wider environment provided game, fish, nuts, berries and plants – 'uncommonly healthy', and vastly superior to the contemporary urban diet.[74]

Food apart, animals were indispensable to the subsistence economy. Crops depended on animal manure; wool, leather and horn provided clothing and utensils; hill ponies performed the heavy work, transporting peats, turf and timber, performing carriages for labour service and dragging stones for floodbanks. Horses also pulled the eighteenth-century Badenoch ploughs – indeed, the Reverend James Maclean, a Badenoch man, condemned the 'barbarous practice of ploughing with four garrons abreast'.[75] Furthermore, livestock paid the rent, both in kind – butter, cheese, poultry and sheep (even a small farmer's rent could include 14lb butter and 28lb cheese) – and in cash, 'the only method they have of making money'.[76] This also enabled the purchase of the few essentials like iron and salt that could not be produced on the davoch.

But livestock too suffered environmental constraints. Grass pasture constituted just 2 per cent of the total land in Badenoch – surprisingly low for such a pastoral region.[77] Dodgshon believes that the most efficient grass:arable ratio was 80:20, firstly because it took a high ratio of pasture to generate enough manure for the arable, and secondly, huge quantities of grass and hay were required to sustain livestock in winter.[78] However, the Badenoch surveys indicate an overall grass:arable ratio of roughly 50:50, with some farms actually having less pasture than arable – Sherramore had just 16 acres grass to 47 acres arable.[79] Animal husbandry thus depended heavily on Badenoch's great expanse of moor, hill and mountain for grazing.

Estimating livestock numbers is difficult. The term 'cow' often referred only to the milk cows, with their followers (all those not in milk or calf) being taken for granted. As two to four followers per milk cow would have been normal, a reference to one cow could actually mean three to five beasts. As Badenoch cattle generally calved only every second year, a cow might have a new calf, a two-year-old and a four-year-old, the last being sold to the drovers.[80] Hence, to sell a beast every year, a tenant required two cows breeding alternately. For small tenants unable to keep followers this long, calves might be sold annually to the tacksman, or simply given in lieu of rent. The only surviving Badenoch souming (the official allocation of stock proportional to rent), from Cluny in 1771, detailed 519 cattle in total, 175 milk and 344 yeld (in this context, all non-milk, non-breeding cattle, whatever age or sex), a ratio of two followers to one cow.[81] From these figures it is possible to estimate some 2,000 to 2,500 cattle in Laggan parish, and 4,500 to 5,000 across Badenoch. Such numbers, of course, simply reflect the official souming, actual totals probably being much higher.[82]

More significant, however, is the number held by individual tenants. The davoch of Gaskinloan (Plate 3) comprised one tacksman farm and four runrig townships with sixteen tenants. Its total souming was ninety-six cattle – twenty-four cows and seventy-two followers, a ratio of three to one. Therefore the number of cattle per tenant (after discounting the tacksman's thirty) ranged from two to six in proportion to rent. Sheep numbers were low, reflecting their relative insignificance within the domestic economy: only 144 on Gaskinloan (1.5 sheep to every cow), allowing the tenants between three and nine sheep each. Thus, on the township of Drumgaskinloan (one of the four runrig farms), Donald MacCoynich, paying just 13s 3d rent, might have possessed two cattle and three sheep; Thomas Macpherson, paying £1 2s 3d, perhaps four cattle and five sheep; while Lachlan Macpherson, the highest rented at £1 15s 6d, would have had a minimum five cattle and eight sheep.[83]While these numbers reflect wealth divisions within the same runrig farm, none of them could have sold more than one cow per year.

In other regions, numbers appear to have been higher. In Strathavon, James Robertson reckoned that 'a man who pays £3 sterling of annual rent will perhaps have 20 black Cattle, 3 or 4 Horses, 20 Sheep & 10 Goats'. Allowing for rental differences, this was double the Cluny ratio.[84] Similarly, Walker noted in the Hebrides a tenant equivalent to those on Cluny would have four cows plus followers (twelve to sixteen in total), while Marianne McLean also recorded ten cattle per tenant in Barrisdale.[85] The discrepancy may reflect the scarcity of winter provender in Badenoch, or simply that these tenants, as Robertson critically observed in Strathavon, were oversouming. Keeping more animals than permitted was universal, and the Drumgaskinloan farmers could easily have doubled the permitted quota. Indeed, Finlay Macdonald, the troublesome Presmuchrach tenant, kept triple the permitted souming, and George Brown noted at Delfour that 'The hill is greatly overstocked with both Cattle and sheep, as there are so many small tenants'.[86]

Keeping larger numbers, however, magnified the problem of the long Badenoch winters. The Gordon estates tried to ban all beasts from the township 'winter grass' from 12 August until 12 November to preserve the pasture.[87] Thereafter, the stubble, grass, meadow and woodland of the township became one vast common where all livestock, by traditional right, grazed together through the winter.[88] At Raitts, Bishop Forbes described 'one of the largest Meadows I ever beheld', some 600–700 acres (Colour plate 3), from which hay was harvested for those animals housed inside, though such riverside meadows were highly vulnerable to the autumn floods.[89]

Climate and altitude combined to prolong the winters, with potentially devastating effects. William Marshall, an English improver, described one such scene: a 'most desolate and distressing picture . . . pasture and meadow lands gnawed to the quick'; the ground 'strewed with the dead carcases of sheep'; cattle 'in a starving state . . . barely able to crawl out of the way'.[90] Fodder was a constant worry to the estates: Henry Butter, in Cluny – 'Winter provider very Scarce in that Country'; William Tod, on Gordon lands – 'the Provider will not last above two weeks more'; John Macpherson of Invereshie – 'a scarcity of provider is dreaded'.[91] In desperate times, the preservation of livestock was paramount for both tenant and estate: in one winter Invereshie purchased 10,000 stones of hay, costing £250, to save their own and their tenants' cattle.[92] Long winters also affected rentals, Invereshie again worrying because tenants had 'bought so much provider in Spring that the Martinmas [rent time] will bear hard on a few of them'.[93]

Snow also took its toll. Though sheep were particularly vulnerable, cattle and even horses could succumb. Quantifying annual losses is impossible, but the worst years featured in estate records. The Dalwhinnie innkeeper suffered the 'Smothering of above Two hundred of his Sheep from the drift of Snow' in 1784. A few years later Gallovie lost over 1,000.[94] John Dow explained the consequences of one such winter to Tod: 'The Lose [of livestock] of the late Storm of Snow is not yet known but it is very Considerable upon this Side of the watter . . . I am much afraid you will Get Bade payments [rent] this year.'[95] For the tenants of Gaskinloan such losses could spell disaster, for replacing a cow in the 1760s was equivalent to one or even two years' rent – yet without one they were doomed.

Overwintering cattle elsewhere was not an option for most. Those at Lynwilg, however, where proximity to the Cairngorm massif entailed the harshest of climates, sent cattle to the 'Low Country' in Morayshire, but did so without cost by striking a reciprocal deal with the farmers there, 'taking their Cattle in to Grass in Summer.'[96] For the remote tenants on Invereshie the laird offered a wintering service, keeping sixty-five of their cattle on the home farm, though at a cost of £20.[97] But the majority of Badenoch farmers could only rely on what limited fodder was available, and pray for an early spring. Failing that, purchasing hay – irrespective of cost – was the only option.

Pastoralism was obviously crucial to the subsistence economy, affecting all from cottar to laird, yet it too was at the mercy of the environment, livestock deaths being just as devastating as crop failure. Thus the survival of the animals, and hence of the people themselves, depended primarily on the supply of winter fodder – and the only way to achieve this while maintaining a sufficiency of beasts was to exploit moor and hill to their fullest potential. Ironically, the success of both arable and pastoral farming was totally dependent on the vast Badenoch hinterland, 'often reckoned in miles.'[98] Described in 1798 as 'a wilderness of mountain pasturage', it constituted the remaining 96 per cent of supposedly 'waste' land, valued at only one old penny per acre, yet without which even the best arable, at 10 shillings per acre, was rendered worthless (Colour plate 4).[99]

Transhumance

Lachlan Macpherson, tacksman of Ralia, understood the importance of those Glas-choire shielings in Glen Banchor in a way that no modern historian or farmer ever could. His own grazings in Drumochter had just been removed by the Commissioners of Annexed Estates, and, along with his neighbour, Duncan Macpherson of Nuidemore, he petitioned them detailing the importance of those shielings. 'There is not a ffarm in all this Country which has not got a Shealling annexed to it, And if the Possessor of Ralia in particular had no Shealling to resort to . . . it is altogether needless for him to attempt to Occupy it [the farm of Ralia].'[100]

It was an unequivocal statement of the shieling's centrality within the subsistence economy – yet one that has been largely ignored. Even when such major issues as estate management, land use, sheep and clearances are under discussion, transhumance rarely receives more than a passing mention. Furthermore, the role of the shieling has generally been treated as peripheral to the main agricultural cycle.[101] Attention has been overly focused on arable crop production, while the often romanticised image of shielings has perhaps led them to be regarded as little more than a pleasant summer interlude to the annual drudgery of the farming year. I.F. Grant, for instance, described the shieling time as being 'a happy one for the beasts as well as for the people', and having a 'particular charm' – undoubtedly valid comments, though hardly an analytical assessment of their economic significance.[102]

But to the eighteenth-century mind also, transhumance was a divisive subject – a pastoral paradox caught between the rationality of the Enlighten-ment and the emotionality of Romanticism. To the improver, transhumance was primitive, a symbol of inefficiency to be rejected in favour of more progressive methods. Southern condescension was encapsulated by James Hall, describing Highlanders in their pastoralism as 'resembling the Cherokee Indians, and most other nations only verging towards improvement'.[103] In similar mode, William Lorimer, mentor to Sir James Grant, condemned the Highlanders as being like 'the wild Scythians or Tartars' in their pastoral lifestyle – and in those green oases, fertilised by generations of cattle, he saw the potential for new, permanent arable farms.[104]

A new, softer – and less patronising – mood was, however, gaining momentum. Adam Smith's *Theory of Moral Sentiments* and Henry Mackenzie's cult novel *The Man of Feeling* encouraged the growth of overt sentimentalism in polite society, while throughout Europe James Macpherson's Ossianic trans-lations helped launch the Romantic movement.[105] On the Continent, a parallel philosophical concept emerged from writers like Rousseau: the Noble Savage and the cult of Primitivism – a romanticised belief in the virtues of an earlier, simpler society, a golden age free of the corruption of contemporary urban life. Instead of emotional austerity, society craved sentiment and romanticism – and Fingalian heroes striding through a landscape of Celtic mysticism were comfortable bedfellows for the Noble Savage, the Highlander presenting, in Charles Withers' memorable phrase, as a 'contemporary ancestor'.[106] The

Highlands, indeed, became a focal point of intellectual romanticism, their perceived backwardness the embodiment of Primitivism; the shieling itself, a physical symbol of that golden age – the last vestige of an ancient pastoral idyll.

In such romantic indulgence, none excelled Mrs Grant of Laggan, writing fondly of 'these vestiges of primitive life', where 'the true Pastoral Life commences'.[107] As a local farmer, Mrs Grant was well aware of the *true* pastoral life, yet, for her late eighteenth-century readership, she clothed it in a veneer of sentimentalism:

> Now hark! What loud tumultuous joys resound,
> From all the echoing rocks and valleys round;
> And hear! The sage oraculous declare,
> 'Tis time the *summer-flitting* to prepare':
> The *summer-flitting!* Youths delighted cry,
> The *summer-flitting!* Lisping babes reply.
> Now all is haste, and cheerful bustle round,
> To reach the wilds, with plenteous herbage crown'd.[108]

The veneer, however, must not obscure the reality, for even though the 'summer flitting' was indeed eagerly anticipated and fondly remembered by the tenantry themselves, the system of transhumance was no mere summer jaunt to the hills, but underpinned the entire local economy.

The most obvious and vitally important reason for shielings, as one young herd acknowledged, was 'keeping up the Cattle from the Town to save the Corns'.[109] But their significance went far deeper, as Duncan Macpherson of Nuidemore explained, starting with the fertility of the arable: 'Without a Sufficient Stocking of all kind of Cattle, for manure', he could not grow a sufficiency of crops, and 'without Some Shealling or Hill grass no such stocking can be kept in a Highland Country'.[110] He continued by outlining local deficiencies concerning cattle: 'In all these Highland Countries, particularly in this, the produce of the ffarm does not maintain their Cattle above Five months of the year'. Hence, to avoid starvation, the bulk of the livestock (the yeld beasts) had to be sent to the hills 'in Aprile from whence they do not return till November'. His third point concerned the milk cattle. Most of the year, the lower grazings near the farm were preserved for them, but, 'even in the best of Seasons when the Farm Grass is exhausted, the Milk Cattle are Sent to the Hills once or twice in the year, untill the Grass at home grows up', without which 'the consequences must be fatal to them'. A more personal point concerned the regular flooding of the Spey, for both family and animals resorted to the shielings 'when the ffarm Grass is . . . Overflowen with water'. He finished with a blunt assessment of the integrated nature of farm and grazings, that if he lost any part of his shielings, high or low, 'the remainder becomes of no Earthly use to the ffarm'.

Ralia's complaint was in similar vein, adding that without shielings he would have to sacrifice arable land to produce hay.[111] He further commented that shielings were the 'Custom in the Country', and that 'It is a thing entirely new in this Country that a Farm should have no Shealling or Summer Grazing' – a clear implication that the Commissioners, as outsiders, understood neither the Highland economy nor the consequences of their actions. Significantly, Henry Butter, the annexed estates' factor sent to investigate the complaints, agreed with every point, concluding that without these shielings, the 'number of cattle must be considerably Lessen'd and their ffarms consequently of less Value'.[112]

Lieutenant Macpherson of Biallidmore raised similar concerns when the Duke gave his shieling at Dalenlongart on Loch Ericht to Robert Dundas (Lord President of the Court of Session) for a 'shooting hut'. Macpherson described his shieling as 'the principal Support of my own and Tenants Black Cattle & Sheep during the greatest part of the Spring and Summer half year, and the only support of our Hill Horses through the whole year'.[113] He pointedly concluded, 'it is really of more Consequence to my possession *than any stranger can possibly imagine from a superficial view* [author's italics]'– another condemnation of the outsider's failure to understand the economic system. Once again, an estate official, this time the Duke's factor, William Tod, supported these claims.[114]

Shielings became increasingly problematic across the Highlands as estates sought to maximise income by converting them into independent farms. Badenoch had already experienced some such conversions. In the seventeenth century both Glen Tromie and Glen Feshie contained 'summer-towns' (an old term for shielings, the 'winter-town' being the home farm), though these were, unusually, used for cultivation rather than livestock. In one of these, Lynaberrack in Glen Tromie, Thomas Macpherson explained that 'no winter dwelling' was to be built there, and that the inhabitants of the summer-town were, after harvest, 'to lead the Cornes thereof . . . to the In Country viz Killihuntly and Invertromie'.[115] Lynaberrack was clearly being used as temporary summer arable, with the farmers returning with their crops before winter to their permanent townships lower down the glen. Then, from 1 November to 1

March the upper glen became the Duke's winter playground, as Macpherson explained: 'the deare of the forrest of gaick [were hunted] in the moores & woods above Kyllehuntly'. By 1750, however, leases show that the old summer-town of Lynaberrack, and others like Achleum in Glen Feshie, had already become permanent farms.[116]

When Alexander Taylor began his survey of Badenoch in 1770, he was instructed to examine the shielings, 'to point out such parts as are fit for culti-vation [and] to erect them into new settlements for small tenants'.[117] This had already been implemented on the Duke's Strathavon estate in 1768, when leases required the cultivation of shielings.[118] In Strathspey, Sir James Grant, under the guidance of his mentor, William Lorimer, enthusiastically converted their summer pastures into permanent farms – though not with total success because, without shielings, tenants struggled to meet rental demands.[119]

Taylor clearly made little progress for Alexander Low's 1803 survey again condemned the local shielings as an 'idle & unprofitable practice'.[120] Yet, he reluctantly concluded, they were still essential to the local economy: 'this practice of Sheeling has been done away with in other Highland Districts', but in Badenoch 'the Argument in favour of Sheallings . . . carries with it great Plausibility, &, in some instances, Probability'. He acknowledged that transhu-mance 'takes off the Bulk of the Stock in Summer, & allows the Pasture at home to grow *rough* for Winter'. Furthermore, he accepted the climatic reality that most local shielings could never become permanent farms – 'those Tracts allotted for Sheallings are unfit for Wintering', even for commercial sheep farms. Hence, despite his ideological contempt, he proposed maintaining the shieling system until some alternative could be decided.

James Robertson, an advocate of improvement, but one who clearly under-stood the integrated economy, viewed the system more positively. Only through shielings could the total environment be effectively utilised: 'They have no other way, in the system of farming they follow, to depasture their distant grazings'.[121] He praised the management of the grazings: 'no other method seems to be equally just, or equally convenient', before castigating those who 'ridiculed' the system as 'persons who take a superficial view of their manners and customs'. He further rebuked the outsider: 'no person, without incurring the imputation of rashness, can call people unhappy, to whose sentiments he is an utter stranger'. In this robust defence, however, Robertson, too, fell into the romantic trap, describing how, after a happy day at the shielings, 'the whole hamlet retires to rest, and drown their fatigues in the soundest slumbers, on a bed of heath, whose mellifluous fragrance perfumes the whole dwelling.'

Transhumance was dependent on two factors. Firstly, the Highland black cattle of the eighteenth century were much lighter, slimmer, hardier and nimbler than today's breeds (one-third to one-half the weight of a modern cow), and so were ideally adapted for exploiting the rugged and boggy terrain of the Badenoch mountains. Indeed, the bigger, heavier breeds beloved by the improvers could never have reached the distant hill grazings, far less coped with the conditions, and significantly, Robertson noted that in Badenoch, even into the 1800s, 'a preference is given to the real Highland cattle'.[122]

The second key point was the grazing cycle itself. Though grazings and shielings have become largely synonymous, they originally had different connotations. The hill grazings encompassed the entire mountain hinterland of the davoch for communal use by tacksman and subtenant, usually comprising two or three different zones. Within these grazings were situated the shielings proper, the green oases, fertilised by generations of cattle, containing the bothies or huts. To utilise the different zones effectively, especially when several miles apart, farms required shieling bothies in each. As a further complication, different livestock had different grazing requirements – not just the cattle, horses, sheep and goats but also the separation of the milk or breeding stock from the yeld animals. Thus emerges a scenario of constant movement between the different zones and shieling sites with different animals – a system of perpetual transhumance that enabled maximum exploitation of different vegetation in different areas at different times of the year.

Mrs Grant of Laggan, who, with her minister husband ran the farm of Gaskbeg, revealed glimpses of this shieling usage in her letters: the women at the shielings 'changing their residence so often as they did in summer, from one bothy or glen to another'; 'her shepherd is in one glen, and her dairymaid in another with her milk cattle'; Ronald, a herd, coming down from 'the high hills, where our sheep and young horses are all summer' – three different animal categories simultaneously utilising three different parts of the domain.[123] Ralia also distinguished between his high and his low shielings, while Robertson described how families 'changed their residence more or less frequently, according to the extent of the hill-grass'.[124]

Most local farms, like those of the upper Spey in Laggan, did indeed have two or three separate shielings: a huge outrun from the farm serving as both a near shieling close to the head dyke and a mid one still contiguous but a few

miles distant, while all had a separate far or high one often many miles away
(Figure 4). Garvamore, for instance, had 'moor and moss ground lying South
from the Cornfields'; adjoining to the west of this and stretching for a considerable distance, a 'Hill Grazing called the Sheallings of Corry Laggan and Corry
Vein'; and 4 miles away on the other side of the Spey, a 'Hill Grazing in
Drummin called the Shealling of Sheiskanan Bain'. At Crathiemore the number
of shieling sites indicates even more clearly the intricacy of the system: hill
pastures 'lying North from and adjoining the Arable Lands'; 'on the East side
of Ault Marky, called Reanuillanich & Rea Ault Tarsen' ('rea' or 'rie' indicating
a residential shieling site); 'on the West side of Ault Markie, north from the
former and along the march of Strath Herick called Reanault Aur [and] Rea
Ault Darg', all the above being in a contiguous outrun from the farm; and a
separate 'Hill Grazing in Drummin called the Sheallings of Rea Ault Vanan
[with two separate shieling sites] lying on the South side of Loch Spey and
along the march of Lochaber about 8 miles Northwest of Crathy More'. The
total hill grazings of Crathiemore comprised 7,032 Scots acres (c.3,600
hectares/14 square miles) with at least six separate residential shieling sites,
and all valued at just £15.[125]

On Cluny Mains, the near shieling in Strath an Eilich (less than 2 miles
from the farm) bordered with and was actually lower in height than the arable
ground of the neighbouring Glen Banchor township of Dalnashalg, not surprisingly bringing the complaint that 'the Cluny Cattle eat even into the Corns of
Dalnashalg'.[126] At Gaskbeg, Mrs Grant was able to watch 'the dairymaids
descending like mountain nymphs from the Corry-buie' – a shieling close
enough to be clearly visible from the home farmhouse, while the fore-
mentioned 'high hills' were their distant shielings, 13 miles away near the source
of the Spey.[127] The township of Glengynack (above Kingussie village) itself at a
height of about 1,000 feet, had three distinct shielings in an unbroken outrun
from the farm northwards up and over the Monadhliaths to the River Dulnain:
the first just one mile away on the Allt a' Choire Bhuide at 1,300 feet, the second,
2 miles beyond that on the Allt Mor at 1,800 feet, and the third, on the Dulnain,
about 5 miles from the home farm, at nearly 2,000 feet (Figure 3 and Colour
plate 5).[128] Others had to travel further: Biallidmore's distant shieling was on
Loch Erichtside 15 miles away; Dalchully's even further, for they rented a field
at the west end of Loch Laggan for resting their cattle overnight.[129]

The utilisation of the different grazing zones reveals a considerable degree
of sophistication. The general perception of a short-term summer migration
to the shielings with the milk cows fails to recognise that this was but one cog

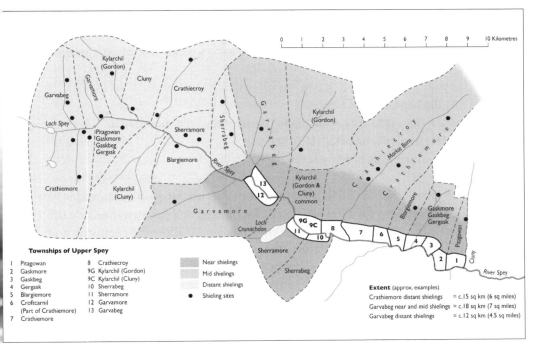

Figure 4

The townships, shielings and grazings of the upper Spey. (*Source*: Adapted from George Taylor, Plan of Badenoch, 1773, RCAHMS, SC1082428.) Taylor's map identifies the contiguous and distant grazings of each farm; the approximate division of the former into near and mid shielings has been added to reflect the evidence for cyclical movement within these vast outruns. The mid shieling zone of Garvabeg (top centre) is depicted in Colour plate 4.

in a much larger wheel. Macpherson of Nuidemore used his shielings from April to November, while Biallidmore similarly mentioned the 'Spring and Summer half year'.[130] Hence the grazing cycle itself needs to be analysed. In winter, the entire livestock, excepting the semi-wild hill horses, which according to Biallidmore remained on the hill all year, grazed the whole range of the township lands in common. Spring, however, saw the hill grazings take centre stage.

The first move traditionally occurred at Beltane, the first day of May, once the fresh growth appeared, and before the open rigs were sown. The by now semi-starved livestock – yeld cattle, sheep and goats, and, after ploughing, the farm horses – were sent out to different shieling sites depending on location, altitude, weather and, of course, the grass itself.[131] There they would graze off the coarse winter vegetation while fertilising the pasture on the lower shieling sites, tended, if at all, by herds and grasskeepers – a scene evocatively captured in 'The Drovers' Song':

> At the beginning of May
> when the cattle are on the high ground of the cold mountains,
> calves in plenty will run about the fold,
> with young girls herding them.[132]

At the same time, the milk cattle moved to the nearest pastures outside the head dyke, either returning each night for milking and housing, or using the near shieling huts, as at Corrybuie on Gaskbeg. To allow the cleansing and rejuvenation of the shieling grass, the yeld animals were moved from there around 25 May into the higher corries, either remaining there or even moving up onto the plateau as conditions improved over the summer.

In early June – the 'summer flitting' – the whole family moved to the shielings with the milking stock. The specific date when Cluny was permitted to occupy the Benalder shielings was 9 June, while the Glen Feshie folk moved to theirs a day later.[133] This was the first practicable time to move, not only because May was devoted to the vital task of peat-cutting, but because the high mountain grasses were only just rejuvenating. The duration of the summer season varied according to the location of shieling sites, grass conditions and weather patterns. The average was four to six weeks, time enough to allow the township grass to recover before the milk cattle returned. On one occasion Mrs Grant explained that her husband could not hold communion till 6 August because the shieling folks did not return till the 2nd – even the good Lord had to move to the rhythm of the grazing cycle – but another year the people stayed a week longer because 'the grass continues so good'.[134]

The summer flitting, however, was clearly not a one-off visit. In another letter dated 10 September, Mrs Grant mentioned cows and dairymaids having been at the Corrybuie shielings for ten days previously. So, her milk cattle, having returned from the distant shieling in early August, were sent out to the nearer one a month later for a short stay.[135] Similarly, Alexander Kennedy told how the 'tenants Milk Cows used to go [to Dalwhinnie] three different flittings during the Summer and Harvest'.[136] Ralia's system was different: in the 'Months of June & August . . . he Sends his whole ffamily & Milk Cattle to the Hill where they continue for a Month at a time', returning to Ralia in between. Patrick

Robertson, who shieled on the Atholl side of Drumochter, confirmed this practice: his cattle 'continued there till about midsummer, when they were brought down to his farm, having continued there about three weeks, and were then sent back to the shealing'.[137]

While these migrations were between farm and shieling, there was also continual movement between shielings. Malcolm Macpherson shieled 'the first part of the Summer Season at . . . Altancraggach', but for 'the latter part of the season' he moved to the shieling at Gerarie, both on Drumochter just 2 miles apart.[138] Daily migrations also occurred. The Presmuchrach tenants pastured between Altancraggach and Delachurn during 'the first part of the Day', obviously moving elsewhere later; at Benalder, 'it was customary . . . to drive their Cattle up to the Corry each day', returning in time for the evening milking; while the Invereshie tenants had 'a right to a day's pasture from their shealings . . . into the forests [of Glen Feshie] the cattle returning every night to their respective sheals'.[139] Milk cows naturally had the best grazing: Alexander Kennedy was ordered to keep the yeld cattle 'constantly . . . in Corrour and up the Faro [a remote high ridge] separately from the Milk Cows'.[140]

As time progressed the cycle reversed. The milk cows returned to the low grounds in August or September, while the yeld animals gradually moved down to the mid and then lower shielings as grass and weather dictated. The yeld beasts returned to the township mid November (the Glenbanchor date being 11 November) though this obviously depended on successful completion of the harvest.

The sophistication of the system is revealed in a shieling 'calendar' from Lochgarry on the south side of Drumochter.[141] Apart from the home farm the grazing zones were 'the strath', a 'low shieling' (unnamed), two mid shielings, and a distant or high shieling with the mountain plateau above it. Cattle were moved between these on nine different occasions between May and November, each stay varying from ten to twenty-eight days. On 1 May, or earlier if weather permitted, the yeld animals went directly to the distant grazing at the north-west corner of Loch Garry where they remained for the next five or six months, rotating regularly between the lochside shieling of Coire Essan, the corrie itself, and An Cearcall, the long high ridge above. There they remained 'till froast and Snow obledges them to come down to the Saunoch' (one of the mid shielings) where they were again to be kept 'as long as froast and Snow can admitt of', finally returning to the farm itself as late in November as possible.

The movements of the milk cattle were more complex. Their first move on 1 May was beyond the head dyke to the strath. On 25 May they moved to the mid shieling, Ruynasaurach, on 13 June to the low shieling, on 23 June to the high shieling of Coire Essan, on 20 July to the two mid shielings, Ruynasaurach and Saunoch, on 2 August down to the low shieling again, on 21 August back to the mid shieling of Saunoch, returning to the strath after 3 September, and then the home farm after harvest. As all these sites were used at least twice in the rotation, 'grasskeepers' were sent to protect the pasture in readiness for the return visit – complex enough, even before sheep, goats and horses were factored into the cycle. The system must have operated with more flexibility than this timetable suggests to allow for fluctuating weather conditions if nothing else, but it still provides a remarkable insight into the type of shieling management hinted at in the Badenoch records.[142]

This constant transhumance was essential to the pastoral process. The effect of systematic grazing and dunging on the different shielings was clearly understood: John Williams recommended to the Duke in 1769 that 'removing their Sheel-Booths on to a hethery know [knoll] every two, or at most three Summers, will sufficiently tathe [fertilise] any piece of hether, & make as good grass as any'; the Duke's leases of 1777 incorporated that very point; and James Robertson explained how hillsides 'covered with heath . . . became as green as a meadow, to the extent of several acres around the huts, by the manure of the cattle'.[143] Similarly, the regular rotation of shielings allowed pasture to clean and regenerate before the next visit, while returning to the home farm in midsummer would improve the township grazing by reducing the coarse grass, fertilising it and thereby extending its growing season. It was, thus, a well-honed and sophisticated system designed to extract maximum return from a hostile environment.

•   •   •

Communal grazing inevitably created a conflict of co-operation and self-interest within the community. While the sixteen tenants of Gaskinloan all cultivated their own individual arable rigs within their four separate townships (Plate 3), all sixteen simply grazed their livestock in common along with those of the tacksman, on the farm's vast moorland outrun. At their distant shieling at Loch Pattack, all the Gaskinloan stock mingled not just with those from neighbouring davochs but also from other estates (Plate 4). With no physical boundaries it required considerable tolerance and co-operation to manage grazings covering many square miles of wilderness, especially as the yeld beasts were not always herded. Macpherson of Biallidmore (a Gordon tacksman whose distant grazings bordered with the Cluny farm of Gaskinloan) explained, 'I am not in the practice nor Indeed able to afford Constant herds in the open Hills', and Lachlan Macpherson of Ralia confirmed that 'the distant grazings were until very lately little attended to'.[144]

The system operated through 'Good Neighbourhood', a general acceptance that livestock would inevitably stray onto others' grazings. After one grazing dispute between the Atholl and Badenoch tenants 'they aggreed to Live good Neighbours as their predecessors had done'.[145] Such mixed grazing was deemed 'promiscuous', leading to the wonderful complaint that 'The Dalnashalg folks eat the grass promiscuously'.[146] This 'tolerance' did not, however, convey legal rights. Finlay Macpherson, who shieled at Delachurn on Drumochter, stated that although Atholl cattle often grazed the Badenoch corries, 'they were not turned back as they were all in good Neighbourhood, but that they had no right to pasture there'.[147] The Delachurn cattle themselves were granted a tolerance 'to pass over the water of Truim and pasture as forward as that they could come home in due milking time' – a right specifically denied to their sheep and goats.[148]

The rising economic importance of pastoralism, however, led to a more possessive mindset. Patrick Robertson commented that 'there was little anxiety entertained about the preservation of the pasture . . . before sheep farming was introduced'.[149] But even before that, the increasing value of the cattle trade necessitated grass keepers to drive off and poind (impound) straying livestock. There were devious attempts to establish new territories through grazing someone else's land 'without interruption' (without your cattle being driven off). John Macpherson of Invereshie warned his brother about the Brae Ruthven folks continually using the Invereshie shieling at the Water of Bran in Glen Tromie: 'I have no doubt that by this manoeuvre, they mean in time to claim a privilege of Pasture there'.[150] When the Duke of Atholl poinded some Badenoch cattle from Drumochter in 1770, James Ross reckoned it was quite deliberate, 'with a View to prevent Seven Years uninterrupted possession – as I see the last poinding of the same kind was in Aug 1763'.[151] Seven years' uninterrupted grazing presumably established legal rights to pasturage.

Erecting bothies on another township's grazings was a clear attempt to establish possession, so the rightful occupiers naturally retaliated, and estate maps recorded where bothies had been 'thrown down' as evidence in territorial disputes (Plate 5). Such acts usually occurred within a legal framework, as when 'Paul of Clun came with a Notary Public and break down a Bothie which Cluny had built'.[152] It was largely a symbolic act. Atholl's men, for instance, were specifically instructed 'to take a Divot off the Bothie at Torcht as it was too nigh the Duke of Athole's March'.[153] Similarly, in Glen Feshie in 1727 where Mackintosh's men had built several bothies on Gordon lands, the Duke's tenants responded with 'a Court Interruption' which involved 'taking down a part of the ffeal or some of the materials off which the bothies were built'.[154] Such actions, however, could prove hazardous, for in this instance the Gordon men found themselves 'violently hindered' by a Mackintosh party armed with 'Guns, pistols Swords and Durks' – prompting the aggrieved response that this was 'in contempt of the Laws against wearing such weapons'.

•   •   •

Land surveyor William Tennoch's brief statement, 'To these distant Grazings they drive up all their Sheep and Cattle In the Summer, and there make quantities of Cheese and Butter', serves as reminder that shielings were integral to subsistence – the combined produce of cattle, sheep and goats being a crucial factor in the domestic economy.[155] On his travels, John Walker noticed that, though mountain pastures produced lower yields, the milk was much superior, creating butter of 'exquisite flavour and sweetness', and cheese 'richer than any other cheese in the kingdom'.[156] Women were also busy with other subsistence tasks at shielings like Delachurn, where Bishop Forbes observed 'a Woman big with Child, spinning at the Mickle Wheel, and another Woman carding the Wool for her'.[157]

Male tasks included hut maintenance, herding and grasskeeping, but primarily summer was the time for cutting and transporting the timber, turf, divot and thatch necessary for structural repairs to the vacant wintertown dwellings. Statute labour duties (compulsory road repairs) were also fulfilled at this time.[158] But the shieling season, especially at more remote sites, also provided opportunities to supplement the larder with produce from hill and loch. Mrs Grant explained one reason for returning from the shielings in early August (the twelfth being the official start of the shooting season): 'the time arrives when they dare no longer fish and shoot'.[159] The presence of corn kilns at Delachurn in Drumochter and Allt a Chaorainn in Glen Banchor, and stills as at Allt Unaig behind Kingussie, suggests that whisky was also a shieling product, particularly after the outlawing of small stills in 1786.[160]

Shielings provide another insight into the social hierarchy, for all classes used these pastures. Some tacksmen maintained their own grazings: Breakachy kept the Torcht 'for the Pasture of his own Catle . . . and gave grass to his tennants elsewhere'.[161] But Delachurn reveals a more integrated community. There the typical rudimentary bothies of 3–5 metres long were intermixed with more substantial buildings of 6–8 metres and even one or two of 12 metres, obviously requiring cruck-framed roofs. Most were distinctively 'L-shaped', probably accommodating a dairy room or storage compartment. Bishop Geddes confirmed the existence of substantial structures on Drumochter, describing 'a genuine shealing house . . . about 30 feet long', with cruck frame.[162] Robertson explained that these shieling communities reflected the social mix: 'The huts in which they lived were in proportion to the affluence and rank of the different possessors: some indeed mean enough, but some others consisting of two or three apartments, besides a proper place for milk' – hardly surprising if tacksman and subtenants were shieling in the same territory.[163]

Conclusion

To the contemporary critic the eighteenth-century Badenoch economy was easy prey. Whether to a southerner like the Reverend Hall or an improver like Lorimer it was, simply, primitive. But such critics were far from impartial. They were outsiders with their own agenda, one of progress and commercialism to which the concept of mere subsistence was anathema. Nor could perceptions be divorced from ideology – if the Highlander was a savage, the backwardness of his economy was a *sine qua non*. The most vocal critics were those improvers who equated progress with the southern model: men ignorant not just of the region's environmental constraints, but also of its traditional agricultural system.

Humans had, after all, farmed in Badenoch – and survived – for 5,000 years. Harnessing the cumulative wisdom of many generations, they had evolved strategies for coaxing life's necessities out of their fickle environment. What the outsider saw as conservatism was perhaps born of an innate understanding of that environment and the seasonal rhythms imposed by it – or perhaps he was simply blind to what he saw. To one passing traveller, Drumochter appeared as 'Siberian wastes', yet every inch of those hills was somebody's grazing, and the more astute Bishop Forbes saw 'All along Herds of black Cattle, and numbers of young Colts running wild', tended by bustling shieling communities (Figures 5a and 5b).[164] Economy was very much in the eye – or mindset – of the beholder.

Historiography also has focused too heavily on the deficiencies of Highland agriculture, measuring it unfavourably against the Lowland British model of improvement rather than considering it within the wider European context of transhumant peasant farming. Such critics have indeed been condemned for their 'uncritical acceptance of improving propaganda which sets the worst of traditionalist farming against the best of commercialised agriculture'.[165]

A true assessment of the farming system depends not on dissecting its component parts but on appraising its totality. Arable and pastoral were not separate, conflicting entities, but, through transhumance, worked in harmony. There was nothing in this worthy of condemnation, for rotational summer grazing was the most effective way to utilise their environment – in the same way that Alpine and Scandinavian communities operated their 'summer farms'. Swedish transhumance, for example, was 'a strategic choice made by the peasants to use the landscape resources in an efficient and sustainable way'; in the Swiss Alps, it 'effectively coordinates the use of limited land resources which are dependent on seasons'.[166] Both countries also employed rotational grazing over three different summer-pasture zones – similar to the central Highlands, though generally assessed in far more positive terms.

Subsistence in Badenoch, likewise, came not from one particular food source but from the totality of produce. As annual grain shortages were inevitable, so a seasonal dietary system evolved encompassing both cereal and dairy in varying degrees – again, typical of all predominantly pastoral societies. There was, too, an inbuilt safety net. The long-standing family bonds of the township community provided a mutual support and security that was impossible within the rapidly expanding urban environment, while the Badenoch mixed economy provided a degree of security lacking to the specialist arable farmer.[167]

Figure 5a (opposite top)
The vast and supposedly waste lands of the Drumochter hills, with the principal farms situated on the more fertile and lower riverside lands to the north.

Figure 5b (opposite bottom)
The same Drumochter hills showing the hill grazings of the farms in 5a, revealing the total exploitation of this seemingly empty landscape. (Source: Adapted from George Taylor, Plan of Badenoch, 1773, RCAHMS, SC1082428.)

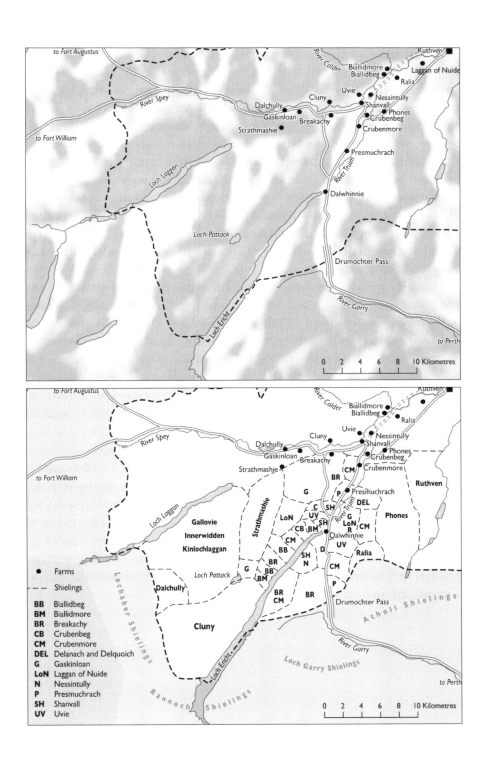

Top map labels:

to Fort Augustus

River Calder

Ruthven

Biallidmore
Biallidbeg
Laggan of Nuide
Ralia

Uvie
Cluny
Nessintully
Shanvall
Phones
Crubenbeg
Crubenmore

River Spey

Dalchully
Gaskinloan
Breakachy

to Fort William

Strathmashie

Presmuchrach

River Truim

Dalwhinnie

Loch Laggan

Loch Pattack

Drumochter Pass

River Garry

to Perth

0 2 4 6 8 10 Kilometres

Bottom map labels:

to Fort Augustus

River Calder

Ruthven

Biallidmore
Biallidbeg
Ralia

Uvie
Cluny
Nessintully
Shanvall
Phones
Crubenbeg
Crubenmore

River Spey

Dalchully
Gaskinloan
Breakachy

to Fort William

Strathmashie

CM
BR
G
C
SH
P
Presmuchrach
DEL

Ruthven

Phones

Gallovie

Innerwidden

Kinlochlaggan

Strathmashie

LoN
UV
SH
CB
BM
CM
BB
G
LoN
R
CM
Dalwhinnie
UV

Ralia

SH
N
D
CM

Loch Laggan

Loch Pattack

Dalchully

G
BR
BB
BM
BR
CM

BR

P

Drumochter Pass

Cluny

Atholl Shielings

Lochaber Shielings

Loch Ericht

River Garry

Loch Garry Shielings

Rannoch Shielings

to Perth

0 2 4 6 8 10 Kilometres

Legend:

● Farms
- - - Shielings

BB	Biallidbeg
BM	Biallidmore
BR	Breakachy
CB	Crubenbeg
CM	Crubenmore
DEL	Delanach and Delquoich
G	Gaskinloan
LoN	Laggan of Nuide
N	Nessintully
P	Presmuchrach
SH	Shanvall
UV	Uvie

These potential benefits cannot, however, disguise the inherent limitations of the economy: market isolation, topography, altitude and climate all conspired against any degree of stability or long-term security, let alone improvement. Yet, despite these deficiencies, Badenoch did have the capacity to sustain a population of around 5,000 people, albeit on a rudimentary level, while providing the additional wherewithal to meet cash rental demands. To that extent at least, it proved relatively successful in overcoming its many constraints. How long it could sustain this self-sufficiency would depend not just on underlying forces such as population, climate and market trends, but also on the human factor, for it would prove vulnerable to externally generated notions of 'improvement'. Indeed, any disruption of the vertical farm alignment would destroy the fragile equilibrium between people and land – and hence between people and subsistence.

Fragility was, of course, the nature of the agricultural economy. Like any pre-industrial peasant society, it was, to return to Devine's words, 'delicately and precariously balanced'. While it provided a sufficiency in good years, potential disaster was never far removed, and the annual fear of harvest failure must have haunted the mind. Hardship was not uncommon, however stoically accepted, and before the century's end Badenoch would, more than once, suffer the ravages of famine. Such patterns of sufficiency and dearth, however, have to be seen within the context of eighteenth-century European peasant lifestyles, rather than as some unique product of Highland backwardness, or worse, the gross inadequacy of the region's indigenous populace.

When recording his farming activities during the 1770s, 'Old Balnespick' never failed to add, at the beginning and end of both sowing and harvest, the words, 'by the blessing of God'.[168] It may just have been the foible of a devout old Presbyterian: it could also have been a simple recognition of the extent to which a subsistence economy was at the mercy of its environment. There was, however, plenty scope for men of Balnespick's class – and, to a degree, those of lower rank as well – to exploit that fickle environment for their own gain as commercialism began to take hold in Badenoch.

Chapter 3
The Commercial Economy

September 1767: two powerful noblemen were locked in dispute over possession of the Drumochter hills, the Duke of Gordon on the north side, and the Duke of Atholl on the south. James Gordon, head officer on the Gordon estates, described how thirty-five years earlier his predecessor, James Gordon senior, had walked him over the entire estate march (boundary), including the 3,000-foot Drumochter plateau, to identify the boundary markers – no mean feat for a man of eighty-seven. The younger man explained how 'James Gordon [senior] gave the Deponent [James junior] a Blow on the side of the head at different parts of the March, that he might remember the March more particularly, and mentioned to the Deponent, that his Predecessor in office had done the like to him'. A colourful anecdote, but the lesson was deadly serious, because, as the older man warned, 'they had such a powerful antagonist as the Duke of Atholl'.[1]

Contemporary maps confirm Atholl's ambitions. The traditional boundary was the mountain called the Torcht or Boar of Badenoch, but on Atholl estate maps it provocatively appeared as the 'Duke of Atholl's Boar' (Plate 6a and b). The Badenoch tacksmen, however, were similarly 'endeavouring to Encroach on the Marches of Lochgarie', and 'still kept possession, at least came back soon after being driven off'.[2] Such competition illustrates the increasing importance of this seemingly waste mountain landscape, and not just at ducal level, for those hills were equally contested by laird, tacksman and tenant – primarily for the burgeoning commercial cattle trade that was growing rapidly in the years after the Union of Scotland and England in 1707. Indeed, the very factors restricting the regional economy now became assets. The vast hinterland presented unlimited grazing potential, while isolation mattered not to a commodity that transported itself to market. Furthermore, Badenoch was ideally placed for the great Lowland trysts (cattle markets).

Progress in the Highlands has largely been attributed to the proprietorial classes – 'commercial landlordism', with landowners 'fundamental in accelerating social change'.[3] It was also seen as coming from outwith the region: 'commercial pastoralism entered the Highland zone from the south and east', or even that 'market forces drove the Highlands in the direction of pastoralism'.[4] Commercial pastoralism in Badenoch, however, was driven not by landowners or outsiders, but by the indigenous tacksman class who exploited the opportunities created by market forces with vigour, initiative and no little acumen – just as industrial entrepreneurs like Richard Arkwright and David Dale exploited those same forces within the textile industries of northern England and Lowland Scotland. The key to understanding both the nature of commercial pastoralism in Badenoch and the role of its indigenous tacksmen lies in analysing the principal components of the business – cattle farming, commercial grazing, land hunger, and droving – with the inevitable challenges and tensions resulting from a commercially driven economy.

Cattle farming

'Grass parks are much wanted in Badenoch, much more so than in any place', reported George Brown in 1771 – 'the inhabitants are mostly all dealers in Cattle and would give any rent for Grass parks'.[5] While highlighting the predominance of cattle, Brown implied that this was more so in Badenoch than other regions. Interestingly, his proposal to convert the Spey's rich arable haughs into grass parks ran contrary to contemporary agricultural thinking. Clearly, commercial pastoralism was already well-established within the region, as further evidenced by those tacksmen who had acquired substantial territories with vast grazings, like the Benchar Macphersons with their 25,000 acres of hill ground.

In the early 1700s there was already evidence of substantial herds. In 1709, one writer complained of the ruination of Gaick, once 'the flower and Garden of all the Duke of Gordon's fforests' (deer forests rather than woodland), though now 'it is past Deserving the name of a forest, Because the forsaid plains and Insyde is possest by two or three Gentlemen . . . who dayly pasture there . . . with a great number of Cowes, oxen, horse, sheep, wedders, goats'.[6] Further east, in the Forest of Mar, figures from 1729 suggest that tacksmen were keeping herds of 100 to 200 cattle, far beyond mere domestic needs.[7]

Precise cattle numbers are hard to ascertain. The 1771 souming for Cluny estate recorded for the tacksmen of Cluny Mains, Laggan and Nuidemore respectively, numbers of sixty, ninety-four and fifty-four.[8] Mackintosh of Balnespick had seventy-five cattle in 1768; John Macpherson of Inverhall fifty-one in 1770; George Macpherson of Invereshie fifty-four in 1786.[9] Lachlan Macpherson of Dalchully sent twenty-two cattle for wintering in 1773, representing only the surplus which he could not feed himself, while Lachlan Macpherson of Ralia was wintering over 120 cattle in Gaick, a figure excluding his milk or breeding stock.[10] Most remarkably, however, Andrew Macpherson of Benchar noted in 1784 that to clear a £200 debt he had 'sold Cattle to that same amount' – at current prices, seventy to eighty beasts, suggesting a very substantial total herd of 300 or more.[11]

Reported losses from the *creach* (cattle-raids), also indicate high numbers. When Cluny Macpherson set up his famous 'cattle watch' in Badenoch in 1744, he mentioned that, in a single year, local farmers with a rent of only £15 were losing £100 worth of cattle, with the whole region losing ten times that value – huge losses, considering that a cow then was worth little more than £1.[12] Five years later a similar complaint suggested that 'the Country of Badenoch had been annually skaithed … in upwards of a thousand pounds sterling' through the thieving of the Loch Laggan Macdonells.[13] Though almost certainly exaggerated claims, if the region was sustaining even a fraction of those losses, total cattle numbers must have been substantial.

Herds were, of course, normally acquired by more legitimate means, through breeding or purchase. Cattle could be taken in lieu of rent in times of hardship – William Tod, the Duke's factor, being instructed, 'If they have not Money, I should have no objection to your taking Cattle from them'.[14] Animals were also seized as payment for debts, though clearly not always a wise transaction: 'an exceeding bad Cow and Stirk . . . which his son got from a Desperat Debtor . . . in Badinough'.[15]

But no matter how profitable, tacksmen could keep no more beasts than could be sustained on the 'wintertown' from November till April. As late as 1803, Alexander Low commented in his survey of Badenoch: 'The whole of the District is evidently suited for Stock, but unfortunately for it, there is a deficiency in the quantity of arable Land for raising Winter food for that Stock.'[16] Various ploys to circumvent the problem were attempted. Subtenants could be made to overwinter the tacksman's cattle – in 1774, Balnespick recorded that the Macphails 'have seven head of my cattle to winter which will amount to one pound one shilling', later deducted from their rent.[17] Dalchully sent cattle westwards to Torgulbin for 'foddering' at 5 shillings per beast;

Invereshie sometimes wintered his in Strathspey; Balnespick, Ballachroan and Benchar all sought farms in Lochaber, presumably for the milder climate and earlier spring grass.[18] John Dow did secure one such farm, Fersit, for £60 (actually dearer than his home farm of Ballachroan), installing his brother as manager.[19] When Benchar requested Kilmonivaig in Lochaber for wintering, Tod acknowledged 'it would indeed be of the greatest Importance to him as such – there can be no objection to him having a farm in that Country – he will pay any Rent.'[20] The desperation for winter grazing demonstrates not only the importance attached to increasing cattle numbers, but also the investment tacksmen were willing to make to maximise profits.

Cattle were not, of course, the only commercial livestock. Herds of semi-wild ponies, 'capable of enduring incredible fatigue', roamed the Badenoch hills well into the nineteenth century.[21] Even before the '45, Cluny Macpherson was commercially breeding a herd of 'some hundred mares' on Benalder.[22] In 1763, Bishop Forbes observed on Drumochter 'numbers of young Colts running wild, 5 or 6 of them frequently after one and the same Mother . . . the most enduring Horses of any, when well broke.'[23] These ponies actually fetched higher prices than cattle in the 1750s (£2 10s to £2) with the bonus that they ran free most of the year – indeed, Macpherson of Biallidmore left his hill horses on Loch Erichtside 'through the whole year.'[24] Ponies were often sold close to home. In 1777, John Maclean of Pitmain sold a dozen within Badenoch and six to Ross-shire for a total of £120.[25] But market demand went much further. Robertson noted that ponies 'were sent down in droves to all countries in Britain, annually, for sale', while on the neighbouring estate of Rannoch, the factor reported that they were 'mostly sold into England . . . and are particularly used about Newcastle for the coles etc.'[26] Though there is no proven link between Badenoch and the English coal mines, it would certainly have provided an obvious and lucrative market.

Sheep and goats also formed part of the livestock trade. Commercial sheep farming in Badenoch was undoubtedly born in the 1760s, again driven by the indigenous tacksmen. The earliest example was at Catlag, where Captain Duncan Macpherson (Breakachy's son) proposed 'turning the whole Hill into an inclosed sheep pasture', adding, to demonstrate his innovative approach, 'A Method of Improvement, which has not as yet been attempted in that Country.'[27] Others were quick to see this new potential. In 1771, George Brown recorded that the Pitmain moorland was already 'a good sheep walk [farm], and Mr. McLean [the tacksman] keeps a flock of wedders constantly in it, and they seldom or ever come down from the hills'. It was Brown's only use of the term 'sheep walk' in his survey, while his reference to sheep staying on the hill implies a flock of blackface sheep, for the smaller native breed were generally housed at night. Macpherson of Benchar was also 'keeping a huge flock of wedders' on his lands, while Invereshie had an established sheep farm in Glen Feshie by the 1760s, with a 'lamb herd' looking after sixty-seven lambs, and a 'wedder herd' with 274 wedders – primarily the 'custom wedders' paid in rent.[28] These early Badenoch sheep farms must, however, be viewed in context. Unlike the huge sheep walks of later years which resulted in widespread clearances, they were evolving within the framework of the mixed farm economy: merely another string to the tacksman's commercial bow.

As commercial pastoralism expanded, the tacksman could obviously not manage the increasing numbers himself. Sometimes professional herds were employed: many of the witnesses testifying over the hill grazing disputes were herds or grasskeepers. Finlay Macpherson from Presmuchrach herded in the Drumochter hills for thirty years, tending cattle from Lochgarry 'in the Summer and Harvest Season', while looking after 'Malcolm Macpherson in Crubenmores Catle during the winter and spring'.[29] Bowman farms were also established, where the tacksman or laird leased a fully-stocked farm to a trustworthy tenant (the bowman), in return for a fixed payment of rent, dairy produce and calves. While the tacksman retained ownership of the original stock, the bowman was entitled to any calves or dairy produce surplus to the rental.[30] Breakachy and Cluny both used bowmen in the first half of the century, while Invereshie farmed his sheep on this system in the 1760s.[31]

Profitability is hard to gauge, but because drovers would generally not take cattle under four years old, substantial herds were required to sustain annual sales. Balnespick's cattle stock in November 1768 totalled seventy-three – twenty-nine breeding cows, ten calves, fourteen at two years old, thirteen at three, five at four, and two of five or older. The lower number of four-year-olds suggests he had already sold eight or nine that year, possibly intending to sell the remaining five later. Thus Balnespick, one of the biggest tacksman-farmers, was selling only eight to thirteen cattle annually out of a herd of over seventy. Later figures confirm this: in 1774, he sold thirteen, but a year later only six, perhaps reflecting a decrease in the total herd due to economic conditions.[32] Such numbers would not create substantial profits. In 1750, ten cattle a year might have brought a modest return of £15, and in the 1770s, £20 to £30, but the wintering costs of a herd of sixty to seventy beasts, as well as drovers' fees, had to be set against this. Balnespick's thirteen cattle in 1774 would, in reality, not have covered even half his farm rental of £84.

Livestock sales were, of course, supplemented by the dairy. I.F. Grant noted that in 1783 a Ross-shire farmer with twenty milk cows sold 25 stones each of butter and cheese for £14 13s 4d, a significant bonus.[33] Such quantities were not unusual, for Miss Nelly Mackintosh, the formidable tacksman of Kincraig, sent 20 stones of cheese and 3 ankers (roughly 30 gallons) of butter to the market at Dunkeld in 1788, entrusting the sale to two sheep drovers, the Cattanachs of Strone.[34] The anticipated profits, however, never materialised: Miss Nelly had been cheated. She railed at her lawyer that the younger Cattanach did 'fugitate [run away] and eloped hiddenly to the loss of all his Creditors.'[35] Later, after seeing him flaunt a set of new clothes, her indignation overflowed – 'were they fit for a common tenant's son? Did he wear scarlet in his short coat Riffled shirts & other habiliments above his rank?'[36] She hounded Cattanach for three years until he was finally incarcerated in Inverness tolbooth (prison). Fraud apart, Miss Nelly's case demonstrates the potential importance of dairy produce in the commercial economy, while offering an unusual glimpse into women's status in contemporary society.

Livestock sales and dairy profits would have secured the tacksman no more than a modest annual income, but as his rent was generally covered by what his subtenants paid him, the pastoral return was total profit. Furthermore, as the Reverend James Hall noted, it was achieved with little effort from the farmers, who 'gain money with less trouble by tending them [cattle] than by the laborious business of ploughing, harrowing, etc' – similarly in Lochaber where John Williams, a mineralogist surveying the Gordon estates, observed that 'The Gentlemen . . . will only mind their Cattle, the management . . . being attended with less expence & much less attention to themselves.'[37] Commercial ambitions were, however, limited by geographic and environmental parameters – Sutherland and Argyll, for instance, exported salt beef by coastal transport, an impossibility for land-locked Badenoch.[38] The most significant obstacle, however, was seasonal: selling even ten to twenty beasts annually required the overwintering of large permanent herds – and these simply could not expand beyond the farm's fodder potential.

Commercial Grazing

Breaking the environmental shackles required both circumstance and enterprise. If there was an abundance of hill pasture for half the year, then success lay in exploiting that facility. The other half of the equation lay in the 'low countries' where the conversion of grasslands to arable during the Agricultural

Revolution left a desperate shortage of grazing during the growing season.[39] The tacksmen were not slow to marry the two.

At Easter Lynwilg, George Brown noted, 'The Principal Tacksman is in the practice of taking in what they call Gaul cattle, or Cattle in summer to Grass from the Low Country.'[40] *Gall* (foreign) cattle – also called strange, outlandish, low-country, and grassing cattle – were brought in from the Moray coast and Perthshire to graze the Badenoch hills from spring to autumn. Most farms in the region followed this system: indeed, Brown only mentioned one, Pitchurn, that did not.

The practice was long established. John Roy Robertson referred to the pasturing of '600 Cattle . . . in Corrydoan for fifteen or twenty days each year' (Colour plate 6a and b), dating it back through oral tradition to 'the beginning of the bad years in time of King William's Wars [1688–97]', after the ousting of King James VII.[41] Similarly, Thomas Macpherson in Tullichierro remembered 'that Donald McHornish [tacksman of Dalnashalg] was in the life of pasturing Gaul Cattle in the first part of the Season at Ri Lossich', possibly in the 1680s.[42] In 1728, Cluny Macpherson promised the Duke 'to take in no cattle into the Shealing of Inveralder [in Benalder Forest] Except such as properly belong to my self & possessors [tenants]' – implying that the practice was already commonplace.[43] Duncan Campbell, herding in Drumochter since the 1730s, described how he had seen 'low Country Cattle Grasing in Corrydoan and that they were Herded there night and day.'[44] That same corrie was also used by Breakachy for his 'Grassing Catle.'[45]

A letter from some Morayshire farmers in 1766 gives an insight into this trade:

> for a number of years past We are in use of Sending Oxen and Cattle
> to Alexander McDonell of Tullochcrom [Loch Laggan] on Summer
> Grass and in the Course of our dealing ffound he did all manner of
> Justice in grasing our Bestials . . . [It] would be Laying us under the
> Greatest Hardships where to provide ourselves so well in Sumer Grass
> or with a man that would use us so discreetly.[46]

That nineteen farmers signed the letter reveals the extent and importance of this grazing facility, for the logistics and costs of driving large numbers of cattle 80 miles in each direction were considerable (Figure 6). Nor was this an informal arrangement, because Macdonell 'always made the agreed satisfaction for any Beast casually lost', implying a contractual compensation scheme.

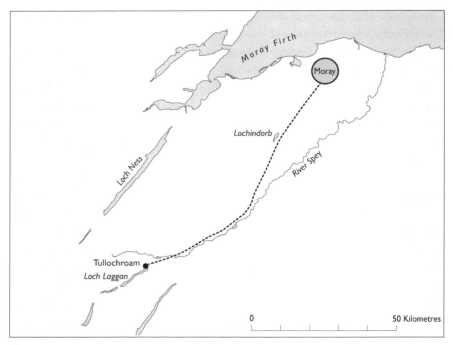

Figure 6
The route taken by the Morayshire *gall* cattle, showing the rendezvous at
Lochindorb.

A dispute in 1765 over a stolen cow revealed further details. The documents referred to 'the greatest part of the Cattle a-grazing in that Country [Laggan] and particularly those Grazed by [Tullochroam]' being driven home after harvest, implying considerable numbers.[47] Angus McGilivandrich, a herd from Brae Laggan, also explained how the cattle were 'Drove Down to the place of Lochindorb in order to be returned to their respective owners'. Tullochroam himself accompanied the cattle to this halfway rendezvous, presumably to collect payment from the Moray farmers.

The income generated from such transactions is impossible to calculate. According to Andrew Wight, the rate for Perthshire cattle sent to the Highlands in 1778 was 'from one to four shillings per head', while in 1794, Nairnshire farmers were being charged up to 1s 6d per beast for three months 'in the glens and mountains in the Highlands'.[48] As there were 11,000 cattle in that county alone, nearly all summering in the Highlands, this was obviously a significant trade.

How many were pastured in Badenoch is not known. In Strathavon, individual tenants were taking in as many as one hundred Lowland cattle, with beasts from fifty different farms being brought in together.[49] However, much higher numbers were quoted by the Lochgarry herds who grazed low-country cattle on Drumochter. Alexander Robertson had '600 Head of Cattle Graseing in Corrydoan'; Patrick Robertson 'had some years seven eight and nine hundred Cattle and one year a thousand'; and Patrick McIlguie recalled that he 'had near a thousand head of Cattle up the Grass that season'. All three were grazing the fore-mentioned Corrydoan as part of a rotational system similar to the shielings, staying two to three weeks there until the cattle had – not surprisingly – 'eated the Grass quite bare'. These cattle were additional to their own stock, for Alexander Robertson's huge herd of 'Grassing Cattle' were kept separate from 'the other Catle belonging to Lochgarry'.[50]

Such figures might, of course, be exaggerated, but they are consistent with contemporary drove numbers. Besides, it is inconceivable that any herd could control such large numbers of cattle, often from numerous different owners, without knowing exactly how many he held from each. All cattle bore their owner's mark (usually tar) and Alexander Canach explained that while in the hills they 'surrounded [the stock] once a fortnight in order to count them'.[51] When returning in autumn, these herds were obviously accountable to the owners for every beast.

Gall cattle were not exclusive to tacksmen. Because no costs were involved, ordinary tenants could exploit this small commercial window. The tenants of Glengynack township, for example, used their shieling on the Dulnain to 'take in Gaul cattle for eating the Grass', as did those of Easter Lynwilg, while those Presmuchrach tenants who converted their arable rigs to grass in the 1770s were also targeting the grazing market. Invereshie's attempt to ban his tenantry 'from bringing in any Strange catle horses Goat or Sheep' because of the danger of overgrazing, shows that the common people were indulging in the practice to boost their income.[52] If they were then taking in the tacksman's cattle for winter feeding (as with Balnespick), it further demonstrates a well-managed farm economy, with all-year-round benefits for the tenantry. Summer grazing remained profitable into the next century, for George Brown's 1804 report on upper Glen Feshie recommended that any tenant would prosper if he 'will take in what is called Gaul Cattle'. He calculated that 400 black cattle could be grazed there from June to August, and even if the rent were 100 guineas, the tenant would still be 'handsomely paid for his pains and Labour'.[53]

Badenoch's summer potential was exploited in other ways. Lachlan Macpherson of Cluny 'not only buys in cattle to pasture but takes in Cattle upon Grass Maill'.[54] Purchasing stock for summer grazing then selling on in autumn would obviously bring easy profits, while 'grass-mail' – renting pasture to commercial graziers – also brought good income with little or no expense to the tacksman. The importance of this business was revealed when cattle prices crashed in 1771, forcing Archibald Macdonald of Fersit to give up his farm because there was 'no demand for grass by Grasiers as formerly ... Those that have taken grass from me for years past from the South Country have renounced the Same'.[55] Depressions apart, this was another commercial opportunity open to the common people, like the Lochgarry tenants who 'set their shealings [on Drumochter] for rent' to Lowland graziers.[56] There is no questioning the profitability of such arrangements, but Macdonald's case illustrates the inherent vulnerability of the cattle economy.

Large-scale cattle farming seems to have resulted in early clearances in Argyll and Perthshire according to John Walker, who observed in the 1760s that 'many tenants were turned out of their possessions' to create such farms.[57] On the Duke's Lochaber lands there was an interesting experiment in hybrid stock farms, converting all the arable to grass, then keeping sheep on the higher ground and cattle on the lower, inevitably leading to substantial clearances.[58] There is, however, no specific evidence of cattle-related depopulation in Badenoch: Hugh Macpherson of Uvie did class himself as 'a dealler in cattle', and he did remove his subtenants in the 1750s, but whether the two were connected is not clear.[59] Indeed, the region seems to have maintained a reasonably successful balance between the needs of commercial and domestic pastoralism.

A further strand of commercial grazing came via the professional droving fraternity. Two Mackintosh drovers from Inverness-shire regularly rented the Drumochter hills for the season at the rate of £5 per corrie, likewise Breakachy's brother, Angus Macpherson of Flichity, another big commercial drover. John Macpherson, a herd, described how Flichity 'keeped Catle there from the beginning of the Season till he carried them off for the ffairs', while another herd, Angus Stewart, noted they were held in the 3-mile-long Corry-doan, filling it 'from one End to the other' – clearly a substantial drove. This enterprise was not without its hazards however, because Flichity 'lost more Catle yearly over the Rocks of Corriecragganach [Sgairneach Mhor] and Mackronach [Mharconaich] than the value of his rent', and soon abandoned the scheme (Colour plate 6a).[60]

Money was also extracted from drovers *en route* to market by renting official overnight stances for the cattle as at Garvamore and Druminlaggan, while the inn at Dalwhinnie was particularly profitable 'as the great Droves of Cattle from the North have no other halting place'.[61] William Tennoch recommended enclosing proper stances, not only 'very valuable', but – an added bonus – 'with such hudge Droves of Cattle the soil would be greatly enriched'.[62] While the profits from stances generally went to the tacksman, ordinary farmers once again capitalised by renting their roadside shielings. The Strathmashie tenants 'were in use of lodging droves on the North Side of the Burn of Sloch . . . and received payment for them'; Finlay Macdonald from Presmuchrach was privately renting the township pasture to passing drovers; at Dalnaspidal the tenants 'used to exact money from the droves when passing through the grazings, for pasturing thereon', sharing the proceeds between them.[63]

Charging for overnight stances appears to have been a relatively new form of commercialism. In 1773, drovers complained that 'till of late years, the hill grass, especially in the Center of the Highlands was of much less value than now by which means Drovers were allowed to . . . pasture near the Road where most convenient for them, without payment'.[64] However, because of the huge rise in value, they now 'cannot find Grass for their cattle'. With Badenoch's vast hill resources and the huge numbers of droves funnelling through the region, here was another source of income to be exploited at all social levels.

While in some parts of the Highlands the commercial success of droving led to the permanent settlement of shielings, the opposite appears to be the case in Badenoch. Here, the wealth of the professional cattle dealers depended totally on maintaining as much hill grazing as possible to facilitate their commercial grazing and droving operations.

Land Hunger

Overgrazing and the consequent degrading of pasture became a constant worry. As tacksman of Sronavadie in 1757, Breakachy was warned 'Not to be a Burden upon the Tenants of Strathmashie by Bringing too heavy a Load of Cattle upon the possession', but years later he was still at it, having 'so overstocked his Grounds [on Drumochter] that Sir Roberts [Menzies] tenants are quite oppressed'.[65] George Brown similarly criticised the Lynwilg tacksman who 'overstocks his own pasture', likewise the tenantry of Delfour.[66] This was presumably why Macpherson of Pitchurn refused to keep *gall* cattle, and why Invereshie had tried to ban them.[67] Overgrazing could reduce the value of local stock with a resultant drop in income. Short-term economic gain for the tenantry could easily become a long-term loss for the estate.

The Gordons responded quickly to the cattle boom, even leasing precious hunting forests for grazing. Though Dukes Cosmo and Alexander were generally apathetic towards agricultural improvement on their Highland estates, cattle provided an easy cash bonanza with little effort or initiative on the landowner's part. Traditionally, the forest grazings were a lucrative perk of the forester, Cluny Macpherson having the exclusive rights to Benalder, and Breakachy to Drumochter. But as early as 1729, Brigadier Mackintosh of Borlum (laird of Raitts) had commented how 'The few Mountains and Wastes left' were now 'rented out, to graze black Cattle on', and Lachlan Shaw confirmed that deer forests were 'everywhere laid open for pasturing cattle' by 1775.[68] Drumochter had been leased to Shaw Mackintosh (the Brigadier's son) in the 1720s 'for Pasturage to Catle'; at Benalder, the Duke 'let the whole forest as a grazing' in 1752; that same year, Glen Feshie Forest was leased to George Macpherson of Invereshie for pasture.[69] The only one not sacrificed was Gaick, Duke Alexander's favourite hunting reserve, a cryptic note in the 1771 survey simply stating 'kept for deer' – though hundreds of cattle were actually grazing there illegally.[70]

Disputes naturally increased. Grazing pressures meant cattle wandered into deer forests where poinding (seizing cattle for grazing illegally and fining the owners) was inevitable. Invereshie organised permanent herds because his tenants' beasts were straying into neighbouring forests, which 'Has been more prejudiciale to them by pay[ing] Trespass money and there travell and Expence on Reliving [relieving] them in Atholl and Mare [Mar]'.[71] John Macpherson of Invernahavon explained that when the Atholl folks 'brought in Catle from other Countries . . . he would be harder on them & accordingly did poind some of their Catle'.[72] Poinding, indeed, became a lucrative business: John Maclean, when forester in Gaick, made £100 in just one year from fines on trespassing cattle, double the rental of his combined farm of Pitmain and Kingussie.[73] But the rise of poinding suggests an erosion of traditional values; a more aggressive society in which the communal concepts of good neighbourhood and tolerance gave way to a more commercially oriented self-interest.

Such disputes were common – but not just at tenant level. When a party of sixty Atholl men rounded up the Badenoch cattle in Drumochter and drove them back to Blair Castle to demonstrate their control over the disputed land, William Tod, the Duke's factor, authorised John Dow 'to catch as many of theirs as we could treat with them on more equall Terms'.[74] John Dow happily obliged, seizing '75 Head of Athol Sheep by way of Reprisals'. This Gordon–Atholl rivalry over Drumochter, as much about prestige as money, spawned four major legal cases between 1727 and 1819. The disputed land, 4,700 acres of hill grazing, including the oft-mentioned Corrydoan, was actually valued at less than £10 in 1771![75] What this local 'hundred-years war' cost is not known, but a small dispute between Sir Robert Menzies and the Duke of Gordon (over the Benalder–Rannoch march) landed Menzies with £38 15s 10½d legal costs for land worth just £5 10s.[76] But Tod knew the importance of these grazings far exceeded mere monetary values: 'The Badenoch Folks cannot live at all if the Duke of Atholl gets the part of Drummochter His Grace's Folks claim'.[77] The Gordon lawyers also recognised the significance of this remote wilderness: 'Its future worth now that the value of Highland property is so rapidly increasing is incalculable'.[78] Indeed, William Lorimer (mentor to Sir James Grant of Grant) had observed fifty years earlier how the rising value of pasture was making landowners 'very jealous of their Hills or Common'.[79]

Tacksmen, inevitably, led the 'land-grab', often at the expense of their tenantry. John Dow represented the ruthless face of commercialism. The tenants of Dalannach complained of his commandeering their grazings: 'The repeated violence in poinding their cattle from off their own bounds, Forceing his own Cattle in and making a highway through their Infield Ground and Corns'. As factor, Tod was forced into legal action 'to prevent John Dow's distressing the Tenants of Dellanach', where he (John Dow) had 'placed a Man on Purpose to prevent their pasturing on the Ground they claim as their own who distressed them by dayly poinding'.[80]

But grievances went far beyond the bullying of small tenants, for the gentry were at each other's throats. Taylor's survey of the Gordon lands in Laggan listed fifteen different hill grazings disputed by local tacksmen, with the obstreperous Hugh Macpherson of Uvie personally engaged in four.[81] Confrontation was inevitable. In June 1734, Invernahavon 'utterly destroyed and threw down' Breakachy's bothy at Balsporran in Drumochter while a family was in residence – 'The poor women and children were exposed to bad weather . . . and were so alarmed at the threats . . . that they were frightened to stay'.[82] Breakachy immediately rebuilt the bothy, 'ordered the women back . . . and maintained a guard for a week'.

Alexander Kennedy, a young herd, witnessed a standoff between two other Macpherson tacksmen, Strathmashie and Laggan of Nuide. When Strathmashie drove Laggan's cattle off a shieling near Dalwhinnie, Laggan retaliated. He 'came up with his Cattle, and brought all his people with him', and then, 'sent notice to the Tacksman of Strathmashie to let him to know that he and his people were there with their Cattle', adding defiantly, 'if he [Strathmashie] would come and drive them off, that he might'. Though they remained most of the day, 'no person came from Strathmashie to challenge them'. Victory, however, was short-lived, for when the Laggan folk had returned home, Strathmashie simply continued to drive off their cattle.[83]

Laggan was involved in another confrontation with his neighbour Duncan Macpherson of Nuidemore, again at a Dalwhinnie shieling. Both tacksmen were present, each with his herd-boy: Laggan's herd was Andrew Macpherson, while Nuidemore's was Donald Macpherson who recounted the incident. The shieling burn was in spate and the two tacksmen and Andrew stood on one side with young Donald on the other. Nuidemore shouted to Donald to 'drive over the burn five stirks' belonging to Laggan, which were grazing on his side. Donald did so, but Laggan immediately ordered his herd Andrew to drive them back across the burn. Donald, clearly relishing the situation, 'turned them again, [so] that they landed upon the other side'. As the poor beasts were driven back and fore across the torrent, tempers rose. Nuidemore grabbed Laggan's herd Andrew, berating him with a torrent of Gaelic abuse. Perhaps Donald or the clerk, out of politeness, toned down the oaths, the translation being rendered as a somewhat improbable, 'Stop my good fellow, and let the beasts pass'![84]

Another colourful episode, but that members of the Macpherson elite would, in each of these instances, confront each other in these remote hill pastures, even acting with gross inhumanity, illustrates not only the importance attached to these lands, but the extent to which, once again, individual interests had displaced traditional clan values.[85]

•   •   •

The legal testimonies, or depositions, of characters like Donald Macpherson, Alexander Kennedy and James Gordon of the boxed ears, provide a rare insight into the common folk of Badenoch: it is, indeed, the only time they talk with authentic voices, for their few written documents were probably penned by teacher or minister. Their depositions were recorded to settle disputed boundaries, 'As pointed out by Old men, that their fore ffathers &

themselves have been long ffarmers & Herdsmen on the Ground'.[86] There is no small irony that the fate of two great aristocrats lay, at least to a degree, in the hands of their humblest subjects.

After being sworn in and 'purged of malice', herds, dairymaids, cottars and tenants gave their testimonies.[87] The transcriptions (often with a rhythm emanating directly from Gaelic) were recorded, judging by their idiomatic flow, word for word. As such they constitute the oral history of eighteenth-century Badenoch – a unique, though largely ignored, glimpse of life through the people's eyes. Much of the detail on the hill grazings, both domestic and commercial, comes from these depositions – an intimate picture of deer forests and shielings, of estates and people. But there are also the incidental gems: how, 'in the year of Killiecrankie [1689]' Badenoch folks hid in the remote shieling of Corrievachkie 'to preserve their Catle from the flying Armies'; the time when 'Lord George Murray and Lochiell with several other Gentlemen had a Deer Hunting in Corrydoan'; measures to prevent poaching by disarming 'whosoever he Shall find Carrying arms in the said fforrest', seizing 'Guns Dogs and Netts', even killing 'all dogs Disturbing the game'; and a woman's fear of being raped by soldiers after Culloden.[88]

There were evocative depictions of the marches themselves: 'the ridge of the hill as wind and weather shears', the 'Quaking Ash tree', the 'chair stone' on Drumochter Pass, removed – most inconsiderately – by General Wade in 1729 for the new road.[89] There was the folk memory extending back into the seventeenth century: Donald Macpherson, aged seventy in 1735, who remarked that, when a youth, he had been shown the marches by a man 'as old then as he is now', or the elderly John Macpherson who claimed that he 'had occasion to frequent these Bounds since he was capable of putting on his Cloaths'; and the haunting memories of King William's 'bad years'.[90] Nothing, however, surpasses old James Robertson's testimony. When asked how to determine the watershed on Drumochter Pass, he responded that it would be the point where 'if you was to empty a pale of water upon the top of it, part of it would run to the county of Inverness and part of it to the County of Perth' – a process on Drummochter's vast boggy summit that would surely have enshrined the old man as Badenoch's own Sisyphus.[91]

These depositions provide a social context that resonates with a positive timbre; not the downtrodden, impoverished or idle peasantry perceived by the outsider, not a populace complaining of its lot, but an articulate people – local worthies – actively engaged in the annual cycle of securing their liveli-hood. Similarly, from an economic perspective, these accounts support the image of a vibrant cattle-based economy in which tacksman – and, to some extent, tenant – were exploiting their environment in a kind of commercial transhumance.[92] The wealth generated by this economic pastoralism would, for some, be sufficient to maintain the desired social status: but for the more ambitious, far greater riches beckoned by stepping out of the world of cattle farmer into that of cattle drover.

Droving

Charles Gordon, the Duke's rather punctilious Edinburgh lawyer, was struggling to balance the spiralling demands of estate expenditure against the unpredictability of its income. Angrily, he complained of having to conduct the Duke's affairs 'as if I were Begging an Alms [charity]'.[93] Particularly frustrating was the irregularity of the Highland rents: 'I cannot keep thinking its strange that the Edinburgh Demands, where . . . Punctuality is expected from all Ranks, should be devolved upon Badenoch Drovers.' He was not alone in his exasperation, for the entire ducal lifestyle appeared at times to hinge on those same drovers.

The drovers who took the cattle to distant southern markets were the lifeline of the Badenoch economy, converting the subsistence farmer's cattle into rent, while providing an outlet for the burgeoning commercial trade. The trade was clearly evident in the seventeenth century – old John Macpherson recalled in 1735 'going to a South country mercat with his Father, when he was very young and his Father very old.'[94] After the Treaty of Union in 1707, the business expanded steadily, becoming a major source of employment and income from the small-scale local operator to the wealthy dealer with a team of employees. While the local trade had developed as a financial necessity, the big dealers, primarily the clan tacksmen, were operating a high-level capitalist enterprise. When James Ross, the Duke's chamberlain, proposed coming across to arrange new leases with the tacksmen, Tod, the factor, replied that there was no point. 'All the Dealers in black Catle who may be supposed to be the best Offerers [for leases] must necessarily be engaged at the Market and consequently cannot attend you': a significant comment not only on the personal involvement and wealth of the drover-tacksmen, but also on their value to the estate.[95]

Nevertheless, small-scale drovers were crucial to the subsistence economy. Often of lowly origins, they used the trade to climb the social ladder – like

Donald Macdonald, who, though 'descended of indigent parents, without education or any visible fund of subsistence, obtained some Credite and commenced a Drover'.[96] Similarly, the McEdwards on Invereshie estate – Angus who 'bought most of the cattle that were to be sold twixt Feshie and Trommie' (the Invereshie farms), and Duncan, whose cryptic scribbles in a battered notebook give a brief glimpse into his methods.[97] In 1783, Duncan was buying beasts for the Michaelmas Tryst at Falkirk: from Lachlan Kennedy in Knockanbuy, three cattle for £4 12s; from Donald Kennedy in Glenan, one for £2 8s; from James Martin in Soillerie, seven for £14. In total he bought forty-two cattle for £96 19s from at least twenty-three different local farmers, evaluating the worth of every beast, and driving a separate bargain with each.

The agreed price, however, was generally not paid up front. Andrew Mor Macpherson, 'a Cattle Dealer on a Small Scale . . . bought a Number of Beasts from the poor Tennants in the manner customary in this place, without paying Money, or granting Security for them, till he should return from the Markets in the South'.[98] Lacking the security of even a drover's bill, the tenant was totally at the mercy of the small drover – who, in fairness, had little financial security himself.

Occasionally, however, the boot was on the other foot. When demand was high, as during the wars between Britain and France in the 1790s, tenants could exploit the market, dictating their own terms to the drovers. The Reverend Anderson remarked to William Macpherson of Invereshie, in 1796, that 'You would think yourself an inhabitant of some opulent Province in South America', to see the ordinary tenants 'asking and receiving, five, six & seven pounds stirling for their small Beasts of black Cattle' – his astonishment confirming the uniqueness of the situation.[99] On another occasion, when the Cattanach sheep drovers told a local farmer he would not be paid till they returned from market, he threatened to remove his beasts. Rather than risk losing a profitable sale, one of them 'took the money out of his pocket and paid [it] instantly'.[100]

Usually, however, purchase was by promissory notes which became a paper currency, often used to cover rents.[101] Tod, for example, complained in 1776 that 'I am getting nothing but Drovers Bills for my Rents and I do not know when they may be paid'.[102] It was a complex system, as James Robertson explained: 'the cattle are given away upon a conditional contract; that if the price rises within a limited time, the seller will receive so much more; but if the lean cattle fall in value, the drover will get a deduction'.[103] Actual payments, indeed, often fell short of the initial agreement.

Market fluctuations were crucial, as Tod explained: 'the Price of Catle for the remaining Part of the Season will be determined by the Fate of a Mercat which holds to Day at Falkirk'.[104] Falling demand, or a surfeit of cattle, enabled English merchants to force prices down: 'the Dealers took very much the advantage of the last bad mercat, and bought the few Cattle they took with them at their own Prices'.[105] Naturally, droving costs were deducted. James Martin in Soillerie, for example, 'paid the price he made of 26 head of Cattle att Falkirk Tryst after Deducting the Expence of Droving and his Trouble', showing that the tenant got the net price after sale and deductions, rather than that originally negotiated.[106] Whether, as Robertson suggested, tenants benefited from unexpected price increases is uncertain, though comments such as 'Cattle and Sheep give great prices so I expect that you will have no arrears this Martinmas' may indicate that this was the case.[107]

However crucial the small local drover might be, the regional economy was driven by his commercial counterpart, and Badenoch was well endowed with men of that ilk. Lachlan Macpherson of Ralia, one of the most successful Highland drovers for half a century, Alexander Macdonell of Garvabeg, Allan Macpherson of Shanvall, John Dow – 'a Drover and dealer in Sheep and Cattle to a very considerable amount' – and many others operated successfully both in an individual capacity and in business partnerships.[108] Indeed, the significance of the Badenoch drovers was indicated in a Gaelic poem from Wester Ross, 'The Drovers' Song', which devoted a whole verse to them (the only ones to be specifically named), referring, with some poetic licence, to 'the Badenoch men with herds from the moor to the sea's edge'.[109]

Even before the '45, Donald Macpherson, tacksman of Breakachy, ran a highly successful partnership with his uncle, Malcolm Macpherson of Cruben-more, and probably also with his brothers Hugh of Uvie and Angus of Flichity, who were also major cattle dealers. Numerous examples of these droving partnerships exist. In the 1760s, John Dow teamed up with Uvie (his future father-in-law) and Lachlan Mackintosh of Shanvall in a 'Co-partnery trade of purchasing Catle in this and the low Country, and of disposing of Them, by Sale, in the South Country, and in England'.[110] Thirty years later, John Dow was still plying his trade in partnership with Lieutenant Evan 'Uvie' Macpherson of Cullachy (Uvie's son, so his brother-in-law) and Colonel Duncan Macpherson of Bleaton (Breakachy's son, so first cousin to Evan). John Dow was also in partnership with Captain Hugh Macpherson of Inverhall (his stepson, and nephew of Evan) and Captain Charles Macpherson of Gordonhall (his stepson-in-law and brother-in-law of Hugh).[111] Lieutenant Evan had also been in a separate partnership since 1786 with the Reverend John Kennedy (brother-in-law to both Evan and John Dow), later joined by Colonel Duncan.[112]

While these partnerships were built round intricate family links, the overlapping partnerships suggest a wider syndicate of clan gentry working in loose co-ordination and acting as mutual cautioners (guarantors) for deals and loans. It has been suggested that the Macphersons were still marrying strategically within the clan with the express purpose of 'represent[ing] the larger interests of the *clann*', rather than simply furthering 'the fortunes of individual families'.[113] But, though such marriage patterns were clearly still prevalent, these droving partnerships displayed no altruistic concern for the greater good of the clan: on the contrary, the clan network was being harnessed to further the capitalist ambitions of the individual. Nor, indeed, were all partnerships clan- or family-based. In Laggan parish a huge partnership involving Allan Macpherson of Shanvall, Alexander Macdonell of Garvabeg, Lachlan Macpherson of Ralia, Evan Clark of Nessintully and Angus Macdonald of Strathmashie (the first three being amongst Badenoch's wealthiest drovers) appears to have been based more on location than familial connections. Shanvall was also in a separate partnership with Evan Macpherson of Muckoull and Archibald Macdonald of Laggan.[114]

Such partnerships were largely financial in purpose, pooling resources and providing the security necessary to engender confidence. Finance came in a variety of ways. Allan Macpherson of Shanvall, one of the biggest local drovers, financed his operation by selling off 'his whole stocking', raising 'one hundred and twenty pounds ster[ling]' – a gamble clearly reflecting his confidence in the business.[115] Military incomes proved crucial – all five members of John Dow's later partnerships were either serving, Fencible, or half-pay officers. Banks played an increasing role, and with the Royal Bank and British Linen Bank opening Inverness branches in 1775 and 1785 respectively, raising capital became ever easier – John Dow securing credit facilities of £500 from each.[116] The partnerships provided guarantees for credit: Lieutenant Evan Macpherson requested 'the accommodation of £500 Sterling for three or four months, and Proposes Colonel Duncan Mcpherson of Bleaton and Captain John Macpherson of Balchroan [John Dow] to join him in a Bill for that Amount'; Captain Charles Macpherson of Gordonhall acted as cautioner along with two more of the clan gentry, Charles of Sherrabeg and Lieutenant Duncan of Nuidemore.[117] On another occasion Hugh Macpherson of Inverhall underwrote Angus Macpherson of Flichity to a remarkable £2,280.[118] The gentry also provided substantial personal loans to friends and relatives through Bills of Exchange.[119] It was a complex web of financial interdependence that would later haunt them.

The next stage was the acquisition of cattle. Drovers naturally took cattle from their own lands and tenantry, but local supply could not satisfy the commercial dealer. Animals were sought wherever possible and the tacksmen-drovers would frequent local cattle markets such as the ones at Ruthven (situated below Knappach) and Grantown. Often they travelled further afield. Lachlan Macpherson of Ralia, for instance, wrote that in May, 'I shall have to go to a mercate in Sky.'[120] Alexander Macdonell of Garvabeg also went regularly to Skye himself, though at other times used a chain system – a Macdonald in Skye sold to a Robertson who then sold on to Macdonell. On another occasion Garvabeg secured a drove from a farmer in the north in lieu of a debt: 'advise him to settle with me in cattle. . . I would perhaps be in his neighbourhood buying Cattle'. English dealers came north to buy from him directly, employing him or his men to take the beasts south: 'John Mackintosh in Crathy, I sent last week as far as New Castle with an English Dealer that was here and bought a parcale of Cattle from me.' Occasionally he worked for commission: 'I was buying [cattle] for an English Company where I had only 2/ [2 shillings] per head Commission'– not a high profit, but at least secure. Garvabeg would even bid against other drovers in his desire to secure cattle: in 1796, he paid £80 for a score of cattle to take south, 'which was two shillings a head more than the other drovers offered for them' – another indication of local confidence in the trade.[121]

The shrewdness of the professional drover is evident in Lachlan Macpherson of Ralia's deliberations over cattle belonging to Sir James Grant of Grant.[122] Ralia wrote to Sir James, 'I have considered them very minutely', explaining that he was rejecting all the young beasts as 'not fit for droving', also four oxen 'which do not answer at our south Country mercates', and another four young oxen which 'fits the mercate here best'. He offered to take fifteen oxen, but on his own terms: 'You may think the price rather low but as the Southern part of England which is the proper spot for the sale of Cattle of their weight is much hurt with a drought I cannot afford more. Nor will they answer our mercates later.' What emerges is Ralia's astute assessment of the cattle, his understanding of different market demands, his awareness of grass conditions 500 miles away, and his confidence in offering a man of Sir James's stature below the expected price.

The response was equally enlightening. Sir James accepted Ralia's offer, albeit reluctantly, 'because you have always acted Genteelly with him'.[123] But he proposed 'that if the sale answers better than you expect you will give him Twenty Shillings Sterling more at least for each of them'. That Sir James trusted not only Ralia's assessment of the market situation, but also his integrity over the extra 20 shillings, perfectly illustrates the importance of the drover's reputation.

Badenoch's importance as a droving centre undoubtedly benefited from its geographical situation. Proximity to the trysts meant cattle spending less time on the hoof, thereby maximising time on the hill pastures and reducing weight loss *en route*. While local beasts obviously summered on the Badenoch hill grazings before the droving season, those brought in from further afield could be rested and fed there before continuing the journey – Garvabeg grazed a herd from Portree on his own extensive pastures at Drummin on the upper Spey for twelve days before moving on.[124] But the region's location benefited not just the local dealer, for its centrality and vast grazing potential funnelled many of the northern drovers through its bounds. With up to 30,000 cattle being sold at a single tryst, Falkirk was handling as many as 100,000 beasts annually, many thousands of which must have passed through Badenoch, for almost every route from the north and north-west passed through the region: Alexander Irvine, indeed, commented that all cattle 'must go round by either Fort William or Pitmain' (Figure 7).[125] Significantly, when Glen Feshie was advertised for sale in 1806, the target was not the sportsman, but the cattle-man:

> It must be an object well worth the attention of dealers in Cattle in all Corners of the Kingdom – Grazers from England & the South of Scotland might find their account in making it a Depot for cattle bought in the North during the Summer & Autumn.[126]

The concept of the vast upper reaches of the glen serving as a 'depot' or halfway house again suggests the gathering and holding of huge droves in readiness for the late-season markets.

The most significant local drove road – described by Donald Mackay who had first used that route in 1762 – ran from the top of Loch Ness over the desolate Monadhliath plateau at heights of over 2,500 feet, crossing the Findhorn and Dulnain straths.[127] The road then ascended Carn Dulnain, traversing the summit of Beinn Bhreac above Kingussie, descending the east side of the River Gynack, before turning west along the north shore of Loch

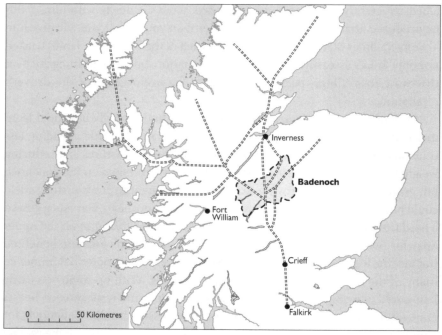

Figure 7
Droving routes from the north and west funnelling through Badenoch.

Gynack (exactly as shown on George Brown's 1771 map), crossing the Calder, fording the Spey above Ralia bridge, then heading up the Truim to Dalwhinnie and Drumochter (Plate 7a). Another major route came through the Corrieyairrack, before taking the drove road from Feagour to Dalwhinnie. Droves coming via Inverness tended to follow Wade's road before heading westwards to join the above road at the Dulnain, or continuing south through their favoured mountain pass, Glen Feshie, Gaick, Minigaig or Drumochter.

Droves varied in size. Bishop Forbes noted droves in Drumochter of 150 to 300 cattle and one of a mile in length, but they could be much greater – John Dow, for instance, taking 'a pretty large drove of 800 head of Cattle, Stotts, Cows and Runts'.[128] Allan Macpherson of Shanvall regularly purchased 'on his own Accompt . . . about eight or nine hundred [beasts] twixt Cattle & horses', which he acknowledged 'might be valued from two thousand to two thousand ffive hundred pounds Sterling', a staggering personal investment made nearly every year in addition to his partnership droves.[129]

Timing also varied. For English buyers the season started early. In 1775, one of the great Yorkshire dealers, who claimed to buy annually £30,000 worth of Scottish cattle, conducted business with two Badenoch drovers in Aviemore in the month of May.[130] Robertson also mentioned English drovers coming north in late April or May (the same month Ralia headed for Skye), ready for the June market.[131] Tod confirmed this was the first of the year, for in January 1770 he explained to James Ross that no further rent could be collected till June, 'the first Mercat for their Cattle'.[132] Generally, however, the Badenoch droves targeted the late-season trysts at Falkirk, Crieff and Doune. Garvabeg conveniently avoided a summons from his lawyer on 4 September because he had, 'a drove sitting to the road for the ffalkirk tryst which I must attend upon that very day'. He also took cattle to Doune as late as mid November – 'the last time this season'. Ralia was another who was clearly going south regularly, writing that he had been 'in England with my Michalmas Drove [end of September]', while Angus Macdonald, Strathmashie, was at the Lowland markets in both October and November.[133]

Though potentially hazardous, droving could extend into winter. The sheep-drover Cattanach, having been at the Lowland markets on 30 November 1788, was again heading south on 14 December 'with another drove and will not return by the latter end of next week [Christmas day]' – a remarkable testimony to the hardiness of the Highland drover.[134] But such enterprises could prove fatal: in Angus McEdward's late November drove of 1795 'one of his drivers . . . was lost [died] in the Snow. . . one night when attending the Cattle – and Donald Clarke had nearly shared the same fate', prompting John Macpherson's hope that it would 'cure him [Angus] from attempting the like in future, so late in the year'.[135] Profit clearly outweighed risks as John continued: 'there is such a demand in the South, that notwith-standing the Storm, the dealers are driving Sheep and Cattle every week'. It shows, however, that between the spring demands of the English dealers and the late Scottish season, the active drover could be buying and selling over a seven- or eight-month season, with several trips south per year.

The Badenoch gentry appear to have accompanied their droves to market. Garvabeg, Ralia and John Dow certainly collected and took the cattle south themselves, even into England, though whether they slept rough with their drove or retired to hostelries at night is not clear. They did, however, always attend the markets personally, for success depended on personal contacts and trust. It was a high-risk business, for securing good deals in a highly compet-itive market involved many a gamble. Working for a wealthy English merchant or buying on commission might have brought safe, though modest, returns, but for the independent drover seeking to maximise his profits, things were not so secure. For him, experience, initiative, intuition, and not least, reputation, were the vital ingredients of success.

One drover, having procured over 400 cattle in Lochaber, advertised privately in the *Caledonian Mercury*: 'They will be at Torwood before Friday 30th [June] and sold off on that day in such lots . . . as purchasers incline, for ready money'.[136] Sometimes, deals were arranged before the markets officially opened. At Falkirk in October 1795, for example, it was reported that 'The greatest part of the cattle were *bought up* by the English dealers, before the usual time for opening the market'.[137] Others tried to play a waiting game – a risky strategy, as in October 1788 when cattle prices on the opening day were high, 'but the Market had a considerable Fall the two last Days, equal to Twenty per Cent On the first Sales'.[138]

John Dow provides an interesting insight into the financial world of the drover. In October 1766, he and his partner, Lachlan Mackintosh, were heading home with substantial cash from their sales at the Michaelmas Crieff tryst. Stopping off at Truell market near Blair Atholl, they decided to reinvest some of their profits – 'as in a Company Concern, purchase Cattle for the Markets to be held at Stirling, or Down [Doune]'.[139] In payment, they firstly offered British Linen Bank notes, but, when the seller seemed suspicious of that currency, they immediately produced the equivalent in Glasgow Thistle Bank notes which proved more acceptable. John Dow then headed south again to dispose of the new stock. This continual reinvestment process is further illustrated by the case of Donald Macdonald.[140] He and his partner bought 'a parcel of cattle' in 1784, selling it within fourteen days. 'Immediately after this they bought about 200 or 300 in another parcel', selling some straight away and the rest the following spring, the profits again being immediately converted into more cattle. On another occasion he 'bought 28 head of black cattle and 12 fillies mostly upon credit', sold them at Doune, 'and again purchased a few cows', to sell at the next Doune market.

Another gamble was whether to go furth of Scotland. James Ross recognised the motive: 'the Drovers had no occasion to have gone forward into England, if they had chosen to be satisfied with moderate profits'.[141] But settling for moderate profits was not in the nature of the Badenoch tacksmen. In 1767, John Dow, with his partners, Mackintosh and Hugh Macpherson of Uvie, headed for Falkirk with 800 cattle, both he and Mackintosh taking along additional beasts of their own.[142] But at Falkirk, 'the Market not answering their Expectations They resolved to drive Their Cattle to England'. John Dow took the drove south, firstly to Carlisle, before finally selling at Temple Sowerby in Cumbria, some 240 miles from home.

Marketing in England was risky, for the anticipated higher prices could be negated by the additional costs. On the extra journey from Falkirk to England, John Dow's personal expenses amounted to £8 8s 1d; for a man who drove the cattle the additional cost was 9s 3d (six days' drive, two nights' watching, and return money); grass at Carlisle cost £2 12s 6d, while four lame cows abandoned at Carlisle cost a further 6s 4d.[143] This extra expense was confirmed by Donald Mackay from Sutherland. His droves from there to Falkirk cost 1s 2d per beast with a daily rate of 10d to 1s per man, while from Falkirk to England it rose to 1s 10d per beast and 1s 3d per man, each of whom had an additional allowance of 5s 'return money'.[144] Nor did this additional expense guarantee better prices, as Tod noted: 'Our Drovers are on their way home – they did not sell nearly so well at Carlisle and Newcastle as they might have done at Falkirk.'[145]

In September 1780, Ralia wrote to Tod from Carlisle describing a disastrous experience in England, illustrating not just the risks of droving but the honour of the drover.[146] Ralia already had one unsold drove in England from his previous trip, and was having to rent grazing for them. On his next trip south in September he turned down a potential buyer at Falkirk – 'I thought their offer very low' – and headed for England again. Once there he discovered that 'the times are worse than I had any apprehension of'; English dealers were offering less than half the previous year's price of £7; 'very few were sold here and at such prices as I am ashamed to mention'. He contacted a Yorkshire dealer with whom he had done business in the past, but again rejected the offered price.

Ralia eventually sold twenty of his cattle at £2 2s each, but the situation had since deteriorated: 'To my shame . . . I have not been able to bring them to the offer I rejected.' He added despondently, 'I wish I may be able to give you the price of a tanned hide for your stots, the best offer I had for 10 of the best of yours, the same number of Clunys & 40 four year old Sky Stots was 30sh.' In desperation he concluded, 'I could not get myself humbled to this degree without a further trial', so remained in England, combining his current drove with the previous unsold one, until the next market, 'where if I have any offers they shall be sold' – clearly implying, no matter how low.

The letter's significance lies not just in Ralia's failure in England, but in his personal response. He clearly feared for his reputation: 'I scarce think you will suspect me [of dishonesty]', but nevertheless he detailed his misfortunes by way of excuse. The words 'shame', 'ashamed' and 'humbled' further reveal the embarrassment of failure, and, underlying that, the consequences to those back home who depended on him. Tod understood the reality, starkly warning James Ross, 'there is no demand for Catle at any Price and as we have no Provinder for them in Winter we shall be ruined'.[147]

Unsold cattle were a drover's nightmare. Wintering beasts in the Lowlands or England was expensive, but returning them to farms that had no fodder would be catastrophic. In 1778, Ralia had been left with 500 of his drove unsold.[148] Angus Macdonald of Strathmashie had to bring unsold beasts back from Falkirk, before taking them south again just eight days later to catch the November market at Doune – the last chance before winter.[149] Andrew Gollan, one of Garvabeg's drovers, took a herd of horses to Falkirk in spring, but 'could not get them sold at any price'.[150] He rented pasture all summer in the hope of a sale until 'he had not one sixpence to pay for the grass or his own maintenance', Garvabeg eventually sending him money to bring the horses home. Gambling on market prices, however, was not just the prerogative of the wealthy drover – even the poorest farmers were tempted to hold out for higher prices. But such audacity could backfire, as John Macpherson of Invereshie noted: 'Greed prevented the people from selling their Cattle, the early part of last year – and the latter part of the Season, prices fell, and no demand – of Course, the Cattle remained on their hands.'[151]

Despite the risks, droving was generally a lucrative trade. Donald Macpherson of Breakachy and his cattle-dealing family accumulated enough wealth to purchase at least five estates for various relatives.[152] Indeed, when the impoverished laird of Raitts, Edward Mackintosh of Borlum, married into the Breakachy family, his creditors rejoiced: 'Borlum by his Marriage with Breakachy's Daughter Is connected with Moneyed people' – an interesting reflection on the social hierarchy for she was but a tacksman's daughter.[153] The potential gains of droving were also illustrated by Angus McEdward from Invereshie who made over £2,000 in one season in 1796; John Dow, who was able to lend £1,000 to the Duke in the mid 1780s; and Allan Macpherson of Shanvall, who spent up to £2,500 a year buying stock, clearing £758 profit in a single drove in 1793 – huge sums at present-day values.[154]

The potential for disaster was, however, never far away, one lawyer observing that droving, of all businesses, was 'the most subject to sudden reverses of fortune, not only from the nature of the subject dealt in, but from the necessity of giving considerable credits'.[155] For the small-scale drover like Duncan McEdward occasional collapses were almost inevitable. In 1784, bankruptcy proceedings were initiated, though whether he was actually bankrupt or had simply absconded (later being condemned as a 'notorious villain') is unclear. Whichever way, he gallantly left his wife to face the creditors and sell the household possessions.[156] As many as 120 small tenants from Badenoch submitted claims on his estate, varying from £1 to £3, just the price of their one or two cows.[157] While the amounts appear inconsequential, to the runrig farmer this represented a whole year's income. The point was emphasised by the Reverend John Anderson after Andrew Mor Macpherson, another small-scale drover, suffered bankruptcy, 'leaving the poor tenants without a shilling'.[158]

Nor were the big cartels immune, for integral to the clan network was its domino effect. When creditors eventually called time, it was often too late – the drovers' bills that had passed into circulation simply could not be honoured. In 1793, John Macpherson of Invereshie wrote to his brother William:

Hornings [legal proceedings against debtors] are up though for incredible Sums – one thousand pounds agt Evan Ouvie, the Colonel and John Dow his Cautioners – several Hornings against John Dow for one, two, three, hundreds – and one for near Six – I suspect Capt Charles and Inverhall are deeply in with him.[159]

A subsequent letter revealed the full enormity of the droving collapse:

The Colonel [Duncan Macpherson of Bleaton], Ballachroan [John Dow] & Evan Ouvie are gone to the devil – Evan is in Jail at Edinburgh his debt amounts to £9000 – the Colonel and John Dow who could hardly clear their own credit are very deeply bound for him which must kick up their heels – Inverhall is also in with him considerably – his property is to be sold this week.[160]

As the dominoes fell, John Dow was summoned to Edinburgh 'to say his Catechism before his Creditors' to the tune of £4,330.[161] Allan Macpherson of Shanvall went down for at least £800 (possibly double that), Garvabeg for £1,600, and Evan Macpherson of Muckoull and Archibald Macdonell in Laggan for unspecified sums.[162] Captain Hugh had to sell Inverhall (Invertromie), Colonel Duncan had to part with all his property, and Captain Charles eventually lost Gordonhall.[163] John Anderson foresaw the long-term consequences:

'Nor is the loss of Credit the worst – our *Badenoch Character* among our neighbours is become infamous – and I am sorry to add, with too much Justice.'[164] Trust – the drover's greatest asset – had been destroyed. Nevertheless, the bankrupt drover's ability to resurrect himself appears much akin to the limited company of today, for Garvabeg was active on a big scale again within two years – only to collapse finally in 1808 with debts of £4,000.[165]

The impact of the great droving collapse on the community, especially on the lower tenantry, was again immense, as Anderson noted: 'this has crashed a Number of our poor entirely.'[166] John Stewart from Sherramore apologised for a debt unpaid because 'we were disappointed in getting money from those we sold our Cattle to this year'; similarly, John Macpherson from Blargie – 'nothing but the faloor [failure] of our Drovers in this Country have been the means of not paying you . . . We are very much distressed in this Country owing to our Drovers giving way.'[167] The point was further illustrated in the list of Allan Macpherson's creditors: 'Alex Macpherson tenant in Coraldie price of 1 cow £2 10s . . . William Macpherson Wester Lynwilg a quey & a stot [young cattle] £3 3s . . . John Davidson Kincraig £1 10s.'[168] At best there was a partial return: Garvabeg 'offers only a Composition of 10/- [10s] in the pound', while Allan Macpherson 'has not Subject to pay 6/8 [6s 8d] in the pound'; at worst, as with Andrew Mor, there was simply nothing at all.[169]

The success of the drovers was vital, not just for the tenantry, but also for the wider estate economy. In December 1781, John Macpherson of Invereshie informed his brother that 'The drovers have not yet opened their purses; so that the rents come in but very slowly'; but in November 1785, rentals seemed secure because 'most of them [tenants] already have received payments for the cattle etc sold by them'.[170] The Gordon estates suffered most from uncertain droving returns because of rapidly increasing expenditure. The rich north-east farms still paid corn rents ('all the Meal and Bear [bere] paid in by the Tenents'), so ready money came largely from the Highland estates of Badenoch and Lochaber which had already converted customs into cash rents thanks to the cattle trade.[171] Those rents, however, were wholly dependent upon the drovers.

Charles Gordon's fore-mentioned frustration regarding the Badenoch drovers was shared by James Ross, the estate chamberlain. Ross complained frequently: to Tod over his 'disappointment of money from your [rent] Collection . . . especially as I depended on a very considerable supply for carrying on the summer Operations about [Gordon] Castle'; to the architect, that he could not pay for timber, 'As the Highland Rents are very backwards this year'; to Charles Gordon, that Badenoch's failure to deliver rents meant he could not 'answer weekly demands for masons etc'[172] He even refused the Duke's personal request for cash in 1775: 'The Highland rents answered so ill that it is not in my power to make any remittance to your Grace'[173] Ross explicitly linked financial problems with droving in a letter to Charles Gordon: he could not provide cash because of 'a very great short coming of the Martinmas Rents [November] – occasioned by the failure in the sale of Cattle', though it might be possible in February, 'when I hope the Badenoch Drovers will enable the Tenents to pay'[174] When times improved, he wrote pointedly to Tod: 'Happy to hear that your drovers are returned with plenty of money. I hope it will have a good Effect in your Collection'[175]

Ross's constant harping to Tod over drovers and rents brought blunt responses, for Tod – farmer as well as factor – understood the reality. Rents simply could not be paid on demand: 'there will be no cash among them till the *Return* of the Market'; while on another occasion, 'you can have no dependence upon any Help from me . . . Our drovers went to England from Doune Market, and we have heard nothing of them since'[176] That Tod could, at times, be just as frustrated by the droving fraternity was evident in a follow-up to the last letter just two months later: 'The Drovers have not yet paid a Shilling in Badenoch'[177]

The relationship between estate and drover reveals the tenuous and tortuous nature of the Highland economy. The Duke and his administrative triumvirate of Tod, Ross and Gordon – and indeed the entire Badenoch community – were totally at the mercy of the drover. But he in turn was subject not just to the whims of the London market, but to government policy, and even international relations. As such, it is a salutary reminder of how even the humblest of tenants in a remote Highland community were increasingly locked into a global economic structure. Nonetheless, the rewards of the cattle trade were high as the Ross-shire composer of 'The Drovers' Song' poetically recognised, ending his verse on the Badenoch drovers:

If they stand firm for their price,
The king himself is no better off than the farmer![178]

Conclusion

The Badenoch economy, from cottar to nobleman, was predicated on cattle. Robert Macpherson of Benchar (military chaplain to Fraser's 78th Highlanders), writing from the banks of America's Mohawk river in 1758, encapsulated the importance of cattle to his native Badenoch. Fearing the effects of new legislation permitting the import of Irish beasts into Britain, he wondered thoughtfully, 'What now will become of the poor Highlands, their very sinews of life is I may say cut.'[179] His fears, fortunately, were never realised, for fifty years later the 'sinews' of the Inverness-shire cattle trade were not just still intact, but, according to the agricultural writer Robertson had become a net gain: 'The cattle . . . sent annually to market from this county, are the great source of wealth to the people, & far exceed the money sent out of the country to purchase meal.'[180]

Though commercial pastoralism had undergone a dramatic expansion, it was open to criticism for an apparent lack of diversification. But the economic front was not as narrow as it appeared. Cattle, sheep and horses fulfilled different market needs, and the variety of saleable commodities – meat, dairy, hides and wool – at least offered some breadth, while rapid urbanisation and the increasing military needs of the British Empire ensured a steadily expanding demand for livestock. Furthermore, summer grazing provided guaranteed returns irrespective of southern markets, for Lowland cattle always required out-pasturing during the arable season. Though periodic collapse was inevitable, the general trend was of an ever-expanding pastoral economy, reflected in that competition over remote mountain pastures.

The driving force behind this commercialism was the indigenous tacksman class. It was neither run nor financed to any extent by the outsider: nor was it led by clan chief or landlord. On the contrary, the initiative to exploit the emerging market opportunities came from within the Badenoch community. Far from being 'parasitic middle ranks', the tacksmen in fact became entrepreneurial leaders, self-confident, enterprising and opportunistic, quick to absorb the skills of the marketplace, alert to every facet of the livestock trade.[181] Having grasped the potential of the market, they exploited it with the restless energy and opportunism that were hallmarks of Britain's commercial revolution. Through the medium of cattle, clan tacksman was metamorphosing into capitalist entrepreneur.

Underpinning this transition, however, was the clan itself. Though politically dismantled and suffering social disintegration, it was, nevertheless, the familial ties and loyalties of clanship that helped forge and finance the great droving partnerships. As such, the clan was re-emerging as a commercial institution, albeit for the benefit of the new tacksman bourgeoisie, for whether farmers, graziers, or drovers – or in many cases, all three combined – there was money to be made. The influx of wealth brought significant social and economic benefits: higher living standards, investment in agricultural improvement, and an increase in estate revenue. Significantly, there were also opportunities for the lower tenantry to dip a toe into commercial waters: employment as herds and drovers, *gall* cattle to be grazed, shielings to be rented out, and the occasional chance for market speculation or even to impose their own price demands on the dealers. The Badenoch experience, indeed, completely undermines the traditional stereotype of the conservative Highlander reluctant to embrace change, for this was a community, at all social levels, keen to seize whatever opportunities came its way.

Though lucrative, the commercial cattle trade was undoubtedly susceptible to market fluctuation – a fact not lost on the gentry, some of whom would seek to diversify their interests, exploring alternative paths to prosperity.[182] But there was never any doubt that, in Badenoch at least, cattle managed by indigenous tacksmen remained economically supreme into the next century. In his spiritual reflections while travelling through Badenoch, Bishop Forbes succinctly captured the essence of the local economy: 'All along, the words of the Psalmist came often into my mind, "And Cattle upon a thousand Hills".'[183]

Chapter 4

1750–70:
Reorganisation and Improvement

Incarcerated in Edinburgh Castle after the 1715 Jacobite Rising, Brigadier Mackintosh of Borlum, laird of Raitts, produced his famous treatise on agricultural improvement. He hoped, perhaps forlornly, that 'the virtuous Design to begin and pursue Inclosing and Planting their Grounds, would inspire our Nobility and Gentry to leave off going so oft to London' – a jibe at the post-Union Anglocentricity of the Scottish gentry.[1] Borlum, however, was no mere theorist, for General Roy's map of the 1750s shows Raitts to be the most improved estate in Badenoch (Colour plate 7).

'Improvement' was, of course, integral to eighteenth-century Enlightenment philosophy, transforming the landscape for both economic and aesthetic reasons, reshaping the random world of nature, imposing civilisation on the environment.[2] Such improvement was not just fashionable, but 'socially prestigious'.[3] Agricultural improvers like Archibald Grant of Monymusk provided practical models, organisations like the 'Honourable Society of Improvement in the Knowledge of Agriculture in Scotland' (1723) provided a national forum for debate, while literature such as Borlum's *Essay* maintained a continuous flow of ideas.[4] In the Highlands, however, improvement had an added sting – in the telling words of one of Scotland's leading Enlightenment figures, Lord Kames – 'civilising so many Barbarians'.[5]

Whig propaganda, indeed, attributed the rise of Jacobitism to that barbarity, thereby opening the door to their own panacea, the ideological twins of 'improvement' and 'civilisation' – assimilation to southern values. Allan Macinnes described post-Culloden policy as both 'punitive civilising' and 'exemplary civilising': the destruction of Highland distinctiveness firstly through organised brutality, and secondly by providing a model of progress on those estates forfeited after the '45.[6] A third category, collaborative civilising, might also be appropriate as Highland landowners wishing to demonstrate their 'British' credentials 'civilised' from within. For such landowners, Jacobite or Hanoverian, acceptance of the ideology of progress served the dual purpose of rehabilitation and economic opportunity – and clanship was increasingly perceived as 'an insurmountable obstacle' to that progress.[7]

Improvement is generally seen as a top-down reform imposed by landowners and outsiders, as with the comprehensive estate reorganisation by Archibald Campbell, 2nd Duke of Argyll, in the 1730s, or Sir James Grant's later remodelling of Strathspey under the guidance of his southern mentor William Lorimer.[8] Within Badenoch during the 1750s and 1760s, the notion of top-down progress naturally brought markedly differing responses across the three principal estates – Gordon, Invereshie and Cluny – not just in the agricultural sector, but also in the attempted diversification into industry. Significantly, however, economic initiatives in Badenoch, though somewhat sluggish, came neither from the principal landowner nor any improving south-erner, but, as in the cattle trade, primarily through the efforts of the local gentry adapting the new ideologies and methods to their own requirements. Attempts by the Duke and the forfeited estate officials to impose social recon-struction from above inevitably provoked clashes with the clan gentry. The lower classes also experienced grievances over land and clearances, though they did receive a vital boost through the annual cycle of seasonal migration to the Lowlands – which in turn became another source of confrontation. Across the social spectrum, however, the most significant impetus for change in these two decades came not from within the region, but from increasing global tensions particularly the outbreak of the Seven Years' War in 1756.

The Gordon Estates

The second Duchess of Gordon, according to Borlum, 'deserves the first Place in the Catalogue of Improvers' for introducing English methods into Aberdeen-shire.[9] Like most landowners, however, the Gordons' enthusiasm for reform did not spread much beyond their home domain. Indeed, unlike the proactive approach of their counterparts in Argyll, neither Duke Cosmo nor Duke Alexander revealed any ideological vision of improvement – a problem further aggravated both by their *laissez-faire* approach and by their absenteeism.

The Estate Commissioners (managers) certainly planned radical reforms, starting immediately after Culloden with the need for rehabilitation. Removing 'rebel' tacksmen was proposed, but Duke Cosmo was reluctant, perhaps due to pro-Catholic sympathies, or simple reality because 'Severall papists of Substance live on his estate who pay their rent very well'.[10] Incorporating loyal oaths into leases was also suggested, 'preventing homage to any person But the King', though such formal declarations were irrelevant after the amnesty of 1747. Thirdly, there was to be an assault on clanship itself, removing the tacksmen and bringing in outsiders: 'to break up the Connexion of Clansmen and for that End to Divide the Highland Duchuses among the Subtenants, holding Each of them immediately of the Duke and bringing in Scattered names into Every Duchus Tack' – much as in Argyll in the 1730s.[11]

The Commissioners formalised their ideas in 1750, suggesting that Cosmo should 'New Modell this part of the Estate', primarily raising rents and breaking Macpherson dominance.[12] The first was pragmatic, Badenoch having 'run into a higher Arrear than any other part of the Duke's Estate'.[13] The tacksmen, they complained, 'receive punctual payment from their Subtennants to the full Extent of their Respective Rentals', but 'don't pay the Rents so received in to the Duke . . . [Instead] They maintain themselves and their familys upon those rents'.[14] Donald Macpherson of Breakachy and his uncle, Malcolm Macpherson of Crubenmore, for instance, constantly evaded the rent for Presmuchrach, to the obvious frustration of the factor: 'I never Got a farthing of these arrears . . . They always had some Flume flame [flim-flam] Tale or other to Tell of Some kind or other'.[15] The Commissioners did actually succeed in increasing the Badenoch revenue. No tacksman could secure a new lease without paying all his arrears. Furthermore, rents were raised by around 30 per cent, partly by 'comparing the Subtenants Rents payable to the master', so the tacksman had to pay the Duke at least what the subtenants paid him. But increases were also achieved, using 'their private Information and Intelligence in which they were very successful' – a rather Machiavellian scheme of getting the rival clans to value each other's lands, with the added bonus of increasing tension between them:

> encouraging the different humours of the different Setts of MacIntoshes, Macdonnells and Macphersons and playing them again[st] one another . . . By this means they came to the knowledge of what Rentally the different Possessions could bear.[16]

Indeed, William Tod, the Gordon factor, was still using the trick of 'a competition between the two clans [Mackintosh and Macpherson]' as late as 1789 as a means of securing a higher rent for the farm of Pitchurn.[17]

Further success came through another devious policy, introducing secret bidding for farms to further increase rentals – 'that no person should know what was offered by another, . . . the different offerers bidding upon one another in this private manner'.[18] The policy effectively destabilised both tacksman and clan, for, given the significance of *duthchas*, secret bidding was a potent weapon encouraging tacksman to bid against tacksman. One man's *duthchas* became another's gain, breeding uncertainty and suspicion, and thus undermining the unity of the clan.

Andrew Macpherson of Benchar exploited this scheme to secure Macdonell land in the Braes of Laggan by making 'such high offers . . . for the [territory] possessed by the Macdonells as £500 of Grassum [down-payment] and double Rent'.[19] The 1752 rental confirms both grassum payments of £584 and double rents equivalent to an additional £912 over the nineteen-year lease – a total bonus to the estate of £1,496.[20] It is further testimony, not just to the wealth of the Badenoch gentry, but to the returns expected from the investment. Secret bidding, however, was a double-edged sword, for to secure their *duthchas,* many offered far beyond what the land could yield. The tenant of Sherrabeg offered 30 per cent above his current rent to secure his farm.[21] Lewis Macpherson, long-standing tacksman of Dalraddie, found himself trapped between *duthchas* and rental, between heart and head, it being 'somehow deeply Rooted in the minds of Highlanders to hold [onto] . . . any lands in the possession of there forefathers'. Because of this he had offered too much, causing him to 'strugel hard to the prejudice of his little personal Interest to pay the augmented Rents'.[22]

The commissioners achieved one further success, tackling 'some lucrative Wadsets on the Estate'.[23]Inflation meant that these old wadsets could actually be redeemed cheaply, enabling the estate, rather than the wadsetters, to benefit from rental increases. John Macpherson of Pitchurn was obliged to pay rent after being made to exchange his wadset for 'a personal Bond by his Grace'.[24] The redemption of the Kingussiemore wadset in 1751 illustrates the benefits. This was an 'improper wadset' where the wadsetter paid £2 11s as surplus rent. After redemption, the tacksman had to pay the full rent of £25 – a £400 increase over the nineteen-year lease.[25] Furthermore, eliminating wadsets brought these quasi-lairds back under estate control.

The estate's 'New Modell' did not all go smoothly, however. The Commissioners again proposed removing all tacksmen in arrears, either through the process of law or the military power of the state: 'a very proper opportunity When the King's troops are in that Country And their assistance can be easily

obtained'.[26] Instead, the subtenants should 'have tacks directly from His Grace
... And this wou'd secure their rents to be paid directly to his Grace, And
prevent their being Intercepted' by the tacksmen – a policy that would
instantly have destroyed the socio-economic basis of clan power. The plan
was, however, quickly abandoned, for the Commissioners realised that it could
not be implemented without 'endangering the Duke's Interest and putting his
Rent . . . on a very precarious footing, by throwing it in small parcels into the
hands of a number of poor people unable to make regular payments'. A multitude of small, impoverished farms would not secure the Duke's future prosperity, and besides, sidelining the tacksmen would mean that their substantial
arrears would be lost. Thus policy defaulted to the *status quo*: tacksmen
subletting their land and collecting the rents therefrom.

The complexities of removing tacksmen, however, went far beyond mere
financial concerns because of the tenacious survival of *duthchas*, already
implied in the intriguing concept of a 'duchus tack'.[27] The Commissioners
encapsulated the dilemma in one highly significant phrase: 'Certain tacksmen
commonly called Douchassers'.[28] The term 'douchassers', which resonated with
social and cultural overtones, was used repeatedly, seemingly investing them
with an authority, almost an aura, beyond the ordinary tacksman. Significantly,
the term was still being used by William Tod, the Duke's factor, as late as 1789,
suggesting the enduring strength of this cultural connection to land in
Badenoch.[29]

Indeed, far from dismissing *duthchas* as an antiquated concept, the
Commissioners trod extremely warily:

> Tho . . . It wou'd be more desirable that these Douchassers were wholly
> Removed, In respect of the power they Assume in the Country and a
> Right to possess without any Tack from his Grace . . . this power may
> make it very difficult to Make it a proper Measure to Remove them
> all at once.[30]

The idea that tacksmen in 1750 still had 'a Right to possess without any Tack
from his Grace', is astonishing – a recognition that land tenure might emanate
from clan rather than estate. There was also a clear acknowledgement of the
tacksmen's power, particularly in the Commissioners' apprehension over
removing them.

Nor was this the Commissioners' only retreat. Well aware that the
Macphersons were easily 'the most numerous and powerfull' of the local clans,

the estate was concerned that 'their chief point of view was to rout out the other two, So as to be the sole Possessor of the Country themselves'.[31] Any extension of Macpherson power and territory was obviously detrimental to Gordon interests, but the estate once more shied away from confrontation, fearful of antagonising the clan gentry, those 'most likely to fform a Party in the Country to prevent the Execution of any part of this Plan'.

Inevitably, these tortuous attempts to enforce structural change triggered a prolonged power struggle between the estate and the 'douchassers'. The Duke's Commissioners were clearly trying to assert their authority, to break the dominance of the tacksman over his domain, even to break Clan Macpherson itself. Yet, considering the estate's financial, legal and political muscle, their reluctance for a showdown with the clan elite was remarkable – even more so their deference to clan traditions and rights at the very time when government was hell-bent on destroying clanship. Even in the shadow of Culloden the residual power of clanship loomed large. Though bidding, redeeming wadsets and exploiting inter-clan rivalries had undoubtedly strengthened the estate's position, the ultimate consequence of this deference was that the future of the estate, in practical terms, still rested with the tacksman. Social reconstruction had been jettisoned for economic and political pragmatism.

Of improvement the estate made little mention, apart from granting nineteen-year leases with the vague requirement to improve 'whatever improvable grounds are in the said lands'.[32] While financial assistance was offered for enclosures made with 'sufficient drystone dykes', stipulating that farms 'would again rise in the Rent by this Improvement' was perhaps counterproductive.[33] The non-specific, permissive nature of these limited improvements supports the notion of an estate that had abdicated responsibility to its tacksmen, though, in fairness, there was as yet no clear understanding over how best to reform Highland agriculture.[34]

By 1771, improvement had indeed made little headway, judging by George Brown's survey report: 'very poor thin gravelly soil'; 'Inclosing this part would also be a great improvement, and there are plenty of stones on the ground sufficient for that purpose'; 'houses in a ruinous condition'; 'the meadow ground . . . is at present in bad order . . . for want of draining'.[35] Similar problems emerge in the offers for new leases at that time. Alexander Macpherson of Strathmashie promised to 'build a head dyke thereon and proper Houses of Stone and lime and Make a proper Channel for the River Mashie . . . Also he will make Drains and Such other Inclosures'.[36] That Strathmashie as yet had nothing as basic as a head dyke reveals how little had been achieved since 1750.

The minimalist nature of improvement is revealed at the duke's farm of Moy in Laggan, where even the surveyor recommended only the construction of a head dyke 'to preserve the Cornfields from the Cattle in the Hills', arguing that 'it would be quite unnecessary to subdivide them [the cornfields] into different Inclosures'.[37]

There were, however, islands of improvement. At Garvamore, Captain Lachlan Macpherson built enclosures with stone dykes, new houses and steadings 'with stone and lime walls', while 'draining several mosses . . . now converted to hay and arable ground'.[38] Hugh Macpherson of Uvie also boasted of his innovations since taking the family farm in 1752:

> He being then an active young man, and at the same time a dealler in cattle, resolved to try a method unknown to his predecessors & until then unattempted upon any of the Duke's farms in the Country. The high rent having obliged his subtenants to remove he took the whole into his own hands & in the space of two years inclosed & subdivided every inch of it, which with bringing to Culture about five and twenty ackers of heathy, woody, stony & mossy ground within these Inclosures has hitherto enabled him to maintain his family & make as ready a payment of what was esteemed a racked rent as any tenant in the Lordship.[39]

Uvie had created a substantial tacksman farm, the land divided and enclosed, new ground broken in, probably for his cattle business. These were indeed the first documented improvements of their kind in Badenoch. But such reforms inevitably brought depopulation. Uvie's explanation was somewhat disingenuous since he was clearly rack-renting his subtenants just as the Duke was doing to him. Whether formally evicted or squeezed out by rents is immaterial – Uvie, one of the clan elite, had effectively cleared his land to implement his improvements.

In his extensive survey, George Brown praised only one tacksman – John Maclean of Pitmain. Originally from Badenoch, Maclean worked for the Duke at Huntly before taking over Pitmain in 1752. He claimed he had been head-hunted to provide 'an Example to introduce such Improvement among the people that have hitherto done nothing that way', improvements that would 'both beautify the Country, and Considerably add to the Intrinsic value of them'. Furthermore, when people saw the 'beneficial effect of such Industry . . . it will naturally prompt them to do the best they can'.[40] It was the language of both Enlightenment and exemplary civilising.[41] Maclean was clearly part of the estate plan, a progressive tacksman introducing new and profitable methods to the Badenoch tacksmen – a more subtle approach to undermining the 'douchassers'.

As early as the mid 1750s Maclean was embarking on his remarkable improvements in Pitmain (and also the neighbouring farm of Kingussiemore which he took over in 1758), starting with the extensive floodbanks on the Spey – the first of their kind in Badenoch. In 1771, Brown recorded his achievements:

> Mr. Mclean has laid out a deal of money on building houses and inclosing the Low grounds . . . The haugh is a very fine field and very extensive, there is a considerable part of it inclosed and drained, which has turned out very well... The first two or three cropts has indemnified the tenant for his trouble and expence. The inclosures . . . are very good and Substantial.[42]

Taylor's 1771 map of Pitmain reveals the rectilinear fields reclaimed from the floodplain – the 'Clover Park', 'Drain Park and 'Swine Park', with annotations like 'ground lately grubbed from Allars [alders]', indicating the nature of improvements (Plate 8a and b). Arable acreage increased from 20 acres to 120 acres; lime was extensively used, a massive 538 cart-loads from nearby Dunachton in July 1770 alone; the region's first sheep walk was established.[43] Maclean's personal outlay already exceeded £800, and though far from complete, his farm was easily the highest valued in Badenoch.[44] Improvement again, however, brought depopulation. In the 1720s, at least twenty subtenants had worked Pitmain and Kingussie: by 1771, only three remained.[45] Between eighty and a hundred souls must have been rendered landless, though many would have remained as Maclean's essential labour force – Taylor's map, indeed, mentions land uncultivated 'since the houses were removed'.[46]

Maclean, however, was no single-minded farmer. When the military road was realigned on the north side of the Spey, he seized the moment, convincing the Duke that a new inn was essential for the well-being of travellers. Pitmain – 'an excellent inn, [with] a spirited landlord' according to Andrew Wight – became the hub of all social and business meetings in the area, opening yet more doors for Maclean.[47] Nothing evaded his entrepreneurial tentacles: not just farmer and innkeeper, he was the Duke's forester at Gaick, depute-factor to William Tod, engineer for the Spey flood prevention schemes, architect for the rebuilding of Garvamore Inn on the Corrieyairrack, ('the only one in the Country that can do it to the Purpose'), and cess-collector, appointed specifically to retrieve £165 worth of unpaid taxes.[48] As Justice of the Peace he contributed to the wider judicial and administrative work of the region; for instance, along with his neighbour John Dow, 'clearing the Country of Borlums Gang [the local banditti]' – a feat acknowledged in James Ross's rather grudging comment, 'they do deserve thanks on that account'.[49]

Maclean, however, became over-confident, abusing his position as forester by grazing his own livestock in the forest and breeding horses there, selling mares worth £120 in just one year. He regularly poinded other beasts straying into the forest, fining their owners, thereby earning another £100 in a single year.[50] His successor John McHardy commented wryly, 'Tho the expence of keeping it when in Mr McLeans Custody was small, yet, his profits were great.'[51] The under-forester was more blunt: 'McLean . . . used unknown freedom with the Forest by keeping a number of horses in it . . . [also] killing your Grace's Deer . . . which he did in greater numbers than any of his Predecessors . . . and . . . Ripeing [reaping] every kind of advantage that could derive or be devised in virtue of the Forest.'[52] No doubt the inn was well stocked with venison. Duke Alexander, however, was not amused, and Maclean was eventually removed from Pitmain.

This fall from grace should not detract from Maclean's achievements. James Robertson's observation, 'The fields around Pitmain which belong to the Inkeeper, are better cultivated than any I have seen North from Perth', was just one of many tributes.[53] Many a local, too, enjoyed Maclean's hospitality, no doubt exchanging pleasantries over his private life, for Maclean threw his prodigious energy into five marriages to closely related wives, with so many children that he earned the nickname, 'the Father of Confusion'. John Anderson, his son-in-law, pithily remarked on Maclean's limitations in accountancy: 'though the honest man can beget Sons and Daughters at threescore and ten, He does not make so good an appearance with pen and Ink.'[54] His real importance, however, was to show what individual enterprise could achieve even in such inhospitable environs. Today Pitmain's fields with their huge drainage ditches and massive floodbanks still testify to Maclean's efforts, while below the farm a triangular shape delineated by road and trees (almost certainly planted by Maclean himself) still marks out the garden of the inn as depicted on Taylor's map – a garden plentifully stocked with fruit trees, raspberries, strawberries, and a remarkable 287 currant and gooseberry bushes.[55]

Maclean's reforms highlight Gordon failures. By handing the initiative to the tacksmen, even if hoping for Maclean's example to rub off, the estate missed out on the rewards of systematic reform. The proactive plan of 1750 had in fact foundered on the rocks of ducal indifference, for the commissioners frustratedly complained that the 'new model . . . hath not been Carried into Execution, By Reason that his Grace [Cosmo] went to London without coming to any Resolution'.[56] For the next two decades, the estate could do little more than collect its rental dues while the tacksmen exploited the region's economic potential.

For the tacksmen it was an opportunity gained – 'civilising' would not be enforced on them by government or duke, but would be achieved largely on their own terms. Their victory lay in maintaining the *status quo*: their autonomy within the *duthchas* intact, perhaps even strengthened by the estate's eggshell approach, their control over subtenants undiminished, and their social status secure. Untrammelled by onerous restrictions and demands, they were free to develop their own commercial interests. Most, however, did not follow Maclean's route. Indeed, they could never have matched his success, for the inn was his market, converting his produce into ready cash from his patrons without worries over distant markets or fluctuating prices. More significantly, however, the cattle trade – the tacksmen's natural medium – was yielding considerable profits without requiring the great effort, cost and risks of improvement schemes.

Invereshie

On Invereshie estate the contrast could hardly have been greater, for through-out his long lairdship George Macpherson was a resident, financially prudent, hands-on improving landlord – albeit a conservative one. As a Whig loyalist, he well understood the philosophical and political connotations of improve-ment, and his post-Culloden involvement with the Hanoverian regime suggested a degree of 'collaborative civilising'. Such notions were reinforced by his marriage to Grace Grant of Ballindalloch (sister of General James Grant), drawing him into a network of Grants who were renowned improvers.[57] But George Macpherson was more pragmatist than ideologue, driven by the desire to preserve the estate both intact and in credit. The Invereshie improvements were uniquely shaped by the laird's intimate knowl-edge of every farm and individual on his lands: most tenants held directly from – and were thus accountable to – the laird himself. It was, for the Highlands, an unusual personal relationship that neither the vast Gordon estates nor the forfeited Cluny lands could ever have enjoyed.

Macpherson was in many ways a traditionalist, making more extensive use of the old feudal labour services than other landowners, much of it for the benefit of the estate – like the improvements to buildings and river defences, bulwarking the Feshie as early as 1732.[58] Using the old to implement the new while raising the estate's value through free labour underpinned George's approach. Farm improvements were also introduced at minimum cost through individualised leases – not the generalised ones of the Duke, but a specific improvement contract between landowner and tenant, detailing the exact reforms and labour required from each farmer.

Invereshie's earliest extant reforming lease dates from 1734, long before government 'civilising', and long before more eminent reformers like Lord Kames, the Duke of Buccleuch and Sir James Grant introduced similar ideas. But the date is not the only remarkable feature, for, though just a poor tenant farmer, Angus Macpherson was given Lubenreoch 'with full power to labour and Make arrable land . . . for the space of nineteen years'.[59] Indeed, George gave nineteen-year leases to every tenant irrespective of class, a security enjoyed only by tacksmen on the Gordon estates. Furthermore, this was a new arable farm carved out of moorland, an improvement generally associated with the later eighteenth century, sometimes classed as 'internal colonisation'.[60] Most interesting, however, was the rental policy. The first seven years were rent-free, to break in the land, enclose it and erect buildings. Thereafter, Lubenreoch would be valued by 'two honest men mutually chosen . . . from three years to three years of the [remaining] twelve'. So, after seven free years, Angus's farm would undergo an independent triennial valuation, the rent increasing in proportion to the improvement. A similar detailed lease of moorland reclamation with graduated rent for Dalwhinnie on the small Badenoch estate of Invernahavon from 1733 suggests that Invereshie was not alone in such progressive measures.[61]

During the 1760s, the Reverend John Walker praised similar improving leases in Ross-shire and Aberdeenshire, and particularly Lord Kames' reclamation of Kincardine Moss through long leases with graduated rentals: yet Invereshie pre-dated this by thirty years.[62] These graduated leases became a standard tool on Invereshie for arable expansion and moorland reclamation, though incremental steps were pre-specified in later leases. Angus Macbean in Lynvragit, for instance, was to pay annually for the first five years a reek hen and a dozen eggs; the next five, a hen, eggs and £5 Scots; the next four, a hen, eggs, a wedder and £8; and for the last five years, hen, eggs, wedder and £10.[63]

George was clearly restructuring the estate. In 1752, the davoch of Killiehuntly contained twenty-eight farmers, including three multiple-tenant farms, and some small single-tenant units. A year later the multiple-tenant farms had gone, replaced by sixteen single-tenant farms and two joint tenancies (each with just two tenants), a total of eighteen small farms.[64] By the end of the century, only four of the eighty-six farms across the entire estate were joint tenancies, the remainder being small individual holdings, many on new land.[65] At Invermarkie on the east side of Glen Feshie at least fourteen small farms were squeezed in between the Cairngorm massif and the River Feshie along a stretch of just 3 miles. Some of these 'new improvements', according to the Duke's forester, had been established in the ancient forest of Glen Feshie itself, which Invereshie leased. The forester complained that George had 'let out the Winter [lower] fforest and made arable ground of the Same', so that 'the woods of Glenfeshie was Destroyed by Garthing burning & Selling each [tenant] making his own use of what wood was within his Garth [plot].'[66] Converting prime woodlands to arable might have benefited Invereshie: it would certainly not have featured in the Duke's schemes.

George used leases to direct the precise improvement for each farm. In Lynvragit, Angus Macbean had to 'leave a Firehouse [dwelling house] Barn and Sheep Coat ... wind & water tight'. Donald Gollonach and his neighbour John Kennedy had to

> Make a sufficient Ditch of Two hundred and twenty yards below the bigging of Achleanbegg and to Drain the Moras and Improve the same in arrable ground and to Inclose by a Dead hedge from the bigging in straight line ... & to improve all the Improveable ground within Said Garth and to have the Ditch Completely finished in two years.

Alexander Gordon in Farletter was required 'To keep & have folds for his Catle great and small, to Manure his Ground, to plant potatoes yearly in New Ground'.[67]

The most unusual tack was Tomfad (Badenoch's most remote farm) in 1767, where George Macpherson and the tenant, Alexander Macintyre, shared the burden of improvement.[68] Macintyre was 'to Inclose the one half of the said Ground ... and the said George is to Inclose the other half ... at my own expence'. Similarly for the buildings: 'I ... George Mcpherson promise to Build ane fire house and a Barn to the said McIntyre ... and Cover the Same with feall and Divote', while Macintyre was 'to build a bire and a Coat himself att his own Expence, and the Fire house and Barn to be at mine'. Macintyre was not obliged to reimburse the laird or pay interest on the improvements. George's magnanimity is puzzling.[69] Perhaps Tomfad was too remote, too big an undertaking for a single tenant, or Macintyre simply could not afford the improvement. To the laird, however, it was obviously a worthwhile investment – a farm that would, in time, repay the initial outlay. Equally unusual was the building of a separate byre (normally located within the dwelling house) – the only Invereshie lease with this requirement. Perhaps the remoteness and altitude of Tomfad (over 1,200 feet) necessitated extra byre accommodation, or perhaps it was primarily a stock farm utilising the vast grazing outrun that stretched southwards to Atholl.

The Baron Court enforced the reforms, 'for the good of the Tennents Beter improvement of the ffarms occupied by them and the Melanders [cottars] under them'.[70] Forbidding tenants from taking building turf from the township pasture, from cutting timber without permission, and from muir-burning – all punishable by fine or imprisonment – was simply good practice. Tenants were to provide communal fox-hunters to protect sheep, and herds to prevent livestock straying. Even peat-cutting was regulated to stop tenants digging random pits which caused the 'Destruction of their own Catle of all kinds by falling into the seperat pots they Dig', while the top layer of turf was to be replaced in the dug trench 'for the Beter Growth again of the Mosses' – a recognition of the need for conservation. Contrary to Lowland practice, George forbade enclosures: 'Multiplicity of ffences and dead heddges is Destructive to growing woods' – henceforth only head dykes could utilise timber fencing to protect crops from livestock. Tathing (systematic grazing and manuring within enclosures) was also specified, cattle and sheep being folded throughout summer and autumn 'upon new Improveable ground' – a modification of the old 'outfield' system to create permanent new arable fields. Invereshie also leased upper Glen Feshie from the Duke from 1752 – a huge summer-grazing reserve both for his own commercial use and the shieling needs of his own tenantry who all paid a share of the 'forest rent'.[71]

In 1766, the Baron Court detailed the earliest known local use of potatoes as a farm crop, a decade ahead of their common use in Atholl.[72] Their use was explicitly and exclusively for breaking in waste ground: 'to plant . . . their potatoes yearly in New Ground and none in their Cultivated Land or Leys already Riven in'. Furthermore, the cultivation of this new crop was largely devolved to the lowest ranks: 'Cottars having houses & holdings from the Tennents'.

They were instructed to grow their potatoes for two consecutive years on the new ground to clear it of stones and scrub; thereafter, the land reverted to 'their Master' (the tenant for whom the cottar worked) who was then entitled to 'Labour the ground so to be Cleared, [and] who is to have the third and subsequent crop thereof'. This was a clear estate improvement strategy: cottars breaking in virgin ground with the new cottar food crop in order to prepare the land for the more highly valued – both economically and socially – corn crop grown by the tenant farmer. That the court designated even a humble tenant as 'the Master' of the cottar further demonstrates how the hierarchical nature of society reached down to the very bottom rungs of the ladder.

Though not on the scale of his Lowland contemporaries, George Macpherson gradually transformed the estate from the early 1730s, creating an infrastructure on which his son John later capitalised. Long leases, graduated rentals, targeted improvements and assistance to tenants typify George's shrewd management: small, independent farms with long-term security would, after all, provide the incentive for self-improvement, rewarding the laird through the gradual rise in estate value. But these small farms, many carved from the inhospitable lands of Glen Feshie, should not be equated with the West-Highland crofts which were deliberately made too small for self-sufficiency.[73] With no industrial potential like kelp or fishing to supplement income, Badenoch farms had to be viable in their own right. But nor were they comparable to the larger units of Lowland or Morayshire agriculture, for George clearly intended to maintain as many small independent tenants as the estate could support, consistent with contemporary belief in the benefits of a numerous population. Interestingly, the MP Edward Ellice, who knew the area well as a Glen Feshie shooting tenant, later attributed Badenoch's survival during the difficult 1830s and 1840s to those small independent holdings, which he categorised as midway between the crofts of the west and the substantial tenant farms of Banffshire.[74]

Though Invereshie experienced no major clearance, reform was not achieved without grief, for social upheaval was inevitable, perhaps evidenced in the number of cottars and tiny crofts that appear in later rentals – ninety-four cottar families to sixty-nine tenant farmers in 1817.[75] Tenants undoubtedly resented the heavy labour services, rents were often in arrears, while, for some, reorganisation brought a drop in status from farmer to cottar or labourer. Significantly, however, all tenants held their own land directly from the landowner with security of tenure and moderate rents – far superior to their subtenant neighbours on the Gordon lands. Above all, and unlike many of his more illustrious contemporaries, George Macpherson achieved it without crippling either his tenantry or the estate.

Cluny

On the forfeited Cluny estate, issues were more complex. Though annexed by the Crown in 1752, legal complications prevented the Commissioners of Annexed Estates from taking control until 1770. Thus the Barons of Exchequer ran the estate, with their clear socio-political remit: 'applying the rents and profits thereof for the better civilizing and improving the Highlands . . . and preventing disorders there for the future'.[76] This was 'exemplary civilising', assimilation through improving agriculture, industry and education. With the post-Culloden economic legacy and the ever-present Hanoverian military, winning 'hearts and minds' would, however, prove difficult.

Further complications arose from the ambivalent situation of the Cluny family themselves. While the chief was an attainted rebel, his family was not. Indeed, Cluny Mains was held from 1746 until the restoration of 1784, firstly by Cluny's wife and brothers, Major John and Captain Lachlan, and after 1770 by his son Duncan. Though tenants of the Barons rather than owners, the family connection with the estate remained intact. Significantly, General Bland, Commander-in-Chief for Scotland, observed in 1747 that the Macphersons were 'more under the influence of their chieff than any clan in the north'.[77] With that chief's presence, albeit fugitive, looming over the estate for nine years, his family's continued residence, and his brother-in-law, the shrewd and powerful Donald Macpherson of Breakachy, as estate factor, the Macphersons would prove as obstructive to the Barons as to the Duke.

The first controversy concerned rents. For seven years the tenants had continued to pay rent to Lady Cluny rather than the government. In 1752, William Ramsay, the Barons' factor, was eventually ordered to reclaim the 'arrears' of £935 from Lady Cluny and the forty-four tenants on the rent-roll – a ridiculous demand considering the poverty levels, with twenty-eight tenants paying under £2 annual rent, with another thirteen between £2 and £4.[78] Eviction notices were served (to no effect) on the entire estate.[79] James Small (Ramsay's replacement) then threatened 'to prosequte Lady Clunie . . . for recovery of the rents . . . and to turn her out of her possession', before proposing that the tenants should pay the entire sum and reclaim it from Lady Cluny.[80] Small tried, again unsuccessfully, to appeal to Breakachy's conscience, that 'the ffriends of the Cluny ffamily will fall on ways and Means of paying that money, rather than See So many poor Wretches Sent to Misery on their account'.[81] When Small tried confiscation in lieu of payment, he was again thwarted: 'I also attempted to Poynd [seize goods], but the Messenger could find none of their Effects; either they had been put out of the way, or their neighbours Swore falsely'.

The tenants protested against 'this Rigorous claim of double payments'.[82] No-one had told them to pay to the Crown – 'they made such payments bona fide to Lady Cluny . . . who took the same care & Charge of the Estate as she was in use to do before her husbands attainder'.[83] So, to 'persons of their low Rank and situation in life', it appeared legitimate, especially as no-one had pointed out their error until 1752 – a clever, though somewhat disingenuous, proclamation of innocent confusion, deflecting blame onto bureaucratic incompetence.

The tenants also played on their hardship:

> In the present calamitous Situation the Country is in, they having scarcely wherewithal to support themselves and their Families . . . the only Consequences . . . would be laying the Estate waste and the exposing the Petitioners, with their Wives and Families, to the Miseries of Famine.[84]

Furthermore, many of their men had just been recruited for the Seven Years' War. Were they 'to be imprisoned, or their small Remains of Goods seized upon, while they are deprived of the Help of their Children and Relations . . . they must be reduced to the lowest Degree of Misery and Ruin'. Famine was the last thing the government wanted, especially if aggravated by its own financial demands, and even more so when it desperately needed Highland manpower for its imperial wars. Small eventually conceded that 'to prosecute the poor people . . . with Rigour would have been the greatest Oppression, at least it would [have] appeared so [to] the Ignorant Country People and been an ill recommendation to the Annexation at its first Setting out'.[85] It was a wise move, though many years too late, for the issue had indeed become an 'ill recommendation'.

The Barons were equally unsuccessful in their improvement remit, reform again devolving on the tacksmen. Donald Macpherson (Laggan of Nuide) made 'considerable Improvements . . . by Stone Inclosures, Drains & Ditches . . . Planting, Altering the Course of prejudicial Rivulets, Bullworks against the

Spey, and thereby taking of new ground at a considerable expence'.[86] William Tennoch, the surveyor, acknowledged his effort, almost despairingly. The land at Milehouse could 'never be much improven, as its surface is made up of a number of Small knows, or hillocks full of Stones', while the improvement at Balintian (Nuide, not Glen Feshie) was 'a very Singular attempt to raise Corn in that part of Badenoch where Corn never grew before', though 'it can never grow so as to yield much profit for his labour' (Colour plate 8a and b).[87] Walking these two desolate settlements now, it would be hard to disagree. Indeed, Tennoch inadvertently highlighted the futility of Lowland-style improvements in such a difficult environment.

Breakachy's son, Captain Duncan Macpherson, was another improver. After returning from India, he embarked on his improvements at Catlag on the davoch of Gaskinloan in 1766. Having cleared stones and brushwood, he enclosed his cornfields with stone dykes and even 'hired Masons from another Country for that purpose'. He also proposed the first dedicated sheep farm in Badenoch. The factor acknowledged Duncan's reforms, 'without any [financial] encouragement' from the Board, adding significantly that he was 'an example to the people of that Country in point of Improvement'.[88] Here was the desired 'exemplary civilising', but financed by the tacksman (probably out of his military and Indian revenues) rather than through any government assistance. Indeed, the Barons sometimes blocked tacksman reforms. Allan Macdonald of Gallovie offered, in return for a twenty-one-year lease, to enclose his farm so that 'the lands will yield near double Rent', but, in spite of the generous offer, he was offered only the standard three-year lease.[89]

The ordinary Cluny tenants also undertook improvements. The runrig tenants of Milton of Nuidebeg had taken over the running of that farm while their tacksman, another Lieutenant Macpherson, was on active service during the Seven Years' War. Finding the farm 'entirely waste, without a gooded Rigg', the tenants initiated improvements over a period of six years, building eight houses, 'bringing the ground to good heart by proper Tillage & Muck-manure; Clearing it of a Deal of Stones . . . And bringing in New Ground that never was before Laboured'.[90] At Drumgaskinloan, another runrig farm, the six tenants also desired improvements. There was no head dyke, 'which is of very great hurt to them, and Indangers their whole Cropt perhaps to be distroyed in one night in Harvest', so they offered to build one at their own expense, 'providing they are not removed within seven years'.[91] They also requested help for building floodbanks to protect their riverside arable, explaining that continual flooding must 'make their possessions less Valuable & lessen his Majesties

Rent'. Seven years later, however, Tennoch reported that this farm still desperately needed a head dyke, and that the river still did 'unspeakable damage both in Seed time and Harvest when swelled with heavy rains' – clearly showing the Barons' failure to provide the requested assistance.[92] Even if not always successful, the desire of the ordinary tenants for improvement demonstrates the potential for agricultural reform from below.

Once again, improvements came at a cost. Donald Macpherson of Nuide (formerly of Cullinlean) evicted some half-dozen tenants from the townships of Milehouse, Drimininich and Elandow in 1758.[93] Captain Duncan of Breakachy requested a lease of the other Gaskinloan townships, involving the removal of at least sixteen families, magnanimously (in his view) offering that 'many of them will have an opportunity of being employed' by him, while the rest would be given a year to move – a request refused by the Barons.[94] But those runrig tenants of Nuidebeg who had worked so hard to improve their farm were not so lucky; when their officer-tacksman returned from the war in 1764, all were served with removal notices.[95]

The Barons' only success lay in promoting education for 'the numerous poor children . . . who can have no access to the benefit of anie publick school'.[96] Though a rather politically correct curriculum – 'Training of poor children in the principles of religion and Loyalty to his majestie' – the local population welcomed the opportunity. By 1759 there was a boys' school at Gaskinloan, while at Cluny, May Angus was teaching 'young Girls to read Sew and Knit Stockins'.[97] Later, the tenants of Nuidebeg and Biallidbeg petitioned that they were 'so happie to have a parochial School in the town of Ruthven . . . for teaching their Boys', but were disappointed that 'they have no School for the Education of their daughters'.[98] Their petition specifically requested a school 'where they [the girls] may also learn the English language': the tenantry were learning to play the 'civilising' card for their own ends.

These girls' schools were, of course, fulfilling another aim, the promotion of industry. Apart from Ramsay supplying lint for the apprentice spinners at Cluny, the Barons' attempt to establish a local textile industry was another failure.[99] Cluny had built a waulk mill (for shrinking cloth) back in 1742, but ten years in government hands had left it so ruinous that the miller requested help:

[John Mackay] Has been now fifteen years Walker in Cluny he being the first that Ever was There, and this the only Walk Miln in the Braes of Badenoch or betwixt that and the Western seas . . . [As it] has not been repaired for these fifteen years the whole of it is gone to absolute Ruin, and for this year past has done no sort of work, to the great prejudice of the Countrey, as it takes up so much of their time in walking [waulking] their Cloaths with their feet upon a board.[100]

Once again the Barons failed either to support an existing local initiative or fulfil their own aims, for the mill remained unrepaired in 1762.[101] Furthermore, they offered no support to Duncan Grant's attempts to develop the textile industry (see below).

The Barons' administration did, however, yield one surprise when their factor, James Small, a Gaelic-speaker from Perthshire, championed the people's rights. John Macpherson of Invernahavon had prevented the tenants of Biallid-beg (a Cluny farm) from cutting peats, 'the usuall Servitude [customary right] they have upon the Mosses of Invernahavon', even going so far as 'taking the Spads from Belidbegg people'.[102] The tenants protested that it would 'Render his Majesty's said Lands Waste & without Tenants'.[103] Small supported them because without fuel the township simply could not survive – a reminder not just of the precarious relationship between subsistence and environment, but the degree to which the tenantry were at the mercy of the gentry.

The Biallidbeg tenants were caught in another dispute involving Hugh Macpherson, tacksman of Uvie. Uvie had seized their common grazing and 'even went the length to apprehend their cattle on their own undoubted Bounds'. They had retaliated – 'a Sort of Riot or Scufle' – so Uvie went to court, to 'Litigate', as Small noted sharply, 'with all the Interest and address the Clan McPherson were capable of'.[104] Small defended them, 'at the earnest desire not only of the poor Opprest Tenants, but that of every lover of Liberty in that Country'. The tenants won, and Uvie was ordered to 'abstain from all bad Neighbourhood'.[105]

During the case, Small observed: 'the lower Class of Tennants in Badenoch, are entire Slaves to the Principall Tacksmen, or Gentlemen – This is the first attempt ever made by them towards freedom'.[106] The concept of freeing the commonalty from the tyranny of the gentry, with emotive phrases like 'every lover of Liberty', was hardly typical of eighteenth-century official-dom. Indeed, Small's employers would surely not have been comfortable with either his rhetoric or his anti-gentry crusade. The clan elite was certainly ruffled, for Small was warned 'that supporting the Comon People there against the Gentlemen was like raising and inciteing a Mutany in a Regt [regiment]'.[107]

A similar challenge to tacksman authority came from the Nuidebeg tenants who simply refused to leave when served with notices of removal by Lieutenant Macpherson in 1764. Their defence – that they had worked hard to improve their farms and houses in his absence, whereas he was 'no proper farmer' – unsurprisingly failed, and they were eventually evicted in 1769. Macpherson's response, that the tenants were 'litigeously inclined' is further proof of a growing assertiveness amongst the lower orders.[108] At Laggan of Nuide the tenants even attempted (unsuccessfully) to have their tacksman, Donald Macpherson, removed.[109] Protest against tacksman tyranny was, of course, not unique to Cluny. The Strone tenants complained about their tacksman, Andrew Macpherson of Benchar, but not publicly, 'being very much affraid of there present master'.[110] The Dalannach tenants accused John Dow of 'many acts of Oppression and harsh usage . . . [and] Threats to exercise his power and Superior Strength upon their persons almost at every occasion', while another petition accused the Duke of letting to 'private gentlemen who oppresses your poor husbandmen to a degree that they are worse than slaves'.[111] William Tod, the Duke's factor, after removing Lachlan McIntosh as tacksman, was pleased to have set 'the poor Wretches [subtenants] free from his intolerably Slavery'.[112] Oppressive tacksmen were, of course, nothing new: the change lay in the common people's increasing assertiveness against their clan superiors, and, interestingly, the support they received from the factors.[113] Such protests, however, were risky, for after complaining to the Duke the Dalannach tenants feared that they would not be given tenancies by any of the local gentry as they were now 'reckoned to be Rebeles in the Country'.[114]

The most problematic aspect of the Barons' administration was the clearance of the Loch Laggan estate of Aberarder.[115] Ranald Macdonell of Aberarder and his brother Alexander of Tullochroam, leaders of a Catholic enclave in the Braes of Laggan, were evicted in 1770 along with eighty subtenants and replaced by a single tacksman, Robert Macpherson (Colour plate 9).[116] The Barons' principal objective was, of course, upholding the Protestant monarchy, and in spite of amnesties and oaths of loyalty, Catholic tenants were still being removed a decade after Culloden.[117] Yet this was over twenty years later, when both government policy and general opinion towards the Highlands had softened considerably.

Furthermore, these lands were the subject of a protracted legal wrangle between the Macphersons and Mackintoshes, with the Court of Session in 1761 and 1763 upholding Mackintosh claims to ownership.[118] It was not until 1770, after some shady dealings involving James Macpherson (of Ossian fame), that the House of Lords finally awarded ownership to the Macphersons –

significantly described by William Tod as 'unexpected', though bringing 'great Joy to the Clan'.[119] The Macdonells justifiably criticised the Barons for pursuing the evictions 'at a time when no person was entitled to make any Such application'.[120]

Equally confusing was the policy regarding depopulation. Removing tenants, even when reorganising runrig farms, was generally avoided.[121] Indeed, wholescale depopulation, as the Macdonells argued, contravened the terms of the Annexing Act.[122] In addition, the Seven Years' War had highlighted the importance of Highland soldiers to British military needs, and the annexed estates were now seen as a vital source of manpower. Replacing nineteen families with one farmer would hardly contribute to that policy.

The Macdonells had, of course, been active Jacobites, even assisting the fugitive Prince in 1746 – but so too had their Macpherson neighbours. The brothers had also been accused (albeit in a semi-anonymous letter) of replacing the local inhabitants with 'persons of wild character, and abominable practices ... nests of thieves, still in the practice of stealing and outhounding cattle'.[123] In 1759, James Small had renewed the attack, describing Loch Laggan as 'a wild out of the way place, formerly as great a Thieving Country as Rannoch', contrasting it with Cluny, whose people were 'poor honest Creatures, from whome a great deal was always Stolen by even the Lochlaggan people'.[124] Small asked the Barons to take over Aberarder – using that loaded phrase, 'for Civilising the Country'. Matters rested there until the appearance of Parson Robert.

Robert Macpherson, one of the Benchar family, had been chaplain to Fraser's 78th Highlanders during the Seven Years' War. Now returned on military half-pay and seeking a Highland farm, he petitioned the Barons in June 1766 for 'the Lands of Aberarder and Tullochcrom ... as now possessed by Ronald & Alexr McDonells'.[125] Why Robert targeted the *duthchas* of his near neighbours, men he had known since birth, is unclear. Perhaps Small suggested it – an ex-army Protestant minister would, after all, be the perfect 'civilising' agent. The factor strongly recommended him, condemning the Macdonells as 'Esteemed bad ffarmers', while praising Robert's (as yet unproven) farming skills.[126] On being granted the lease of Aberarder, Robert asked Henry Butter, the new factor, to remove the entire population.

The Macdonells mounted a strong defence, ably supported by their advocate, the young James Boswell, firstly denying Small's accusations as 'false and malicious', while casting aspersions on Robert's 'sobriety' and 'knowledge of agriculture'.[127] They offered to match Robert's rent and implement whatever improvements Small demanded. More interestingly, they pitched the argument in broader social terms: *'Justice, equity and humanity'*. These farms were 'by far *too large for one Tenant'*, and the brothers were

> both married men and have large families, whose sole dependence is on the petitioners industry ... They have no place to go to, nor nothing to enable them to support a young and numerous family – Mr Macpherson is a single man, has no burden and draws half pay as Chaplain of a Regiment.[128]

They backed their case with impressive testimonials. The ministers of Laggan and Alvie (irrespective of religion), the Mackintosh chief, the sheriff-substitute, numerous Inverness-shire gentlemen and Justices of the Peace, nineteen Morayshire farmers and, most significantly, twenty Badenoch gentry – including ten Macphersons, some of whom were Robert's relatives – all testifying to virtues such as 'Gentlemen of Veracity & honour'.[129]

In his court submission, Boswell argued in more emotive terms, almost a prequel to nineteenth-century sentiment: 'the distress which about Eighty persons Servants, Children Cottars must be put to ... will be without example in this Country. They are to be driven out of their habitations without refuge or resource'.[130] In a hearts-and-minds appeal, he argued (justifiably) that clearance was counter to the aim of 'ensuring a happy tenantry' – the Barons should 'in these times of disquiet ... rule with a gentle hand ... to conciliate the minds of those under their Care [rather] than to drive them away from their Abodes like felons and fugitives'.[131] His final point, that 'Few instances have hitherto happened of turning out the ancient possessors of Highland Estates', hinted at traditional clan rights to land, while implying that such wholescale evictions were as yet unusual.

Initially, both Sheriff Court and Court of Session overturned the eviction orders, but after a prolonged legal battle the House of Lords eventually ruled in Robert's favour in 1770.[132] The entire tenantry was subsequently cleared, though not without a last act of defiance, for Tod reported that they 'have been foolish enough to deforce [oppose] the Shiriff by a Party of 100 men & as many Women'.[133]

The underlying reasons remain obscure. Robert's determination and apparent vindictiveness seemed at odds with both his military reputation and his later demeanour, as indeed was his disregard for the Loch Laggan folk – as incoming tacksman he could have renewed their tenancies. One contemporary critic specifically blamed Robert for turning out, without means of support, 'every subtenant and cottar to the number of 80', while Tod's comment that 'Parson Robt . . . is determined to have the McDonells driven from both sides of him, at whatever Expence', suggests some protracted family or clan feud.[134]

But Robert did not act alone, for his old boyhood friend, James Macpherson, now at the zenith of his political influence in London, was lurking in the background. During the court hearings, James had come to Edinburgh specifically on 'Lochlaggan matters', already predicting the successful outcome, and he had also been secretly involved in the fore-mentioned decision to award Lochlaggan estate to the Macphersons.[135] James's involvement possibly stemmed from nostalgic notions of clanship – he hoped 'to acquire *magna cum gloria gentis* [with great glory for the clan] the lands for the chief', though it may also have been part of a wider clan vendetta.[136] Either way, installing a Macpherson in former Macdonell territory was the ultimate prize.

The Barons' motives were less clear. Humanity aside, clearance was contrary to their overall objectives, to the Annexing Act itself, and even to national interest. Profit was not a factor because Robert's fifty-seven-year lease was 'at the old rent'.[137] Nor was it agricultural improvement because Robert could hardly match the Macdonells' experience. Fraser-Mackintosh maintained that Aberarder was cleared for sheep, but this was never part of the Barons' wider strategy.[138] In fact, Robert intended cattle farming, for in 1767 (when his lease officially started) he spent £400 buying cattle and employed twelve farm servants to manage them, repeating the process in vain in 1768 and 1769.[139]

One observer, having studied the court papers, suspected a deeper political agenda:

> They are to be turned out of these possessions . . . because they are MacDonalds and are said to be Papists. No such thing as disaffection to King or government is alleged against them, they were not in arrears of rent, nor did they wish to hold their possessions on easier terms than the other tenants.[140]

Considering Small's 'civilising' appeal, Robert's ministerial background, and his appointment as a Royal Bounty Missionary (preaching in Gaelic to remote communities in the Catholic-dominated 'Braes'), it is certainly credible to interpret Aberarder as the deliberate depopulation of a Catholic estate. Between this unsavoury episode, the rent fiasco and the lack of improvements, the Barons' administration of Cluny was distinctly unimpressive. Their only real successes lay in the promotion of education and in James Small's support for the Cluny tenantry – the latter not even being official policy.

Employment

Crucial to the concept of progress was industrial enterprise, keeping supposedly idle hands busy, providing supplementary income and boosting estate coffers. Textiles, supported by the government's Board of Trustees for Manufactures and Fisheries, naturally took centre stage, with the Board's agent, Duncan Grant, a Gaelic speaker from Strathspey, pointing out that the Badenoch people were 'great Strangers to manufactures and Industry'. He initially proposed developing the native woollen industry – 'it makes little odds what kinds of Cloths are made, providing they are well wove of their kinds, whether plaiden, Stuffs, Serges, Tartans, Camblets, Blankets or Cloth commonly called Grays'.[141] But the industry suffered a dearth of weavers, Grant colourfully suggesting that they were 'look'd on as Cowardly and unmanly, as not engaged in the Heroism of the times – and the Tylers [tailors] probably from the same cause and their more unmanly exercise, bore a share of this ignomony'.

Though Scotland's principal industry, linen fared even worse. The only flax sown in Badenoch was by a few poor women producing a very coarse cloth for domestic use, and fine linen had to be imported from the Lowlands.[142] At first, Grant had to bring in spinners from elsewhere at high cost because of the lack of local skills.[143] In 1758, he had petitioned the Commissioners of Annexed Estates for help to establish the industry on Cluny estate, suggesting Milehouse of Nuide as the base, and requesting a farm where he might 'sett the Country an Example of farming [and] Raise a little Flax'.[144] With financial support from the Board, the Commissioners and the SSPCK (Scottish Society for the Propagation of Christian Knowledge), Grant promoted the linen industry in Badenoch, with reasonable success in the early 1760s. His emphasis was naturally on training the local people in the requisite skills, as in this advert for a local spinning school in 1761:

All *young Women and Girls,* are to be admitted into the SPINNING-SCHOOL . . . and to be instructed there *gratis* in the Art of *Spinning* Linen Yarn from Flax in all its Ways and Methods, and in *reeling* and putting up the Yarn.[145]

In that year alone roughly eighty girls were taught to spin, with a further sixty the following year, and on completion of their eight-week course, all were given spinning wheels and reels (for winding the yarn) benefiting the local carpenter to the tune of '180 wheels & 220 reels to Duncan Grant's Pupils' by 1762.[146] The industry clearly crossed the social divide, for in 1764 sixty-five more wheels and thirty-one reels were given out with both 'Captain Lachlan Macpherson's lady' and 'Janet Lesly in Croft of Glen Banchar' being recipients.[147]

Itinerant workers were brought in to instruct locals like Angus Macpherson of Laggan in the art of flax-raising, while Lachlan and Donald Macpherson, discharged soldiers from the Seven Years' War, were not only taught to weave, but were supplied with looms to establish a weaving shop in Ruthven.[148] Other new skilled jobs included the various processes of flax-dressing such as scutching and heckling (preparing the fibres for spinning), and the manufacture of wheels and reels. To encourage local production, lintseed was supplied free to the poor or at a subsidised price for the better off. In 1764, over 500 pints of seed were distributed to 118 different Badenoch families ranging across all the estates, again including both gentry like Captain Lachlan Macpherson of Clunie and the humblest of the peasantry like Grisal Cattanach in Lagnaha in Insh.[149] Prizes were offered as a further incentive.

The initial response was positive. As early as 1761, the Board were praising Grant's success, and two years later commented how the local flax industry had 'increased every year and thrived Remarkably under him'.[150] They noted the enthusiastic support of George Macpherson's son William in encouraging the industry on Invereshie estate, and more significantly, that 'the Common People begin to find that money can be made'.[151] Grant's summaries of production confirm this, with the number of spindles of yarn in Badenoch and Strathspey rising from 427 in 1759 to 12,435 by 1763.[152]

But the scheme struggled. The initial reluctance of a farming population to take on the discipline of industrial labour had to be overcome, while teaching spinning in isolation proved fruitless: 'their Instruction turned out to no purpose when they had neither Flax, nor Linen Weavers, nor any Body to employ them in Spinning or buy their yarn'.[153] Marketing again proved prohibitive, for Badenoch remained 'one of the most Inland Countries of Scotland, at a great Distance from all Places of Trade and Commerce', and yarn surplus to local needs had to be transported to Grant's base in Forres or 'down to the Low Countries by the Highlanders themselves, or picked up by the Hawkers'.[154] Grant complained that 'The Carriages of Lint to & Yarn from the

Highlanders are very expensive & many inconveniences attend them in bad weather', referring to his own losses of horses and carts because of 'Stormy weather & bad roads', the cost of provender, and the consequent delays – he 'could never expect to have my Lint returned in Yarn from the Highlands in less than 6 months'.[155]

Furthermore, many of the gentry were hostile. The six-month feeing system for servants made it hard for women to attend spinning schools or men to take weaving apprenticeships, and their employers were reluctant to release them. As early as 1761, the Board had criticised 'the opposition the spinning meets with from the Gentlmen and Farmers [in Badenoch] who being difficulted by the scarcity of servants occasioned by the great Number taken out of the Country to the Army [the Seven Years' War], Complain that the spinning makes theire servants still scarcer and heightens their Wages'.[156] Several years later, Duncan Grant was still complaining of employers who 'spread a thousand falsehoods to frighten the Girls, [including] Stories of their being . . . transported'.[157] Though the Board tried to secure the support of the Duchess of Gordon (Lady Katherine), Grant was sceptical: 'There is little Reason to expect any Encouragement from the Family of Gordon considering their present Situation . . . If the Proprietor of a Country does not attend to it's Interest others will be the Cooler'.[158]

Ultimately, however, the industry's fate was determined by financial problems. Grant's annual requests must have seemed a bottomless pit, and, moreover, the Board's limited resources were focused on the western rather than the central Highlands.[159] As funding began to decline in the mid 1760s, the local industry suffered – not helped by Mackintosh of Borlum's accusations of embezzlement against Grant in 1765.[160] George Macpherson of Invereshie and William Mackintosh of Balnespick wrote in support of Grant, fearing the withdrawal of government finances would mean depriving 'so great a multitude of poor People of the Resource generously bestowed upon them', whereas a few more years 'would bring it to such maturity as might enable it to subsist by its own Strength without any assistance from the Public'.[161] Though a very limited degree of subsidy continued, the withdrawal of government support meant that the Badenoch linen industry, as a commercial venture, had largely collapsed by the end of the decade. Nevertheless, the local populace must have continued to benefit, at least on a domestic level, from the acquisition of both the new skills and the equipment, particularly the art of spinning.

Textiles were not the only failure. While timber abounded in eastern Badenoch, there was little commercial forestry at this time. Indeed, the Duke was more interested in mineralogy, employing an eccentric Welsh mining engineer, John Williams, to survey the region. Williams enjoyed little success: 'In all the rocks I have searched . . . I saw not the least mineral appearance worth notice, which maked me very doubtful I shall meet with nothing valuable in that way here.'[162] His diaries were, however, filled with wild entrepreneurial schemes – a machine to dredge the River Spey, draining the fourteen-mile-long Loch Ericht, and diverting the River Truim to flow southwards into Perthshire instead of into the Spey. Dams and sluices, forestry and sawmills, shielings and agricultural improvements, all fired his restless imagination – another manifestation of that rational Enlightenment mindset which sought to tame the environment, to 'civilise' nature.[163] In reality, Williams' dreams revealed the quixotic nature of Badenoch's industrial potential.

Lack of local opportunities resulted in seasonal migration – a process largely born of poverty.[164] One local farmer, indeed, remembered 'the poor Creatures who were necessitated to go to the south to shear the harvest' – with the added bonus that those migrants would, for six months or more, be consuming someone else's corn, easing the burden for families back home.[165] The real importance of this annual migration, however, was the influx of specie into a cash-poor community, a vital factor in preventing both famine and depopulation. Necessity was not, however, the only factor driving the annual exodus, for it was increasingly fuelled by the desire of the lower orders for better living standards, emulating the gentry in however small a way, and even indulging in the latest southern fashions. For many, particularly the women, it was also the only chance to taste life outside the *Gàidhealtachd*.

Badenoch's geographical situation undoubtedly facilitated this annual quest. Mountain passes that rendered trade difficult proved no obstacle on foot, with Perth itself, and the rich farmlands of Fife and the Lothians, easily accessible. Tom Devine estimates that at least one member of every family from the southern and central Highlands would go south annually, including perhaps half of all young women – a huge exodus.[166] Badenoch numbers were probably similar, certainly substantial enough to provoke a reaction from the local gentry who were, after all, the employers.

In April 1769, the Badenoch gentry met at Pitmain Inn – thirty-seven lairds, tacksmen and farmers, representing four different estates, and including the three local ministers. After four days' deliberation they issued a quasi-legal edict describing their 'unhappy pernicious and Distressed situation', further dramatised with words like 'Calamity', 'desolation', 'hardships and evils', 'hurtful Consequences'.[167] The edict eventually detailed the cause of this apparent

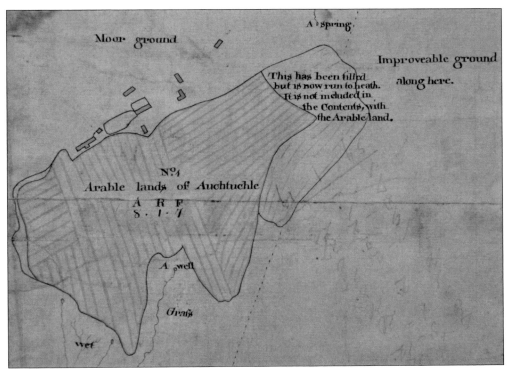

Plate 1. The runrig farm of Auctuchle, part of Pitmain, showing the township, the unfenced rigs and the surrounding rough pasture. (Source: NRS, RHP1859, William Taylor, Pitmain, 1771. Courtesy of the Duke of Richmond and Gordon.)

Plate 2. The large barn at Uvie, with its opposing doors for threshing and winnowing. (D. Taylor)

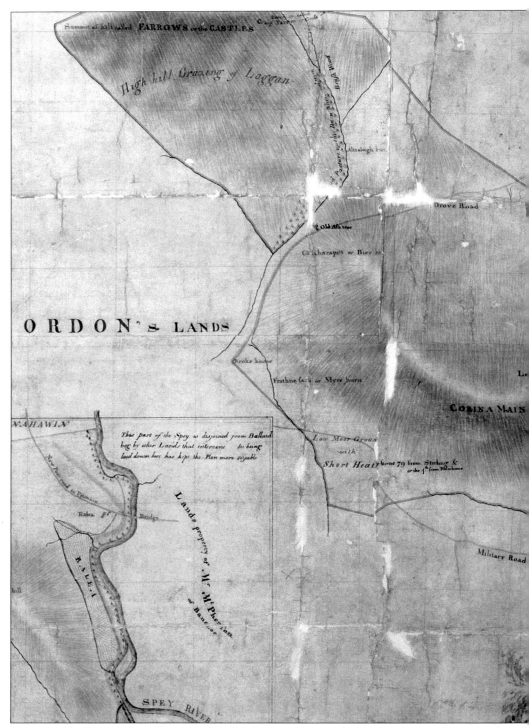

Plate 3. Gaskinloan with its four townships by the River Spey and its huge communal grazing outrun. (Source: NRS, RHP3489, Plan of the Annexed Estate of Clunie. By William Tennoch, 1771. Crown copyright, National Records of Scotland.)

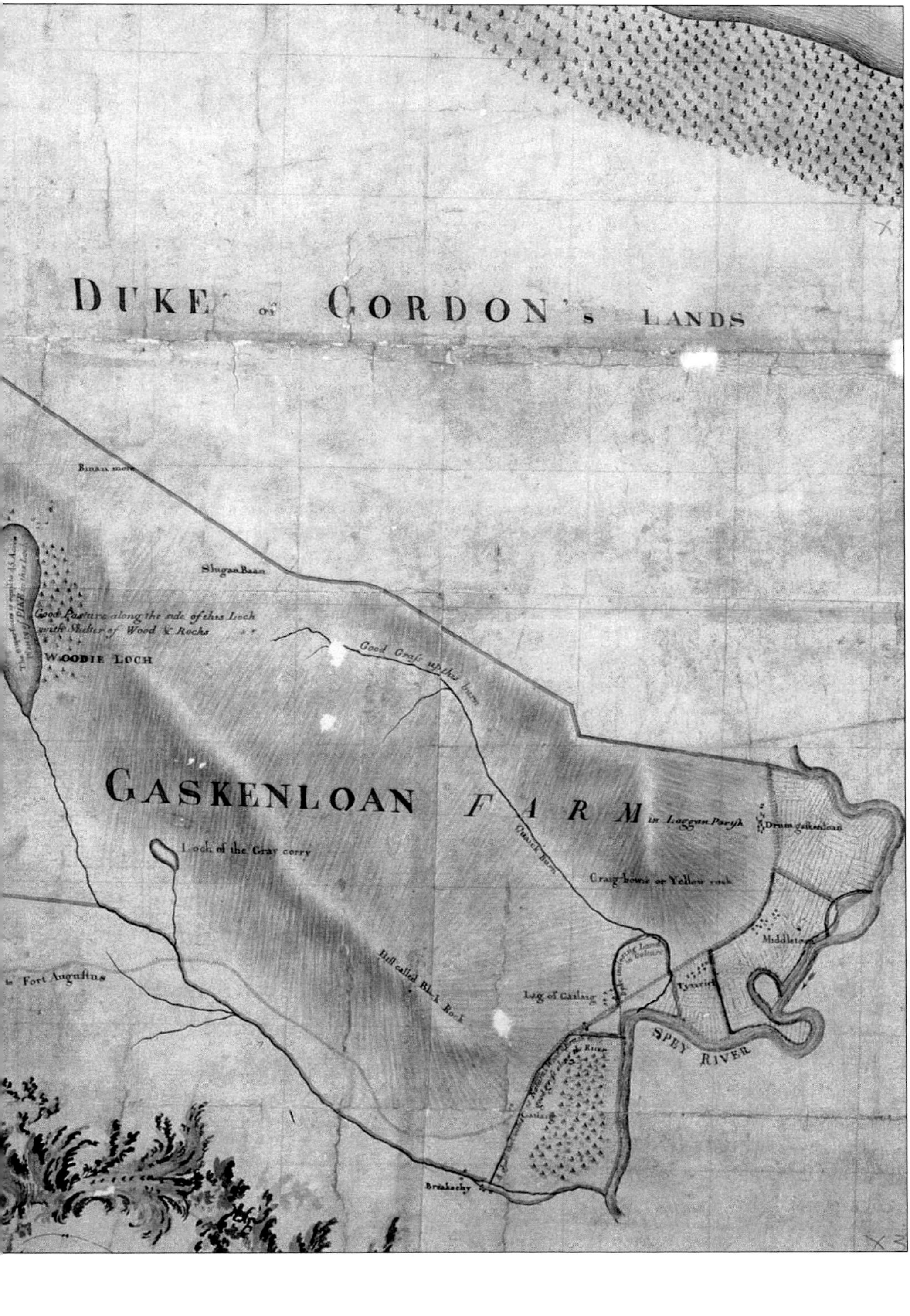

DUKE of GORDON's LANDS

Binan moor

Slugan Baan

Good Pasture along the side of this Loch
with Shelter of Wood & Rocks

WOODIE LOCH

Good Grass up the burn

GASKENLOAN FARM in Loggan Parsyh

Drum gaskenloan

Loch of the Gray corry

Craig bowie or Yellow rock

Middleton

Fort Augustus

Hill called Black Rock

Lag of Catlaig

Tynarick

SPEY RIVER

Breakachy

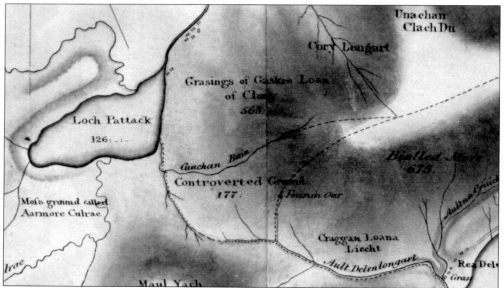

Plate 4. The distant grazings of Gaskinloan at Loch Pattack, adjoining with Biallidmore's grazings bottom right. (Source: RCAHMS, SC1082428, George Taylor, Plan of Badenoch, 1773. © Courtesy of RCAHMS. Licensor www.rcahms.gov.uk)

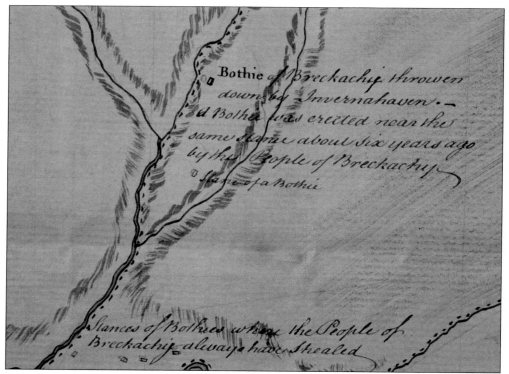

Plate 5. The throwing down and reclaiming of one of Breakachy's shielings. (Source: NRS, RHP31711, Controverted ground between Breakachy and Dalwhinnie, 1806. Courtesy of the Duke of Richmond and Gordon.)

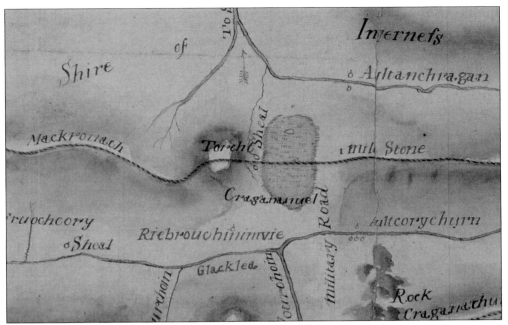

Plate 6a. Gordon Estate map showing the Torcht, the Boar of Badenoch. (Source: NRS, RHP4064, Plan of the controverted marches betwixt the annexed estate of Lochgarry and the Duke of Gordon's estate of Badenoch. Courtesy of the Duke of Richmond and Gordon.)

Plate 6b. Atholl Estate map claiming the Torcht as the 'Duke of Atholl's Boar'. (Source: The collection at Blair Castle, Perthshire, Map of Perthshire from Mr Stobie's Map, 1784, copied 1 Sept 1819.)

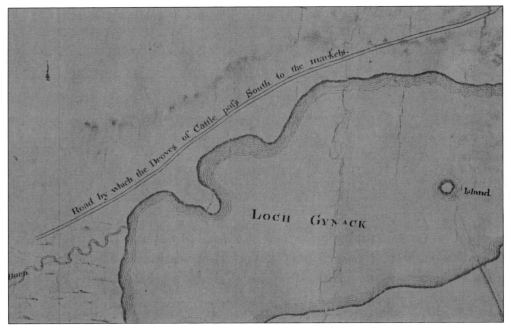

Plate 7a. The principal drove route from the north passing Loch Gynack above the modern village of Kingussie. (Source: NRS, RHP1859, William Taylor, Pitmain, 1771. Courtesy of the Duke of Richmond and Gordon.)

Plate 7b. The old drove road today, now an estate track, running along the north shore of Loch Gynack. (D. Taylor)

Plate 8a. Pitmain in 1771, showing John Maclean's improvements. (Source: NRS, RHP1859, William Taylor, Pitmain, 1771. Courtesy of the Duke of Richmond and Gordon.)

Plate 8b. Pitmain today, apart from the railway almost exactly as in 1771: Maclean's great drainage ditches and the 'canal' running across the bottom are still perfectly clear. (Image: TerraServer.com/DigitalGlobe.)

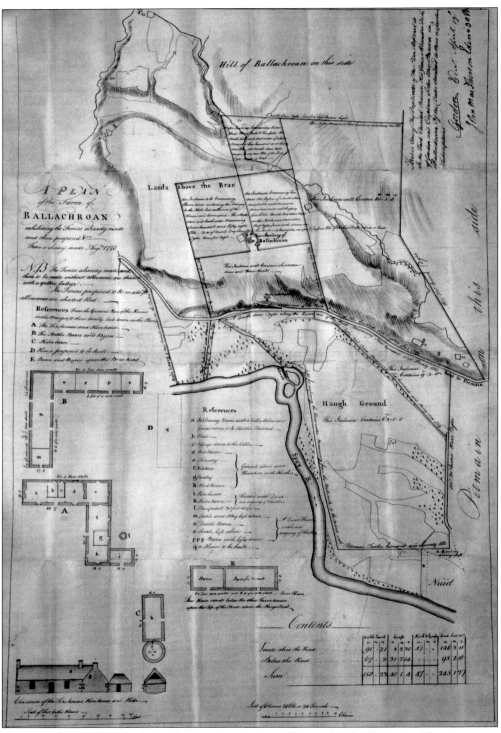

Plate 9a. John Dow's Ballachroan improvements, 1778. (Source: NRS, RHP94411, Plan, Ballachroan, 1778. Courtesy of the Duke of Richmond and Gordon.)

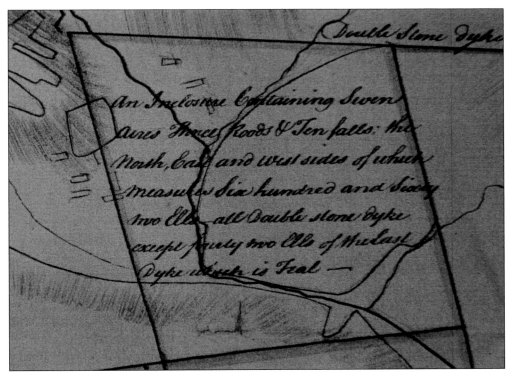

Plate 9b. One of the Ballachroan improvement dykes running right through a runrig township. (Source: NRS, RHP94411, Plan, Ballachroan, 1778. Courtesy of the Duke of Richmond and Gordon.)

Plate 10. The reconstructed Gordon Castle with its 172 metre frontage. (Source: Goodwood, PD25, Nattes, *Scotia Depicta*, Plate VI, October 1799.)

Plate 11a. A tacksman's house c. 1792: John Dow's Ballachroan with its arched doorway.

Plate 11b. The surviving arch of Ballachroan. (D. Taylor)

Plate 12. Captain Lachlan Mackintosh's house at Kincraig. (D. Taylor)

Plate 13. A late eighteenth-century cruck-framed turf house at Lynwilg in Badenoch, probably in the process of its triennial re-thatching whereby one-third of the roof was replaced each year. (Source: *The Literary Magazine and British Review*, 1792.)

Plate 14. A 'miserable Hutt built with sods'! A reconstructed eighteenth-century Badenoch turf house at the Highland Folk Museum, Newtonmore. (D. Taylor)

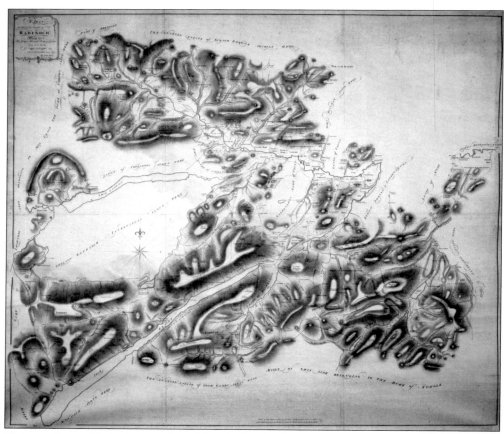

Plate 15. George Taylor's 1773 plan of the Gordon lands in western Badenoch, the map from which Figures 4 and 5 were adapted. (Source: RCAHMS, SC1082428, George Taylor, Plan of Badenoch, 1773. © Courtesy of RCAHMS. Licensor www.rcahms.gov.uk)

catastrophe as 'the absconding and away going of servants' – the cycle of seasonal migration which was creating a labour shortage and fuelling inflationary wages: 'the extravagant fees & Hyre exacted by and of Necessity given to severall unskillfull servts of both sexes remaining in the Country'.[168] There were, however, deeper reasons, for they complained that this was happening 'without the leave and Consent of the Proprietors and Tacksmen – to the manifest Detriment of our rights & Interests and evident obstruction of our Farming and other Labours'. This was clearly about control – social as well as economic. The existence of similar documents for Strathdearn and Lairg suggest not just that this was a universal Highland problem, but that there was a degree of communication amongst the gentry and Justices of the Peace across the whole region over how to combat it.[169]

The Badenoch response was severe. All seasonal migrants would have their cattle confiscated, seriously undermining the benefit of their earnings. Family or friends housing them on their return in November would be fined £1. Those employed locally on the six-month feeing system would have their wages withheld 'untill they assertain and prove that they are Engaged and bound to serve some other person *in this Country* [author's italics]' – migrants would thus forfeit their previous half-year's wages. Finally, anyone not employed locally would be declared 'free and idle vagabonds', and hence forced to work under the vagrancy laws. To try to win the community's support, they promised anyone informing on seasonal workers 'adequat reward for their trouble', with fines being divided, 'one half to the informer'. Furthermore, just as they had opposed the spinning schools, this cartel of gentry seized the opportunity to impose a sliding scale of wages across the region. The best male workers would receive a maximum of £1 for a six-month fee with 'two pair of Brogs good and sufficient' worth 3 shillings a pair. Women received just 5s 7d for their half-year, plus their brogues, ironically worth more than their cash wage.

The elite nature, size and duration of the meeting, along with the employment of a Notary Public, and the attendance of the three parish ministers, show this was no mere sabre-rattling. The draconian response to seasonal migration was clearly an exercise in social control, the gentry reasserting their authority and crushing the emerging enterprise of the common people. Yet it reveals a rather myopic self-interest, for, to the region's poor, this annual injection of cash was a vital lifeline, not least in meeting rental payments. Significantly, the elite of the two rival clans, Macphersons and Mackintoshes, had joined forces to preserve their collective economic interests against those of their former clansmen. Class had become more important than clan.

The Military

Alexander Campbell, servant to George Macpherson of Invereshie, 'now Souldier in the Regiment of Hylanders Commanded by the Honourable Collonell ffraser' had one last duty before embarking:

> Considering that I am forthwith to Leave my native Country, and that my return to it again, if ever, Is most uncertain: Doe Therefor, and for the Love and affection I have and bear to my Nephews after named make this my Latter Will . . .[170]

He bequeathed his nephews four hill ponies, his total worldly possessions. In this one brief document Private Campbell marched in – and out – of history, his fate unknown. But his will did survive, its starkness encapsulating the essence of the Highland soldier. What made men like Campbell fight for a government against which so many had recently rebelled, a government pledged to destroy their society and culture? But not just the commonalty – what prompted so many local gentry to lead men like Campbell to glory or death in pursuit of Britain's imperial ambitions?

Britain's entry into the Seven Years' War in 1756 plunged her into conflict with France in both North America and India, the urgent demand for military manpower bringing forth two new Highland regiments under Simon Fraser and Archibald Montgomery. It heralded a new era of opportunity avidly seized by many in the Highlands: not only a chance for post-'45 rehabilitation, but a chance to forge a new relationship with the British state. Lady Katherine, the dowager duchess, demonstrated the loyalty and importance of the Gordons in 1759 by raising what would become the 89th Regiment of Foot, led by her new husband, General Morris, with her three young sons all holding commissions.[171] Cluny's family was equally enthusiastic, for the restoration of the estate was their ultimate goal. John Macpherson (Cluny's brother) immediately left military service in Holland for a captaincy in Fraser's 78th Highlanders, while in 1761, Cluny's son Duncan, aged only thirteen, was offered a commission with the clear message, 'Your Dilligence & Success in recruiting will greatly recommend you.'[172]

The tacksmen, however, had less need for rehabilitation, having suffered little from their Jacobitism. For them, war simply provided another opportunity to enhance their social and economic status within the British Empire. Amongst those acquiring commissions were John Dow, John Macpherson of

Invereshie, Duncan Macpherson of Breakachy and Lachlan Mackintosh of Balnespick. Young Robert Macpherson of Benchar was also fast-tracked from his divinity studies at Edinburgh to Gaelic-speaking chaplain in Fraser's Highlanders, enjoying a better press than subsequently at Aberarder – a 'very respectable chaplain . . . indefatigable in his clerical duties', according to General Stewart of Garth.[173]

Not least among the army's attractions was the universal appeal of adventure, travel and glamour. Parson Robert looked back with embarrassment at having been 'so easily Dazled by a Red Coat, a Laced hat, and a little common place sort of wit, chit chat & Flummery'.[174] His exasperated young friend, John Macpherson of Invereshie, was motivated more by personal ambition: 'Glenfeshie is not the fittest [place] in Univers for a young man to pass his time in that intends to push his way in the world.'[175] More seriously, the army provided a lifelong career, not only commencing at a remarkably early age, but without the academic study required for other professions. It also provided economic independence, especially for younger sons unable to access land, while conferring a universally recognised status throughout the Empire. Furthermore, the Highland regiments, even though not clan-based, enabled the officer to maintain his cultural identity in language and dress within a nationally recognised – and celebrated – context.[176]

Badenoch's history would become closely intertwined with this new officer class, returning after the war on a lifetime half-pay pension. A half-pay lieutenant received £42 annually and a captain £68, a vital new form of inward investment.[177] Between the end of that war in 1763 and the outbreak of the American War of Independence in 1775 these officer-farmers would have received an approximate peace-time dividend of £500 and £820 respectively, often substantially exceeding their rental. Captain Alexander Macpherson paid £20 annual rent for Druminard while receiving £68 half-pay, a handsome surplus.[178] Captains Duncan Macpherson of Breakachy and Lachlan Macpherson of Garvamore both invested in improvements, thereby redistributing some of that military income through the community as wages, while others like John Dow undoubtedly used it to underpin their droving activities.[179] Highland gentry were, as Andrew Mackillop argued, using the military as 'a crucial financial prop' – though the term 'prop' hardly does justice to the significance of this income in the Badenoch economy.[180]

In 1773, eight of the seventeen Gordon farms in Laggan parish were held by half-pay officers (including Parson Robert), paying 55 per cent of the total rental – a high proportion, perhaps because Laggan was the Macpherson heartland.[181] In Kingussie there were only two half-pay officers on Gordon farms contributing 20 per cent of the rental, and in Alvie, just one, again paying 20 per cent. In total, however, half-pay officers still contributed over 40 per cent of the Duke's Badenoch rental in 1773, and the figure was probably higher because military incomes derived from other family members are not included – Donald Macpherson of Breakachy, for instance, though not himself an officer, had two sons who were.

Officership, however, also brought financial problems. Commissions were expensive, an ensigncy costing £200, a lieutenancy £400, and a captaincy from £500–£1,000 – a substantial investment considering the annual rental for an entire davoch was between £25 and £75.[182] There were also hidden costs. George Macpherson of Invereshie, having secured a commission for his younger son John, had to pay him through military academies in London and Paris.[183] Costs grew with the boy's taste for luxury – a sword with silver hanger, silver buckled shoes, silver cutlery, servants and coach-hire.[184] Dr John Mackenzie, his brother-in-law, condemned the extravagance: 'he unluckily thinks himself a man of such consideration that he must keep company with Inglish men of fortune that happen to be in the place where he is setled', adding dismissively, 'the young man has no fortune being only a Lieut on half pay, with no other prospect'.[185] Later, John himself expressed the universal dilemma of the young Highland officer thrust into a cosmopolitan military environment:

I know the impossibility of keeping company with my brother officers . . . on my pay, & I assure you William [his brother] that I cannot think of remaining in the Corps when I have it not in my power to live with the officers. You say many do live on their pay I own it, but they live entirely by themselves, & never see any company & are so entire strangers to what passes in the Regt. as if they lived a hundred miles from it . . . I have not been able to keep myself quite free from debt [in spite of] what assistance I got from my father . . . in a few years I shall be over head & ears in debt.[186]

This troubled relationship between frugal father and worldly son serves as reminder that establishing an army career could bring with it 'expectations . . . that resulted in luxury, hedonism, excess and despair', though, for most, the half-pay bonus still made it a valuable long-term investment.[187]

War also enticed the common people. The lure of adventure, foreign lands and uniform were a powerful attraction, for the red coat could dazzle the young labourer just as it had the young parson. Yet Alexander Campbell's testament resonated with foreboding rather than excitement. Had he been forced? Pressure was undoubtedly being applied. The Impress Act of 1757 persuaded some to enlist before they were seized; the annexed estates' factors, including James Small, were instructed to help 'in raising a Body of Forces'; landlords, tacksmen and officers were actively recruiting by means fair or foul in the hope of gaining commissions, favours, or political status.[188] When Simon Fraser formed the 78th Highlanders, his familial connection (brother of Lady Cluny) made Badenoch fertile ground, especially with Cluny's brother John as captain. But competition was intense: Captain Mackintosh had recruited '38 young men of the name of Macpherson, from Badenoch' for the 42nd Regiment; Montgomery was also active locally, enlisting, amongst others, John Dow; Malcolm Macpherson of Phones, though only a 'gentleman volunteer', brought out twenty-five men from his own small estate alone.[189] With this intensive recruitment, intimidation and force must have played a part, especially as a tacksman could achieve officership by providing a fixed quota of recruits, generally his own subtenants.

The Badenoch tenantry were not, however, simple victims of forcible recruitment, for war came at a propitious time. Poverty was rife: the post-Culloden depredations had left many struggling, economic opportunities were limited, and by 1757 famine was looming.[190] Government bounties of £3 to every recruit – two to three years' annual rent at Gaskinloan – provided a strong incentive, and as recruitment declined, bounties rose. In 1759, the Duchess was offering £4, and by 1761, when young Duncan Macpherson of Cluny was struggling to raise his own company, the figure was probably higher, for the tenants quickly realised their worth.[191] His uncle, now Major John, complained when recruiting for Duncan that 'men were hardly to be got and recruits so much wanted for the publick service', that it had cost him 'the greatest part of £1400 for which he cannot expect the least Retribution'.[192] The Cluny tenantry had clearly demanded a high price for their enlistment. Furthermore, war guaranteed a steady wage over several years – a significant asset for the poorer classes who provided the majority of recruits.[193] Perhaps, as happened in Breadalbane, some even negotiated promises of land though there is no actual evidence of this in Badenoch at this time.

Between recruiting, poverty and adventure, Badenoch gave many (perhaps hundreds) of its young men to the army. The Cluny tenants' petition of 1757 implied a local labour shortage because 'so many of the able-bodied young men' had enlisted, a point echoed by the Board of Trustees regarding the 'scarcity of servants' in the local linen industry.[194] Parson Robert also mentioned the intensity of recruitment: 'the difficulties we met with in recruiting Montgomeries and our regt [Fraser's] was so great that it would be idle for any to think of coming after us . . . I imagined the Highlands cou'd not send out such vast numbers.'[195] When young Cluny tried to raise one hundred clansmen for his commission in 1761, he managed only sixty-four – his uncle, Simon Fraser, suggesting that 'the Country of the Macphersons cou'd not afford so many.'[196] If that was all the clan could raise, the available crop had clearly already been harvested. Fraser, however, was angry. Supporting their chief was 'no more than they ought to have done' – they had 'behaved excessively ill' and should be fined for their failure. His continuing belief in the unquestioned loyalty of clansmen to their chief seems naive in light of events before and after Culloden: more significantly, the letter implies that the tenantry had refused to follow their chief, further illustrating the splintering of the clan.

Extensive recruitment undoubtedly brought benefits. Fewer mouths required feeding, the reduction in labour must have increased local wages, and money was being sent home from America. From his meagre pay a soldier could save one or two (old) pence a day, equivalent over a year to at least the annual rent or two cows.[197] Some did better than others: Murdoch Cameron from Lynwilg was 'among the Richest in the Company', but Polson from Kinrara was 'none of your savers'.[198] Even for some of the wounded there were lifelong Chelsea pensions of 5d a day – received by at least fifteen Badenoch soldiers, including John Macdonald from Lynwilg, suffering from 'scurvy and age', and Donald Cattanach from Benchar, who 'lost his left eye'. At £7 12s annually, this compares favourably with local yearly wage rates and was three times the rent of a typical runrig farmer in the 1750s.[199]

Deaths were, however, inevitable. At Louisburg, 'The Poor Highland Regt was terribly maulld . . . Lt Evan McPherson killed and Willie Grant Rothy [Rothiemurchus] wounded . . . the other Losses of that Regt are too numerous for this Place', wrote Parson Robert, while at Quebec, 'our whole officers except three or four were killed or wounded'.[200] From just one Badenoch company, he named five wounded and ten dead – Donald Macdonald from Crathiecroy, John Macpherson from Glentruim, John Macpherson from Ruthven, James Wilson from Pitchurn, representing losses across the entire region. Robert hoped to recover £5 12s (six times the local cottar rent) from James Campbell of Glen Feshie 'for his family'. He was collecting the assets of the dead to be sent home in one batch, 'in order, I suppose, that there may be a flourish about it in the Newspapers at home' – the universal need for a positive spin during war.[201] It was but small compensation, however, for such losses could threaten the very survival of families at home.

When peace came in 1763, the government offered 50 acres of land to any soldier (200 acres for officers) wishing to settle in America – an extent beyond comprehension to a Laggan farmer. Furthermore, in Parson Robert's hyperbole, Nova Scotia was 'the best Lands in the known World and the Climate far from being a bad one', while for hundreds of miles the land was as flat as the 'Isle of Bancher' (the haugh ground of his home farm, now Newtonmore's shinty pitch, the *Eilan*).[202] Many, including some Macphersons, seized the opportunity – opting to become 'independent-minded settlers' rather than return to the ranks of subtenantry.[203] Between losses and land, only 20 per cent of recruits returned to the Highlands, and though no exact figures for Badenoch as a whole exist, on Phones estate only two of the original twenty-five came home. Some returning soldiers received crofts on annexed estates like Lovat, but there is no evidence of this at Cluny.[204]

War's immediate benefits were economic, whether jobs and income for the tenantry or careers for the gentry. For the ordinary soldier, however, there was no long-term dividend and life reverted to its pre-war rhythm. Nonetheless, war had changed him: he had been part of a conquering British army, his exploits lauded by the media; he had been assimilated into the heart not just of the British establishment, but of the Empire itself; and his awareness of his own worth was considerably increased.[205] For the gentry the benefits were far more significant: their return to tacksmanship in the *duthchas* was considerably enhanced both by their membership of the military elite and their guaranteed income, cushioning them from the vicissitudes of Highland agriculture while facilitating their entrepreneurial schemes.

The most significant consequence, however, was the ideological shift: Highland savage had become British hero. In 1760, the Commissioners for the Annexed Estates broadened their initial aims of civilisation and loyalty to include the 'propagation of a hardy and industrious race, fit for serving the public in war'.[206] If the Highlands were to become a breeding ground for soldiers, maintaining substantial numbers of small tenantry was essential. It polarised the debate over the region's economic future: the large commercial farm bringing depopulation, or the less economic small unit sustaining high population – a debate that would become more focused as recruiting demands increased in subsequent wars.

Conclusion

While the ideology of progress, improvement and civilising permeated society, theory and reality were not easily reconciled during these two decades. Only Invereshie undertook any serious estate reconstruction, establishing a model of self-sufficient peasant farms under a benevolent local laird. The Gordons, however, provided neither a clear economic plan nor the investment necessary for improvement – similarly the Barons on Cluny. On these estates, improvements were led not by outsiders or landowners, but by the local tacksmen, who naturally focused on their own interests rather than those of the wider estate or community. Such improvements, however, were sporadic, and though some tacksmen invested considerable money and effort, only Maclean achieved noteworthy success. For most, exploiting the traditional profits of droving or the new opportunities of military service proved simpler and more lucrative.

For the peasantry, economic progress was a more remote prospect. Those on Invereshie achieved modest gains under the aegis of George Macpherson, but the vast majority in Badenoch derived little benefit from agricultural improvement. Aspirations on Cluny were thwarted by the Barons' lack of support, while the Gordons simply abandoned their subtenantry to the mercy of the tacksmen. But demands for education, attendance at spinning schools, military enlistment, seasonal migration, the Nuidebeg improvements, and, of course, the initiatives in commercial pastoralism discussed previously, all demonstrate a desire for self-betterment. Even the poorest citizens wished to taste the wider benefits of the British state, broadening horizons and enhancing lifestyles. The 'civilising of Badenoch's barbarians' was indeed as much self-induced as imposed by government agencies.[207]

More significant than economic improvement, however, were the consequent social tensions, particularly those arising from the confrontation between the Gordon estates and the Badenoch tacksmen. The estate's failure to impose its authority in 1750 inadvertently strengthened the tacksmen in their traditional status, leaving them the dominant force in the region for the next two decades. Integral to this victory was the clan. At a time when clanship in general was suffering a twin-pronged military and legislative assault, Clan Macpherson, paradoxically, was flexing its collective muscle, effectively outmanoeuvring both the Gordon estates and the Barons. But this was not the Highland clan of old. With a fugitive chief dying in exile in 1756, leadership had devolved to the tacksman class which effectively commandeered the clan as an exclusive club of Macpherson gentry for promoting and protecting their own interests.

The sense of alienation from this new elite clanship exacerbated the existing grievances of the rank and file.[208] The general resentment over tacksman oppression, particularly over rents, services and the erosion of traditional rights, had been heightened for some by the trauma of landlessness arising from improvement, eviction and clearance. Further aggravation resulted from the gentry's attempts to prevent seasonal migration and impose wage controls. That these abuses were perpetrated not by outsiders but by those same clan tacksmen with whom they had marched in 1745 could only have increased that feeling of alienation. The widening class divide was evident in the growing assertiveness of the common people, seeking redress from higher authorities like the Duke, or, ironically, appealing to the Barons and the courts – institutions of the Hanoverian state – for protection against their erstwhile clan leaders. Nothing, however, better illustrates the disintegration of clan society than the reluctance, even refusal, of the Cluny tenantry to enlist with their young chief in 1761.

As the self-interest of the elite increasingly overshadowed any residual obligations to the lower orders, clan society was irretrievably fractured. Traditional bonds gave way to class antagonism. Clanship was indeed being more thoroughly dismembered by the Macpherson tacksmen than by any government legislation.[209] But the power of these tacksmen, especially within the collective security of the 'new' clan, made further confrontation inevitable in the next decade when the young Duke Alexander tried to re-impose estate authority.

143

Chapter 5
The 1770s: A Turbulent Decade

Across the Highlands the edifice of clanship was crumbling at an ever-increasing pace as former chiefs appropriated clan lands for lucrative sheep walks, thereby sacrificing the economic and social status of both tacksman and tenant. Tenurial insecurity and rising rents, exacerbated by depression and famine in the early 1770s, caused many of those tacksmen, particularly on the western seaboard, to emigrate to America, often accompanied by substantial numbers of their subtenantry.[1] It was a massive social upheaval, depriving the Highlands not just of population in general, but of community leaders, managers and entrepreneurs, with, of course, their wealth and expertise. This 'west-coast' pattern, however, was not the universal Highland experience.

While Badenoch undoubtedly suffered much upheaval during the 1770s, it featured neither tacksman-led emigrations, nor invasive sheep walks: instead, the indigenous gentry largely retained their traditional lands, still with their subtenantry and their cattle.[2] But though enjoying a considerable degree of continuity, the region nevertheless experienced a period of dramatic internal turmoil. Economic depression and climatic deterioration brought devastation in their wake. Estate policies regarding rentals, leases, reform and authority further destabilised the social fabric, though tacksman improvement schemes allow a more positive interpretation. The imperial dimension again brought its own mix of problems and benefits through the American War of Independence (1775–83). This social turmoil was, of course, fuelled by multifarious forces – impersonal ones outwith human control, but also those of human agency, whether the needs of an empire, the whims of a duke, or the desperation of the poor.

Many of these impersonal forces were, of course, universal to the Highlands: that different regions followed their own paths was largely due to the human element. Hence, Badenoch's distinctive path through the decade was largely down to the fragile relationship between tacksman and estate. Because Duke Alexander's interests centred primarily on Fochabers and London, the management of the Highland estates was delegated to two key officials appointed in 1769 – the oft-mentioned Ross and Tod.

James Ross, chamberlain, cashier and manager at Fochabers, a man of immense energy and ability, astutely directed policy. Though 'much a Stranger to Highland Countries', he had the wisdom to listen to elder statesmen like Andrew Macpherson of Benchar: 'I will ask Your Opinion . . . being convinced that Nobody in the Country is capable of giving better Advice.'[3] Meanwhile, William Tod, from Banffshire, became factor for Badenoch and Lochaber. Establishing himself at Ruthven, he adapted well to both the Highland environment and the nature of its society, wittily remarking to Ross in 1772, 'I am already so much a Highlandman . . .'[4] Tod was integral to the community: resident factor and farmer, raising his family there, while sharing – and hence understanding – the tribulations of everyday life. He was indeed that rarest of Highland characters – a compassionate factor.

These two moulded estate policy until Ross's death in 1782 whereupon Tod moved to Fochabers, remaining a key player until the next century. The Duke was deeply indebted to these two young men – equally so the historian, for both were prodigious correspondents: Ross meticulously expounding every aspect of policy, warts and all; Tod more rambling, but describing every facet of community life, interlaced with local gossip and pithy asides. But neither was a yes-man, so their letters resonate with sincerity and integrity, frustration and emotion – and, not least, criticisms of their noble employer. Their correspondence provides the framework of this chapter, not least in detailing the economic difficulties that buffeted the region throughout the 1770s.

Economic troubles

The early years of the decade were little short of disastrous, beginning with a severe market depression. Though cattle prices were on a long-term upwards trend, rising at least fourfold during the eighteenth century, periodic slumps nevertheless had dire consequences for such a predominantly pastoral community. In 1770 Tod had problems collecting rents because the previous year had been 'so ill for the Sale of Cattle.'[5] Prices remained low throughout 1770; by mid 1771 they were 10 shillings down – a 20–25 per cent drop; in October newspapers reported 'very low prices' at Falkirk ('20s a head' down), pushing at least one local dealer into bankruptcy.[6] As tacksman and subtenant suffered, the depression rippled through the estate economy, forcing Ross to inform the Duke that it was 'almost impossible to get money out of the Highlands owing to the bad Sales of cattle'.[7]

A partial recovery in 1772 was quashed as unscrupulous southern buyers, playing on recent bad markets, forced prices down, before Tod again complained of 'the low Price of Cattle' in February 1773.[8] Such a sustained collapse was almost unprecedented. While the years 1773 to 1775 saw 'very high' prices, 1776 brought a market 'even worse than was expected . . . there are but a few Hundreds of the North Country Cattle sold, and they below prime Cost' – a gloomy picture confirmed in the media.[9] Prices recovered briefly next year, but by October 1778 Falkirk values had halved and Tod feared there was 'no Chance of their getting a Beast sold this Season at any Price'. Six months later Parson Robert confirmed there was still 'no price for any kind of Stock'.[10]

Six years of poor prices in one decade undoubtedly bit deeply, destabilising the traditional economy. Yet the local cattle dealers were in no way to blame – it was simply that an unpredictable London tail was wagging the Highland dog. Landowner and tacksman rode the depression well enough, but it bore hard on the small tenant, whose troubles came not alone.

•   •   •

Exasperated by Ross's nagging over rents, Tod responded angrily: it was impossible 'to make a highland Farm do its own Turn', adding, with a personal *cri de coeur*, 'instead of paying Rent at present, we would need to be paid for living in these Countries'.[11] That one sentence encapsulated the devastation of the period. Since the early 1700s, climatic conditions had been improving to the obvious benefit of all Highland farming communities, but around 1770 a deterioration in the climate (the last fling of the 'Little Ice Age') occurred, not just resulting in 'a fairly steady drop in temperatures until about 1820', but also bringing 'very volatile climatic shifts'.[12] This climatic phenomenon is corroborated by a dendrochronological study of the northern Cairngorm region, showing that from the late 1760s to the early 1800s there was a gradual decline in the mean summer temperature.[13] In an area of marginal mountain arable any sustained temperature drop would obviously have serious consequences, further restricting the already short growing season, curtailing the spring and autumn grazing cycle and increasing the demand for scarce winter fodder resources. Climatic cooling in itself impacted heavily on the local economy, but equally damaging was the turbulent weather accompanying it.

With remarkable correlation to the scientific data, newspapers reported unusually severe weather, including a 'great storm of snow . . . excessively deep' in Badenoch at the end of April 1770 – 'such a season has hardly been remembered there at any time'.[14] The Gordon records reveal the full impact of the deteriorating weather starting early in 1770, and intensifying drastically over the next three years. Indeed, the effects of climatic turbulence are rarely absent from the records from then until the 1830s.

Both Ross and Tod were continuously requesting meal from March 1770 onwards, indicating harvest failure in 1769.[15] Bad harvests were nothing new, but this one triggered a calamitous succession. Early in 1771, large quantities of meal were again required, suggesting the 1770 crop also had failed.[16] Then, in May 1771, Tod reported from Badenoch, 'the most violent rains for eight days past', so intense that 'it has killed many of our cattle here'.[17] George Brown, the surveyor, confirmed that the deluge had 'hurt their corns very much . . . in many places the seed carried off'.[18]

The 1771 harvest was disastrous: in Lochaber, 'their whole Cropt is rotten', while in Badenoch, 'not a single Bole in the Lordship fitt for seed'.[19] Ross informed the Duke there would be no Highland rents because 'the almost total loss of their Cropt' coincided with collapsing cattle prices.[20] When the following year opened with a winter so severe that cattle across the region died from storm, frost and starvation, the Duke's Highland estates slid inexorably into famine. In mid March Tod reported that 'the poor People are dying at the Rate of a dozen a Week in this Corner, I suppose owing to the want of, and the badness of the meal'.[21] Disease inevitably took its toll: 'hundreds [in Lochaber] . . . carried off by a feverish Disorder'.[22] By the end of March, Tod's despair was clear:

> I wish from my Heart that we could find a Supply [of meal] here – I verily believe a third of the poor People must die of mere want, before the new Cropt comes in – Many of them are already done with their meal, they have but half Seed for their Land. The Provinder will not last above two weeks more, and yet the Weather has not admitted of our beginning to our labouring.[23]

The long winter and the seed shortage, followed by a lengthy summer drought and a September flood in which 'the poor People . . . lost their whole Cropt of

Hay', ensured another miserable harvest in 1772. Even the normally lucrative corn mills ceased operating.[24] In February 1773, Tod faced stark reality: 'there is the immediate Prospect of a Famine – the poor People, rather than starve, are eating the Corn with which they should sow their land', prompting his bitter remark about being paid to live here.[25] Even the London papers reported that 'the poor people in Badenoch and Lochaber are in a most pitiful situation for want of meal', bleeding their cattle to survive.[26]

Good harvests in 1773, 1775 and 1776 brought some respite, but autumn floods and 'violent frosts' damaged the 1774 harvest, while, in November 1777, the Spey ruined 1,000 stones of Tod's hay and drowned his corn 'three feet deep with water'.[27] Next year, flash floods in Laggan, 'more Extraordinary and Distructive than ever was known', destroyed all the buildings on Breakachy, though the tacksman, Lachlan Macpherson of Ralia, seemed more concerned for his wine: 'the seller [cellar] is almost still water up to the jests [joists] but I believe bottles etc are pretty safe'.[28] Worse, three-quarters of the arable of the neighbouring runrig farms was buried under 'large Stones, Gravell and sand from the adjacent mountains', never to be cultivable thereafter. [29] Another 'miserable harvest' in 1778 was followed by heavy livestock losses in a winter blizzard.[30]

The estate struggled to cope. Tod had no doubt that meal from the Duke's granaries was vital in 'preserving the Lives of many of the poor People', preventing hundreds from fleeing the region.[31] But this was not simply estate beneficence. The meal was not purchased specially for the starving Highlanders: it was the corn rent paid by his north-east tenants, which would, admittedly, have been sold on the open market.[32] But it was still sold, even during the famine, to the starving tenantry at a price of 15s a boll, nearly 2s higher than was being charged on the annexed estates, and 1s 4d above the previous year's price.[33] Baillie Macpherson in Fort William was refused permission to sell at 8d below cost price because 'the Duke sees no good reason to do this . . . they will not grudge the price'.[34] Even the transport cost from Aberdeenshire to Fort William was charged though ships were already sailing to Ballachulish to collect slate for Gordon Castle.[35]

The Duke somehow expected the Badenoch tenants to pay with 'ready money only'.[36] Frustratedly, Tod responded, 'You can hardly expect Payment': people simply had no money – they were already owing the previous year's meal money as well as two years' rent. Tod, the pragmatist, had in fact already distributed meal to the hungry who had promised 'to pay any Price you ask . . . with the Interest thereof', for all meal distributed on credit during the famine was subject to interest. Transport caused further problems, for meal had to be collected from Huntly (72 miles) or Fort William (48 miles) using the long carriage services.[37] Tod warned that the starving tenantry simply could not undertake such a journey, besides which, 'the Horses in this Country will hardly be able to get that Length'.[38] The estate compromised on the River Avon, still 40 miles distant.[39]

The crisis deepened as supplies dwindled. Somewhat understatedly Tod wrote: 'It is a very great Disappointment to the poor People, your not having more Meal, as hundreds of them are still in great Distress.'[40] John Dow had ordered 60 bolls for his Ballachroan tenants but received only 36.[41] Desperate tenants who had struggled as far as Huntly returned empty-handed.[42] Ross apologised that supplies were 'so far short of the demand . . . owing to our being quite exhausted at Huntly.'[43] His suggestion that the Badenoch folk could purchase any meal left unsold at Fort William – an unlikely scenario – was hardly reassuring. Extra meal was acquired from Ireland, Atholl, and the Lowlands, though this was perhaps more down to individual initiative than to the estate.[44] Alexander Macdonell (formerly Tullochroam, now at Garvamore) went personally to Ireland, adopting, as Tod wryly commented, 'the character of a distressed persecuted Papist', but clearly cut no Hibernian ice, for he returned empty-handed.[45]

Famine reveals the oft-criticised tacksmen in a more favourable light. They were central to relief operations, calculating the needs of their tenantry, liaising with Tod over requirements and arrangements, helping with the collection, carriage and distribution of meal, even acting as financial guarantors for their subtenants.[46] Most fulfilled this role honourably, though Lachlan Mackintosh of Balnespick was clearly racketeering, selling meal at 50 per cent over cost price to 'the Poor People who have the misfortune to be his tenants', thereby making 'unconscionable profits on his share of what was allotted for Badenoch.'[47]

Population inevitably declined through starvation and disease, but also through migration. Tod warned in 1773 that the consequence would be 'some hundreds more of their Families leaving the Country, whose Lands must fall into the Hands of their Master [the tacksman]' – implying many had already left.[48] Some may have headed for America, but there is no evidence of substantial emigration from Badenoch at this time, so most probably followed the familiar route south – years of seasonal labour facilitating permanent settlement. Indeed, Tod later commented that the poor 'must no doubt remove to the low Countries.'[49]

The tacksmen themselves confirmed this exodus. Mrs Macpherson of Wester Lynwilg complained: 'The late Course of Bad years has Reduced the Tennentry in my Neighbourhood to so low circumstances that I cannot get but a very small Part of the Daugh [davoch] land I hold subset'; many of the Delfour and Kinrara tenants had 'gone a begging'; Easter Lynwilg's tenants had 'left & ceded all their holdings'; half of the Ruthven tenants 'have left their houses within Two Years past & the . . . [rest] are absolutely determined to give up'; those at Turfadown 'have already verbally renounced their lands'; and at Biallidmore, 'most of my tenants already Reduced & left the land to myself, and the rest, in a tottering condition'.[50] Without the rents, farming and labour of the subtenants, many of Badenoch's tacksmen found their *duthchas* economically untenable.

During the famine, Tod's emotions were clear, but James Ross, too, reacted angrily, pointing out to the Duke that 'The distress of the poor, in all corners, calls loud for compassion and Assistance – Instead of the Expence of some Carousing expected on the Marquis and Lady Madelinas birthday [the Duke's children]'.[51] If that were not bold enough, he advised: 'It would be very good in Your Grace, to order a few Bolls of meal be given in Charity among the poor of every parish of Your Estate', ambivalently adding that such a reminder would not be necessary had the Duke been at home to witness the distress himself! The following year he bluntly told the Duke to find cheaper food for the hounds: 'I grudge the Quantity of Victuall they consume – especially in this time of great Scarcity'.[52] Hardship or not, the Duke rarely missed the annual Leith races, where the Duchess raised a 'subscription purse' of 60 guineas, not for her Highland poor, of course, but as prize money for the races – somewhat undermining the image of a paternalistic aristocracy.[53]

That Badenoch's difficulties in the 1770s resulted largely from insuperable climatic forces and market depression is unquestionable. All classes were, in varying degrees, victims of circumstances beyond their control, though the Duke's rental losses simply cannot be mentioned alongside the appalling suffering of his tenantry. While hindsight enables a greater understanding of these impersonal forces, the contemporary tacksman and tenant were unequivocal in laying blame on a very personal force. Duke Alexander had just imposed two consecutive rent increases at the very moment the regional economy was in freefall.

Estate Policy: Rentals

A 1773 critique of Highland landlordism captured the interrelation of personal and impersonal forces, attributing the suffering to 'hard seasons on the one hand, and the severity of the masters on the other', before targeting the landlords: 'Nothing can exceed the avarice . . . of the proprietors in the Highlands, for some time past, in raising their rents; to double, triple, and quadruple, and often more.'[54] Such rack-renting has been defended by some in the historical fraternity – Eric Cregeen commenting on the 5th Duke of Argyll's increases, 'what is remarkable is not that he asked more but that his demands remained so moderate', while Bruce Lenman even suggested that 'a steady screwing up of real rent levels' was 'the single most effective device for compelling tenants to modernise their social relationships and agricultural methods.'[55]

Not so, however, for Duke Alexander's increases of 1770 and 1771 nearly tripled the previous rental of 1750, with some individual farms like Breakachy and Pitchurn rising fourfold, and Moy nearly fivefold.[56] Such increases were far from 'moderate', and any suggestion that they were an 'effective device' of estate management is totally implausible. Indeed, their introduction at a time of such economic devastation and hardship suggests, at best, gross insensitivity.

The justification was, of course, to capitalise on rising livestock values, but comparing monetary rentals with cattle prices reveals that this was no fair equation. Between 1750 and 1771, rents rose nearly 180 per cent while cattle prices, even at their pre-collapse level, only increased by approximately 70 per cent (Table 3). The Duke's Badenoch rental in 1750 would have required the sale of roughly 340 cows: in 1771, had there been no depression, 560 would have been needed. During the 1770–1 depression, however, the number would have risen to 930. For an individual farm like Strathmashie the figures would have been: 1750 nine or ten cows, 1771 (pre-slump figure) twenty, and at the actual price, thirty-three. Whether measured in cash, percentage or cattle, rents were rising vastly in excess of prices.

While the Duke claimed that he 'does not Wish to get more Rent for his land, than industrious sober people can afford', a fellow aristocrat, the Duke of Atholl, disagreed: 'I am afraid he [Alexander] is Racking his Poor People tenants etc too much.'[57] Atholl continued – either with a moral perspective sadly lacking in his peers or simply having a jibe at the young Duke's expense – 'We should not forget that our Present Rank, fortune, Ease, and Independence has been purchased by the Blood of the Ancestors of our present dependents & Tenants.'[58]

Table 3

Rental increases on the Gordon estates in Badenoch, 1750–71.

	1750	1752	1770	1771
Estate rental £s	505	662	962	1,400
Incremental percentage increase		31	45	55
Cumulative percentage increase		31	92	177
Cows required if no slump in price	340			560
Cows required after slump in price	340			930

Note: Calculations based on prices in local estate papers and newspaper reports. Though only approximations (because of market fluctuations, age, quality) they are a general indicator.

Source: NRS, GD44/51/732/9, Rental, 1771.

Tacksman and tenant blamed rent increases for their distress: Lachlan Macpherson of Dalchully – 'the wretched Bargain I have of my Tack'; Mrs. Macpherson of Nessintully – 'The present rent of my farm is unsupportably high'; John Clerk of Ruthven – his land was 'near triple rented'; the Balmishag subtenants – 'it is not possible . . . they can hold the place at the present advanced rent'; Donald Grant, the Kinrara boatman, was simply 'over raxed already'.[59] Tod agreed: the estate rental 'was undoubtedly too high, even had the times been favourable'; 'their possessions are set above the value'; 'it is too high as on all the places you gave . . . last year'.[60] Even Ross agreed: 'I would be for bringing down their rents at once to what their possessions are really worth'.[61] Unfortunately, one person did not concur: 'The Duke does not enter much into the Humour of discounting Rents'.[62]

It was a short-sighted policy. Tod collected only £45 out of £1,300 in Lochaber in 1771, and in Badenoch £400 out of £1,400 in 1772 (the difference perhaps reflecting the greater affluence of the Badenoch tacksman class).[63] Next year's arrears were again 'prodigious', amounting by 1774 to nearly £3,000 for Badenoch.[64] Tacksmen like Dalchully, Biallidmore and Lynwilg 'renounced their possessions upon account of the high rent', and vacant farms remained so.[65] When Torgulbin was advertised in 1772, 'no Body would have it, on [account] of its high Rent'; similarly with Uvie, 'there is nobody very keen to get his farm'.[66] The estate was forced to negotiate, but concessions were not substantial – fewer than half the farms in Laggan benefited and by 1774 total reductions amounted to just 12 per cent of the estate rental.[67] Tod indeed was instructed to be selective and make concessions 'as small as possible & . . . only for one year'.[68] The tacksmen naturally fought their case. Benchar refused to levy the rent set by the Duke for the township of Strone, arguing that he had raised it 'to all the height I would think prudent to do', and the estate conceded.[69] Interestingly, when Benchar later negotiated another discount, he did not apply it universally but gave it, like a means-tested benefit, to 'those of the tenants who are most reduced' – another example of the tacksman as social manager.[70]

Despite these concessions, the Duke was clearly rack-renting his estate at a critical time, not only increasing hardship, but undermining the social and economic fabric of the region. That these increases were supporting the reckless pursuit of aristocratic luxury and power did little to allay the grievances. Alexander, however, had stirred up a veritable hornet's nest – another confrontation with the clan tacksmen.

Estate Policy: The Tacksman

Tod's fear was mounting. Tacksmen were threatening to renounce their farms. 'We cannot afford to lose them', he wrote – hardly the stereotypical view of that particular class, who, according to one historian, 'appeared to have no function in the new system and were dispossessed by the landlords'.[71] It was, however, a shrewd assessment of the estate's dilemma. By chance, depression, weather and rising rents coincided with the end of the nineteen-year leases. Though the perfect opportunity to re-assert the estate's authority, it was a policy fraught with risk. These were the tacksmen who had defied the estate in 1752, now wealthier, relishing their semi-autonomous state and quick to defend their rights – as Tod well knew: 'There is not a man in Badenoch worth £50 but has his Agent in Edinburgh with whom he advises before he does any thing of the least Moment'.[72] Challenge meant confrontation – and triggering a tacksman exodus would spell disaster.

The estate seized the initiative. Over the winter of 1769–70, Ross prepared for 'warning out [removing] the Badenoch people'.[73] Serving removal notices prior to new leases was, of course, standard tactics, giving the estate leverage over negotiations. Ross instructed Tod in 1771: 'It is certainly right that You push the Removings as far as tenable, without hearing of a Compromise', though advising caution, 'but it would be better to compromise, than to be defeat at last'.[74] Tod's request for 'some thousands' of printed removal notices

– 'they can hardly send us too many of them' – indicates the scale of the operation.[75] Ross again told Tod: 'be very determined & steady with the Badenoch
people', but repeated the warning 'never to Attempt anything that will not
carry through & being once attempted, it must be thoroughed [carried
through] at any Expence'.[76] Both men clearly understood the potential for
confrontation.

The estate increased the pressure by targeting troublesome individuals.
Donald Macpherson of Cullinlean, one of the wealthiest of the clan elite, was
taken to the Court of Session over his arrears and was evicted in 1770. Clearly,
no Macpherson was beyond the Duke's reach.[77] Lachlan Mackintosh – a
member of the powerful Balnespick family – was also removed from his
Laggan farm on the grounds of his 'tyranny'.[78] More worrying still, the farm
was temporarily given to the subtenants, as was Presmuchrach in 1773 when
its tacksman was removed.[79]

Introducing outsiders was another ploy to weaken the clan hierarchy. Tod
warned that if the tacksmen proved obstructive, 'His Grace will be induced to
introduce more Strangers among them'.[80] This was another risky manoeuvre
– three Lowland farmers had been brought into Lochaber, but they 'had many
of their Cattle Stolen, or destroyed of late, and are in danger of being totally
ruined'.[81] Tod tried to mitigate such hostility in Badenoch, for the three new
tacksmen who were introduced in the early 1770s were all Highlanders.[82] Two
were half-pay officers (one married to a daughter of Invernahavon) and therefore deemed reliable, but the most significant was John McHardy, an estate
appointee who was awarded Crathiecroy in 1770. Though a Gaelic-speaking
Highlander whose father was the Laggan dominie, that did not diminish the
local people's desire 'to distress him . . . [which] they have all the Inclination
in the World to do'.[83] Even in this diluted form the intrusion of outsiders caused
resentment, though it succeeded in its purpose of unsettling the tacksmen:
Benchar, the most respected of the clan elite, 'seems to Dread the Duke will
not see it proper to continue it [his tack] with him'.[84] It was a calculated strategy,
for Ross advised Tod that 'keeping up the Spirit of Interfering about the
Badenoch lands' would help focus minds when new leases were offered.[85]

The prospect of new leases further worried the tacksmen. The surveys
conducted by Brown and Taylor would inevitably lead to further rent increases
and onerous new conditions. In Lochaber the Duke had already imposed a
twenty-one point plan, eliciting a witty response from Colin Campbell:

Why do you propose 21 new ones to the good folk that never could keep the old Ten, when they say yours are by far worse to keep; and the penalties more certain, and you make no allowance for repentance after three years; but the good old ten we break till death bed and yet hope to escape.[86]

Leases indeed became a running sore as the Duke procrastinated, firstly waiting for the surveys, then holding off year after year in the hope that 'they recover from the Loses of the late bad Seasons & are in better condition to take leases' – obviously to impose higher rents.[87] The consequences were disastrous. The local gentry, even the most affluent and diligent, were for six years reduced to virtual tenants-at-will, paralysed over improvement and investment. Benchar bluntly informed Ross: 'It is needless to tell you how much the want of leases has contribute, with other unhappy circumstances, to the present ruinous state of the country.'[88]

Rising rents, new leases and threats to status provoked the expected confrontation. In 1770, Ross warned of a 'plan for a struggle against the Duke in Badenoch' led by John Macpherson of Inverhall, which Duke Alexander believed was 'the Consequence of a Concert among the Clan . . . to take advantage of him.'[89] Though it was quelled by isolating and threatening Inverhall, rent rebellions continued with leading tacksmen like Breakachy and Uvie demanding reductions, even trying to dictate terms. Ross noted the rising tension: 'they seem to push rather hard at present – which will not do with the Duke.'[90] More worrying than rents, however, was the threat of renunciations.

Captain Mackintosh, tacksman of Gaskmore, had already 'turned his plowshare into a sword', abandoning his farm in favour of the army. By spring 1773 at least a dozen or so tacksmen had tendered renunciations and Tod feared 'at least half a Dozen more.'[91] This was, of course, just as much a tactical manoeuvre as the estate's removal notices, and Tod knew it would only be used if the tacksmen 'cannot make bargain to their satisfaction'. In the prevailing economic circumstances, however, the mass renunciation of so many tacksmen was a deeply worrying prospect.[92] Was this in fact the feared 'Concert among the Clan' strategy to force the estate's hand? Such tactical renunciations were certainly happening on the neighbouring Grant estates in Strathspey from whence Tod had just heard of the renunciation of the 'People of Six Davochs who had determined to go as a Body to America if they did not get the proper Deduction [of rents].'[93] Intimately aware of the brewing disquiet in Badenoch, Tod was right to be concerned, for mass renunciations generally meant mass emigration.

Tod expressed his fears: 'I am not fond of these Emigration Schemes at all
. . . I was still more alarmed today, at being told of its having got the Length of
Badenoch.'[94] An emigration leaflet – 'that has put all their Heads agog in the
West Highlands' – was already circulating locally, seductively advertising St
John's Island (Prince Edward Island) in British North America.[95] Having
witnessed the substantial emigrations from Lochaber in 1771 and 1772, Tod
feared the truth of Colin Campbell's warning: 'if the Spirit of Settling colonies
in America is only kept up two years longer, you will certainly see waste lands
in the Highlands.'[96] Tod was determined this would not be Badenoch's fate.

Renunciation and emigration were the estate's 'Achilles heel'. Breaking the
tacksmen might be the goal, but driving them out was unthinkable. Finding
replacements of substance and quality would be difficult, so many of that class
having already left the Highlands – and the famine-ridden Badenoch of early
1773 was hardly an attractive proposition.[97] How would southern farmers cope
with the severity of the environment or the subtleties of the hill grazing regime
on which cattle – and hence estate income – depended? Sheep farmers might
be the answer, but none as yet had shown an interest. Furthermore, it was far
from certain that any southerner could effectively assume the social and
cultural role of tacksmanship in an area like Badenoch.

Perhaps Tod's greatest contribution to the estate was his appreciation that
the estate simply could not afford to lose its tacksmen. Many, like Lynwilg,
earned the comment, 'a good tenant and should not be parted with', while his
sentiment on the threatened departure of Benchar and Breakachy was simple
but profound – 'we will *miss* them'![98] Conciliation was necessary. He warned
Ross, 'they must all be kept in Humour; at whatever Expence till the Times
grow better.'[99] Ross agreed: 'they are certainly Good tenants . . . they ought to
be encouraged to stay'; 'rather than lose him . . . I think he should be indulged';
and in a highly significant comment on Breakachy and Uvie – the most
obstreperous of the clan gentry – 'tho they are troublesome, they are very
substantial tenents, *which is of great consequence in these times* [author's
italics]'.[100]

It was in fact the powerful Breakachy family who led the resistance.
Donald Macpherson and his son, Captain Duncan, with Donald's brother,
Hugh Macpherson of Uvie, epitomised the powerful, independent tacksmen
that the estate was determined to break. Believing they were untouchable –
for they were the above-mentioned 'very substantial tenents', and, as Tod
commented, 'seem to know their own Importance thoroughly' – the family
defied the estate over rents and conditions.[101] As tensions escalated through

1771 and 1772, Captain Duncan withheld his rent as a bargaining counter.[102] Tod prepared for a showdown: 'I shall have no Objection to a Tryal of Skill with them if they please, as I am furnished with some Arguments that they think I do not know of, and which they have been at great pains to conceal.'[103] He planned his strategy carefully, quietly seeking replacement tacksmen. A cryptic comment, 'I should like to have Ralea home before I do anything with them', revealed his attempt to line up the wealthy drover, Lachlan Macpherson of Ralia, for Breakachy.[104]

Tod took a firm stand over Uvie's lease: 'He must subscribe to every Article in the Terms . . . or it can be no Bargain.'[105] Then, when Captain Duncan threatened renunciation, Tod called his bluff, causing an immediate retraction.[106] The 'negotiations' had their lighter moments – Breakachy plying Tod with drink in the hope of discovering the estate's plans, and even threatening to spread his 'large Dunghill . . . upon an adjacent piece of Cluny estate' rather than on the Gordon farm of Breakachy!'[107] But Tod's frustrations were evident: 'I have now begun to lose all Temper with Breakachy and Ovie and if the Estate was my own I would certainly extirpat the very Seed of them, if I should never find Tenants.'[108] Reluctant to lose such wealthy tenants, however, the estate again compromised.

In 1773, Ross and Tod took a harder line. Tod tried to isolate the troublemakers: 'if we could get all the other Folks secured, they might be allowed to take their Swing.'[109] Captain Duncan still expected to be 'preserv'd on his own terms': Ross replied that he would 'be glad [if] he continues at Breakachy', but not 'upon the terms he proposes.'[110] That was Ross's bottom line – though he wished to retain Breakachy and Uvie, he 'would not yield to their imaginary Importance.'[111] The estate simply had to be paramount. Tod, with replacement tacksmen now in waiting (Ralia for Breakachy and Lieutenant Shaw of Dalnavert for Uvie), meticulously prepared the legal ground. The brothers were offered their farms, rent and conditions non-negotiable. When the usual renunciations followed, Ross accepted them, writing firmly to Breakachy: 'I am sorry that you & your Son have thought proper to leave Breakachy considering how long your family has possest it upon very reasonable Terms.'[112]

It was a remarkable victory: Donald Macpherson, brother-in-law of 'Cluny of the '45', leader of clan resistance, wealthy cattle dealer and hereditary forester to the Duke, a shrewd and skilful negotiator who was a constant thorn in the flesh of both Gordon estates and the Barons, had been ousted from his *duthchas* without either formal eviction or messy lawsuits. That his replacement was a fellow Macpherson coveting the rich pickings of Breakachy, must have made Tod smile – self-interest once again undermining concerted action. With this warning shot reverberating through the clan, Tod concluded individual negotiations with the other tacksmen, offering rent concessions to bring them back onside, including those who had earlier sent in renunciations.

With clan opposition broken, at least temporarily, the years 1774 to 1776 were comparatively peaceful, though rents, leases and emigration remained dominant concerns. The Duke, still seeking 'a *low Country Rent* in Lieu of a highland one', obstinately continued with annual leases, refusing to consider anything beyond a seven-year term for the future in case the economy improved, or perhaps, as in Glenavon, simply 'to keep them in fear'.[113] Tod pointed out the folly – the policy was 'much against His Grace's Interest as well as that of the Tenant'.[114] Ross tackled the Duke directly: 'in Badenoch where there are many People of Substance and accustomed to a nineteen years Lease I am doubtful if a Tack for a Shorter Period would go down'.[115]

Ross worried that the Duke's intransigence could yet push the Badenoch tacksmen into emigration 'if the leading People there do not get Leases upon agreeable Terms'.[116] As yet more Lochaber tenants threatened to leave in 1775, Tod confirmed Ross's fear: 'the Spirit of Emigration has even got in here [Badenoch] where one would least of all have expected it' – perhaps believing that the region's inland isolation or the strength of *duthchas* feelings might make it immune to such pressures.[117] Reports came from a small neighbouring estate that 'most of Rothiemurchus's Tenants are gone' (possibly because rents more than doubled in just ten years), while the Duke himself had failed to dissuade a party of Strathspey emigrants from leaving, though offering 'to accommodate them with Lands if they would stay' – possibly the 200 emigrants who 'rendezvoused at Aviemore, and marched off to Greenock'.[118] Such fears, however, diminished with the government's prohibition of emigration on the outbreak of the American War of Independence in 1775, thereby depriving the tacksman of his principal negotiating threat.[119]

With estate debts spiralling, Ross also started to explore the possibility of sheep in 1775 – perhaps again a tactical ploy, for Border sheep farmers assessing the region's potential would cause further ripples. Early in 1776, the Duke at last proposed a new sett and Tod seized the moment with a provocative advertisement inviting offers for every farm in Badenoch and Lochaber (excepting John Maclean's Pitmain), proclaiming that in addition to corn and cattle, the land 'would answer well for breeding sheep'.[120] Nineteen-year leases were suddenly on offer – to attract outsiders presumably – with entry in three months. Whether seriously seeking outsiders, or just pressurising the tacksmen into settling quickly with more competitive rents is not clear – but it certainly brought a reaction. Tod commented wryly, 'You cannot imagine what Offence that Measure has given the Clan.'[121]

A threat too far, perhaps, for the clan again closed ranks to boycott the new sett. Ross informed the Duke: 'not one of them has given in proposals for a Lease, notwithstanding of the impatience they expressed formerly to get Tacks', adding later that they were 'in concert not to take Leases but at a Low Rent.'[122] Exasperated, he warned Tod: 'If the Gentlemen of your Country chuse to be backward in making proposals for Leases I am now determined to be as little forward in making advances to them.'[123] He continued, implying that there had been an element of bluff, that he had not previously intended 'to introduce strangers among them', but was now sufficiently riled to introduce 'some substantial industrious people among them who understand the management of sheep'.

In March 1777, the stalemate was unexpectedly broken when Lieutenant Alex Macpherson of Strathmashie lost his family *duthchas*. All decade he had wrangled over the rent of his farm (valued at £50, but in his view worth only £35), but then Angus Macdonald from the neighbouring Gallovie family offered the full value.[124] The estate immediately accepted. Ross was unsympathetic: 'Lt Mcpherson came rather late – but he had himself to blame', pointedly adding, 'I hope it will be a warning to some others.'[125] He later justified the estate's actions:

> When a number of them appear into concert to force the Duke into their *own terms*, there is a necessity to endeavour to disconcert their Measures so far as to bring them at least to *reasonable terms*, And in the course of the Struggle some individuals must suffer – Strathmashie happens to be the first in Badenoch . . . others are in danger who perhaps, are little apprehensive of it.[126]

As Ross suspected, the Strathmashie affair undermined the clan 'concert', and gradually the tacksmen returned to the fold, reluctantly accepting the new leases.

Though both sides were left embittered by this long attritional struggle, victory lay with the estate. The 'douchassers' had effectively been broken: important they would undoubtedly remain, but their independence and collective power had been seriously undermined. The Ross–Tod axis had proved crucial not just to the estate's success, but to Badenoch's future identity.

Both men had acknowledged the economic and social importance of the tacksmen within the community, often defending their interests – particularly over tenurial security – even when it meant opposing Alexander's wishes. But recognising the tacksmen did not mean surrendering authority: neither chamberlain nor factor would allow the estate to be held to ransom by individual or clan. Their aim was to redefine the relationship, the tacksman remaining the linchpin of the estate, but clearly as middle-manager, subservient to the Duke's demands.

The estate's success was largely down to Tod. An astute negotiator, he appears to have been well-respected and trusted. Not only was he one of the community, but he had worked tirelessly to provide famine relief, had been willing to compromise over rents and arrears, and had shown respect for traditional clan rights. His strategy, however, was classic divide and rule. Threats of outsiders and sheep undermined the clan gentry, many of whom, already suffering financial difficulties, felt vulnerable and insecure. Individual troublemakers and ringleaders were, with Ross's support, targeted and removed. The others were then won over through negotiation and concession, exploiting the cultural power of *duthchas.* Tod realised, for example, that Alex Macpherson of Biallidmore's renunciation, in which he specifically stated that he was the 'nineteenth generation upon this spot', was in fact a plea for help, and compromising over his financial embarrassment would ensure his continuation as tacksman.[127]

Duthchas and clanship were integral to estate strategy. That clanship had been a constant thorn is evident in Tod's comment that Uvie had used 'all the Law, and all the chicane, he and his clan were masters of' against the estate.[128] But clanship provided a point of attack, and not just through bringing in outsiders. In the early 1770s, Tod again exploited inter-clan rivalry by trying to establish Macphersons like Ralia, Benchar and John Dow amongst the Lochaber Macdonalds: 'to preserve the *Balance of Power* in that Corner, which however it may appear to a low Country man [a dig at Ross], is absolutely necessary', and would 'at least keep Sandy Keppoch in Order for us [Alexander Macdonell of Keppoch]'.[129] In 1776, Ross reversed the policy: 'some of the McDonalds . . . will take a Survey of Badenoch – and rouse the Mcphersons a little, from their present security of not being interfered with'.[130] Giving Strathmashie to Angus Macdonald may well have been part of that process: that it had the desired effect is clear from Tod's comment that the Macdonalds 'do not injoy their Victory in Silence'.[131]

That Badenoch remained in the hands of its indigenous tacksman families is testament to Tod's skill. He took particular credit for preventing mass emigration, one of the features that most distinguishes Badenoch from other Highland regions: 'I have furtherto got them all kept in tolerable good Humour; and by a seasonable Discount of a Rent . . . I have prevented a Single man from leaving His Grace's Estate, while many of the neighbouring ones are laid waste.'[132] Tod had thus preserved the traditional leadership, expertise, and above all, the specie that would have been drained out of the community had this social group emigrated as happened on the west coast.[133] Most significantly, while the tacksmen remained in their ancestral lands, the nature of tacksmanship itself had been redefined.

Estate Policy: Improvement

Difficult though the 1770s were, agricultural improvement continued, with leases the key to reform. Invereshie estate had already established nineteen-year improvement leases as standard practice, but the most progressive policy came from the much-maligned Commissioners for the Annexed Estates who had finally gained legal control over the estates of Cluny and Lochlaggan in 1770. Parson Robert was granted a virtual lifetime lease of fifty-seven years, while the Macphersons of Laggan, Nuidemore, Catlag, Ralia and Cluny received terms of forty-one years, with even the small tenants of farms like Gaskinloan and Biallidbeg getting twenty-one.[134] Furthermore, the rental increased only 25 per cent between 1752 and 1784.[135]

The Cluny leases were tied into improvement. The tacksman had to invest five years' rental over the first seven years and improvements were specified – Nuidemore, for example, had to provide ditches, bulwarks and stone dykes.[136] The Commissioners also reinvested the estate rental in improvement schemes, Laggan farm receiving £12 15s 11d annually for twenty-one years.[137] Similarly, the common tenantry were assisted, those at Gaskinloan receiving £4 annually throughout their twenty-one years, on condition they abandoned runrig ('each keeping his own part') and kept the farm 'without division'.[138] Vouchers show that tacksman and tenant alike were assiduously building dykes in the late 1770s, the seven tenants of Gaskinloan constructing 205 roods (over 1,000 metres) over nine years.[139] Premiums were specifically given to encourage potato cultivation.[140] Without doubt, the security of long leases, stable rents and financial assistance must have encouraged even the poorest of tenants to undertake improvements. This was, of course, the 'exemplary civilising' of post-Culloden strategy, albeit some twenty-five years late, but again it shows the Highlander, when provided with opportunity and support, willing to initiate reforms – a focus undoubtedly sharpened by famine.

The contrast with the Gordon estates could hardly have been greater. The Duke's leases, eventually issued in 1777, were short-term and contained little on specific agricultural improvement apart from a primitive rotation of three consecutive corn crops on ground that had been limed followed by four years' pasture.[141] While the estate did undertake certain major projects like flood defences and straightening burns, these were often charged to the tacksman with interest. Furthermore, a suggestion that the Duke should provide lime for local tenants – a potentially vital improvement – was never implemented.[142]

Individual initiatives like Maclean's Pitmain improvements continued through the 1770s. Even those thorns in the flesh, Breakachy and Uvie, had 'at a very high Expense Built and ffinished neat ffarm Houses, and made most Extensive Dykes and Enclosures.'[143] John McHardy, the new tacksman of Crathiecroy, also impressed, though initially suffering from both the hostility of his neighbours and the economic downturn. Tod wisely supported him, lending £34 10s for seed and provender, explaining to Ross, 'I can assure you from Experience that it is no easy matter to plenish a Highland farm.'[144] It paid dividends, for McHardy was later praised as 'a very eminent improver to be in that wild country . . . thorn fences in excellent order, dividing the valley from the hill, and stone fences on the higher grounds, a kiln for burning lime, cows remarkably well shaped.'[145] Evictions, however, inevitably accompanied such improvements, though the estate's report that the Crathiecroy tenants were giving 'trouble about Removing', and had 'reclaimed [appealed] against the Decreet of Removing', gives another glimpse of growing assertiveness.[146]

The best case study, however, is John Dow Macpherson, the 'black Lieut', who had become tacksman of Ballachroan in 1770.[147] Tyrannical towards his social inferiors, he was also belligerent and cantankerous with his peers. Even old Malcolm Macpherson, laird of Phones and famous veteran of the Seven Years' War, suffered: 'I was really in danger of my life if I refused signing the summons . . . He told me privately if he could not won at you by Law he would make use of his hands.'[148] Ross was wary: 'John Dow seems to be very trouble-some & you should keep him in Order . . . See you be certain of your proof where he is concerned.'[149] Yet Ross was determined 'to fix him as a Tenent upon the Estate'; he was 'a very intelligent usefull man'; and not least, 'a substantial man & pretty punctual [with rents].'[150] Significantly, Ross 'suggested to the Duke & Dutchess the propriety of taking notice of him – and I think

they were as attentive as could be Expected'.[151] Again the estate was demon-
strating its appreciation of good local tacksmen, even if 'troublesome'.

Like most tacksmen, John Dow's rent was covered by his subtenants, half
the farm being 'sett to tenants who pay more rent than the whole he pays your
Grace's factor'.[152] John Dow had argued that £40 was all that Ballachroan was
worth: if his subtenants were paying more than that from only half the farm,
they were clearly being rack-rented – not by the Duke, but by their tacksman.
Free of rent worries, John Dow could invest his cattle, droving and military
proceeds in improvements – acquiring some notoriety in the process. Local
legend tells of crops so luxuriant that satanic pacts were rumoured, though
his extensive use of lime might provide a more rational – if less exciting –
explanation.[153] Though his actual arable exploits are not recorded, the presence
of three barns (totalling over 1,600 square feet) with additional haylofts
indicates substantial harvests, probably fodder for the cattle that were his
primary interest.[154]

Unusually for a Badenoch farm, Ballachroan's only hill grazing and shielings were in the corrie directly above the farm, so John Dow leased the
substantial grazings of Fersit in Lochaber, both for its summer shielings and
milder winter pastures.[155] Ballachroan itself had byre accommodation for over
seventy cattle, suggesting a very substantial herd between the two farms.[156]
Under his management, it became one of the foremost grass farms in
Badenoch, providing butter not just for James Ross's wife in Fochabers, but
even for the Duke and Duchess.[157]

John Dow's improvements progressed rapidly. By 1775, he was well
through a building programme costing £400, with a further £100 required 'to
clear the land above the brea of the Stones and Baulks'.[158] In 1778, Tod
described the huge earthen 'flow dykes' along the Spey and the Aultlarie,
bringing the valuable haugh grounds into cultivation.[159] The now-completed
buildings comprised 'an exceeding good and sufficient House, with a Kitchen
. . . a Kiln, a Stable, a Barn, and four Byres . . . all built of Stone and Lime'
(though still with divot and heather thatch), plus another 'Barn and a large
Byre . . . above the public Road'. A stone dyke ran alongside the public road,
and a head dyke was planned to demarcate farm and hill. Ten acres of the
upper farm had also been cleared, levelled and enclosed (the impressive stone
dykes still standing exactly as on the farm plan), with more underway – 'and
all without Allowance', meaning self-financed (Plate 9a). Unlike many of his
contemporaries, John Dow invested his money wisely rather than frittering it
on luxuries.

John Dow fought for a nineteen-year lease, rejecting a 'very advantageous' offer from Ross.[160] To strengthen his case, he commissioned two surveys of Ballachroan in 1775 and 1778, eventually securing his lease with a £20 reduction (one-third), conditional on continuing to finance his own improvements.[161] The lease stipulated his permanent residence, farming two-thirds of it himself, and if, as indeed happened, he were summoned 'furth of the Kingdom' on military service, his wife must run the farm or forfeit the lease.[162] The estate clearly wanted larger farms managed by resident tacksmen, abolishing the practice of multiple tacks – Tod had already stipulated that the tacksmen 'ought all to be bound to reside constantly, themselves, with their family'.[163]

The lease sheds further light on women's status. As daughter of Hugh Macpherson of Uvie and widow of John Macpherson of Inverhall (both notoriously troublesome), John Dow's wife, Ann, clearly had pedigree in handling domineering men. Indeed, when widowed in 1770, she had successfully run Inverhall estate for her children. In 1778, however, she caused consternation by planning to follow her new husband's regiment to America – jeopardising the residential clause of the new lease.[164] After familial discussions, John Dow noted (perhaps with relief) not only that 'Mrs Macpherson was fully reconciled with the plan of staying at home', but would manage the farm '& I am hopefull as she has been used to an active life that she will have no dificulty in Carriing on the part of Farming'.[165] Her management skills were as ruthless as her husband's according to Thomas Macpherson, a subtenant: 'Mrs Capt. John McPherson . . . has done everything in her power to distress him and his ffather . . . her Resentment being implacable and Irrevokeable as well as that of her husbands', begging the Duke to suppress such 'tyranny and oppression'.[166]

Like his neighbour, Maclean, John Dow had fingers in many pies – improver, cattle dealer, drover, officer. He also proposed trying sheep 'as I can have a Good Sort from my Friends in England' (presumably droving or military contacts), and was importing flaxseed from Riga.[167] He was factor on Phones and Flichity estates, applied to be forester in Gaick (with an eye to its extensive grazing) and was a Justice of the Peace.[168]

Removals were again inevitable. In 1730, there had been at least fourteen tenants farming Ballachroan, in 1771 just six or seven, and the 1778 plan shows a new enclosure imposed over an old township (Plate 9b).[169] John Dow epitomised the entrepreneurial, if not always desirable, face of tacksmanship, repaying the estate's faith through the extent and success of his reforms. Far from being unwilling or unable to adapt to new ideas, these Badenoch tacksmen were quick to adopt whatever improvements suited their own particular situation and inclination.

•   •   •

Writing to Edinburgh lawyer, Alexander Tait, in 1775, Ross wondered if wealthy sheep farmers could 'be tempted to Settle' in Badenoch and Lochaber, dangling the bait that 'as there are no Leases on Badenoch . . . His Grace could accommodate them with any extent of Ground'.[170] It was a dual-purpose initiative, undermining the tacksmen and boosting revenues. This flirtation with sheep, however, reveals another divergence from events in other parts of the Highlands at this time. Sheep farms were, for instance, being established in Mar estate in the eastern Cairngorms, in Morvern, in Glenorchy and in western Inverness-shire, leading to clearances and emigration.[171] The perception of an all-consuming northwards colonisation by sheep, however, is inaccurate, for, despite Ross's initiative, the Gordon lands in Badenoch did not follow the general pattern.

On the advice of William Fraser (another Edinburgh lawyer), Ross invited Adam Hunter, a Tweed-dale sheep farmer, to advise if the land was 'proper for Sheep Husbandry'.[172] Fraser wisely suggested that the Duke or Tod should go into partnership with Hunter, otherwise people would resent him 'as a new man brought in to raise rents, & take every opportunity to distress him'.[173] Rather optimistically, Fraser described Badenoch as 'the likest country to Tweeddale that I have Seen only the hills of one is black & those of the other green' – a colour difference that might prove rather significant, not to mention 2,000 feet in height and a somewhat harsher climate! But Fraser's enthusiasm was understandable because 'in the Sheep country there is no such thing known as bade payments [rent arrears]'.[174]

Tod was to show Hunter around, not only to 'procure all useful information & Intelligence for the Dukes interest', but also, in light of the earlier troubles in Lochaber, to 'convince him that Strangers would be protected and in safety to Settle in your Bounds'. Tod felt optimistic: 'he seems better and better pleased with this Country'.[175] In 1776, Ross contacted other Borderers: the Duke was keen to introduce sheep, 'believing that it would be of general benefit to the Country', and leases would be 'upon very reasonable Terms . . . particularly Badenoch as the leases are all out at Whitsunday'.[176] He also tried Captain Ross, who wanted a Lochaber farm, offering a 'Cheaper bargain of Lands in Badenoch, if their Situation & Climate would answer your purpose'.[177]

Still unsuccessful by 1777, Ross contacted David Cubison, another Ayrshire sheep farmer interested in Lochaber. If he chose Badenoch instead, 'there would be less difficulty to get you a settlement', and moreover, 'all the Duke's Lands in Badenoch are open, except a few'.[178] In a significant reference to the recent troubled relations Ross added that the Duke 'has some reason to be displeased with the Badenoch People, and will be less Scrupulous about removing them'.[179]

Ross's overtures were in vain – southern sheep farmers showed no interest, preferring Lochaber. Their rejection of Badenoch was probably influenced by the extreme climate and the long overland routes to market, though local hostility to outsiders was no doubt another factor. But the Duke's own ambivalence, caught between economics and paternalism, was hardly encouraging. Writing to Cubison, Ross described 'his Grace's sympathy for the present Tenents . . . he cannot find it in his heart to turn out a number of them, unless he has it in his power to settle them conveniently elsewhere'.[180]

Tod himself was not enthusiastic. Depopulation, 'the Consequence of the present Rage that so universally prevails for Sheep Husbandry', worried him.[181] But he also believed the bubble would burst: 'the Certainty of the Markets being soon over stocked with Mutton and Wool, made me always averse to the Encouragement of that Plan except in a very modest Degree'. Whatever the reason, the great wave of sheep sweeping the Highlands largely bypassed Badenoch in the 1770s.

Rather than moral or economic concerns, it was imperial affairs that killed this initiative. As the American War of Independence intensified in 1778, the demand for soldiers increased, and the Duke decided that his future – and hence that of his Highland estates – lay more in the patriotic rearing of men than sheep. Ross later explained to Cubison that he would have received a Lochaber farm in 1778 'had not His Grace in the course of Recruiting that summer, come to a resolution not to remove any of his People, nor to give any Encouragement to the introduction of sheep in that Country'.[182] It was a significant decision: Duke Alexander remained hostile to sheep walks until well into the next century.[183]

Meanwhile, the local gentry – so aggrieved by the estate's wooing of the Lowland sheep farmers – were not averse to such a move themselves. Some, of course, already kept substantial flocks, but, in 1776, Benchar was negotiating 'with a Sheep Farmer from the South, for his Place of Glenbanchor'.[184] In 1779, McHardy was doing the same in Crathiecroy, while also requesting a lease of the neighbouring farm of Sherramore in time for 'issuing out the Removings [to be] in readiness for stocking it'.[185] Whether these schemes materialised is unclear, but there is no doubting that the first definite sheep walk run by a Lowlander was Aberarder, Parson Robert's Lochlaggan farm, which he sublet in 1779 to Andrew Mitchell from Ayrshire: 'The intention I have had, for some years past, to lett this Farm to a South Country Grazier is lately accomplished'.[186] Mitchell's rent to the parson was almost ten times higher than Robert himself paid to the Commissioners![187] Ironically, at the very time the Duke turned against sheep walks, some local tacksmen were looking to introduce them for their own commercial benefit, with scant regard to their depopulating consequences.

While the impact of sheep in the 1770s was minimal, agricultural improvement was gradually transforming the landscape with ditches, dykes, floodbanks, and stone steadings – the physical infrastructure for future improvements, whether arable or pastoral. Much of this improvement was doubtless driven by the needs of the expanding cattle trade, producing the fodder to sustain larger herds through the winter. But improvement also had its social and aesthetic dimension, as the local gentry acknowledged the more 'civilised' landscape emerging in the regular fields of Pitmain. Improvement was as much fashion statement as economics. For the poorer tenantry as well, progressive estate management on Invereshie and Cluny encouraged improvement, not, of course, for fashion, but as a basic security against any recurrence of famine.

Military

While imperial necessity applied the brakes to sheep farming, it created other opportunities, not least through the American War of Independence. From Duke to cottar, the outbreak of war in 1775 again brought potential benefits. For the gentry, commissions beckoned. Veteran half-pay officers like John Dow and John Macpherson of Invereshie returned to duty as captains, Duncan Macpherson of Breakachy rose from captain to major, while Duncan Macpherson of Cluny achieved a colonelcy. Others quickly followed as Captain John (Invereshie) noted from America: 'Several gentlemen joined the army lately even from Badenoch & Strathspey'.[188] As the war escalated in 1778, Ross notified the Duke of yet more Badenoch officers: 'no less than nine McPhersons and about as many Badenoch & Lochaber McDonells, named to Commissions'.[189] When John Dow entered the Duke of Hamilton's Regiment in January 1778, his brother-in-law, stepson and nephew accompanied him as officers. The economic benefit of such commissions is evident as John Invereshie sent £100 the first year and £50 annually thereafter from America to help clear his father's debts, while offering £50 more to his brother William.[190] For others, like Macpherson of Biallidmore's son, social graces and status were more significant: 'it will introduce him to genteel Company, and give him an opportunity of acquiring Accomplishments which may be usefull'.[191]

Sacrifices were made to get on the commission ladder. Ranald Macdonell (formerly Aberarder, now Moy) sold his cattle to purchase his son's commission, thereby falling into arrears: 'my Son Sandy required all the money I could Draw for my Cows'.[192] Local connections proved beneficial. From America, Invereshie offered to 'do all I can for Evan Macpherson of the 42nd', though higher-ranking patronage pulled more strings.[193] General Grant of Ballindalloch, a doyen of the British establishment and uncle to Captain John Invereshie, helped a few young hopefuls: 'I was certain Gen Grant would soon provide for him [Benchar's son]'.[194] Others, including John Dow and his relatives, owed their success to the 'London Macphersons (Fingal and the Nabob) [who] seem to have much to say with the Hamilton Folks . . . they have used all their Influence . . . to push forward the Clan' – at least eight local gentry gaining commissions through James Macpherson's patronage in 1778.[195] Now a government propagandist, 'Fingal'was also promoting enlistment through patriotic pamphlets, 'sent to everybody here by the Government', noted Tod, 'I found one waiting me which had come by Post – gratis'.[196]

But not all seized the chance. Captain John commented that many of the Badenoch half-pay officers did not rejoin: 'I wish some of the Country half pay lads had come over here . . . I think it was not worth their while to leave their farms without superior rank to what they had'.[197] A guaranteed half-pay pension in the comfort of home was, for some, more attractive than the rigours of conflict, but, as John acknowledged, the costs of full-time officership rendered it uneconomical without promotion, while re-enlistment at the same rank did nothing to enhance social status.

Many of the commonalty also exploited war's opportunities, though some were driven by hardship. In 1775, young Cluny had already 'got about 70 men', and Major Duncan Macpherson (formerly of Breakachy) was determined 'not [to] be left behind on the recruiting Service'.[198] Major Duncan and Lachlan Macpherson of Ralia were, according to Parson Robert, 'indefatigably active' in enlisting men.[199] 'The Country was full of People, and the Times were so bad that many of them were starving, or obliged to go to the Low Country to serve as Labourers.' Major Duncan sent recruiting officers southwards 'who soon picked up all the Natives of this [country] That had struggled thither'. Tod commented that Duncan was taking men 'of all ages & Sizes', and within months of the war starting warned that 'there are but few remaining'.[200] Further intensive recruitment occurred at the start of 1778, Ross alerting the Duke that, with all the newly commissioned officers, 'It will be impossible to prevent their getting men – so that you may expect Your Highland Estate will be drained of 4 or 500 men'.[201] Charles Gordon referred to '150 Highlanders chiefly mustered by the Macphersons' in Hamilton's alone.[202] By April, however, recruitment was diminishing. Even the notorious John Dow was having 'very litle Success in this Country – Benchar's Son and the other Folks have had still less'.[203]

Bounties rose far above the government allowance of £3. Major Duncan, even in 1775, 'does not scruple five guineas of Levy Money'.[204] In 1778, John Dow was offering 10 guineas, Captain Leith £15, while Ross mentioned 20 guineas and Parson Robert 30 guineas – 'if a man say he will be a soldier he shall have his price be what it will'.[205] With Cluny rents ranging from £2 to £4, such figures had considerable attraction. Bargains could also be struck: Macintyre at Presmuchrach, Macarthur at Garvabeg and Macqueen at Beglan in Glenmore all secured leases in return for enlistment.[206] Military income brought further benefits: in 1780, a sergeant received land in Pitchurn because he 'returned with a Pension – he has also made some money, and is recommended as a good Tenant'.[207]

For the Duke, it was more about political influence. In 1777, he belatedly sought permission to raise a regiment. Ross was horrified, for the estate already faced enormous debts.[208] Regiments were costly, most potential recruits had already been enlisted, and bounties were soaring, never mind clothing and equipment. Ross again rebuked his employer: 'wishing that Your Grace would not spend so much time or money in London . . . and exert yourself to protect your People and make them usefull at Home', adding as warning, 'It is now so late, and the difficulty and Expence must be so prodigiously encreased'.[209]

The government's rejection of the Duke's regiment temporarily allayed Ross's fears, but French entry into the war in 1778 brought the spectre of invasion and Alexander's new proposal for a thousand-strong regiment for home defence, the Northern Fencibles, was readily accepted.[210] Andrew Macpherson of Benchar shrewdly assessed its importance: 'as it is [the Duke's] first essay for support of government in the military line, they, as well as the nation in generall, have an attentive eye upon the progress and will be apt to judge of his future ability by the success attending this particular instance'.[211] He also recognised its potential local significance: 'The more his consequence is established with the administration he will have it more in his power to doe for his Dependants.'

Ross was still worried over the 'considerable Expence', but also feared it might 'drain the Country too much of necessary Servants'.[212] The Northern Fencibles did indeed become problematic. Recruitment in Badenoch was sluggish. Ross found the failure of officers 'to raise even half their Quotas . . . extremely mortifying', but believed the regiment would fail unless the Duke 'suspend his Amusements for a Season and turn his thoughts & attention wholly to that Business'.[213] Numbers improved, however, when religious barriers were removed for the Duke had 'no objection to a Catholick', and even dropped the word Protestant from the attestations (oaths of allegiance).[214] When the Comprehending Act, for 'laying hold of all the Fellows in the Country of bad Characters', was introduced, the regiment was finally completed.[215] Of the 1,000 men, however, only 150 came from the Duke's own estates, and of those only one quarter were from Badenoch.[216]

As feared, the regiment proved expensive. Though his enlistment bounty was only one guinea, there was another 'Twenty shillings for each Recruit – out of which he must be provided of necessarys'.[217] Costs rapidly mounted, especially as bounties were inevitably exceeded. Aesthetics added to the burden – not just kilts and jackets, but black ostrich plumes, buckles for shoes, even a black silk napkin for each man.[218] The expense of raising the regiment in 1778 amounted to over £6,000, with an additional £3,500 in 1780.[219] Further costs arose because Alexander was being 'scrupulously nice on the quality' of men, and Charles Gordon begged him 'to reserve your weeding until you have supernumeraries'.[220] But for the Duke, this was, as Benchar had suggested, a very deliberate display of 'martial symbolism', a visual statement of his importance to king and government.[221]

The difficulties in recruiting sufficient numbers suggest that the Badenoch tacksmen were, as Mackillop suggests, 'unenthusiastic recruiters'.[222] This apparent reluctance was confirmed by Parson Robert: Cluny and Breakachy apart, 'there was not a Gentleman in this Country, except Capt. John Ballachroan for a week or two in the beginning, who took an active Concern'.[223] Apathy was so great over the Northern Fencibles in 1778 that Tod summoned all the local tacksmen to Pitmain Inn with lists of their available tenants – hoping, with his usual diplomacy, 'to be able by the Help of some Bottles of

Wine, and a few Threats and Promises to induce them to comply with my wishes'.[224]

Badenoch's failure to support the Duke's regiment had complex causes. William Macpherson of Invereshie simply believed that raising the requisite numbers would prove too heavy a financial burden on the tacksmen.[225] Parson Robert, however, now 'the Oracle and Adviser of the whole clan', shrewdly saw the underlying causes – the breakdown of traditional social values and relationships. 'Neither the Honour of the Country nor attachment to the Duke of Gordon can easily procure a decent number of Volunteers in this Country', clearly reflecting the tensions between Duke and tacksmen.[226] Furthermore, Robert feared it gave the Duke 'great Reason to complain of his Tenants in this Country, and it will confirm the prejudices he already appears to have unhappily conceived of them' – echoing Ross's earlier comment to Cubison (the sheep farmer) regarding the Duke's displeasure with the local tacksmen.[227]

Parson Robert also recognised that 'the Spirit of Clanship has absolutely ceased', and with it the traditional loyalties that would previously have ensured successful recruitment.[228] Tacksmen no longer felt any obligations to Duke or chief, but, as Robert noted, neither did the lower orders to the gentry who were 'very much fallen off in their Circumstances' and suffering a 'Decrease of their influence amongst the Common People'. The latter were now 'aspiring at Independence, and trust to there own Industry and Protection of the Law more than to the precarious Support formerly afforded them by there Demagogues or Heads of Tribes'. Most of the Benchar tenants, for instance, had 'absolutely refused to go with their young Master'. It was a perceptive analysis of social change, all the more valuable for having come from one of the clan elite – and without the benefit of hindsight.

Reluctance over recruitment, however, was rooted in basic economics as much as in social tensions. The region was simply, as Ross had feared, being over-recruited. Invereshie was 'pretty well drained of men', and Parson Robert agreed that the shortage of labourers was 'Deplorable'.[229] Indeed, Tod's gathering at Pitmain revealed that by mid 1778 the Duke's Badenoch lands contained fewer than 200 men suitable for military service, 'so much has this Country been drained during the last three or four years'.[230] The local economy – ploughing, harvesting, peat-cutting, and services – was still heavily labour-intensive. Without the requisite manpower neither township nor tacksman farm could function, and the consequences were potentially devastating.

There was no good time for recruiting. To Invereshie, spring was 'a very unfavourable time till the seed is put in the Ground', while for Benchar, 'the harvest is surely a bad recruiting season'.[231] As factor, Tod was again caught between estate and community: 'if the Duke does not allow the Hands he has already got to return for a Month or two, the Harvest Work can never be properly accomplished'.[232] He described his own experience, how his horses had 'lain idle these eight Days owing to my not being able . . . to procure Hands to work them'. Indeed, the spring sowing would have failed if 'it had not been for Athol Refugees', fleeing, ironically, from their own recruiting parties.[233] McHardy feared the effect on wages: 'with the Scarcity of men . . . they cannot be got cheaper now'.[234] Tacksmen's worries were so great that they even paid to have 'pressed' men released from service.[235]

Wine or not, Tod's meeting with the tacksmen proved fruitless – 'they have unanimously declared that it has not hitherto been in their Power to influence a single Man of their Dependents to enlist': indeed, Macpherson of Invernahavon's son felt obliged to surrender his Fencible commission having failed to recruit 'a single man'.[236] The common people's antipathy to the Fencibles was partly due to the low bounty. As George Macpherson drily explained when referring to the amounts offered recently for the line regiments, 'a Guinea will not sound well in there ears'.[237] But Parson Robert again saw deeper causes – a 'Change of Spirit among the People', that burgeoning sense of independence. Furthermore, he blamed the duplicity of the military: 'They have been so often cheated that they scarce know whom to trust' – specifically mentioning those Highland soldiers who had enlisted for a term of three years or the duration of the war, but had been redrafted into other regiments where they were 'bound for Life'.[238] There were also fears of Fencible men being sent overseas. Captain John, Invereshie (now in Edinburgh), indeed had just written home about the 'poor devils' in the Seaforth mutiny of 1778 who had believed they were being sent to India.[239]

But, for them too, the domestic economy was the biggest factor. It was one thing for younger sons to enlist voluntarily: quite a different matter for the breadwinner. Benchar held back one recruit whose wife and seven children 'will starve if he is not allowed [to] gather his little Crop for their winter subsistance'; Murdoch Macpherson from Nuide begged twenty days' leave because his family were too young to undertake the harvest; and Tod feared that recruiting men from the poorest classes might force their dependants to go 'a begging thro the Low Countries'.[240]

As volunteers dwindled, Ross worried that 'very unlawful methods will be practised . . . & many fine fellows will be drag'd out of the Country'.[241] The most infamous recruiter was John Dow – the Black Officer. He had been active with

Breakachy and Cluny in 1775. Then early in 1778 he raised his own company for Hamilton's, another sixty men for the regiment, and sixteen more for his nephew.[242] The following year he produced seventy men from as far as Ireland for Sir William Maxwell (the Duchess's brother), acquired for 10 guineas each by his 'Dubline Kidnaper'.[243]

John Dow's methods brought notoriety. Captain Shaw of Uvie complained that a recruiting party had broken into his house 'to drag one of my servants from my wife . . . to make him a Recruit for . . . Capt John McPherson [whose] Rugged Banditti Insulte my wife and otherwise used her so ill that an Abortion Insued'.[244] Another man taken by the same party was dragged 'for three days from Glen to Glen & from sheal to sheal in a starving condition as he would not drink whiskie' – an interesting reflection on the mores of the recruiting party. Increasingly concerned, Ross wrote: 'We have many Reports of horrid oppression & Cruelties committed in that Country – which have gained more credite since we heard of the conduct of a Party of John Dows'.[245] As the 'clamour against Captain John' grew, Sir James Oughton, Commander-in-Chief for Scotland, declared that 'if Captain McPherson had been in the Country, they certainly would have brought him to a Court Martial as guilty of many unmilitary practices'.[246]

The Black Officer's reputation was confirmed when the Reverend John Gordon of Alvie vented his rather unchristian wrath on the people for not volunteering.[247] The Duke's tenants were 'Low-lifed People . . . generallie a Stupid obstinate ungratus Generation'; any family who refused to provide a son should be evicted; and anyone failing to volunteer would be 'an open Prey' to John Dow. He ended with a pointed threat: 'leting Capt McPherson [John Dow] lay hold of one or two will make them run to the Duke'.

Forcible recruitment occasionally met with community resistance. When a Lieutenant Shaw, an outsider, tried to recruit a local man, McBean, under the Press (Comprehending) Act, he was met by a mob led by John Dow's wife. Shaw colourfully described the encounter:

> Captain John Dow McPherson's lady appear'd on the head of upwards of sixty men and women with staves and stones . . . Their Godess declar's McBean should not move a step further . . . . I behaved with all possible politeness to her, being a woman . . . her violence led her so far as to call me an eternal scounderal etc.! . . . an unguarded spark kindled in my breast that led me to tell her that none but an ill bred hissie durst tell me so.[248]

The same lady's forceful nature was further revealed by Thomas Macpherson who had deserted from her husband's company. Thomas complained that he was 'seized by Mrs Capt McPherson upon the highway & Confined & his Horse & packs left by her where she apprehended him' – a truly formidable lady![249]

Such desertions were an inevitable consequence of the illegal recruitment in 1778, and many fled to the hills. 'Considerable parties of Deserters . . . were lurking in . . . parts of Lochaber . . . all armed, and consequently very dangerous' – roaming the remote Monadhliath mountains right into Badenoch.[250] With dubious wisdom, Captain Shaw of Uvie was sent to arrest them with a detachment of local soldiers. Unsurprisingly they failed because 'a Number of his Men . . . are connected with & wish well to the Deserters'.[251]

Parson Robert was asked for advice. The army would never succeed, he replied, unless 'powerfully assisted by the Gentlemen in . . . the Neighbouring Countries', implying a certain ambivalence amongst the gentry towards the deserters.[252] Military operations being futile in such a wilderness, Robert's strategy was to negotiate with individual ringleaders – wisely arranging for a bribe, a discharge and a free pardon. Robert and a colleague met in remote Coire Ardair on Creag Meagaidh (immediately above his Aberarder farm) to initiate the plan – though his subsequent report, that 'We drunk many Drams together in Corarder Sunday morning', suggests he was little more enthusiastic about capturing deserters than the other local gentry.[253]

War, as usual, had brought dividends for some. The Duke secured his regimental prestige, tacksmen renewed or embarked on military careers securing a continuing influx of government money, and many of the poorer tenantry took the bounties and wages that would help them and their families through further difficult times. But war had also been a catalyst for the increasingly destructive tensions within the social hierarchy. Moreover, it had strained manpower reserves to the limit, undermining the region's economic sustainability – and with it, ironically, the population base on which future imperialist ambitions would be built. War had, in fact, created a conflict of interests not just between community and estate, but between community and nation.

Conclusion

Between prices, climate, power struggles and war, the 1770s constituted a decade of considerable turbulence in Badenoch, yet, paradoxically, little appeared to have changed. The principal estates remained in the same hands, tacksmen continued to administer their lands and manage their subtenants, while the majority of those were still tied to their runrig townships. Furthermore, Badenoch suffered neither the wholescale invasion of sheep nor the huge emigration experienced in some other Highland regions. Yet such an analysis would be superficial for the undercurrent of change was dramatic.

Undoubtedly the lower orders suffered most. Low prices, famine, rackrenting and eviction caused hundreds to abandon their homeland, not as emigrants to America, but as permanent migrants to the Lowlands, seeking work in agriculture or industry. Population inevitably declined. Indeed, the sources clearly reflect the shortfall of tenants and labourers resulting either from migration or war. Nor can this exodus be viewed with the same positivity that Marianne Maclean found in the contemporary Glengarry emigrations, for these Badenoch migrants, fleeing starvation and poverty, were anything but 'extraordinarily self-confident': still less could their flight be described as 'an ambitious alternative'.[254] Indeed, these migrations mark a significant distinction between Badenoch and the western seaboard. The transatlantic emigrations from the west comprised the self-sufficient middling tenantry with the resources and specie to finance the venture, thereby depleting the area's resources and leaving the more destitute to fill the void.[255] On the contrary, many of Badenoch's Lowland migrants in the 1770s (and also the early 1780s) were the pauperised victims of famine, fleeing in desperation, while the more financially secure tenantry remained *in situ*.

For those remaining, the situation was far from unremitting gloom. Population decline actually enabled existing tenants to increase their allocation of land while some of the landless could step up into the ranks of runrig tenantry. A new security came with the long leases on Invereshie and Cluny, especially with the financial support of the Commissioners. Cattle still yielded cash in the good years while the commercial grazing of Lowland and droving beasts continued irrespective of uncertain markets. Labour shortages brought higher wages, while, after 1775, war provided further economic dividends. The desire for self-improvement continued to grow, undoubtedly sharpened by the famine years, while Parson Robert's phrase, 'aspiring to independence', highlighted both their growing assertiveness and the widening rift between commonalty and gentry.[256]

Those gentry, the clan elite, were also buffeted by change. While tenaciously clinging to the antiquated social system from whence derived their power and status, they were simultaneously embracing the economic opportunities of the modern world. In spite of unpredictable markets and the temptations of sheep, commercial cattle remained their economic mainstay. Some espoused agricultural improvement, and the demand for long leases was as much to facilitate reform as for personal security. For others, war and empire provided lifelong careers and incomes. In spite of economic difficulties, the spirit of progress was spreading and the pace of commercialism quickening.

The most dramatic change, however, occurred in the social sector, as the estate went on the offensive. The lesser tacksmen had undoubtedly been weakened by the difficult times, while cumulative rent arrears and the loss of subtenants increased their vulnerability. The security of all was threatened by the Duke's opposition to leases, while the threat to introduce outsiders and sheep further undermined confidence. With the removal of the troublesome leaders of the clan elite, the subsequent disintegration of the clan's collective bargaining power, and the government's ban on emigration in 1775, the tacksmen had little choice but to accept the Duke's terms. Having backed off from confrontation in the post-Culloden years, the estate had clearly re-established its dominance, breaking the traditional independence and solidarity of the clan tacksmen.

The tortuous economic and political circumstances of the early 1770s beg the question as to why the Badenoch tacksmen did not follow their west-coast counterparts to America. The simplest answer is that the gentry as a whole were neither physically driven out by landowners nor replaced by sheep. Furthermore, there is little evidence of a desire to emigrate, and *duthchas* ties do seem to have been unusually tenacious in the region. Though relations deteriorated badly, animosity never reached the point where emigration was seen, as in Moidart, as a means to 'demolish the Highland lairds'.[257] Perhaps the remoteness of the Duke (physical, social and cultural) lessened the antagonism that might have been directed at a more immediate clan chief. Most significant, however, was the diplomacy of the estate officials. Indeed, as the ruthlessness of factors was one of the most common reasons for emigration, Tod's role was particularly important. Crucially, he and Ross recognised that the tacksmen, far from being expendable middlemen, remained the hub of what was still a predominantly peasant economy – not just as the only substantial wealth producers, but as managers, administrators and community leaders. Given the social and cultural nuances of tacksmanship, no outsider, however wealthy, could possibly replace the indigenous gentry without risking the disintegration of the economic and social cohesion of the community.

So the tacksmen remained, but the relationship had changed. Co-operation rather than defiance now paved the way to success – even the irascible John Dow knew that recruiting for the Duchess's brother would facilitate his Ballachroan lease. Furthermore, status came no longer from simple membership of the clan elite, but rather from wealth, which in turn derived not just from subservience to the Duke, but from service to state and empire.

Though change in Badenoch in the 1770s was hardly as cataclysmic as in the west, the traditional fabric of society across the whole spectrum was irrevocably fractured. Though the tacksman might still remain on his traditional land, the tacksman of old was no more. No longer could he assume the arrogance of the untouchable, nor rally the clan in defiance: indeed, his destiny appeared to lie firmly with estate rather than clan. His status, however, had suffered a double blow. That 'Change of Spirit' amongst the lower orders that Parson Robert described meant that the old loyalties binding commoner to tacksman were fast disintegrating. Assaulted from above and below, the very essence of tacksmanship was beginning to evaporate.

Chapter 6
The 1780s: Continuity, Contrast and Seeds of Change

As in the previous decade, the 1780s opened in crisis as Badenoch's economic and social landscape was once again engulfed in famine, plunging the peasantry into yet more desperate times. Parallel to their suffering, the lavishness of the aristocratic Gordons soared to new heights. Between these two extremes the gentry suffered mixed fortunes with some improving their social status, while others succumbed to economic pressures. Yet as the decade progressed there were signs of economic recovery: the droving trade was flourishing, agricultural improvement continued, industry, sheep and sport brought greater diversification, while opportunities abounded for service within the Empire.

Unlike the 1770s, this was not a decade of definitive change – more a gradual evolution within the longer chronological framework, though beneath the surface the seeds of structural change were being sown. It was in many ways a decade that highlights an increasing polarisation within Highland society: deprivation and luxury, small and large estates, bankrupt lairds and nouveau riches, responsible and irresponsible landownership, conservative farmer and imperial adventurer, even tradition and modernity. Woven into this tapestry of opposites were the fortunes and fates of both estates and people.

There was, however, another contrast hovering in the shadows – the emerging dichotomy between image and reality, resulting from the poetic collections published by Badenoch's James Macpherson: *Fragments of Ancient Poetry* (1760), *Fingal* (1761) and *Temora* (1763), loose translations and arrangements of ancient Gaelic verse by the poet Ossian. While Macpherson's personal influence in these works has been much debated, their impact was indisputable as the 'strange cult of Ossian' swept Europe and America, described by one historian as 'a transcendent force in the development of

Romanticism.'[1] As the birthplace of both Ossianic legend and Macpherson himself, the Highlands were inevitably swept along on the tide of this new era of Romanticism. Colonel Thornton might depict the road to Invereshie as 'winding through coppices of birch, exhaling the most grateful, aromatic odours'; Robert Burns might see the Badenoch mountains as 'wild and magnificent'; Mrs Grant of Laggan might sentimentally view 'the meadows, glittering with dew . . . and the curling mists that climb the opposite mountain'. Such Romanticism, however, was strangely at odds with the pervading Enlightenment ethos of 'improvement' and 'civilising' within the Highlands: more significantly, it was in the starkest of contrasts to the famine-ravaged community of the early 1780s.[2]

Famine and Cattle

'These times are truly dismal', wrote Lachlan Macpherson of Ralia in 1783, 'neither favour nor money will procure the necessaries of life for the poor.'[3] This new outbreak of famine was no localised shortage, but a national, even European, failure of corn and potatoes resulting in spiralling food prices. To John Macpherson of Invereshie it was the worst crisis 'since the time of King William'– a famine in the 1690s so severe that it still haunted folk memory.[4]

The crisis began in 1782. In March, Andrew Macpherson of Benchar described 'a dreadful Storm, which has subsisted now without interruption for two months past [and] has created the most dismal Scene of distress in the Country that has happened for very near a century past.'[5] In April, James Ross informed the Duke of a winter 'such as has not been experienced within the memory of man', warning that 'the demand for Victual . . . is amazing . . . there will be great scarcity among us . . . before Harvest'.[6] And it was not only corn. Mrs Grant, shedding her customary romanticism, wrote of her sheep 'perishing in scores'.[7] John McHardy described how 'the greatest part' of sheep, goats & hill horses in Laggan 'are already dead by Smothering', while cattle were 'dying by mere want, and no greater appearance of a Growth of Grass this day [4 May] than in the middle of February'.[8] Nor was it just Badenoch – in the Ross-shire parish of Kincardine, for instance, the 'accumulated distress' of 1782 caused many 'to remove with their families, and settle in the low country', while the nearby lower-lying parish of Easter Logie experienced a 50 per cent population increase as 'whole families came down from the Highlands, on account of the dearth'.[9]

Things did not improve. The 1782 crop was ruined when the unripened corn was buried under a heavy snowfall, the Laggan harvest falling to one-third its normal yield, the resultant meal as 'black as dust'.[10] As 1783 dawned, Tod despairingly wrote to Mackintosh of Balnespick:

> I wish from the bottom of my heart you may be successful in finding Meall – but I beg you may not come over the Spey in Search of it – for we are all starving here already – The Duke proposes importing some Grain – but God knows when it may arrive, or how we shall be able to pay for it'.[11]

In April, John Macpherson of Invereshie explained to Kenneth Macpherson in London how his father, George, had sent a servant with £80 to procure grain 'to keep his own tenants, if possible, alive, till the potatoes would relieve them', but found none anywhere in the north-east, and the money was left with Baillie Grant in Forres to purchase some imported pease-meal. John described how 'many farmers have been obliged to shut their houses, and go about [begging] with their whole families', how people had been reduced to eating sheep that were themselves 'no better than carrion', while fearing that 'there will be many lives lost'.[12]

Kenneth's reply was critical: 'Has not the Great Landed Proprietors with you ordered Grain from abroad, to supply their Tennents – I am afraid, that there is a want of feeling somewhere?' He recounted how the 'ex-pat' Badenoch gentry in London had met to organise charitable relief, adding sarcastically that, while failing to reach agreement, they had 'Sacrifice[d] as many Bottles of Claret & Burgundy as they could carry in Bumpers to the Land of Cakes [Scotland]'.[13] When aid did materialise, the pease-meal that George Macpherson had reserved was taken by the Forres townsfolk – because, Baillie Grant explained, 'the Cry of the Poor People . . . was so great'.[14] More was, however, expected and the Invereshie tenants were told to be there when the next ship arrived, '& those that have ready money will come & be served'. Not only did starving tenants have to make a round trip of at least 80 miles, they also had to pay up front. On Cluny estate the Commissioners organised relief, authorising meal to be sold at cost price or, at the factor's discretion, distributed free.[15]

The Duke, in spite of Ross's earlier warning, only authorised relief in March 1783 –'Bread for his People, in order to keep them from starving' – costing a seemingly substantial £3,885.[16] As before, this was neither purely philanthropic nor altruistic. The grain was sold at cost price (nearly double the previous year), plus carriage, to the starving tenantry. Remarkably, two-thirds of the sum had been recovered before the end of 1783, perhaps, as elsewhere in the Highlands, because of the pride – and sacrifices – of the recipients.[17] Though the estate acknowledged it would probably never recover the remainder, that does not disguise the intention. Furthermore, Ross argued that it was in the Duke's interest 'to save your people from ruin', later reinforced by the new chamberlain, Menzies, pointing out that if tenants were not provided with seed corn and potatoes, a 'great part of His Grace's highland Estate would have lien waste', hence yielding no rental income.[18] An early harvest in 1783 led Menzies to cancel further relief cargoes: 'We have begun to cutt down some barley, which affords plenty of supply . . . the demands from the upper parts of His Grace's Estate [the Highlands] are now but trifling.' – a judgement probably not shared by the Badenoch tenantry who harvested much later.[19]

So desperate was the situation that the state, for the first time, intervened in famine relief, albeit belatedly. In June 1783, fifteen months into the crisis, Parliament lifted restrictions on corn imports, and the Commissioners of Supply were authorised to levy a tax on heritors to purchase supplies. Furthermore, in an unprecedented move, £10,000 was allocated for the purchase of pease-meal to be sold at cost price or distributed gratis at the discretion of the local co-ordinators – sheriffs, gentry and ministers.[20] Though it has been rather cynically suggested that such government assistance was a recognition of the region's importance 'as a nursery for the armed services', it must, in fairness, be noted that there was not the slightest hint of this in either the report of the parliamentary committee or in the numerous submissions from the Highland gentry, their concerns being entirely humanitarian.[21] It is also generally accepted that at the end of the American war the government released supplies of pease-meal surplus to military requirements to ease the crisis, but no contemporary evidence of this has emerged in the parliamentary papers, the estate records, or the local *Statistical Accounts*. Nearly all the pease-meal coming into the Highlands in 1782–3 was in fact purchased from Eastern Europe – 'large supplies from the Baltick are Still Expected' (June 1783) – either out of the £10,000 grant or privately by proprietors and merchants.[22] The infrastructure for relief on this scale, especially to inland communities, was inevitably haphazard. Sheriff Fraser of Inverness tried through landowners and kirk sessions to ascertain the needs of local communities, but the process was slow, the Parish of Alvie not receiving desperately needed relief until December.[23] Yet, for all its difficulties and no matter its source, relief was crucial in averting disaster.

Conditions were exacerbated by the Laki eruptions in Iceland in 1783–4, causing climatic cooling across Europe.[24] If Gaelic folklore would remember 1783 as the 'Year of the White Peas' (because of the huge quantity of imported peasemeal), then the sulphurous fall-out of Laki made 1784 the 'Year of the Yellow Snow', culminating in the coldest winter on record at that time.[25] Though no local sources specifically mention this phenomenon, Invereshie suffered some unseasonally harsh weather, for frosts on the 16th and 26th of August had 'blackened all the Crops of Puttatas'.[26]

Weather problems continued. John Macpherson believed the 1786 harvest was 'the worst I ever saw', yielding even 'less than the Pease Year', potatoes on this occasion preventing starvation. In 1787, he recorded, in June, 'driving ... snow, as hard as it can pelt'.[27] That year's harvest weather was the worst William Mackintosh of Balnespick had ever witnessed – on 9 November, he despaired of his crops, 'as yet two thirds uncut'.[28] The harvest of 1789 again brought 'such dreadful weather' that Kingussie's farming minister ruefully commented: 'it requires the Christian virtues of *Faith* & *Hope* to induce one to think of Farming any more. We shall lose both *Corn* & *Straw*, if there does not come a Change soon'.[29] Balnespick again suffered, reporting on 24 November 'one third of my crops rotting in the fields'.[30]

In these difficult times cattle prices proved crucial. The decade started badly. Low demand in 1780 led to complaints that cattle were selling for less than half the previous year's price, causing 'great distress'.[31] The following year, however, sales were 'much superior', remaining so over the next three years, and with prices averaging just over £2, occasionally topping £3, reasonable returns were achieved, even though the livestock losses of 1782 must have impacted on sales.[32] Surprisingly, there is no record of resultant bankruptcies as happened in Ross-shire.[33] Nor, in spite of suggestions of a collapse in cattle markets in 1783–4, is there any evidence locally of any slump in cattle sales or droving income at this time: indeed, John Gordon, a merchant, noted that 'milk cows sell very high owing to scarcity of meal'.[34] Thereafter, prices improved considerably. In 1785, John Invereshie informed his brother, 'You'l have a good pay'd Rent, as Sheep & Cattle have sold very high', with the cattle 'never in better condition'.[35] In 1787, beasts at Falkirk averaged £5 to £6 compared with the previous year's £3 to £4, Invereshie again recording 'great prices', which continued over the next two years.[36]

A sustained run of favourable markets not only mitigated the effects of disastrous harvests, but boosted confidence across the community. This was the era of large-scale commercial droving financed by seemingly limitless credit, with tacksmen and lairds reaping consistently high profits and punctual rents. For the peasantry too, good prices helped compensate for crop failures – John Macpherson commenting in 1786 that, though the harvest was bad, 'the great prices for Cattle and Sheep . . . cheers them up'.[37]

The effects of the 1782–3 crisis in Badenoch cannot be quantified. Hunger and disease must have increased the mortality rate while encouraging further out-migration. Colonel Thornton noticed 'a much thinner audience' at Rothiemurchus church than during his previous visit – 'the spirit of emigration had seized the people of these parts . . . many handicraftsmen and others . . . had actually left the country', though whether heading southwards or overseas was not specified.[38] Yet, apart from an indicative rise in the Kingussie Poor Roll from 26 in 1782 to 46 in 1784, no concrete evidence of the effects of famine exists.[39] Furthermore, none of the local ministers, Laggan, Kingussie or Alvie, made any reference to the crisis in their *Statistical Accounts* written just a decade later, even though all three were resident at that time. Indeed, though mentioning the hardship and praising the relief measures, the minister of neighbouring Duthil did not mention it amongst the reasons for depopulation in the parish, while over in Strathdearn, though many were impoverished through the high cost of importing food, there was no mention of mass starvation or death.[40] The lack of evidence suggests that the region did not slide into the full-blown famine initially feared by Ralia and Invereshie: the crisis averted by a fortuitous combination of circumstances – the lower population base after the 1772 crisis, the increasing cultivation of potatoes, the rise in cattle prices and the relief measures. That does not, however, deny the appalling suffering of the community in 1782–3, a suffering dramatically highlighted when contrasted with the outrageous extravagance of the Gordons.

Extravagance

In January 1779, Charles Gordon, the Duke's Edinburgh agent, already struggling to finance his employer's multifarious demands, received a letter that clearly got under his skin. He wrote angrily to Ross: 'as a Specimen of the *Urgency* of one of the Mouths to be filled, I send you the Inclosed[;] Lady Charlotte's Demand for her Annuity'.[41] The Duke's eldest daughter did not mince her words:

I write this early to prevent the inconveniency occasion'd by the last payment being so long delay'd. I know from good authority that it is the Duke's pleasure I should receive it when due so shal axcept of no excuse to the Contrarey.[42]

To be addressed thus was bad enough: more galling still that the author was a girl of ten – but it was symptomatic of the malaise afflicting the Gordons, for financial problems permeated estate administration, impinging on the lives of every Badenoch tenant.

Expenditure was soaring. Debts of £29,000 in 1765 had risen to £54,288 by 1773, and Ross warned of 'an Abyss of Debt.'[43] Credit was increasingly hard to raise: in 1770, the Aberdeen Bank had called in a loan of £4,000, and in 1774 'refused to give Cash or Drafts on your Graces Bill.'[44] Ross again warned the Duke of the impossibility of 'raising money here to support the rate of Expence that has been going on these Two or three years past in Buildings, Politicks & other articles', adding pointedly, 'It cannot be done from the Estate.'[45] The admonition went unheeded, and in 1778 debts reached £86,508.[46] 'Malicious reports respecting the Duke's Circumstances' were circulating: 'Fifty thousand pounds due to Lord Aberdeen – The same sum to Baron Gordon – the debt contracted by building seventy thousand pounds – and twenty or thirty thousand by political contests – the whole estate sequestrated.'[47] Ross worried, 'although these reports are false they will have a very bad effect for some time', seriously damaging his attempts to raise sufficient credit to satisfy the family's demands.[48] By 1790, debts had spiralled to £110,000 – a near fourfold increase in twenty-five years – with the annual interest of £2,440 far exceeding the total Badenoch rental.[49]

The rebuilding of Gordon Castle at Fochabers was the estate's black hole (Plate 10). With a frontage of 558 feet (172 metres) and 184 windows it was variously admired as 'one of the noblest palaces in North Britain', 'as magnificent as any in Britain', 'perhaps the grandest in Great Britain.'[50] Its magnificence would, however, be the estate's downfall, for an army of masons, carpenters, labourers and carriers was required for over a decade. Apart from the vast tonnage of stone, cargoes of slate (over 14,000 in one shipment alone) were transported from Ballachullish, while, because native wood was, in architect Baxter's opinion, of 'the roughest, coarsest kind', innumerable shiploads of superior timber were imported from Russia and the Baltic.[51] Ross expressed his concerns to Baxter over 'the great additional number of hands you have sent North', for the unpredictable arrival of cargoes often left workers idle, while further worries arose from providing fodder 'for enough Cattle to drive the Stones, Wood, Lime, Etc that will be needed to keep all your people at work'.[52]

Building expenditure, over £11,000 between 1771 and 1773, remained constantly high.[53] Ross struggled to find the cash: 1770, demanding the Badenoch rents 'as you know Money is much wanted here'; 1771, unable to pay for foreign timber because 'the Highland Rents are very backwards'; 1774, trying to raise £1,000 within two weeks because it was 'Impossible to answer weekly demands for masons'; 1777, another loan because 'the Buildings will be very heavy this Season'; 1779, unable to pay Baxter 'owing to the bad sale of Cattle'.[54] The dependence of the ducal residence on the Highland tenantry's rents was never more explicit.

Moreover, the valuable Forest of Glenmore was stripped of timber: in February 1770, Ross recorded, 'It will be necessary to cutt down a very considerable number of Trees as soon as possible'; in May, an extra 3–4,000 feet above the 6–8,000 already cut; in 1771, 400 hundred more trees felled for floorboards, and so it continued.[55] Then 'the expence of cutting, floating etc must come high', with a costly dispute over floating rights between Loch Morlich and the Spey, for the connecting rivers, Druie (also known as Beanaidh or Bennie) and Luineag, crossed Rothiemurchus land.[56]

Political ambition proved equally burdensome, for the Duke's influence rested on guaranteeing a solid Tory bloc from the north-east constituencies. In the 1773 Elgin Burghs election the Duke was 'determined to spare no expence'; in 1774, he was supporting candidates in Banff, Moray, Aberdeen and Inverness, causing Ross worries over 'the great demands of his Politicall affairs'; in the 1780s, he threw his support behind William Pitt and Henry Dundas, (Scotland's political 'manager', and the Duchess's lover), fighting numerous elections such as the Elgin Burghs in 1780, 1784 and 1790.[57] Costs mounted over the creation of fictitious votes (£1,600 in 1790 alone), endless legal issues (£8,000 in the early 1770s), and financial inducements.[58] Political 'entertainment' proved so heavy that the Duke was advised to reduce 'the frequency of Company at the Castle by reason of Politicks'.[59] The Northern Fencibles further drained finances, leading to another warning 'That no new Political Pursuit, attended with Expence be embarked in'.[60]

Nothing, however, rivalled the family themselves. Between 1771 and 1773 their personal expenses totalled over £27,000 – an interesting perspective on the £3,885 famine relief in 1783.[61] While annuities to Charlotte and her siblings amounted to over £1,400, the real problem lay with their mother, Lady Jane

Maxwell, the 4th Duchess, for whom life was an endless social extravaganza.[62] Captain Hart wrote from Edinburgh, 'The Duchess of Gordon keeps the whole Town alive – private parties almost every day, and on Saturdays amazing publick routs, where I am told there are in generall three or four hundred people', adding that some found it 'disgusting'.[63] While General Grant in London might have been 'captivated by [her] all powerful and fascinating charms', douce Edinburgh citizen David Drummond was scandalised by 'the example of dissipation set by her Grace':

> It is really astonishing to think what effect the conduct of a single person will have on public manners when supported by high rank & great address. She is never absent from a public place & the later the hours so much the better it is often four o clock in the morning before she goes to bed . . . Dancing Cards & Company occupy her whole time.[64]

Debt became so critical that the Duke's advisers imposed restrictions in 1780 – selling the London residence, the Duke and Duchess to receive only £400 personal allowance each, total expenses limited to £5,000 per annum.[65] But next year Ross complained again that he could meet no other demands because 'the Dutchess's Establishment in Edinburgh . . . has drained me so thoroughly'.[66]

Political ambitions greatly increased the problems, for the Duchess became London's 'most powerful political hostess' in the late 1780s, maintaining her status through the next decade, and ousting her arch rival in politics and fashion – not to mention debt – the Duchess of Devonshire, doyenne of the Whig party and former leader of the London elite.[67] Lady Jane's political influence was remarkable. Deliberately exploiting her Scottish and Highland identity through extensive use of tartan – even forcing London society to perform 'Scotch reels' – she galvanised Tory fortunes through lavish balls, banquets and parties. She was 'of Infinite service [in persuading] the Young Men' to support the Tory party, by 'holding nightly gatherings of them in Pall Mall [her London residence]'.[68] Prime Minister William Pitt was a close confidante, and valued her support; as mistress of Henry Dundas, Pitt's right-hand man, she had influence over the choice of parliamentary candidates in Scotland; not least, she was greatly admired by both king and queen. Lady Jane acted unofficially as 'a Whipper-in of Ministers [using] her rank, her sex, and personal attractions . . . to send for members of Parliament, to question, to remonstrate, and to use every means for confirming their adherence to the government'.[69] She was also directly involved in politically sensitive issues like the Regency crisis of 1788, and, ironically, in resolving the Prince of Wales' debt problems.

But celebrity came not alone. Her Tartan Ball of 1787 was ridiculed: 'great people by courtesy and etiquette seem entitled to play the fool in any style they please'.[70] Gossip flew that she had 'lost thirty thousand pounds at play in the course of winter in London – and besides played away eight thousand pounds upon *one* unfortunate game at back-gammon'.[71] Over the next decade her spending spiralled out of control. In 1791, her London debts alone amounted to £9,000.[72] After separation from the Duke, her allowance of £4,000 for the first year and £3,500 annually thereafter inevitably proved inadequate.[73] After practising 'the greatest economy' in 1794, her housekeeping necessities alone amounted to £4,056. In May 1796, her London debts totalled £3,416, and when the estate requested details of all her unpaid bills, she itemised such costs as 6s 3d for laundry bills, while claiming £888 on 'sundries'.[74] So disastrous was the situation that the Duke and his Commissioners held crisis talks 'to prevent the Dutchess from running him deeper into Debt, Having discovered . . . that her Grace had exceeded her allowance, large as it was, to the amount of some thousands'.[75] Between 1791 and 1809 she cost the estate £112,000, 20 per cent of entire estate expenditure.[76]

In terms of 'conspicuous consumption', few could emulate the Gordons.[77] Had their social and political ambitions been funded out of the Duke's own endeavours it could be excused as the foolish squandering of personal wealth, but squeezing it from his impoverished Highland tenantry was tantamount to the same gross economic recklessness that characterised Europe's *ancien régime*. It was not, as has been argued of landowners, that 'rising rents inflated social pretensions', more that rising social pretensions necessitated inflated rents.[78]

The Gentry

Gordon ambitions did indeed bring a further rent rise in 1786. Though a modest 8 per cent, the estate rental had actually doubled since 1770 and tripled since 1750.[79] Harsh times or not, the Duke refused to renew any lease in 1784 'until the arrears are previously cleared up'.[80] Secret bidding brought further inflation. Fearing competition for his farm of Strone, Andrew Macpherson of Benchar offered a rent that 'hurt myself considerably'.[81] His half-brother,

Parson Robert, also threatened by rival bids for Dalchully, had 'been sweated most confoundedly' to secure a renewal.[82] Nevertheless, he appreciated the resulting security, though still only nine years: 'Dear as the Farm is I am very well satisfyed that I am now in no apprentions [apprehensions] of a Removal', for he had a 'dread of interrupting a Course of Life which I found of such a benefit'. Security was worth paying for, as the estate well knew.

The strong attachment to land re-emerged as the Breakachy and Uvie families ousted in 1773 tried to regain their lost domain. In 1779, Hugh Macpherson requested his 'old duchas' of Uvie, but the estate imposed such strict conditions that the family again refused.[83] Then in 1784, Duncan Macpherson (formerly of Breakachy) stated that he was 'Desirous to recover & possess the Duchas of our Predecessors . . . in such a manner as will enable us to keep the men (not the sheep) on your Grace's Estate', offering £435 plus a grassum of £200 for a consolidated group of eight farms (worth only £170 in the 1786 rental).[84] In spite of the generous offer and the promise not to depopulate – pandering to the Duke's military ambitions – the estate declined. The concept of *duthchas* was, however, fading. Macpherson of Strathmashie was desperate to regain the family heritage taken by the Macdonalds in 1778, but his grandson, an officer in India, commented, 'in our days these matters are of no consequence' – even the most fundamental of clan beliefs was suffering erosion.[85]

Though the tacksmen's wings had been clipped in the 1770s, the vacuum of absentee landlordism ensured their vital role as community leaders continued. The letters of the Badenoch gentry (wives and daughters included) reveal a cultured society, though their educational background varied. Mrs Grant commented on 'how plainly people of the middling rank educate their children here', probably attending the parish schools, as did Alexander Macdonell of Garvabeg's children at Gergask.[86] The grammar school in Ruthven burgh (where the young James Macpherson himself had been both student and teacher) had provided a sufficiently good education to help prepare local youths for university.[87] For the more affluent, city schooling was the goal. Some certainly boarded in Inverness, like Captain Lachlan Mackintosh's son William who made 'very little progress' and was consequently sent to England to finish his schooling.[88] Evan, son of the old Uvie tacksman, had received a 'classical education', though where is not known.[89] John Macpherson of Invereshie sent his two boys to Edinburgh – which, though 'both dear and distant', was the only place in Mrs Grant's view to acquire 'a genteel education'.[90] Benchar's desire for his children was 'to expend my little fortune upon their Education', and his comment that 'my son when his Education is finished, may, perhaps, incline to a Country life' implies a city education.[91] Nor was it just boys: Mrs Macpherson of Killiehuntly had been 'educated as a Gentlewoman'; Peggy and Jess Mackintosh at Dunachton (Captain Lachlan's daughters) were sent away for education to Banff, costing £26 for six months' board, education, music books, writing, and music master, with Jess finishing her education in Edinburgh; Peggy Macpherson of Inverhall attended boarding school at Inverness; while John Dow's daughter, Isabella, emerged from her education as 'elegance, vivacity and truth personified' – not quite in her father's image![92]

Some attended university. Parson Robert had studied divinity at Edinburgh in the 1750s, and two of his sons later studied law and medicine. James Macpherson attended both King's College and Marischal College in Aberdeen, and possibly took some classes at Edinburgh as well. John Maclean's son, James, also studied divinity. In 1750, Donald Macpherson, a young Cluny relative, was studying law at Edinburgh; John Macpherson of Pitchurn also had legal training; Alec Macpherson of Drumgellovie was practising law in Inverness at the turn of the century.[93] Books were a valuable enough part of the household to be included in the Invereshie insurance schedule. Reading material was freely exchanged, Tod sending books to George Macpherson, 'which might be new to you', while John Dow subscribed to a 'share of a year's newspapers'.[94] Parson Robert's letters, written from America during the Seven Years' War, contained literary references that his friends at home would clearly have recognised, suggesting, for instance, that he and William (Invereshie) 'in our friendship might thus Resemble Taliacotius's Noses and their parent, Porter's Bum', a reference to Samuel Butler's late seventeenth-century satiric poem *Hudibras*.[95] For others, worldly wisdom was acquired through the cosmopolitan education of military careers. Mrs Grant reflected favourably: 'Our neighbours abound in courtesy and civility, and many of them, having been abroad in the army, are sufficiently intelligent.'[96] Awareness of topical issues is indeed apparent in local correspondence, with Benchar emerging as the social hub: Captain John Invereshie, writing from America, wryly commented of Andrew Macpherson, 'his house I suppose is still the Courthouse, or Coffee house of the Country – where all controversies are decided'![97]

Status was enhanced through positions of responsibility. Four or five tacksmen regularly sat as Justices of the Peace with the local heritors on the Ruthven Quarter-Session Court, dealing with issues as diverse as labour shortages, recruitment, public works, statute-labour, public house licences, arbitration, and the general maintenance of law and order.[98] As kirk elders they not only collected and distributed the poor funds, but served as the region's moral guardians. As such, the tacksman's social profile was little different from the heritor's.

While their ruthless side has been frequently criticised, tacksmen, as demonstrated in their response to the famine of the early 1770s, had an important social role. Alexander Macdonell of Garvabeg wrote to his lawyer to get help for Angus Macdonald, 'not worth a pound in the world', who was being sued for an ounce of tobacco worth only 2d: 'The poor man is in great distress . . . he does not know where to go, or what to make of his family or his cattle.'[99] Garvabeg also paid a debt for a small tenant, gave money to a widow and child, protected a tenant injured after a drunken brawl, and arranged the discharge of an unwilling recruit.[100] He even provided employment for a needy subtenant: 'McIntosh is a poor fellow that I wish to help, and I put this job [droving] in his way merely to support his poor ffamily.'[101] Such community concerns are paralleled in Balnespick's account book.[102]

A taste for fashion was emerging, though meeting with Mrs Grant's disapproval: 'That rage for elegance, that passion for show, that frenzy for false refinement and artificial luxury.'[103] Cluny's new house in 1744 with eighteen 'fire-rooms' had cost £1,000. Though destroyed by Loudoun's troops in 1746, it had been rebuilt in the 1750s, and again in 1783 for £1,500.[104] In 1760, Invereshie was rebuilt with slate roof, with just a few of the bills totalling £785.[105] Not all lairds, however, could afford such improvements. In 1779, the 'Mansion House of Raitts', still with its upper walls of turf, was 'in very great disrepair': in 1787, the rebuilt house still had a thatched roof, and was not deemed 'sufficiently good for constant residence'.[106]

Tacksman houses also revealed the desire for improvement: there was a 'sclater's [slater's] croft' at Pitmain, Balnespick employed a mason and slater for his buildings, while John Dow was constructing a new stone house for himself at Ballachroan in the early 1770s, though still with heather thatch.[107] Twenty years later he built a more impressive residence from the stones of the recently abandoned Kingussie kirk (further blackening his reputation), even reconstructing the arch of the church door as a grand entrance that still stands starkly over the now-deserted farm (Plate 11a and b).[108] Alexander Macdonell of Garvabeg when trying to avoid his window tax pleaded that his 'little house' had 'only seven windows', actually indicating a reasonably sized building. Easily the most impressive tacksman house, however, was that of Captain Lachlan Mackintosh (son of 'Old Balnespick'), a two-storey mansion house at Kincraig with wings, game larder, ice-house and ballroom – sufficiently large that when

Nelly Mackintosh took it over after Lachlan's death she shut off six windows as a tax avoidance scheme (Plate 12).[109]

A modest desire for fashion and luxury pervaded life. Church, city and entertainment all required suitable apparel. Captain Lachlan Mackintosh's inventory reveals the ex-officer's wardrobe in 1786. Amongst the more exotic were 'A Suit of Crimson Coloured Clothes', two 'Regimental Short Coats' and 'Seventeen Ruffled Shirts', though many were now 'much worn.'[110] Diet remained relatively plain, but Mrs Grant sent to Inverness 'for elegancies and superfluities; elegant sugar and superfluous tea', essential for providing 'entertainment for the superior class'. She also noticed the lavish expenditure on food and drink at local roups (auction sales of stock and equipment), 'whether it can be well afforded or not'.[111] Silver accoutrements appeared in the homes of gentry like Invereshie and Inverhall – candlesticks, wine strainer, sugar tongs, spoons, spurs, teakettles, shoe buckles, while a mahogany tea chest testified to fashionable tastes.[112] John Dow bought a feather bed.[113] Young Jess Mackintosh of Dunachton acquired a new-style 'Piano Forte' in 1795, shipped to Inverness by sea – though for the difficult journey to Kincraig she requested that it be 'slung between two horses', fearing that any other mode of transport 'will put it out of tune'.[114]

Human issues were ever-present. Mrs Macpherson of Invereshie voiced the universal fear of a mother for her daughter over the new medical process of inoculation against smallpox: 'But I am afraid of the Consequence, and yet if she takes them in the natural way I shall blame myself for not doing it, in short I am so divided with two opinions that I don't know which to pursue.'[115] Parson Robert, not surprisingly, took a more traditional view of medicine, taking nothing 'Except Port Wine which I have drunk an English pint a Day . . . to cure my Stomach of Flatulency and as the best medicine I have yet found for my Legs'.[116] Heavy drinking was universal. While local whisky was obviously never in short supply, imported liquor was also an essential commodity in wealthier households. In 1771, Mackintosh of Balnespick's rather modest cellar boasted one dozen bottles of port, four dozen bottles of wine and some bottles of rum; the following year, twenty-five bottles port, five bottles of Malaga, and more than two ankers (20 gallons) of rum.[117] After one celebration, Captain John Invereshie complained he had 'suffered so much from my late debauch', while Parson Robert attended a cattle market where 'A Carousing will probably ensue that may curtail two years of his life considering his bad habit of body'.[118] Robert even reminded his friend William of less salubrious youthful pleasures with his 'old acquaintants at Lucky Japps' – an Edinburgh establishment run by 'Honest' Mrs Japp, who had 'enticed more young Nymphs to appear at the Shrine of Venus, than any other priestess ever did in this city'.[119]

Though not the ostentatious luxury of the aristocracy, there was clearly a growing taste for indulgence – perhaps reflected in personal size, with Parson Robert at over 18 stone, John Invereshie, 19 stone ('as fat as a whale'), his brother William, over 22 stone, and John and Evan Macpherson of Benchar described as 'the late fat captain' and 'the present fat captain' respectively.[120] Colonel Thornton recognised the changing tastes even in his few years of visiting during the 1780s, though not with approval: 'Luxury and effeminacy have proportionally found their way hither.'[121] There is indeed little doubt that the lifestyles of the gentry reflected both an increasing prosperity and a desire to keep pace with southern fashion, though, with the additional burdens of education, military commissions, city jaunts, and legal bills, financial difficulties were seldom far removed. But even if the outward trappings of status proved hard to maintain, the gentry as a whole remained secure in their traditional role of community leadership.

Cluny

With all fear of further rebellions gone, the annexed estates were returned to their former owners in 1784. Much criticism has been directed at the management of these estates: Allan Macinnes, for instance, condemns the Commissioners for their 'manifest neglect of improved agriculture', even suggesting that their policies became an 'official model for clearances'.[122] Such criticisms, however, often arise from seeing these estates in isolation rather than in comparison with those under private ownership. That said, Cluny estate's first twenty-four years under the Barons of Exchequer – the double-rent fiasco, the total lack of improvement, and the Aberarder clearance – were little short of disastrous. After 1770, however, the Commissioners did introduce significant improvements on Cluny, not least over rentals. Though the Commissioners have rather astonishingly been criticised for maintaining low rents, the policy protected the Cluny tenantry, rich and poor, from the excessive rises experienced elsewhere – only 25 per cent increase by 1784, compared with 200 per cent for their Gordon neighbours over the same period.[123] Furthermore, the ordinary Cluny tenants had the security of twenty-one-year leases with the reinvestment of rents to help finance improvements: benefits their Gordon counterparts completely lacked.[124] Similarly, the Commissioners gave the Cluny tacksmen forty-one year leases in the 1770s, while at the same time the Duke withheld leases from his tacksmen for six years before reluctantly granting seven-year terms.[125]

There was also a willingness to support the commonalty. David Moncrieffe (secretary to the Barons) told James Small 'to give the poor Tenants all the relief they can', and manipulation of feu duties enabled the factor to reduce rents slightly, while meliorations (allowances or compensation) were granted for house improvements.[126] Small also supported the rights of the poor tenants against oppressive local gentry. Investment in the estate provided further community benefits – annual premiums for potatoes, a new ferryboat at Catlag, a new parish schoolhouse, church and manse, repairs to the waulk-mill, mill dam, and public house at Catlag, and not least, three new schools, including a spinning school with lint and wheels provided.[127] Agricultural commentator, Andrew Wight (admittedly a Board employee) rather exagger-atedly praised the achievements on Cluny by 1780:

> The houses and offices in each farm are neat and commodious. The grounds are inclosed by sufficient stone walls; good pasture; ... barley and oats growing vigorously. ... The people ... sensible that there is no intention to squeeze them [through increasing rents], have taken heart to make the most of their possessions; and they have succeeded accordingly.[128]

The Commissioners are, of course, open to criticism. At least ten small tenants were cleared from the Aird and Milton to expand the Mains farm, and all five tenants from Middletown were removed to provide land for the new Dalwhin-nie innkeeper.[129] Furthermore, the overall financial investment on Cluny was minimal compared with the £1,000 on Strowan and £2,000 on Barrisdale.[130] Nevertheless, in contradiction to the contention that the 'Board made very little impression on its Inverness-shire estates', the Cluny tenants of 1784, both gentry and commoner, undoubtedly enjoyed far better conditions in terms of rent, security and improvement than their Gordon neighbours.[131]

Nor was the return to private ownership necessarily a blessing. Colonel Duncan of Cluny, son of the attainted chief, immediately denounced the long leases, while complaining about his rents being lower than his neighbours'.[132] Criticising both the security and the moderate rents of his tenantry suggests that the people's welfare was not uppermost in the new laird's thoughts. Though there is no complete rental of Cluny estate after 1784, Gallovie reveals the increase on one farm. In 1756, the rent had been £30; at the restoration in 1784, £40 – a rise of only one-third over thirty years. In 1787, Colonel Duncan gave the tacksman, Allan Macdonald of Strathmashie, a new lease increasing the rent immediately to £66 with a further leap in 1793 to £160 – a fourfold increase in less than ten years.[133] Gallovie, stretching the entire length of Loch Laggan's southern shore, was clearly being converted to sheep, and, signifi-cantly, Macdonald removed fifteen tenants in 1788.[134] As Fraser-Mackintosh rather mischievously suggested of Cluny, 'Bad as the factors of the forfeited estates were, I fancy the tenants in Badenoch or some of them would . . . have been glad to see them back.'[135]

With restoration came the last opportunity to rekindle notions of clanship, but the new chief, Colonel Duncan of Cluny, having been born after Culloden, with a fugitive father and a clan in disarray, grew up with neither a role model nor even the concept of chieftainship. His life as a professional officer from the age of fifteen meant that he was more at home in London clubs than in the clan. Indeed, when General Grant enjoyed a drink with some Highland friends, including 'your little chief Cluny', at the British Coffee House in London, he commented that Duncan had 'not been for nearly Eight Years in Badenoch.'[136] His uncle, Simon Fraser, had already warned Duncan, 'he is no Chief who does not make his interest a secondary consideration that ought always to give place to that of preserving the affections of his kinsmen.'[137]

The restoration was naturally welcomed by the clan elite with 'a Grand Ball at Maclean's', and a 'blaze of Bonfires' on the hilltops.[138] Colonel Thornton, the sporting English aristocrat, left a colourful description:

Each gentleman . . . . handed in his tartan-drest partner. The table was covered with every luxury the vales of Badenoch, Spey, and Lochaber could produce; . . . game of all kinds, and venison in abundance . . . . No company at St. James's ever exhibited a greater variety of gaudy colours, the ladies being dressed in all their Highland pride, each following her own fancy, and wearing a shawl of tartan; this contrasted by the other parts of the dress, at candlelight, presented a most glaring *coup d'oeil* . . . The dinner being removed, was succeeded by a dessert of Highland fruits . . . . [then toasts] drank with three cheers, and re-echoed by the inferiors of the clan in the area around us.[139]

While the evening proceeded with Gaelic song, bagpipes and Highland reels, the reference to the 'inferiors' shows that the common tenantry were kept at a respectable distance – the superiority of the clan elite clearly remained sacro-sanct.

Thornton's description of the gathering at Pitmain captures the changing nature of clanship with its conscious display of 'Highlandism', the deliberate and ostentatious cultivation of Highland identity (through dress, tartan, language and music) within the British establishment. Significantly, there is as yet no notion here of a universal clan tartan, with the ladies all dressing according to fancy. Indeed, Donald Macpherson, a merchant in Inverness, was ordering fine tartans 'for the wear of Ladies who are desirous to dress in the uniform plaids of their husbands', suggesting that the new regimental tartans were of greater significance than clan ones.[140]

The changing nature of clan society was further highlighted by the problems of chieftainship. Colonel Duncan of Cluny, according to Mrs Grant, 'took a fancy to live on his estate . . . built a new house, and brought fashionable furniture from London'.[141] But it was simply not for him: 'For half a year he lived hospitably in the halls of his fathers', before returning to London, 'aspiring, as every Colonel does, to die a General'. In 1786, Colonel Duncan Macpherson of Bleaton (formerly Breakachy), now both laird and colonel, and other senior clan gentry proposed a meeting with Cluny, clearly revealing tensions within the hierarchy – an opportunity 'to the Chief & Clan to show each other the reciprocal friendship & attachment which formerly was in a singular manner their Characteristic, & which alwise tended so conspicuously to their honor & interest', adding pointedly, 'It's a pity that such an opportunity should be lost'.[142] Restoring forfeited lands was one thing: restoring former ideals of chieftainship quite another. As both tacksman and chief knew, the Highland world was simply changing too fast.

The Small Estates

Economic difficulties, fashion and lawsuits gradually reshaped the proprietorial landscape. Patrick Grant of Rothiemurchus, entangled with the Duke over floating rights, complained of 'the many drawbacks honest men of small fortunes have in this Country . . . I have neither poverty nor ritchess', but he wished that 'great men would let me alone to enjoy what I have in pace [peace], but some of them prove a greater curs than a Clip[p]ing to the land they live inn'.[143] The Duchess, with a worldly wisdom, warned him against throwing 'money into the hands of the Lawyers from whence it can never return to you'.[144]

First to go was Donald Macdonald of Easter Delfour, who, 'being of an extravagant turn', was bankrupt by 1772, and sold his land to the Duke.[145] The small estate of Phones and Etteridge, with a rental of £86 and debts of £5,000, had also succumbed and was on the market in 1783; similarly the neighbouring small estate of Invernahavon.[146] The most significant, however, was Edward Mackintosh of Borlum's estate of Raitts, which, in spite of the laird's *alter ego* as highway robber, was bankrupt by the early 1770s. Borlum fled the country 'on board a smuggler', with a price of £50 on his head 'on account of some heinous crimes whereof he was accused' – rather wisely, considering his brother was hanged for his part in proceedings.[147] But Borlum's wife, daughter of Donald Macpherson of Breakachy, seems to have done rather well out of her husband's nefarious deeds, for Elizabeth Grant commented rather snidely on 'her ill gotten gear', how she was 'richly dressed for her station', while 'her handsome silks caused many a sly remark'.[148]

The Duke, as principal creditor, eventually forced the sale of Raitts. With both Colonel Thornton and Lord Maitland interested in it as a sporting estate, it might have passed into external ownership. That it did not was thanks to a wealthy son of Badenoch, James 'Fingal' Macpherson, who announced in June 1787 'that it was upon my account Raitts was purchased', paying 8,000 guineas for what was a small, bankrupt Highland estate with little prospect of ever becoming profitable. He also acquired Phones, Etteridge, and Invernahavon.[149] Born at Invertromie, James Macpherson's fame had come from his Ossianic translations. His wealth, however, derived from elsewhere, primarily from his Indian connections, though he also received an annual life pension of £200 for services in Florida and a salary of £800 a year as propagandist for the government, supplemented by academic works like his history of Great Britain which earned him a staggering advance of £3,000.[150]

For all his political cunning and deviousness, Seumas Bàn (fair James), was paradoxically driven by nostalgic clan romanticism. The resurrection of Clan Macpherson was paramount – especially if forever indebted to him. Using his considerable political influence, he helped secure the Mackintosh estate of Lochlaggan for Cluny, installing a Macpherson (Parson Robert) as tacksman; he promoted the careers and fortunes of Macpherson gentry, including the chief himself; and long before 1784 was lobbying for the restoration of clan lands.[151] There is, indeed, a persistent story that the government offered Cluny estate to James who declined it in favour of Colonel Duncan – if true, putting the chief totally in his debt, though it seems unlikely the government would offer it to James when there was a legitimate heir.[152] James's ambition, nevertheless, was a triumphant return to the clan domain, and the purchase of three local estates was a clear statement that the local boy had made his mark, not just on the world, but on the clan. Chief he could never rightly be, but the power behind the throne was a destiny for which he was more than adequately prepared.

Another twist in the Fingalian paradox was that, while fulfilling his dream of Highland lairdship, James largely remained an absentee, for his power and wealth still emanated from London. He wittily commented that having 'surveyed all my *valuable* hills and moors, and drunk almost as much Whisky, as one of their Corries discharges of Water; . . . in prudence, I ought to think of returning to a warmer Climate': in truth it was to deal with 'matters of more importance than my Badenoch concerns'.[153] When resident, though, his presence was welcomed and his hospitality legendary. His close friend, the Reverend John Anderson of Kingussie, punned frequently on the literary associations, describing Raitts as 'the hospitable walls of Fingal', and enquiring of William at Invereshie, 'May we expect to find You at the *Feast of Shells* in the Halls of *Selma this Season*?'[154] Mrs Grant waxed lyrical ambivalence:

> The bard of bards, who reached the mouldy harp of Ossian from the withered oak of Selma, and awakened the song of other times, is now moving, like a bright meteor, over his native hills; . . . He has bought three small estates in this country within these two years, given a ball to the ladies, and made other exhibitions of wealth and liberality. He now keeps a Hall at Belleville, his new-purchased seat, where there are as many shells as were in Selma, filled, I doubt not, with much better liquor.[155]

Changing Raitts to 'Belleville' was but another paradox for a man whose fame was born of Celtic romanticism. While it has been claimed that he was adapting a local Gaelic name (*Bail'-a'-Bhile*), Macpherson was using this continental spelling within a year of purchase.[156] When he commissioned an Adam mansion at a projected cost of £4,000, Mrs Grant reflected on 'how this must dazzle people accustomed to look on glass windows as luxury' – and not just the common people, for such opulence was far beyond the reach of any Badenoch gentleman, chief included.[157]

There is, however, a deeper message in 'Fingal's' return, as he himself recognised: 'I fear the improvements . . . which . . . I intend to give it [Raitts], will never justify, in point of return, the sum which the purchase has cost,' crucially adding that it was immaterial, for 'my resources . . . do not depend on Badenoch rents'.[158] Unlike other local proprietors, climate and cattle mattered not to James: henceforth Badenoch estates would indeed become increasingly dependent on externally generated capital.[159]

Improvement

Improvement on the Gordon estates was still initiated by the more progressive tacksmen whose reforms were highlighted by two eminent agricultural commentators. David Young singled out Hugh Tod of Ruthven (William's brother) and John Dow for their floodbanks, also noting how the latter had increased the value of the Ballachroan pastures twenty-fold. Parson Robert's improvements at Dalchully were 'as good and substantial as any in the low country', including stone-faced ditches and the use of lime, while his farm 'maintains and fattens a vast number of cattle more than when he entered into possession'.[160] The ultimate accolades inevitably went to John Maclean. Andrew Wight described the latest improvements at Pitmain in 1780: '200 acres of low ground adjacent to the river . . . little better than a swamp . . . but now perfectly firm, and bearing good crops of corn and hay. . . . His crops indeed far exceed any in the neighbourhood'.[161] His sheep flock now numbered 1,000, comparable with some of the best dedicated sheep farms in the Borders, while his cross-bred cattle 'draw a greater price than any in that country'. Young agreed it 'might pass for a good farm in any part of the Lothians'.[162] When Maclean moved to Cluny after falling foul of the Duke, his new floodbanks there were particularly admired for being built with stone founds 'to prevent moles from making holes in it'.[163] Such tacksmen were clearly a different breed from those criticised by earlier historians for lack of ambition and 'slipshod methods'.[164]

It was on Invereshie estate, however, that the most interesting developments of the agricultural revolution took place over the last two decades of the century when Captain John Macpherson, having been near fatally wounded at Princetown in 1777 during the American war, took over the reins on behalf of his ageing father, George, and his hypochondriac older brother, William. The extravagant young officer who had once resented the confines of Glen Feshie had matured into 'a very accomplished gentleman' according to Colonel Thornton.[165] Like his father, John lived on the estate, working directly with the tenantry and initiating judicious improvements through personal example.

Top priority was, as always in Badenoch, flood control. John employed a

Colour plate 1. Lynallan in Phones, a typical deserted Badenoch township showing the ruins of a turf house, the scanty arable at over 900 feet, the birch woods, the contiguous moorland grazings and the distant hill pastures. (D. Taylor)

Colour plate 2. The woodlands at Aviemore, providing vital pasture and shelter for livestock as well as raw materials for tanning, tools, furniture and buildings. (Source: NRS, RHP13927, Plan of Bulladern, Aviemore and Grenish by George Brown, 1809. By the kind permission of the Honourable the Lord Seafield.)

Colour plate 3. The great natural hay meadow at Raitts/Balavil, one of the largest Bishop Forbes had ever seen. (D. Taylor)

Colour plate 4. The vast hill grazings of Badenoch comprising 96 per cent of the land – this particular area belonging to Garvabeg in Laggan. (D. Taylor)

Colour plate 5. One of the mid Glengynack shieling bothies. The eighteenth-century environs would have been much greener thanks to the intensive grazing and manuring. (D. Taylor)

Colour plate 6a. The entrance to Corrydoan (now Coire Dhomhain) with the steep corrie of Corriecragganach (now Sgearnaich Mhor) where Flichity's cattle fell to their deaths. (D. Taylor)

Colour plate 6b. Corrydoan seen from Corriecragganach, with the vast Drumochter plateau on which the cattle grazed at over 3,000 feet. (D. Taylor)

Colour plate 7. The Raitts (Raiths) improvements contrasted with the scattered runrig townships of neighbouring Dunachton estate, as shown on General Roy's map of the 1750s. (Source: British Library Maps, C.9.b26/4. © The British Library. Licensor www.scran.ac.uk)

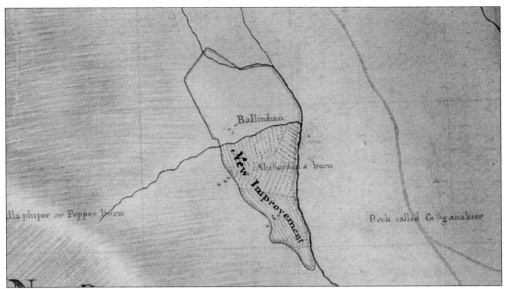

Colour plate 8a. Donald Macpherson's 'New Improvement' at Ballindian (now Ballintian), as shown on Tennoch's map. (Source: NRS, RHP3489, William Tennoch, The annexed estate of Cluny, 1771. Crown copyright, National Records of Scotland.)

Colour plate 8b. The 'New Improvement' today as seen from Ballindian – still an oasis of green pasture in the moorland, though as arable it could 'never yield much profit'. (D. Taylor)

Colour plate 9. A small patch of arable rigs on Tullochroam last cultivated in 1770. (D. Taylor)

Colour plate 10. The great canal of 1790 to drain Loch Insh, now much silted and overgrown. (D. Taylor)

Colour plate 11. The remote shieling of Dalenlongart on Loch Ericht (centre, now under forestry plantation), the first commercial shooting lodge in Badenoch. (D. Taylor)

Colour plate 12. The Invereshie improvements of the 1790s: the reclaimed haugh lands of the River Spey. (D. Taylor)

Colour plate 13. The Duchess of Gordon's original cottage at Kinrara. (Source: Aberdeen Art Gallery & Museums Collections, J. Merigot, Kinrara 1801.)

Colour plate 14. Macpherson's huge Belleville (Balavil) floodbanks. Such defences ran the entire length of the Spey on both sides, and on its tributaries – a testimony to the prodigious labour required in agricultural improvement. (D. Taylor)

stone mason to build floodbanks 'with three roes of fail [turf] and six quarter high of stone'; tenant leases specified the maintenance of the huge drainage ditches (still running in grid patterns through the Insh marshes) on which the Invereshie hay meadows depended; the Spey was straightened to remove the huge Loupouchkie loop which slowed the river's flow.[166] John also organised the neighbouring proprietors, in a rare example of inter-estate co-operative planning, to lower the level of Loch Insh itself to 6 feet below its lowest summer level, digging a long canal (still visible just south of Insh church cemetery, Colour plate 10) to drain its waters back into the Spey.[167]

Reconstruction, repair and reorganisation were undertaken, as at Killiehuntly, 'completing the Offices, repairing the dwelling House, and enclosing and Subdividing the farm'.[168] At Invereshie a new stone steading was built and because of 'the danger of a heather thatch' it was roofed with 'fine slate we discovered above Benchar'.[169] Limestone was transported from Dunachton on the opposite side of the Spey, involving 'the Annual Passage of some hundreds of Horses'.[170] Custom peats provided the fuel: 'we have brought the most Pairt of the peats that was upon the Aurdgale to the Lime Killn [we] Build there & one fil of the Lime Killn of Lime Brunt & is to be filled without loss of time again'.[171] Sown grasses and clover were introduced along with new fodder crops like turnips, and the attention given to middens – John writing during a particularly cold spell, 'we can work at nothing but the dunghill' – confirms the vital importance of these within the Badenoch farm economy.[172] Tenants unwilling to follow John's lead were 'encouraged' by removal threats. The six tenants of Ballintua, having been warned out, promised that if they were allowed to remain, 'we shall follow and adopt any plans he may Judge proper to lay down for us, or any regulations, in dividing the land, improving the commonty, and regulations for pasturing'.[173]

John's emphasis on grass, hay and fodder revealed a fundamental shift. 'Our present mode of farming is a ruinous one', he explained to William, 'I find it impossible to manage our present number of [farm] servants, to *profit* or *satisfaction*'. He proposed instead 'to make it more of a pasture one'.[174] Faced with the inevitable paternal disapproval, John wryly commented that his father was 'not quite reconciled to the laying out of the fields in Grass. Tho' he says very little on the subject to me, he often says to Angus that *Corn* is preferable to Grass and that it is a new fashion to dress fields like a Garden'.[175] So serious was the generational clash that John threatened to leave the estate.

With wool prices doubling during the decade, the emphasis on pasture inevitably spread. A sheep walk was established at Gallovie in 1782 by the

Commissioners of Annexed Estates, later expanded by Cluny; another had been set up by Inverhall in Glen Tromie some time before 1783.[176] James Macpherson may have had similar ideas, for in July 1788 his factor on Phones, John Dow, forced the tenants to 'renounce their Possessions and as a good many were illiterat there was two Notarys signing there names'.[177] When local criticism was mistakenly directed at the Duke, Captain Shaw reminded people that these removals were 'at the Instance of Mr. McPherson the Proprietor'.[178] In 1789, James warned more tenants out of Raitts and Invernahavon, though possibly not enforcing these removals.[179] Indeed, when considering purchasing land in 1783, James had revealed his view of Highland estates: 'you have extensive limits for the shepherd and sportsman, together with an influence among the inhabitants'.[180]

Even the Duke broke his own embargo on sheep. Beset by financial difficulties, he reluctantly leased 10,000 acres of Gaick Forest to Robert Stewart of Garth in 1782 for a modest £80 rent.[181] Having been exclusive deer forest, this new sheep walk had little impact on the tenantry who had never been permitted to shiel there. Some of the Gordon tacksmen were also expanding flocks: Maclean had his 1,000, John Dow enclosed land to 'afourd a safe wintering for 600 sheep', while Mrs Grant wrote of hill grazings at Gaskbeg suitable for 'some hundreds of sheep', probably blackfaces, because 'they require even in winter no food or shelter, but what the hills afford'.[182] These, however, were not exclusive sheep walks, but still operated within a mixed farm economy. Indeed, there was still a degree of local scepticism, Mackintosh of Mackintosh voicing his concern regarding Pitchurn in Badenoch: 'as for a general scheme of laying everything under Sheep Tho at present it proves to be a lucrative one I am far from thinking it will continue long so'.[183]

Similarly sceptical was the usually astute Charles Gordon when assessing the economic potential of the emerging enthusiasm for grouse shooting, suggesting that land values would fall 'when the Keeness for Shooting had abated'.[184] The first significant southern shooting tenant in the Highlands, Colonel Thornton ('an eccentric Devil'), visited Badenoch regularly, staying first at Raitts and then Lynwilg, where he built his own 'temporary residence' nick-named 'Thornton Castle' by the Duchess, though demanding the removal of the subtenantry 'to make room for him' – a warning of things to come.[185] These early sportsmen brought little economic benefit, treating the Highlands as a place where they could 'hunt, shoot and fish, apparently without charge or hindrance'.[186] However, the first commercial shooting let in Badenoch was granted as early as 1784. Robert Dundas (Solicitor-General, and nephew of

Henry Dundas) asked the Duke for 'a spot to build a Shooting Hutt upon', at Dalenlongart on Loch Ericht, where a slate-roofed lodge was erected within a year – now the rather more grandiose Benalder Lodge (Colour plate 11).[187] Though but a token rent, this was a watershed development. For the first time, prime hill pasture – Dalenlongart being Biallidmore's best shieling ground – had been transferred from agricultural to sporting use, thereby depriving the tenantry of the distant hill grazings which underpinned the entire economy.

Industry

Though Duncan Grant's early attempts had largely failed, linen was still seen as vital for economic diversification, and 'the best security for [the Duke's] rents'.[188] In the difficult times of the early 1770s, Tod saw it as 'the greatest Improvement we could meet with . . . We have at this present moment 1000 or rather 1500 women quite idle for want of Employment in that way, and who would all willingly work, if they could get Lint & persons to pay them for it.'[189] Tacksmen like Maclean, McHardy and Benchar were keen on taking the initiative, though Benchar was concerned about the seasonal demands of the industry, for the labour-intensive processes of flax dressing might interfere with 'their other more valuable avocations' (harvesting), while Maclean warned of the perennial problem that had undermined Grant's enterprise – transport, 'the great expence of which has . . . put a total stop to spinning and the Generality buy all the linen cloath they use in other Countrys'.[190] Andrew Macpherson had already been awarded £40 by the Board of Trustees for Manufactures for a lint mill at Benchar, but abandoned the scheme because the grant was retrospective and far short of the actual cost.[191] John McHardy also requested a bleachfield at Gaskbeg in Laggan for his brother James, a weaver keen to learn the bleaching business.[192]

Tod, however, wanted the lead to come from the Duke. Alexander Taylor had been instructed in his 1770 survey to point out those sites 'most convenient for bleachfields . . . and . . . for the situation of a new village', and George Brown in his survey the following year suggested that the 'haugh of Kingussie would be the most proper place, and the most centricle in the Country. It is well watered for the accommodation of Bleachfields and manufactures of any kind'.[193] Tod immediately proposed that the Duke invest his recent rental increment in this project: 'I would have His Grace bestow a hundred or two of his additional Rent, in erecting a Lint Miln, a bleaching House, a House sufficient for accommodating half a dozen weavers and Making a Bleachfield there.'[194] Inevitably nothing happened and Tod approached the Board about the need to address the 'State of idleness which has prevailed . . . for many years past', requesting lintseed, an instructor, and money for a lint mill.[195] The initial response was sceptical, quite naturally wondering 'what Effects appeared in that Country, from the Encouragement given in former years' – all the money previously given to Duncan Grant.[196]

Persistent badgering eventually brought results, with Ross reporting to the Board in 1782 on the success of the previous year's endeavours, though still requesting 'skillfull men for directing the people with respect to the sowing of Lintseed etc and for building Lintmilns'.[197] Ten hogsheads of lintseed were delivered for distribution in Badenoch that year – with inevitable accusations of unfairness when John Dow received four barrels to Benchar's one.[198] Benchar's son John denounced Tod as 'infamously partial', and demanded – what else – that 'the injured insulted Country' should hold 'a publick enquiry into the matter'![199] Protests aside, the distribution of free seed continued with a further purchase of '20 Barrells Riga Lintseed' in 1783, though only to 'such persons of the poorer sort, as are most likely to take care of their crops'.[200]

The Duchess, having been advised by her close friend Lord Kames (one of the Trustees) 'to train the young creatures about her to industry', pushed the development of linen in Badenoch, helping 'to procure us a Lint Mill in this Country which I hope will be of much service to us all'.[201] The mill, costing £115, was constructed through the mechanism of service labour, as Tod explained to George Macpherson: 'We have no way of getting materials led to it but by the Assistance of the Gentlemen of the Country', and Invereshie was given free lintseed in return for providing men 'in Carrying Materials for the Lint Miln & shed'.[202] John McHardy took on the new mill, also establishing a bleachfield in Kingussie, though the business would soon fail as his debts spiralled to over £400.[203]

Linen undoubtedly enjoyed more success in this decade than under Duncan Grant. Domestic production was already well established in some parts, for, in 1781, Mrs Grant at Gaskbeg in Laggan was weaving the 'fine linen which my maids have been spinning in the glens all summer', while, in 1784, her farm produced 'flax in abundance'.[204] On neighbouring Cluny estate the 1784 rental noted that 'they raised some fflax upon the ffarms of this Estate'.[205] Later, William Macpherson of Invereshie claimed that 'Every penny [presumably rent] that I now get was made by the Linnen yarn, and the Tennants are exceedingly desirous to have a Mill upon this Estate'.[206] Though this claim

cannot be verified, it certainly suggests a marked improvement in the production of linen, particularly in the female sector of spinning, and also its increasing importance to the household budget. There is, however, little sign of any
significant commercial development, and after the establishment of the lint
mill there is an indicative dearth of references to linen in the Gordon papers
– undoubtedly hampered not just by transport costs but equally by the Duke's
prolonged delay in establishing the village of Kingussie. Furthermore, the
increasing interest in sheep farming in the area would inevitably shift the focus
away from linen as the region's primary textile industry.

The only other business was timber, centred on the pine forests of
Badenoch's eastern periphery – Feshie, Rothiemurchus and Glenmore. Timber
was undoubtedly being felled and sawn there throughout the century, much
of it for local consumption, though rafts of logs and planks were also being
floated down the Spey to Garmouth.[207] Glenmore Forest was, of course, being
plundered for Gordon Castle, though this was obviously not commercial.

The main commercial forestry was at Rothiemurchus where Andrew
Wight described the woods as 'a treasure, to which Mr Grant gives great attention. Saw-mills are erected, and the timber is floated down the Spey.'[208] From
1770 to 1774, the woods, with both sawmill and boring mill, provided London's
water pipes; thereafter, purely local sales of timber were yielding £370 yearly,
twice the estate's farm rental.[209] In 1785, the Glenfeshie Wood Company, a
much more modest concern, was established at Dalnavert (Mackintosh land)
by Cameron and Carmichael, two enterprising local tacksmen.[210] The Duke's
only major contract was the right to fell 100,000 trees in Glenmore in 1783,
'full grown and fit for the Royal Navy', to the English company Dodsworth and
Osborne, for £10,000.[211] Though the estate chamberlain, Menzies, regarded it
as 'a very advantageous Bargain . . . [which] will make a good slope in the round
sum of Debts', the Duke's greatest asset actually realised less than 10 per cent
of estate debt, the £1,000 instalments barely covering the annual wage bill for
servants at Gordon Castle.[212]

This scheme, however, undoubtedly boosted the economy. At least
eighteen men were employed on the harbour, dam and sluices at Loch Morlich
in 1787, twenty-six more on the road through Glenmore, more again to
deepen and straighten the Luineag, blasting boulders out of the river bed, not
to mention the regular forest work of felling, sawing and floating.[213] A local
Gaelic bard captured the activity: 'Our ears are stunned by the crash of falling
trees and clamours of the Sassenachs.'[214] Within twenty-two years, Osborne
recounted, the Glenmore trees had been turned into 'forty-seven sail of ships'

totalling 19,000 tons.[215] Like linen, however, the industry grew but slowly, and, apart from temporarily boosting the Duke's coffers and providing some localised employment, had relatively little impact on the wider region.

Empire

Empire, whether as military, mercantile or administrative service, was becoming increasingly vital to the economic diversification of the Highlands. Indeed, the peace of 1783, coinciding with famine, was not universally welcomed. For Benchar, 'Scarcity at home, and his Son's [Captain John Benchar's] disappointment from the early peace are rather too much to bear', while John himself was 'preparing both Mind and Body for the melancholy condition of half pay'.[216] For the common people, too, peace could hardly have been worse timed. Some wisely accepted the offer of land in British North America: James Macpherson and his brother John, both from Badenoch (possibly Kinrara) and serving in Hamilton's Regiment, received 100 acres each in Pictou – though how many other local men followed suit is not known.[217] But peace did not close all doors, for Britain was enmeshed in wider colonial struggles. In 1787, ongoing troubles in Mysore in India led to the government raising four new regiments. John Dow was again recruiting for his kinsman Hugh Macpherson of Inverhall, though numbers were low compared with the 1770s – perhaps because, in Captain John Invereshie's opinion, of the 'aversion that Highlanders have to a hot climate'.[218]

Outside the military, mercantile opportunities abounded, with the Caribbean proving highly profitable for some Highland families like the Baillies of Dochfour.[219] Badenoch, however, had comparatively little involvement in plantations and slavery, apart from Jamaica where Donald Macpherson of Phones (brother of old Malcolm) had 'acquired a handsome estate', though his success did not prevent bankruptcy at home.[220] Two of Dalraddy's sons, two of Invernahavon's and one of Breakachy's were also training as planters there, and by 1780 Colin of Dalraddy and William Clark from Garvabeg had both become plantation overseers. Breakachy's son John, however, died so poor that he 'cannot afford him a decent funeral' – indeed, the writer complained of how hard it was to achieve success there.[221] For Badenoch, the Caribbean was clearly no panacea, perhaps simply because the local patronage network pointed east rather than west.

India was indeed the focus of Badenoch's colonial interests. War was seldom absent and with both the government and the East India Company raising regiments, military opportunities were plentiful, and after the cessation of hostilities in America many officers relocated to India. As early as 1759, the Duke of Gordon's 89th Foot had sailed for India, many transferring to the East India Company in 1763. Well-educated officials and clerks were also required for administrative purposes, while the rich resources of the continent provided lucrative commercial opportunities. Indeed, India was potentially a quick fix for those with financial problems or simply seeking an easy fortune.[222] Robert Clive cynically noted of Highlanders at this time, that 'their only concern is to quit your service within a twelve-month with a plundered fortune.'[223]

Scots in general had a totally disproportionate influence in Indian affairs, largely through internal patronage networks.[224] One such network helped Badenoch, particularly the Macphersons, to achieve a remarkable degree of success in this fabulously wealthy colony from the late 1760s onwards. In 1769, John Macpherson of Skye (later Sir John, Governor-General of India, 1785–6) made an astonishing assertion: 'Could you imagine that during all the polit-ical fire and action in this seat of mighty Empire [India] two Macphersons have been the only pillars of Government.'[225] John was one; the other, James ('Fingal') – 'incomparably the first Writer, Satirist and Drolist in the Nation', 'as valuable a man upon the whole as lives', and the 'most useful connection possible.'[226] John was already in India, becoming agent for the wealthy Nawab of Arcot in 1768, while James pulled the political strings in London. Perhaps John exagger-ated the Macpherson axis of power, but that the two co-operated in ruthlessly pushing their own – and the clan – interests is indisputable, often correspon-ding in what James called his 'Putney Heath Gaelic' to veil their schemes. James's cousin and close friend, Captain (later Colonel) Allan Macpherson, Allan's younger brother John (later Lieutenant-Colonel), and their cousin and James's nephew, Captain John Macintyre (later Lieutenant-General), all helped create a remarkable clan network out in India.[227]

In 1771, James helped, amongst others, young Alex Macpherson of Strath-mashie to India. A year later John informed James that Alex was prospering – 'You do good in sending these young men.'[228] By 1774, James had helped sons of Benchar, Pitmain, Breakachie, Strathmashie, Ralia and Uvie to establish themselves in India, even lending the necessary capital himself – for instance, £150 for Charles Macpherson, younger brother of Parson Robert, and 'an old school fellow' of Allan's.[229] James boasted of his achievements: 'I have almost depopulated that Country [Badenoch], by sending officers and men of the clan into the army. You will see Col. Macpherson of Cluny soon in India. *Smis a rain shin air a shon.* [I did that for him.]' – written in rather crude phonetic Gaelic.[230]

Parliament, however, was the ultimate home of networking power as James realised: 'A man . . . cannot possibly serve his friends, but through that channel; and my friends have done too much for me, not to excite in me a resolution of keeping myself, in a situation, which may be useful to them.'[231] In 1780, he became MP for Camelford at a cost of £4,000, thereby enabling him to further his Indian interests with both the government and the East India Company directors in London. Nor was this patronage restricted to India, for James had secured military commissions for eight local gentry in 1778.[232] So extensive was his patronage that he was asked by the Russian ambassador 'to procure six young men, qualified to teach different branches of literature, in a College instituted by the Empress [Catherine the Great]' in St Petersburg.[233] Expectations, naturally, were high. Seeking further promotion, Alex Macpherson asked for recommendations that were both 'warm and strong', even listing the influential people James should contact.[234] Captain John Macpherson of Benchar, on half-pay, blatantly requested a full commission in 1787: 'I should certainly imagine that the *Clan* in London could have no difficulty, in the present state of matters, to procure me a company' – a wish eventually achieved in 1789.[235]

James's real power lay in his influence over Warren Hastings, whose position as Governor-General of India was under serious threat. 'I am well with his [Hastings'] friends here and I hope he will pay attention to my friends there', he told John. In one of his coded Gaelic passages he emphasised his power, 'The whole World here knows that he [Hastings] would fall if my hand did not support him', boldly telling John that if it did happen, 'We will put you in the place of Hastings' – as did indeed happen.[236] In an obsequious letter, Hastings thanked James for 'the essential advantages I have received from your friendly offices . . . how strenuous and indefatigable you have been in defence of my Cause'. He had, in return, 'taken every opportunity of expressing my regard for you, by forwarding the views of your relations and connections in Bengal, and you may be assured that I will neglect no opportunity of serving them in future', promising promotions for James's cousins, Allan and John Macpherson, and nephew, John Macintyre. He finished with further grovelling – 'how earnestly desirous I am of attending to your recommendations . . . and receiving your Commands.'[237]

Once in India, men could become 'extremely rich remarkably fast', through private trade, company contracts and administrative dealings, though also through the 'corrupt behaviour of Company servants'.[238] Such men were, of course, not permanent emigrants, but 'sojourners', intent on returning to their native *duthchas* as soon as they had amassed sufficient capital.[239] Colonel Allan was pragmatic: 'We ought therefore to take care of ourselves whilst in office as the only chance of being comfortable the remainder of our lives', though his comment, 'to get Money – Honestly if we can', clearly implies the opposite.[240] Allan and his cousin, Macintyre, in fact accumulated £62,500 through what were euphemistically known as 'presents'.[241] They were also smuggling diamonds back to Britain – in 1776–7 alone, Allan had sent over £3,000 worth for James to sell in London.[242] Indeed, such contraband may have secured James's parliamentary seat.[243] But speculation was fraught with risk. Macintyre personally brought a consignment of diamonds into Britain, but, being offered only one-third of the cost price, he returned them to Allan in India to try to 'recover the original sum the articles were once valued at'.[244] Macintyre's later comment, 'I am willing to sacrifice my life to retrieve the fortune we have lost', tells its own story.[245] Allan himself lost £15,000 in the bankruptcy of his trading partner, Sir Samuel Hannay.[246]

In spite of these losses, Allan still returned with sufficient wealth to purchase the three Highland estates which later ended up in James's possession (costing nearly £13,000), plus a substantial estate near Blairgowrie for £17,000.[247] Colonel Duncan (Breakachy) also had been able to buy at least three Highland estates on his return, while Ralia's son and Cluny each amassed enough to expand their Badenoch lands the following century. Indeed, most of the local gentry did rather well. One tacksman's sons were 'making money . . . Equal to highland fortunes'; Macintyre too had 'made a great fortune'; Allan's brother, John, died shortly after his return worth nearly £6,000.[248] Those at home benefited too: old John Macpherson of Strathmashie acknowledged the receipt of 'Gold Mohurs [coins]' from Bengal sent by his grandson Alex, though knowing 'nothing about their values'.[249] Significantly, when Alex died in India worth only £2,000, he was regarded as a failure, though that sum was thirty-five times the Strathmashie rental.[250] James himself did immensely well. As agent for the Nawab of Arcot from 1781 to 1793 he received an annual salary of £4,800 plus expenses of £15,000, quite apart from the more dubious transactions – a nabob who never set foot in India.[251]

For the Badenoch gentry India proved a veritable honey pot. Within the small sample of James's and John's letters consulted there were twenty-eight named individuals from twenty different local tacksman families who had benefited from their patronage, often being assisted with each promotional step over many years. The total number helped onto the Indian gravy train is impossible to say. Scarce a family did not have some connection, while others, like Benchar, with four sons in India, had multiple links. The wealth that James thus generated for Badenoch, his own fortune aside, is incalculable. Not all the money, of course, made it home, but Indian profits undoubtedly financed much of the region's economic and social development. Though his reputation and character have been savaged by historians and contemporaries alike, it is perhaps unsurprising that James Macpherson was almost universally popular within Badenoch circles. Even the shrewd Captain John Invereshie wrote to his brother William of 'our friend James . . . the Great Fingal'.[252]

Conclusion

Though there was no dominant theme equivalent to the power struggle of the previous decade, the 1780s nevertheless witnessed the steady progression, albeit with frequently contrasting fortunes, of longer-term trends – climatic difficulties, rising debts, the demise of small estates, the importance of empire, and gradual economic improvement. It was a decade easily perceived in pessimistic terms: a society struggling against climatic difficulties, bad harvests and famine, a society of poverty, bankruptcy and failure – a decade far removed from the romanticised views of those early southern tourists. But – without in any way diminishing the appalling hardship of the famine years – such a view would be unduly negative. Potatoes, agricultural improvement, rising cattle prices, gradual industrial development, and famine-relief measures all enabled the Badenoch community's survival. Indeed, the overall impression by the end of the decade is one of resilience, adaptability and even an emergent optimism.

Though the gentry suffered stock losses and rental failures during the famine, most emerged relatively unscathed, and, despite further rent rises, the 1786 rental reveals only two new tacksmen from outwith the region.[253] Seemingly now at peace with the estate, the tacksmen retained their social status, while commercial enthusiasm remained strong among the entrepreneurially minded. Agricultural improvement and droving remained uppermost, but sheep, linen and timber all began to offer alternative paths to riches. The key to wealth, however, increasingly lay overseas, whether through military or administrative professions. The wealth of empire beckoned, and, largely thanks to clan networks, India became the most lucrative route for

Badenoch's gentry to establish careers with, at worst, steady incomes, and at best, fortunes.

Estate success continued to depend on individual leadership. While Invereshie thrived under Captain John's management, Cluny estate's restoration brought an absentee laird whose policies were not necessarily in the interests of tacksman or tenant. For the Gordon estates the situation was worse. With neither investment nor improvement, and lacking external sources of wealth, the Duke's pursuit of luxury and power perennially drained the region's hard-earned specie – indeed, with the ever-increasing millstone of debt, Gordon days were already numbered. But if the clock was ticking for the Duke, it had already struck for the smaller lairds. The economic climate had undermined the viability of their estates, making it impossible for the small and insecure rentals to sustain any semblance of lairdly existence.

While the decade was largely one of natural progression, it did, however, have its definitive moments. The restoration of 1784, rather than rejuvenating clanship, hastened its demise. Cluny's return to London and his failure to exercise chieftainship as understood by the hierarchy destroyed any romantic notions of resurrecting the clan of old. More significantly, the clan was experiencing generational erosion as ancient traditions came to be held in less esteem than professional careers, while imperial opportunity lured the sons of gentry to a future outside the clan homeland. Equally momentous was Dundas's shooting lease, for, though still in its infancy, sport (like sheep) opened the door to proprietorial commercialism. It was a process that would destroy the very basis of the Highland economy, imposing a horizontal stratigraphy on the vertical alignment that underpinned the traditional subsistence farm. The most definitive moment was, however, James Macpherson's entry into proprietorship – not because of who he was, but because of what he symbolised. He was the first to buy estates in Badenoch with externally raised capital, the first for whom land was an adornment rather than an economic enterprise. Indeed, every parcel of land sold in the region thereafter, even when purchased locally, was funded by external capital. Although the 1780s were not in themselves a revolutionary decade, the seeds of radical change had undoubtedly been sown.

Chapter 7
The 1790s: Years of Optimism

While climatic forces had dominated the previous two decades, the 1790s were driven by political turbulence as the shock waves of the French Revolution of 1789 rippled through Europe. Captain John Macpherson of Invereshie expressed his concerns that, even in remote Glen Feshie, 'The spirit of reform, or *I may say* revolution principles – has got so strong a hold of the people *of this Country* [Badenoch] that little encouragement would *blow the flame*.'[1] This 'spirit' impacted particularly on the commonalty, both in developing a more assertive voice and in gaining opportunities for material improvement. The subsequent war between Britain and France, starting in 1793, dominated the century's end, with the ever-increasing military demands of the nation benefiting the entire community.[2]

A different revolution was, however, sweeping the Highlands in the 1790s, as 'some of the most explosive sheep clearances' occurred through substantial areas of Argyll, Perthshire, Inverness-shire, Easter Ross, Sutherland and Caithness.[3] This time, Badenoch did not escape the trauma of clearance, with the rapid spread of sheep farming into the region profiting, as ever, the few at the expense of the majority. Yet, no matter the temptation of profit, proprietorial attitudes to sheep remained divided.

In the shadow of these major events, the interrelationship of continuity and change was delicately balanced. On Invereshie estate improvement continued to evolve through the decade with remarkable success. The Gordons were further undermined by ongoing financial difficulties, though a more positive note was injected by the Duchess's personal intervention in economic affairs. Amongst the gentry, whether laird or tacksman, fortunes varied as some succumbed to financial imprudence while others gained from economic diversification, not least the sheep bandwagon. Once again, the greatest benefits were externally generated as war not only stimulated the local economy but provided the usual lucrative career opportunities. One of the most significant features of the decade, however, was the improving welfare of that most elusive of social classes, the common people.

Continuity and change also affected Badenoch's leading players. With the passing of the older brigade – community stalwarts like Andrew Macpherson of Benchar (1788), Parson Robert (1791), and George Macpherson of Invereshie (1795) – the dominant figure in the region was Captain John, running an exemplary model of Highland lairdship at Invereshie, though never officially achieving that status. Another key figure rising to prominence was the Reverend John Anderson, appointed minister of Kingussie in 1782. 'A young man of Genius, well versed in point of Literature, and of a most unexceptionable Character', his presence would tower over Badenoch for nearly forty years as minister, improving farmer, businessman, and factor-cum-adviser on six different local estates.[4] Like William Tod in the 1770s, Anderson was a factor who acted with an empathy and compassion that belies the Highland norm. It is the prodigious correspondence of both these men – Captain John's detailed accounts of estate business for his absentee older brother William (heir and later laird of Invereshie), and Anderson's erudite and witty epistles to both John and William – that provide a picture of society as valuable as that of Ross and Tod two decades earlier, and almost unique in its intimate depiction of a Highland community at this time.

Invereshie

Estate correspondence naturally focused on the economy, and weather featured heavily, revealing a pattern of severe winters and bountiful harvests. February floods twice wrought havoc. In 1791, an 'Enormous speat . . . levelled all fence & water Dikes to the Ground'.[5] But a far worse one in 1797 brought a typically whimsical response from Anderson (in Edinburgh at the time):

> Your accounts . . . of what Satan has been doing to the good people of Badenoch since I left you are bad indeed; and if I possessed the power over Him that Your old Friend Mr Gordon [minister of Alvie] did, He should not have been permitted to roam at large, destroying all our Improvements.[6]

When an unseasonably warm spell in late February followed the devastation,

Anderson ironically captured the vicissitudes of Badenoch's climate: 'We have the finest weather that ever was seen. What a heathenish Climate you and I live in.'[7]

More serious were the heavy snows and late springs. In January 1792, Laggan suffered substantial stock losses, while the sheep at Ballachroan and Kingussie were 'in a bad way'.[8] The following winter John commented that 'The tennants flocks have everywhere diminished much in their numbers', while Gallovie had lost 'fully one third' – a thousand sheep.[9] Further losses occurred in 1795 after 'a winter of uncommon Severity'; so scarce was provender in the spring of 1798 that 'most of the tennants are in the Low Country with their Cattle – where there is plenty of Corn and Straw'; the following year 'a thousand sheep were smothered in Glentruim'.[10] Significantly, the correspondence highlighted sheep losses, reflecting the shift within the pastoral economy while confirming the perceived unsuitability of Badenoch for commercial sheep walks, primarily due to the lack of suitable wintering.

Serious though these losses were, much-improved harvest seasons enabled the minister of Alvie to note that there was generally 'a sufficiency for the subsistence of the inhabitants'.[11] From 1791 to 1798 John recorded an unbroken run of successful harvests: 1793, 'the richest crop ever seen'; 1794, 'plenty of meal and Potatoes'; 1795, 'a Capital Crop of everything'; 1796, 'luxuriant' crops; while 1797 brought 'plenty of provision for man and beast'.[12] Anderson, somewhat less enthusiastic, complained of incessant rain in 1795, but still harvested enough for 'a Year's Bread without buying'.[13] Mrs Grant of Laggan confirmed the good reports – 'We had last year [1794], in this corner, the best crop ever remembered, and this year's is at least equal', similarly in 1797 and 1798.[14] Considering that the mid 1790s saw poor harvests and soaring grain prices in the north-east, the sun must literally have been shining on Badenoch – to the extent that John was selling corn to the hungry citizens of Forres in 1796.[15]

Buoyant livestock markets further enhanced prosperity. In 1794, high prices were 'of the greatest benefit to the Proprietors and Tenants', and though a drought in England next year caused concerns (grass shortages there affecting the saleability of Highland beasts), cattle again reached 'uncommon high prices'.[16] Indeed, in late November, John reported 'such a demand in the South, that . . . the dealers are driving Sheep and Cattle every week'.[17] Further increases in 1796 enabled John to clear estate debts and prompted Anderson's bizarre comparison of the Invereshie tenantry with 'some opulent Province in South America'.[18] In 1797, cattle prices were 'uncommonly high' and 'most enormous', one beast at Falkirk reaching the exceptional price of £14; newspapers reported an 'alarming . . . scarcity of cattle', and dealers were even advancing money to secure next season's sheep.[19] John remained optimistic for 1798: 'I should think from the number of Troops, and shipping employed – that Cattle and Sheep will give tolerable good prices this year.'[20] Cattle prices remained consistently high: in the early 1790s up to three times higher than 1750, and four to five times higher between 1796 and 1798. Wool prices also nearly tripled.[21] This huge bonus was, of course, as John readily acknowledged, a temporary by-product of war.

Invereshie's halcyon days were not, however, a passive result of war and weather, but rather a product of careful, progressive management. A 1796 rental reveals the extent of tenurial reorganisation. Apart from the Mains itself, the only large farms were Anderson's Dell of Killiehuntly at £105 and Dalraddie at £42. The remainder consisted of eighty-six small single-tenant farms and four joint tenancies (probably family), mainly valued between £5 and £10.[22] A later census identified a similar number of cottars and labourers, probably displaced tenants.[23] These small, self-sufficient farms – held directly from the laird with improving leases and moderate rents – undoubtedly stimulated reform.

Progress, however, required exemplary leadership, and Captain John's improvement ethos was reaping dividends – indeed, his letters buzzed with reforming zeal. Similarly Anderson's: 'We are draining Bogs – and clearing Fields; and planning a Thousand Improvements.'[24] Floodbanks reclaimed riverside haughs rich enough to 'yield bear without manure' (Colour plate 12).[25] John manned the barricades himself – 'I was for several days attending Bulwarks in the davoch of Invermarky from morning till night.'[26] The Feshie defences involved immense effort: 'all the stones were carried from the Ord, many of them six feet long, all the farm horses were leading them for three weeks – and the Stone Lads are still at Work.'[27] It paid dividends in the great 1797 flood. 'On this farm', noted John, 'the Feshie has done no hurt', while Keppoch (a Mackintosh farm) on the opposite bank was utterly destroyed.[28] Similarly, Anderson's new dyke at Dell of Killiehuntly forced the Spey to the north bank, destroying Belleville land – one man's bulwarks were another's ruin.[29] The resultant increase in crops and fodder from the reclaimed land undoubtedly contributed to the improving conditions of the tenantry during the decade.

Plantations were integral to improvement, and John clothed Tom Dow, the hill beside Insh church, with ash, plane, pine and larch, while enclosing and planting the 'Shian of Keppoch'.[30] Building renovations continued, as evidenced by John's complaint that 3,000 stone slates had been stolen from Invereshie – no mean feat by horse and cart![31] Arable fields and moorland were enclosed; names like 'Clover Park' appeared; turnips, peas, rye grass and potatoes enabled crop rotation.[32] Lime was crucial and John had clearly charmed Nelly Mackintosh of Kincraig, whose farm contained an abundant supply of limestone: 'I am now in great favour with our neighbour Miss Nelly, and have . . . got Liberty to quarry as much limestone there as I please', later informing William, 'you would be astonished to see the quantity of lime stone quarried'.[33] Anderson waxed lyrical: 'You never saw so fine a crop on the Lagmore . . . I saw no Oats so good in the Neighbourhood of Edinburgh . . . Such are the Fruits of Liming'.[34]

Nor was the pastoral sector ignored. John rented a substantial park at Belleville, 'the best Grass in Badenoch', pasturing twenty-seven dairy cows there for six weeks in summer, and three in September, also feeding his yeld beasts there in autumn and spring.[35] John's innovation lay not just in keeping a specialist dairy herd, but in using these riverside meadows as a high-quality shieling. The traditional hill grazings, however, remained integral to the estate. Negotiations with neighbouring estates provided security from poinding – 'there has been no trespass money paid from any of your tennants these two years past'.[36] Then, after securing the remote high grazings of Beinn Bhrotain and Glengeusachan in the Cairngorms for his own non-dairy herd, he reorganised the lower land of Glen Feshie as tenant shielings 'in a way that would be very advantageous to them'.[37] Though he himself maintained a flock of around 1,000 sheep within the general farm economy, John admirably refused to establish a sheep walk 'for fear of hurting the tennants arround it' – again protecting their hill grazings.[38] Sheep were, however, clearly being kept in considerable numbers: 'our three sheep drovers . . . carried no fewer than two thousand sheep across the hill last week – this is their fourth trip'.[39] The tenantry were even conducting their own improvements by cross-breeding with imported blackfaces – a 1791 report complained that the native variety was 'quite adulterated', and indeed that no pure-bred native sheep remained in Glen Feshie.[40]

When touring the Highlands in 1803, the Reverend James Hall noted the clergy's role in improvement – perfectly illustrated by Kingussie's minister at Dell of Killiehuntly.[41] Commencing in 1792, Anderson immediately repaired the house and John informed William, 'You will see a great change in the Dell – The bank is nearly inclosed – and the Parson is busy clearing and dressing the ground below it for a Garden – he is Grubbing and squaring the fields at a great rate – and the Cairns of stones are sent to defend the [River] Trommie.'[42] Anderson also built 'a fine road to the Bridge of Trommie', and within a year had completed both floodbanks and field clearance.[43] Huge ditches drained the Dell's waterlogged haughs, and by 1794, the 'wet park' was 'perfectly dry.'[44] Anderson might complain that 'not being a Man of Money' curtailed his ambitions, but he could at least seek comfort in 'the pleasure to be derived from the View of progressive Improvements' – a classic statement of Enlightenment philosophy.[45] Captain John's tribute – 'so valuable a member of society' – was hardly surprising.[46]

Laird and minister set the tone, and the progress of individual tenants was outlined in John's letters: Evan Clark, Garribuy, 'one of your best and most industrious tenants'; similarly Croftmartin and James Martin of Soillerie.[47] The boatman at Insh had limed his 'little croft near the Kirk'; the Inveruglas tenants had 'made a road into the meadows below Croftmartin at their own Expence, that a Coach and Six could drive on'; Malcolm Clark was negotiating a lease in return for house improvements and enclosures.[48] Such endeavour was rewarded. William instructed his brother 'to give Leases to such of his Tenants as are industrious', and a local tenant's son familiar with the latest Lowland methods was given a farm, 'an honest Lad – whose father paid at Least Forty Rents [on Invereshie] – and who studied farming in the Carse of Gowrie.'[49]

As resident laird, Captain John's letters reveal his familiarity with his tenants: 'James Martin, Pennie the Bandussach and the Bairns are well'; a jocular reference to the local boatman, 'He and I look upon ourselves as great farmers'; even remembering two former tenants who had moved elsewhere and were now 'in a fair way of doing well for themselves.'[50] Hard times, like the winter of 1798, brought estate assistance: 'I shall be able to give a little relief to the most needy.'[51] As trustee for an old widow's meagre legacy, he was 'very attentive to the old woman herself, during her life.'[52] Humanity was further revealed in John's attempts to commute the death sentence on Alex Leslie to transportation to Botany Bay, and to free Angus Falconer from his imprisonment for debt in Inverness tolbooth – 'a poor distressed fellow miserably involved by accidents & misfortunes.'[53] When Anderson secured a schoolmistress from the SSPCK, John recorded that 'the tenants with my assistance are building a comfortable house for her at Inveruglas' – the school soon boasting 100 pupils.[54] Bad tenants, however, were not tolerated: John warned William, 'there are some very bad subjects to be removed', while also complaining that 'no Servants can be depended upon.'[55]

Financial prudence underpinned improvement. Referring perhaps to James Macpherson and the Duchess, John wryly commented, 'The neighbourhood of great and rich people will make me *more guarded than ever*.'[56] Anderson admired his thrift: though still 'an improving Farmer ... [John] now *sitts down to calculate* before he commences his operations', and, even more significantly, 'He adheres rigidly to the Maxim of living within his Income.'[57] Indeed, John kept only one male servant, one riding horse, and hired a chaise for longer journeys: his main extravagances being £63 on clothes in 1795–6, and the considerable cost of educating his children in Edinburgh, not just at school and college, but with a private tutor – a kinsman of Anderson.[58]

The dividends of improvement, albeit assisted by war and weather, were remarkable. In 1794, 'all [were] very happy by the certainty of plenty'; in 1795 – almost unheard of – 'there will be a good deal of meal sold in Badenoch [and] plenty for ourselves'; 1796 had been prolific enough that they might 'thrash the corn for sale'.[59] John gave proof of local prosperity, telling William that 'a number of your people are lodging money in the Bank, some more, some less from £20 to £100 – The Ground Officer £300', while Angus Roy's father 'this day sent £80 to the Forres Bank'.[60] 'The people were never more comfortable than they are at present', and John contemplated rent increases because 'the price of Cattle, as well as every other Article produced by the land, has risen so much in price of late'.[61] But, while appreciating war's dividend, John provided a thoughtful caveat:

> In the midst of our mountains, thank God, we have peace and plenty – and though the heavy taxes affect us, we have no cause to complain. The war has raised the price of Cattle, and if we are prudent and attentive, in place of doing us harm, it has done us good. Yet for the sake of humanity, I wish there was Peace and unanimity all over the Globe.[62]

Since George Macpherson's first improving lease of 1734, the estate had implemented its own distinctive agricultural revolution, moulding Lowland practice into the constraints of a Highland environment, blending arable improvement with the pastoral shieling economy. Indeed, contrary to the assertion that Highland landowners were trying to replicate the improved agricultural society of the Lowlands, Invereshie incorporated and enhanced the very system of transhumance scorned by southern improvers.[63] Reorganisation, however, had destroyed the runrig townships, causing the removal of many tenants, some remaining as cottars or labourers while others headed southwards, like Duncan from Dalraddie who went to Glasgow 'to engage in the weaving linen or Cotton manufacture'[64] The resultant social dislocation cannot be measured, but perhaps because of the gradual nature of reform and the genuine respect for the Invereshie family, the transition was achieved relatively smoothly, a far cry from the contemporary Ross-shire riots which arose from the extensive introduction of sheep. When Captain John died in 1799, he left an estate markedly different from any other in Badenoch, a tribute to his own leadership, energy and wisdom. While historians have argued that the Clearances were inevitable because there was simply no alternative, it is worth noting that Invereshie did provide a different – and far less traumatic – model for the Highlands.

The Gordon Estates

Meanwhile, on the Gordon estates, relations with the tacksmen appeared somewhat strained, judging by Anderson's acerbic comment: 'my Friends of the Clan will never have really Peace or Comfort; and will never be free of some jarring and Interference with the Dirty Mushrooms of the Day, so long as they hold a foot bread of Land from the family of Gordon or pay them groat of Rent'[65] Inevitably, the Duke milked the rising cattle prices with further rent increases in 1796 and 1799 – a 58 per cent rise since 1786.[66] Between 1750 and 1800 Badenoch had in fact suffered a fivefold average rent increase, with Laggan reaching sixfold. Then, in 1808, the Duke nearly doubled the 1799 rental of £2,395 to £4,650, increasing it again in 1812 to £5,375 – a near 1,000 per cent increase since 1750.[67] These increases were admittedly partly due to the spread of sheep walks, but even non-sheep farms experienced increases of between 500 and 1,000 per cent. Though investing nothing in the local economy, Alexander had no scruples about skimming off war's profits.

Those profits had, in fairness, considerably eased the condition of the Badenoch tacksmen. In 1786, Badenoch's rent of £1,512 would have required the sale of roughly 600 cattle: by 1795 rising prices meant that only 380 would have been needed – a substantial bonus for tacksman and subtenant alike. As the 1796 rent increase was imposed during the main price boom, the advantage remained with the farmer. But the 1799 increase coincided with a sudden market downturn, bringing the number of cows required back up to at least 600. While it appears that the Duke was merely maintaining rental parity, a longer-term comparison shows that the number of cattle required to cover the rental had risen from 370 in 1750 to 600 by 1799. The huge increases of 1808 and 1812, far exceeding wartime prices, pushed the number of cattle required to over 700 (Table 4). The new rentals, of course, depended on war prices, but even in the midst of hostilities the market proved fickle: 1798 ended with a 'Want of Sale of Cattle & low prices'; the following February 'stagnation' in cattle sales; in October, 'neither Cow nor Sheep will be taken at any price'.[68] Such fluctuations made it difficult to cope with the level of rent inflation.

The real culpability of Highland landowners, according to Roy Campbell, lay not in rent inflation itself but in 'their failure to put it to productive use'.[69] For Duke Alexander this was only too true: reaping war's dividend as unearned increment, he neither re-invested it nor reduced the family debt. Worse, by creaming off this windfall, Alexander deprived the tacksmen of the where-withal to conduct their own improvement schemes.

Things improved considerably, however, when the estranged Duchess adopted Badenoch as her home. In 1792, she considered 'a Shieling at Badenoch', at Kinrara, eulogising its 'wild scenes of delight, which possess everything in nature that is sublime and beautiful', capturing the intellectual passion for wilderness that was then sweeping Europe (Colour plate 13).[70] Captain John was not enthused: 'Her Grace may change her mind before Whitsunday – *entre nous*, it would be no loss to this Country if she did – Poor Cameron [tacksman of Kinrara] had no idea, that in his old age, he would have been removed from a place he himself had made comfortable.'[71] Once established there in 1796, she adopted, according to Elizabeth Grant, 'a sort of backwood's life', though still playing society hostess. With resident French chef, and local fiddler Lang James's band playing for the mandatory Highland reels, she enticed 'half the London world of fashion . . . to enjoy the free life, the pure air, and the wit and fun the Duchess brought with her to the mountains'.[72] The Reverend John Anderson, acting as factor, was less enamoured: 'I am neither

Table 4
Rent-cow comparison for Badenoch, 1750–1812.

	1750	1786	1791–5	1796	1799	1808	1812
Badenoch rent £ sterling	505	1512	1512	1994	2395	4650	5375
Cows	370	600	380	400	600	665	700

the Lady's retained Counsel; nor Her domestic Chaplain – flattering Her for Preferrment: nor do I know that I ly under any Obligation to Her of any kind', though admitting his opinion was influenced by 'the *Spirit of Wine* that sometimes leads me to speak too strongly'.[73]

One of her sycophantic visitors, John Stoddart, described the Duchess's life, playing on the 'noble savage' ethos. 'People will not believe, that a mind habituated to all the polish and splendour of courts, can find gratification in the simple pleasures of nature'.[74] He acknowledged, however, that domicile in Badenoch, 'one of the wildest of Highland districts, necessarily cuts off many of the accommodations of polished life', bread and coal having to come from Inverness or Perth. Stoddart described the Duchess's landscaping of Kinrara following the latest fashion outlined in Sir Uvedale Price's newly published *Essay on the Picturesque* – 'a textbook to all our discussions on local improvement' – advocating natural beauty and romanticism.[75] In the evenings they discussed Ossian, 'the painter of Highland scenery', and Burns, the 'still more animated painter of Scottish feelings'.[76]

More significant, however, was the Duchess's practical impact. Stoddart again extolled her virtues as 'benefactress to the surrounding country . . . The affability of her manners, still more than the extent of her benevolence, rendered her name universally beloved'.[77] Always a keen advocate of improvement, she now focused on Kinrara. Mrs Grant of Laggan described her as 'a very busy farmeress . . . She rises at five in the morning, bustles incessantly, employs from twenty to thirty workmen every day, and entertains noble travellers from England, in a house very little better than our own'.[78] She later founded the Badenoch and Strathspey Farming Society, awarding 'premiums for all kinds of domestic industry – spinning, dyeing etc.'[79]

Most important, however, was the long-awaited village – first proposed two decades earlier – which the Duchess later referred to as 'Kingussie, my favourite child'.[80] By 1793, there was already a school, courthouse, post office and a lint mill on the proposed site of the village.[81] Once in Kinrara she pushed for its completion, and in 1797 William Tod and George Brown met in Kingussie to discuss the plan. Stoddart noted that 'Her Grace has planned the establishment of a village, at a little distance, whose bakers, butchers etc. may serve all the adjacent country'.[82] On 21 January 1799, the *Aberdeen Journal* advertised the 'New Village at Kingussie in Badenoch'. The following week, Captain John of Invereshie confirmed Lady Jane's role, commenting that the parish's ubiquitous minister, John Anderson, 'has the sole management from the Dutchess of the Kingussie Village that is to be'.[83]

Planned villages were classic Enlightenment philosophy: fashionable, respectable and aesthetically pleasing – planting outposts of southern civilisation into the untamed Highland environment, with the added bonus of market facilities and employment.[84] The advertisement thus stressed Kingussie's potential. 'There is a stream of water [the Gynack] running close to the spot intended for the village, fit to serve a Bleachfield, and to turn Machinery of every kind; and there is a Lint Mill already built on the premises.' Encouragement was offered to manufacturers, shopkeepers and tradesmen, particularly weavers and shoemakers. Significantly, in 1799, the upper part of Kingussie farm had become a sheep walk, and none other than the enterprising minister established the Kingussie Woollen Company.[85] But remoteness once again ensured failure as an early tourist guide noted: 'Kingussie . . . can scarcely be described as a thriving village, as it has no trade or manufacture to maintain a large population.'[86] It was indeed suggested at the time that villages founded without 'means of subsistence' would inevitably suffer 'the most pernicious consequences', degenerating, as Smout later argued, into 'rural slums.'[87]

The Duchess was also assiduous in 'improving the morals as well as the fortunes of those around me', because 'a healthy well-regulated people must be the proud riches of this country.'[88] Indeed, while in post-separation depression she commented, 'The prospect of doing good to these poor Highlanders is the only consolation of my wretched life.'[89] Stoddart recorded how 'she visited individually the separate cottages of the peasants; at one time she prevailed on a great number to have their children inoculated under her inspection; and she was ever ready to give her personal advice and assistance.'[90] She worried over smallpox, 'cold, hunger and dirt carries off hundreds . . . [inoculation with] cow-pox would save many', but it was, she commented – blissfully missing the irony – 'an evil I cannot remedy without money.'[91] Education was another priority: 'I hope I won't lose the school Dr. Kemp [secretary of the SSPCK] promised me in Kingussie – and a high sallary – as everything there is so dear – and no education nearer than Inverness – it is real charity.'[92]

The word enigma barely does justice to Lady Jane: friend to both king and local peasantry; elite society hostess and hands-on social reformer; political intriguer and practical farmer; Enlightenment thinker and sentimental Romanticist; 'Empress of Fashion' and 'the goodwife of Kinrara'; at ease in the opulence of Gordon castle or her smoke-filled cottage; a lover of wilderness for whom it was 'cruel enough to be shut up in these mountains.'[93] Similarly her legacy, for though she was passionately concerned for the wellbeing of the poor, her outrageous extravagance undoubtedly contributed to the rent increases that afflicted their lives. Aggravating the very poverty she was trying to alleviate was a paradox the Duchess never quite grasped.

Lairds and Tacksmen

Fortune dealt varying hands to the other estates. Cluny estate, where the clan chief, Colonel Duncan, returned after retiring from the army in 1796, witnessed the widespread expansion of sheep farming, obviously benefiting laird rather than tenantry. On the Mackintosh lands in eastern Badenoch, improvements were at last underway. John Carmichael, tacksman of Kinraranakyle (a substantial farm of 56 acres arable) was bound by his lease to build a substantial head dyke, to farm 'according to the rules of good husbandry', and to maintain one-fifth of his arable as ley grass, implying fallowing or crop rotation.[94] The presence of some single-tenant farms of 14–16 acres, and some tiny moorland-reclamation 'crofts' at the former Glen Feshie shielings of Rienabruaich and Ruigh-aiteachain also indicate restructuring. But Dalnavert, leased by two absentee tacksmen, was simply left in the hands of the subtenants, and there was at least one communal township still operating, suggesting an estate in the throes of transformation.[95] Reorganisation was also being introduced into the Mackintosh estate of Dunachton in 1792.[96]

At Belleville, James Macpherson's initial glamour was perhaps wearing thin. 'He has lost himself with every Individual in the Country, high and Low', wrote Captain John, later calling him 'a perfect hermit', though offering no explanation.[97] Anderson, however, noted the continuing improvements: 'My neighbour Bellville is amusing Himself . . . making Roads, and Dykes, and Houses and Bridges' (Colour plate 14). The benefits were significant:

> He built his house . . . by native workmen, whom he paid liberally . . .
> he was the first person in Badenoch who gave a shilling a-day to
> agricultural labourers, who had previously received only eightpence
> and ninepence. Scores of them were employed on his grounds, and in
> forming his embankments.[98]

Removals, however, continued, as Glentruim was at least partially cleared in 1792 to 'support a new Arrangement . . . upon that part of his Estate where this ejection is to take place'; more were planned at the time of his death and implemented by his son, James, 'so as to carry into Execution some arrangements' –

frustratingly unspecified.[99] By 1796, the combined estates of Phones, Etteridge and Invernahavon carried only thirteen tenants, but with rents averaging £8 to £12, it suggests small discrete farms rather than sheep walks.[100]

James's thirst for land continued, unsuccessfully offering for Invertromie estate, Glenbanchor, and all the Duke's Alvie lands, before finally purchasing Benchar in 1795.[101] After his death in 1796, Belleville passed to young James, an officer in India with neither roots nor interest in Badenoch, and Anderson oversaw the management. Captain John's criticism aside, 'Fingal' appears to have been popular with his tenantry, perhaps because of the high wages, which might explain the tensions with other local gentry. Mrs Grant's 'obituary' provided interesting insights: 'He was a very good-natured man; and now that he had got all his schemes of interest and ambition fulfilled, he seemed to grow domestic, and showed, of late, a great inclination to be an indulgent landlord, and very liberal to the poor.' She admired his 'genius, taste, benevolence, and prosperity', adding that he was 'the only person of eminence among us . . . certainly worthy of a better fate'. On the negative side, though, success had never brought him happiness; 'his religious principles were . . . unfixed and fluctuating'; he was 'too strongly marked with . . . vanity and ostentation.' She added, with a rather damning generality, 'Tavern company, and bachelor circles, make men gross.'[102]

Other estates suffered. Inverhall was sold in 1794 and Gordonhall in 1797, victims of the droving collapse of 1793. More significant, however, was Benchar's demise. Desperate for ownership of his wadset lands, Andrew Macpherson had managed to buy Clune in 1754, and Benchar, eventually, in 1787, just before his death.[103] His heir, another Captain John (the 'fat captain'), disastrously increased the estate debt by £2,000 before dying in his London house in 1791, to be succeeded by his even more profligate brother, Lieutenant, later Captain, Evan (another 'fat captain').[104] Though his own nephews and nieces, Captain John Invereshie characterised the family bluntly: 'The females, as well as the males are more thoughtless and extravagant than could be wished or expected', and later, 'that Family for Indolence and inattention beats everything I have heard.'[105]

By 1792, Benchar's meagre rental of £349 barely covered the interest on its £8,000 debt. Anderson, acting factor while Evan was on military duties, sold the Glen Banchor townships of Dalnashalg and Tullichierro to Cluny for £4,300 – but to no avail. As Evan's debts spiralled, Anderson sold the remainder of the bankrupt estate to James Macpherson in 1795 for a remarkable £8,000. Benchar's fate encapsulates the Highland problem. Originally clan tacksmen who had acquired a wadset, the Benchar family spent a century striving for ownership of their *duthchas*, only to lose it within eight years through wanton extravagance, and see it pass to one of the clan's *nouveaux riches*. Anderson succinctly concluded, 'where a Small Estate is much in Burden, *in a few years it will consume itself*.[106]

For the Badenoch tacksmen, however, high market prices and military careers made this a decade of opportunity in spite of inflationary rents. Individual enterprise was still evident. John Carmichael of Kinraranakyle was importing 'excellent Rye Grass Seeds . . . [and] three Tons of best New Clover Seeds from Holland' not just for himself, but to 'supply my Friends with good Seeds & on reasonable Terms', while also involved in the Glenfeshie Wood Company, and later, the Kingussie Woollen Company.[107] John Maclean, now seventy-one, left Cluny when Colonel Duncan returned, becoming tacksman of Benchar under James Macpherson, remaining there till his death in 1808. Anderson, now his son-in-law, ruefully commented to William of Invereshie that the indefatigable old man was 'now as anxious planning Improvements . . . and as much interested about liming, and dyking, as if he was only 25 Years of age . . . What Pity, that You and I had not possessed some portion of his Enthusiasm'.[108]

Maclean's old neighbour, John Dow, started the decade well, even commencing as sheep farmer at Dalnaspidal. In 1794, however, he went bankrupt for over £4,000, destroyed by the previous year's droving crash, horrific sheep losses, and a recruiting fiasco. The following year, the entire contents and stock of Ballachroan and Dalnaspidal were rouped.[109] Rather than face his creditors and debtors' prison, John Dow, now aged seventy, had 'fled or absconded [to] a very distant part of the Highlands', which he refused to leave unless given 'a personal protection' by the court.[110] It was a sorry, though perhaps inevitable, end. John Invereshie wrote sympathetically of his namesake's humiliation: 'one will be ready to put a Veil over what he formerly was', while Anderson explained to William that John Dow and family 'are changed indeed from what You have seen them'.[111] Defying bankruptcy, however, the wily old tacksman somehow retained possession of Ballachroan, and in 1798, aged seventy-three, even returned briefly to military duties in Ireland – as Anderson pithily commented, 'he will Still be a Schemer till he goes down to the Grave'.[112]

One of Badenoch's most distinguishing features was the longevity of its indigenous tacksman class, though the estate's desire to retain its most enterprising tenants and community leaders was hardly surprising. Indeed, until southern sheep farmers were convinced of the region's worth, there simply

THE WILD BLACK REGION

was no alternative – alienating the tacksmen could have destroyed the entire social and economic structure of Badenoch. But equally significant was the tacksmen's own attachment to native soils. A study of sixty-six farms across Badenoch between 1750 and 1800 reveals that, excluding a few intruded characters like factors and ministers, 90 per cent were still held by indigenous tacksman families in 1800, comprising just five surnames, Macpherson, Mackintosh, Macdonald/Macdonell, Clark (a Macpherson sept), and Shaw (a Mackintosh sept). In Morvern and Mull, twenty years earlier, the equivalent figure was just 36 per cent.[113] Of the remaining incomer tacksmen, half were native Highlanders, some of whom, like McHardy, already had local connections. Thus only 5 per cent of local tacksmen by 1800 came from outside the *Gàidhealtachd* – a remarkable continuity at a time of such dramatic change.[114]

The picture, however, was more complex. Only 38 per cent of these farms were held continuously by the same clan through that period and only 14 per cent remained in the possession of the same family, suggesting a highly mobile community where neither clan nor tacksmen could hold their *duthchas* in perpetuity – a situation caused by both estate and tacksman. The Duke targeted clan continuity on three fronts: intruding members of rival clans, offering farms to the highest bidder, and removing obstructive tacksmen. Meanwhile, commercially minded tacksmen like Ralia and John Dow did not hesitate to bid for and take over the land of other Macpherson gentry to further their own interests, while others abandoned family lands because of bankruptcy, or to pursue more lucrative careers elsewhere, thereby providing openings for new tenants. But, while most tacksman families had moved at least once within that half century, many did hold the same lands over several decades, and often through several generations. The issue was further confused by marriage, for where a husband moved into his wife's farm – apparently not uncommon in Laggan – it disguised a continuing tenancy.[115]

The pattern of continuity and mobility was in fact shaped by geographic parameters, for tacksman families moved within a very tight locality. As clanship declined, and with it the hold over traditional territories, the narrow confines of discrete clan lands were perhaps being replaced by the broader concept of a regional homeland. The ancient Lordship of Badenoch had become a wider *duthchas*, a distinct geographical and cultural entity within which the looser clan and familial bonds of the late eighteenth century could exist with easy compatibility. Thus, unlike the eradication or dispersal of this class that happened in some areas, and contrary to Devine's contention that there was a new middle class which had 'little hereditary or ethnic connection with the people', the indigenous tacksmen still remained firmly rooted in their Badenoch homeland as late as 1800, even if not actually occupying their specific family heritage.[116]

Diversification

'All these mountains . . . are at present nothing but sheep farms; though formerly black cattle and sheep were raised on them', observed Mrs Murray of Kensington when crossing the Corrieyairrack in 1799 – the valuable Laggan wool now feeding the Yorkshire mills.[117] In this, Badenoch was no different from the rest of the Highlands, as a new wave of sheep farming, boosted by wartime wool prices, swept the region. Tacksman and landowner alike seized the moment.

In 1787, John Dow leased a sheep farm at Dalnaspidal from Atholl estate, but Tod was concerned:

> In spite of the Remonstrances of all his Friends. . . . he very foolishly embarked some years ago in the great undertaking of the sheep Farm of Dalnaspidal. To a *young* man, able to pay proper attention to it . . . I dare say it would be a very lucrative Bargain. But to him, I should be afraid, it must turn out a bad one.[118]

The winter of 1790–1 saw his whole flock 'scab[b]ed & with rainy weather dieing by Hundreds'.[119] Nevertheless, in 1792, he still sold at least one batch of 200 hoggs (young sheep) for £95.[120] But a costly dispute with the Duke of Atholl lost him the vital wintering ground at Dalnaspidal, resulting in losses of 600–700 sheep estimated at 300 guineas. Captain John reflected prophetically: 'The Capt of Ballachroan I believe has near run his race.'[121] As Gordon estate factor, Tod tried to save him from total disaster, offering a generous deal to Stewart of Garth, his Atholl counterpart. Shrewdly and compassionately he blamed John Dow's folly on age: 'None of us are willing to believe ourselves growing old, and he the least so, of any man I know.'[122]

Such failures, even when largely self-induced, reinforced the wariness of commercial sheep farmers. In Alvie, in the mid 1790s, the minister recorded 'only one farm flocked wholly with sheep', while in Kingussie, 'sheep farming has not as yet made any considerable progress'.[123] Indeed, the only exclusive sheep farm in either parish in the 1799 Gordon rental was Kingussie itself.[124] In Laggan, however, the Reverend James Grant recorded 'four or five' sheep farms, supporting 12,000 beasts. There were only two landowners in the parish, he noted, and the Duke, 'has not yet shewn any great disposition to let his lands to shepherds', adding pointedly, 'that nobleman is attached to his people, and fond of nourishing and rearing them'.[125] Thus the proprietor introducing sheep walks was the Macpherson chief, Colonel Duncan of Cluny, who, by implication, lacked the same attachment.

Aberarder sheep walk on the north side of Loch Laggan had, of course, been established by the Ayrshire Mitchells before the estate was restored to Cluny in 1784, but a rent increase of £30 to £190 in just fifteen years had proved its worth. In the late 1780s, Cluny expanded the existing sheep farm at Gallovie on the south side of the loch into one massive sheep walk, later claimed to be the largest in the Highlands. The entire hinterland of Loch Laggan thus became one vast depopulated sheep zone.[126] At least three others followed: in 1796, thirty families were removed from Laggankenneth and Cromra to create Laggan sheep farm at the east end of the loch; Dalnashalg and Tullichierro, purchased from Benchar in 1792, were cleared to create Cluny Mains sheep farm in 1796 or shortly after, later incorporating Biallidbeg as well; and the remote shielings of Benalder were also converted by 1799 – Mrs Murray describing an isolated shepherd family on Loch Ericht who could 'neither speak nor understand Gaelic'.[127]

Though the Duke's aversion to sheep farms remained, banning them proved impossible: 'this Exclusion has been much, if not altogether, Evaded, and indeed it is difficult . . . to enforce Such Restraint upon Highland Tacksmen, whose Glens and Grasings are out of Sight', especially when the ban was 'Contrary to their own Interest and the Example of Neighbours'.[128] The tacksmen were both exploiting their remoteness and re-asserting their independence to capitalise on this windfall. By 1803, Moy, Strathmashie, Garvamore, Garvabeg, Sherramore and Sherrabeg were already established sheep walks with staggering rental increases reaching over 2,000 per cent above the 1751 figures (Table 5).

Significantly, the four farms in Table 5 plus Sherrabeg, Sherramore, Gallovie and Dalchully were all held, *not* by southern sheep farmers, but by indigenous Macdonald and Macpherson tacksmen, though some, as at Loch Ericht, may have employed Lowland shepherds.[129] That they could sustain such rents without the subtenant contributions on which they previously relied explains their enthusiasm for sheep – and also why estate officials appear to have turned a blind eye to this defiance of ducal policy. Between the Gordon tacksmen and Colonel Duncan, the whole of the Braes between Laggan Bridge

Table 5

Percentage increase rentals of some Laggan sheep farms based on the 1751 rental figures.

	1799	1812
Garvamore	500%	1,200%
Garvabeg	650%	1,500%
Strathmashie	750%	2,000%
Moy	1,200%	2,300%

Sources: NRS, GD44/51/732/25, Sett of Badenoch, *c.* 1803; GD44/27/54, GD44/51/732/32/2, GD44/27/6/103, Rentals, 1751, 1799, 1812.

and the Lochaber boundary had, by 1800, become an unbroken run of sheep farms, 'the sole subjects of this realm of solitude', bringing a seismic shift in the pastoral economy of western Badenoch, and with it a very different future for the region, one with huge social repercussions.[130]

Shooting also continued to flourish. Anderson noted that the Kingussie hills 'are much frequented by sportsmen'; at Dalnacardoch, Mrs Murray observed 'the attendants, and horses of sportsmen, who were come to the Highlands to shoot'; while Mrs Grant reported that 'the country swarms with shooters'.[131] Not that they were universally welcomed. In 1792, Sir James Grant advised the Aviemore innkeeper to give preference to 'to genuine travellers as against southern sportsmen'; the minister of Alvie colourfully referred to 'the havoc of the sportsman'; while Captain John complained: 'This Country is threatened with a Vast quantity of Shooters agt the 12th of Augt – I had much rather they paid a Visit to Greenland – however I am happy with the certainty [weather] that they will have no Sport'.[132] The antipathy was perhaps due to the inevitable disruption of hill grazings, but also, as Macpherson of Biallidmore warned, 'There is so much Complaints in Glentrime [Glentruim] against the Damage done by their Dogs to their Sheep already'. Rannoch farmers indeed had already complained that sportsmen's dogs 'frighten their cattle, drive them over precipices, into bogs'.[133]

Though the purchase of sporting estates is generally seen as a nineteenth-century phenomenon, it clearly pre-dates that era in Badenoch.[134] The sale of Raitts and Benchar in the 1780s had attracted the interest of sportsmen, and in 1793, Invertromie estate was glowingly advertised for sale, 'With Excellent Shooting Quarters'.[135] Glentromie lodge, 'a substantial house', had 'for several years been occupied as a Shooting Quarter, by different Gentlemen of rank and fortune'. It was the 'best Shooting Ground in the Highlands', had salmon and trout 'in the greatest perfection', the arable was the best in the region, the meadows produced excellent hay, the river could power mills, there were slate quarries and limestone, and, not least, it was 'well calculated for a sheep walk'. As if all that were not inducement enough, the advert targeted the fashionable cult of Romanticism, depicting scenery and ruins as 'beautiful', 'romantic', 'picturesque', before culminating in the dual thrust that nowhere could better 'gratify the pleasures of the sportsman and the man of taste'. Romanticism and sport were in fact inseparable, for the shooting aristocracy were, ironically, deemed to be lovers of nature.[136]

Meanwhile, estates still sought their industrial *El Dorado*. The Alvie minister depicted a seemingly successful cottage industry: 'The natives are remarkable for the quantity and quality of white plaiding they bring to market', though later contradicting himself by stating, 'They have no idea of trade or manufactures.'[137] In Kingussie, Anderson was negative: the lack of a village market was 'severely felt', requiring wool to be sent by 'long land carriage' to distant manufacturers.[138] Linen had also failed because 'skilful people are not collected in one close neighbourhood', 'bad services in the neighbouring mill [Kingussie]' and 'the difficulty of procuring seed in this inland situation.'[139]

Timber, however, was more successful – 'many thousand pounds worth' according to the Reverend James Hall, much of it for pit props in English coal mines.[140] While Dodsworth and Osborne continued felling Glenmore for shipbuilding, smaller companies also contributed. The Glenfeshie Wood Company, run by tacksmen Carmichael and Cameron, had enlarged its sawmill – 'a very decent machine' – earning them over £200 annually through the decade; Thomas Shaw, another tacksman, having 'bought a Bargain in the Inchriach [Forest]', was also doing well; and Captain John was exploiting the Invereshie woodlands: 'we have a thousand Loggs of as good wood as any in the Kingdom at the Mill and three Saws will be working on Monday.'[141] A year later there were five saws, and when a rival company collapsed, John pounced: 'we may raise our prices, when there is no competition.'[142] The venture, however, was only moderately lucrative, some £200 to £300 a year, and in 1794, John acknowledged, 'The wood business is going on slowly and surely we will not make rich by it.'[143] While local lairds like Rothiemurchus and Invereshie were undoubtedly taking a lead in commercial forestry in the 1790s, tacksman enterprise in this sector was certainly not insignificant.[144]

Surprisingly, whisky was not a particular money-spinner in Badenoch.

Illicit stills certainly satisfied local demand – the Alvie folk being 'much addicted to drinking of whisky; . . . there being no less than 13 houses in the parish, where drams are sold without a . . . licence'.[145] But the region never enjoyed the commercial success of neighbouring Strathspey, probably due to the usual environmental constraints – the inability to grow or transport sufficient quantities of barley. Indeed, the parliamentary committee investigating illicit practices in 1798 was informed that a farmer attempting to establish a licensed distillery in Badenoch had been 'obliged to give up his intention for want of Grain'.[146]

Military

The repercussions of the French Revolution of 1789 dominated the 1790s, whether through the growth of radicalism and political protest, or, after the outbreak of war in 1793, through fears for national security as French successes in Europe posed an ever-increasing threat of invasion. Because of falling recruitment levels – a result of deteriorating pay and conditions – the government had resorted to establishing Independent Companies, one of which was raised by the Duke in 1790 under the command of his son, the Marquis of Huntly.[147] Later incorporated into the 42nd, it was initially drawn from the Gordon estates, including at least thirty-three men from Badenoch, exclusive of those raised privately by local officers like Captain John Macpherson of Benchar.[148] While hardship, adventure and a lingering degree of loyalty to the Gordons helped recruitment, enlistment bounties proved decisive. John Menzies, the chamberlain, was warned that it was 'necessary to give high Bounties from Five to Ten Guineas – You can't Judge what Effect Money has among the lower class'.[149] Duncan Gordon from Glen Feshie reinforced the link between poverty and recruitment: old, infirm, and unable to support his family, he had already enlisted two sons in the army, and in 1790, sent his youngest to the Marquis's regiment with the despairing plea 'to do with him as may seem best to your Lordship'.[150]

In January 1794, Lord Amherst (Commander-in-Chief of British forces) authorised the Duke to raise a regular regiment of 1,000 men (originally the 100th Foot, but later the 92nd), again under Huntly's command. While regiment-raising by this time can be seen as 'a political act directed towards the centre of power in London', the appointment of local gentry as officers would naturally help secure the Duke's rentals.[151] The official bounty was

5 guineas, but even double that proved inadequate: 'It is vain to offer 10 Guineas here – they would laugh at us . . . when they can get 14–15 guins down from other corps', while 'Expence for drink & other Contingencies will also mount up'.[152] Badenoch provided at least forty men, with bounties averaging £15 but reaching £21, and tavern bills of £116.[153] These two regiments cost the estate dearly, though money could be recouped through the sale of regimental commissions: 'The army is at present a great Market – the highest bidders must be looked for and one Coll [Colonel] gets more for Commissions than another, just according to circumstances'.[154] Though military agents Cox and Greenwood estimated the sale of commissions at £22,000, it was an impossible figure for the Duke who needed officers from his own estates, rather than the open market, to ensure the recruitment of Highland soldiers.[155]

War's demands brought the Quota System in 1795 – every county having to provide a fixed number for the navy or face a £25 per capita penalty. But, with the Independent Company, the 92nd regiment, and internal defence requirements, the Gordon estates had already been stripped. Tod voiced his concerns: 'considering what we have all done in the way of recruiting already, we need not look for finding Men – and therefore we shall have to lug out our £25 for each of the men demanded from us'.[156] In Morayshire alone the fines would cost £1,000, but the Duke, to his credit, refused to make his tenantry contribute: 'in Consideration of the Aid they gave [him] and Lord Huntly when recruiting he has forbid me to ask a Shilling from them'. The Ruthven Quarter-Session Court helped raise the quota, authorising local constables to report 'all such persons as are Idlers, disorderly, or immediately out of Service', adding as incentive, 'any person who will give information to the above effect will be handsomely rewarded, and the name of the informer Concealled if desired' – though the success of such methods is not recorded.[157]

Desperation for men gave the initiative to tenants who could secure land in return for enlistment. Trying to maintain regimental strength in 1797, the Marquis appealed for 'young, handsome fellows', offering as inducement 'such farms on his estate as they are inclined to settle upon'.[158] Thomas Macpherson presented his schoolboy son, Malcolm, asking only 'what Lord Huntly offers to every other person . . . a half aughteen of land' (a small croft) on the townships of Gorstan or Pitagowan in Laggan.[159] As the latter already contained two Chelsea pensioners, these farms were possibly being divided into soldiers' crofts as an enlistment incentive. (Pitagowan, now Balgowan, did indeed become one of the only genuine crofting communities in Badenoch, though whether specifically for soldiers is unclear.) Thomas, openly acknowledging that the boy was 'young and weak', was clearly trading his son for land. There were other examples: the father of Alexander Macdonald, 'a Serjaint in the 42nd', had been promised 'an half-aughtenpart Land' in return for his son in 1791, while Donald Robertson had joined the Gordon Highlanders in 1794 on 'the promise of an aughten part of Land in the Farm of Gargask . . . for the support of his wife & Family during his Absence' − a promise that had been honoured.[160] This land may have been offered instead of bounties as was happening in Breadalbane and Argyll, a mutually beneficial arrangement.[161]

Internal defence further depleted both manpower and resources. In March 1793, the Duke again raised the Northern Fencibles, costing nearly £3,000 for the 600 men: the official bounties of £3 reached £15 as officers desperately tried to raise their complement.[162] At least sixty-six enlisted from Badenoch.[163] Through local influence and diplomacy, Captain John secured thirty from Invereshie by ascertaining which farms had surplus young men who might 'benefit by being a year or two in the Fencibles', and then negotiating with their parents, who all 'agreed in the most handsome manner'.[164] But he anticipated problems: 'The people are Fencible mad − so much so that many parts of the Country will feel the want of Servants.' In 1794, Lord Lieutenants were appointed to organise local defence, and 977 Badenoch men responded to the call for a new national defence force.[165] John proudly acknowledged that 'On the Banks of the Spey we are all Steady and Loyal; and have enrolled to a man to Support King and Constitution' − what one historian described as 'national defence patriotism'.[166]

In 1797, a Scottish militia was established specifically for internal defence, men being chosen by ballot, though the better-off could avoid service by paying substitutes. So unpopular was the ballot that militia riots spread across the country, including neighbouring Atholl − 'more serious and more general than you or I had an idea of', wrote Captain John, for the rioters had put 'the Duke [of Atholl] . . . and all of the Gentlemen . . . in a very critical Situation'.[167] Badenoch's militia ballot, however, received media praise for its smooth conduct, perhaps because 'the nature of it was properly explained' by the gentry responsible: Cluny, Grant of Rothiemurchus and Captain Cameron of Kinapole.[168] In Laggan, a fund was even launched to help families pay for substitutes where a balloted member could not be spared. Cluny wrote rather smugly of Badenoch − 'so very different from the turbulent behaviour of our Neighbouring Counties that the Proprietors on Speyside must feel themselves highly gratified in . . . presiding over a People who have . . . proved themselves the most Patriotic and Loyal Subjects'.[169]

The most fanciful defence scheme was Dundas's proposal for a clan levy, a Highland force of 16,000 with each clan led by its own chief, described by Tod as 'raising the clans in the *good old fashioned* way'.[170] It was, however, based on three totally erroneous premises: 'Highlanders have ever been and still are warmly attached to their Chiefs'; using clansmen would cause 'little injury to Agriculture & Manufactures'; the people were 'absolute Strangers to the levelling and dangerous principles of the present age'.[171] A supporting letter reiterated the bizarre notion that Highlanders were 'the only Soldiers . . . not in the smallest Degree tinged with Democratic principles', completely at odds with Captain John's earlier concerns.[172] That the government considered entrusting national security to the very society it had persecuted fifty years earlier shows how effectively Highlanders had rebranded themselves. It also shows how little Dundas and the government understood the Highlands.

Unsurprisingly, the scheme was still-born. Being the most heavily recruited area of Britain – Inverness-shire alone supported eight Fencible regiments, approximately 3,000 men – there simply were not 16,000 surplus men in the Highlands.[173] Cluny expressed his opposition: 'This Country has already been much drained by different Levys, so much so, that if the number now proposed were taken out of it, there would be great dangers of a totall stop being put to the Operations of Husbandry.' Mackintosh of Mackintosh agreed that 'from the great Drain the Country has already sustained it will be almost impossible to raise the Body of Men proposed'.[174] In reality, however, both acknowledged that the clan's military role was obsolete – Mackintosh pointing out 'how little influence the Chieftains retain at this day in comparison of what it was half a century ago', while Cluny suspected the people 'would not readily agree to leave their homes, in the manner proposed'.

Cluny instead proposed expanding the local volunteer system, and more such companies, each operating within its own district to avoid further depleting labour, were indeed authorised in 1797–8.[175] Captain John described how the Badenoch companies were 'raised in different Propertys, and engaged on the condition that their respective Proprietors should march along with them, when called on Service'.[176] Two days a week training at one shilling a day (roughly £5 a year) provided another significant military boost for the domestic economy.[177]

The recruiting frenzy confirms the concept of an 'armed nation', with men encouraged by wages, bounties and land. Indeed, the Duthil minister commented that whereas local men used to enlist only in Highland regiments, 'bounty money now determines the choice'.[178] But forcible recruitment was still significant. When one of the Invereshie servants was seized in Grantown, Captain John angrily demanded his release: 'I look on every one I take a concern in as safe in Strathspey as if they were at my own fireside'.[179] At home, the Badenoch gentry were rounding up the indigent to fulfil the Quota Act, and John Dow was again on the prowl. In 1792, he was apparently the only active recruiter on Speyside, and as Captain John acknowledged, 'has always been successful'.[180] In October, he had twenty-eight men, 'North Country people he and his Mirmidans kidnapped on the road', fourteen providing his son's quota for an ensigncy, while for the rest 'he gets 20 guineas per man from the Capt of the Company'.

John Dow's good fortune – perhaps his judgement – deserted him, however, for in 1793, he 'lost terribly by his recruiting'. Out of a batch of thirty men, fourteen were rejected as unfit (five being under 5 feet 2 inches) and three deserted, but having already paid them bounty money, he lost heavily – £117 for just six of the rejected men. Further disaster occurred when out of thirty-three Irish recruits, six were rejected and twenty deserted – 'he has made a sad business of it', reflected Captain John.[181] Perhaps recognising the manpower shortage, John Dow was primarily recruiting outside Badenoch, similarly Captain Evan (Benchar) in Manchester 1794–5, and Phones in the Lowlands and Ireland.[182]

India continued to offer opportunities, and the bankrupt Captain Evan and two of his younger brothers, Graeme and Robert, all served out there. Despite the declining influence and death of James Macpherson, patronage remained crucial: William of Invereshie wrote to his uncle, General Grant, on behalf of his nephew Graeme, 'to recommend him to some person who can place him in a situation to make the Rupees'.[183] The 'sojourners' already there naturally continued 'to make the rupees' before returning home sufficiently enriched – providing, of course, they survived the venture – to invest in improvements.[184]

Perhaps as many as 40 per cent of Scottish gentry were officers during the Napoleonic Wars, probably even more in the Highlands, and for the Badenoch gentry, officership remained as crucial as ever.[185] In 1795, Lord Adam Gordon asked Dundas for a captaincy, 'without purchase', for the bankrupt Hugh Macpherson of Inverhall, who had been 'very unlucky lately in having been security for his father-in-law [John Dow]' during the droving collapse, and 'is obliged to sell his small property in Badenoch' – the army was in reality the only 'remaining vehicle of social opportunity' for impoverished Highland gentry.[186] Tacksmen also exploited commissions. Cluny asked the Duke for a captaincy in the Fencibles for Donald Macpherson of Gaskmore: 'He doesn't by any means intend to quit his farm, on the contrary it will enable him to pay his Rent more regular' – an obvious incentive for the Duke, even if Macpherson's military commitment was questionable![187]

Mrs Grant of Laggan inadvertently revealed the cynical exploitation of commissions. She and her minister husband secured an ensigncy for their twelve-year-old son, John, in 1795. She not only hoped his education would continue normally, but that, being a Fencible commission, he would be 'sent to graze before he is fit to kill or be killed'. They had, she acknowledged, 'never intended . . . the army as his permanent profession', but still hoped he would be 'allowed half-pay at the conclusion of the war' – a calculated attempt to secure a lifetime income without ever facing danger. Their scheme backfired doubly, however, because Fencible officers were not entitled to half-pay, and John ended up in Ireland, 'his education neglected, his morals in hazard'.[188]

Losses were inevitable. Captain Evan and his brother Graeme both perished in India, the latter at Tanjore in 1797 and Evan at Seringapatam two years later.[189] In Europe, the 92nd lost one quarter of its complement at Alkmaar in Holland on 2 October 1799, among them, the eldest son of Mary Macdonell, widow of the bankrupt John McHardy.[190] The boy being 'their only means of support', she appealed in desperation to the Duke of York for help for her remaining six young children – military service was no guarantee of financial security.[191]

Military careers could indeed prove disadvantageous, firstly through purchasing commissions and maintaining status while on service – Captain John had indeed complained back in 1777, while recuperating from his American wounds, that it was 'next to impossible to live on my pay' in Edinburgh.[192] It has also been claimed that long-term damage was done to the Highland economy because returning half-pay officers made poor farmers.[193] For most, however, this was not the case. Commissions were an investment bringing long-term dividends, and half-pay officers were valued as tacksmen because they guaranteed estate rentals and provided the externally generated capital that underpinned farming improvements and commercial expansion. The classic example was John Dow, an outstanding farmer, improver and entrepreneur, whose military career lasted from 1757 till 1800, moving between full and half pay as lieutenant and then captain. His total military income, excluding his earnings as recruiting officer, exceeded £3,500. Comparing this with his rent demonstrates its true significance. From 1770 to 1800, John Dow's total Ballachroan rent was £1,400, while his military income topped £2,800, leaving him an average surplus of over £40 a year.[194]

Consequently, the entire income of farm, subtenant rents, and droving was clear profit – investment capital for the huge improvements at Ballachroan as well as his commercial enterprises. For those preferring to sell their commissions there was a substantial one-off dividend: Captain John sold his captaincy for £1,500 in 1780, though up to £2,000 was achievable; John Macpherson of Cluny had sold his majority *c.*1760 for £1,400, though by 1771 this rank had become worth £3,500, 'an enormous price'; while William Mackintosh of Balnespick offered his colonelcy for 5,000 guineas in 1783.[195] India, could, of course, yield much higher – if not totally legal – rewards.

Not all military income, however, was reinvested. For officers on active service, much was absorbed in maintaining status, while others, like John and Evan of Benchar, blew theirs on self-indulgence. But for many Badenoch gentry, that income constituted a lifetime subsidy to invest in economic concerns, better lifestyles, or the education and careers of their children. Military revenue indeed proved far more effective government support than the paltry sums invested locally by official bodies like the Board of Trustees for Manufactures and Fisheries or the Barons of Exchequer. Without such revenues, Badenoch – and, indeed, the Gordon estates – would undoubtedly have faced a much bleaker future.[196]

The Peasantry

Highland poverty is often portrayed in negative terms, perhaps because of the word's modern connotations.[197] But defining poverty within the context of a subsistence society in which personal wealth had limited relevance is problematic. After potato cultivation became widespread, extreme hunger was comparatively rare – indeed, no late eighteenth-century visitor depicted a starving society, while modern research confirms that there was 'little or no impression of scarcity of food' in the Loch Ness area in the 1790s.[198] Clothing, plaiding and shoes were largely home-produced, fuel poverty was non-existent, while building materials and labour were free. In most years, cattle generated enough cash to cover rent and supplementary meal, without including textile sales, rising wages, military incomes and seasonal labour.

This in no way suggests affluence, simply that today's poverty is not a yardstick for past societies where sufficiency was wealth, a surplus, luxury. As one of Badenoch's peasant community, Mary Macpherson (*Bean Torra Dhamh*) from Glentruim, understood life on the edge, particularly in widowhood. Yet in her religious hymns she expressed the simple reality – and contentment – of subsistence. Significantly, she did not consider herself poor.

Gar na ghlac mi mòran stòrais,
Cha do chrìon mo chòir gu airceas,
An t-aran lathail fhuair mi 'n còmhnuidh,
'S math gu leòir gun stòr 'chur seachaid.

And although I've not obtained much wealth
My lot has not decayed to poverty:
Daily bread I've always had
And adequate income without saving.[199]

Alexander Campbell echoed that sentiment regarding the Breadalbane peasantry who were 'not affluent, [but] far from a state of poverty'.[200]

The relative prosperity of the 1790s was, of course, war-related. Cattle prices up to five times higher than 1750 benefited everyone – Anderson noted tenants 'asking and receiving, five, six & seven pounds stirling for their small Beasts of black Cattle' in 1796.[201] Military incomes were also crucial from the annual £5 in the Volunteers to full-time wages in Fencible, militia or line regiments. Captain John wrote of 'Fencible Soldiers . . . remitting home money from Hythe Camp [Kent]', and Stewart of Garth referred to regiments as a 'species of savings bank'.[202] Bounties of £15 were worth two to five years' rent, and the bounty payments to Badenoch men in the 92nd in 1794 (including only those recruited directly by the Duke himself) totalled £442, the highest of all the Gordon estates.[203] War undoubtedly provided a 'state subsidy' for the local economy, benefiting poor and rich alike. For the Badenoch tenantry, military income provided between 50 and 100 per cent of the annual rental, though, for the common soldiers, lasting only the duration of the war.[204]

Equally important was the labour shortage resulting from military service and seasonal migration. Robert Grant of Elchies complained of young workers returning from their summer season in the Lowlands and 'debauching the minds of the labouring servants persuading them to go south where they will have more wages'.[205] For Badenoch workers the primary destination was Lowland Perthshire, itself in crisis as rising wages in industrial centres like Dundee and Perth enticed the local workforce, leaving a vacuum in the countryside. A farmer in the Carse of Gowrie explained the consequences:

> The price of labour has, in the course of these last thirteen years, risen to nearly double what it was; . . . nor could the extra-works, such as turnpike-roads, planting, inclosing, draining, etc. be carried on but by the means of strangers, of which a considerable number come here every spring from Inverness-shire . . . each of whom returns to his own country about Martinmas with eight or ten pounds in his pocket.[206]

As the nearest district of Inverness-shire, Badenoch must have supplied many of those 'strangers' – and ten pounds for six months was two to four times the local equivalent.

The gentry expressed their concerns in 1795: 'Although Servants are at present much wanted [here] . . . a great number men and women are about to leave the Country for Service.'[207] To try to prevent this annual drain on labour they threatened eviction: 'the Principal Tacksmen are also determined to remove all subtenants, Cotters or Mealanders who may be guilty of the evil complained of.' The same fate awaited anyone (including their families) who offered shelter to the workers when they returned home: 'They will . . . remove all such persons from their respective propertys.' Even allowing that the high recruitment of 1793–4 and the Quota Act of 1795 put labour at a premium, this was an even more draconian attempt to control the local labour market than that of 1769.

Labour shortages and the higher expectations arising from seasonal migration fuelled wage demands. The six-month farm servants' fee, fixed at £1 in 1769, had increased about fivefold, with casual labourers, too, demanding increases. Anderson commented indignantly: 'A shilling *per* day is reckoned but very ordinary wages. Many receive 15d and 16d and some refuse to work under 18d.'[208] The word '*refuse*' was significant. The minister of Duthil and Rothiemurchus made the point more colourfully: 'Servants during the summer, stroll about idly, and live upon their former half-year's wages, knowing that the farmer must yield to the highest terms when the harvest approaches.' Consequently, 'they are obliged to give high fees, and from this view numbers of servants lie in waiting.'[209] The notion of workers manipulating the gentry to ensure better wages has rather a nice irony to it. Though ministers and gentry expressed outrage, agricultural writer James Robertson interestingly defended the workers: 'The landlord draws more rent than he did formerly for his lands; and the farmer receives a higher price for all the produce of the farm; so that the price of labour ought also to rise.'[210]

Invereshie wages confirm this trend. Murdoch Campbell, a shepherd, received £2 8s wages in 1791, £3 in 1793, £5 in 1798 and £10 in 1801; while John Macdonald, who had been earning £5 a year up to 1796, jumped to £8 from 1797 onwards.[211] Captain John was ambivalent, seemingly pleased in 1797 that the poor 'are getting into easier Circumstances and wages have got so high from the Scarcity of hands – that the young people are making money fast', though next year complaining that wage demands had become 'extravagant in the extreme'.[212] The Reverend James Hall confirmed rising local prosperity: 'Though few people are rich, yet, comparatively speaking, there are but few beggars', and furthermore, 'Pedlars . . . find here a good market; the people often having plenty of money, from the high price they receive for their cattle, sheep, etc.' The minister of neighbouring Rannoch also noted that the 'peasants were better fed and better clad', though suggesting that 'affluence shines now where formerly penury and sorrow hung their heads' was a touch hyperbolic.[213]

With rising prosperity came growing self-confidence, even assertiveness, among the poorer classes, reflecting an emerging political consciousness fuelled, at least partially, by events in France. Though Edinburgh lawyer Henry Mackenzie believed all was safe by mid 1793 – 'In Scotland the people think more deeply than . . . they do in England [yet] even here, Democracy seems for the present perfectly laid to Rest' – many, like Captain John, still feared the spread of 'revolution principles'.[214] The minister of Duthil berated the common people for having 'a fanatical idea of becoming their own masters and freehold-ers'.[215] A year later, John Ross worried that Fencible recruitment had 'all the common people agog about their Rights etc & may tend to spread a Spirit of Discontent to the North of the Grampians'.[216] Furthermore, he added that making people declare 'their Detestation of French Principles . . . will naturally lead them to enquire about them', and on discovering that 'French Principles consist in *Liberty & Equality*, in *having no Dukes or Lords*, & in *paying no Rents*, they may happen not to dislike them'! In 1797, Anderson warned Captain John against anything that might encourage 'Murmuring and Discontent', which 'in the present Moment . . . you will wish to avoid'.[217] The following year, John noted that 'French Principles are gaining ground – even in the midst of our Mountains', adding the practical concern that evictions were proving problematic because 'the people are now become very *Legal* and there is no want of advisers in this Country'.[218] It was a point reiterated by Alexander Clark, Belleville's factor, when summoning the tenantry to initiate removals: 'But some of them did not appear . . . with a view to disconcert matters'.[219] Considering the background of Highland disturbance – the Inverness meal riots, the Atholl militia riots, the unrest in both the Strathspey and Gordon

Fencibles, not to mention the earlier sheep riots in Ross-shire – these concerns were not without justification.[220]

Rising prosperity and confidence were, however, relative. Rentals show many of the peasantry still operating on subsistence level, ranging from £3–£8 on Benchar, and £4–£10 on Invereshie, and although Alexander Low's survey commented on the 'increased size of many of the Farms' on the Gordon estates in Badenoch, his comments more likely refer to the tacksmen than the subtenantry, many of whom remained on runrig farms.[221] Unforeseen circumstances like the 1793 droving collapse still caused financial difficulties. Inflation, which had already triggered protests around the country including meal riots in Inverness in 1793, worsened after the outbreak of war that year, making prices 'uncommonly high', and by 1795 corn was 80 per cent up on 1780 – causing serious hardship in years of shortage.[222] Seen from a middle-class ministerial perspective, the 'inferior tenants' of Alvie were 'very poor', and 'their habitations wretched', whereas in Kingussie it was the people who earned the epithet 'wretched', their dwellings being 'mean ill-constructed huts'.[223] Travellers also sneered at the 'miserable Hutts . . . built with sods' (Plate 13), though this could be just another example of the outsider's failure to understand local culture. When passing through Drumochter, Harriot Macpherson deplored the 'little huts that you would take more for cow houses or pig sties than dwelling houses, as there is neither a window or a chimney in them' – she simply did not realise (or deliberately misrepresented) that these were temporary shieling bothies, not permanent dwellings.[224]

Against this, however, food riots were primarily urban, and more self-sufficient farming communities like Badenoch, with their varied diet of corn, potatoes and dairy produce, were never as badly affected by either shortages or inflation. Only about 2 per cent of Alvie's population and 5 per cent of Kingussie's were dependent on poor relief or charity. While there were undoubtedly some inferior quality dwellings, the Highland Folk Museum reconstructions (replicas of the eighteenth-century Badenoch township of Mid Raitts), reveal substantial, solid and well-insulated buildings (Plate 14).[225] Elizabeth Grant of Rothiemurchus encapsulated this housing polarisation: 'frightful without, though warm and comfortable within'.[226]

A people's welfare cannot, however, be measured solely in material terms, for the wider quality of life and well-being of the community have to be considered. Education was valued and paid for out of meagre incomes. Across the region at least eight schools catered for 350 to 450 children, though lower when children were 'sent to attend the cattle in the hills, during the summer months' – but they were nevertheless 'fond of learning', and most were already bilingual.[227] Crime was rare. Families lived within a mutual support network born of generations of intermarriage and coexistence in communal townships – a support that would sustain them through difficult times like unemployment, widowhood and old age. But beyond that lay an intangible psychological dimension – the 'feel-good' factor that both enriched life and enabled hardship to be borne with greater equanimity.

Mrs Grant, who knew her Laggan peasantry intimately as both farmer and minister's wife, noted their 'cheerfulness', and the genuine excitement of the shieling season – their nearest equivalent to a summer holiday, a luxury unimaginable to the urban worker. 'The people', she wrote, 'look so glad and contented, for they rejoice at going up', echoed by Robertson as 'the season of contentment, of festivity, of health and joy'.[228] This same feeling permeates Gaelic poetry, perhaps because of associations with courtship:

Bidh an coileach dubh 's an smùdan
'Dianamh ciùil duinn air bharr chranna;
'S bidh am fiadh ann 's a' bhùireadh,
Ga n-ar dùsgadh 's a' mhaduinn.

The black-cock and stock-dove
For us make music on the branches;
And the deer in time of roaring,
Will awake us in the morning.[229]

Drudgery was also broken by the bustle of the weekly market days and even more so by the throng of traders and entertainers attending Ruthven's six annual fairs. Shinty was naturally an important diversion – very much a Sunday sport in Laggan in the 1750s. The men – along with their minister, Duncan Macpherson – would start playing early on the Sabbath, before all entered the church for worship, after which the game 'carried on at intervals till darkness put an end to their amusements, when many retired to the neighbouring crofts and public houses, where high revelry was kept up till morning'. The next incumbent, Andrew Gallie, was clearly less successful in holding his congregation, for it was reported that 'shortly after public worship had commenced [the men] retired from the church to have a game', returning in time for the end of the service – perhaps more a reflection on the length of Gallie's sermons than on the devotion of his flock.[230]

Mrs Grant focused her descriptions on harvest celebrations, and the 'gaiety of the Garagask [Gergask] balls where all the belles and beaus of the braes exhibited themselves'.[231] She gave an intimate depiction of the three-day wedding celebrations for two of their tenants: the night before, 'the bride's friends with all the servants, dancing all the evening' (the hen night); then the wedding feast and barn dance with local musicians, where 'the music and dancing were very superior to anything you could imagine'; further dancing 'on the green' next morning, with a 'concluding ball' at night in 'our itinerant dancing-school' – that in itself being an interesting insight into community life.[232] Captain John also paid for a local dancing school at Invereshie and a fiddler for practice.[233] Elizabeth Grant of Rothiemurchus featured similar events – 'harvest home' dances; the annual 'Floaters' Ball'; an all-day shinty match.[234] The Reverend James Hall captured the idea of community as he described being 'whirled about' by a 'beautiful young woman' at a dance attended by 'people from thousands a year to those that were not worth a sixpence, all dancing and happy', commenting that the 'musical grace, and airy lightness of the dancers' surpassed London's finest.[235] Shrewdly, Mrs Grant recognised not only the poor's capacity for enjoyment, but their need for it: 'it was hard to grudge this one day of glorious felicity' to those who were 'doomed to struggle through a life of hardship and penury'. Furthermore, she held her poorer tenantry in high esteem for their 'superior degree both of fancy and feeling' and 'all the love of society, the taste for conviviality, and even the senti-ment that animates and endears social intercourse', whereas the urban poor, by contrast, were 'so gross, so sordid'.[236]

Such images sit comfortably with the cultural milieu of Gaelic poetry and song from Badenoch – 'a true reflex of the life and shadows of a community' – which dwell not on poverty, misery or starvation, but rather explore those notions of 'fancy and feeling', as in these wistful memories of the Drumochter shielings:

'N uair a théid mi mach mu 'n chabhsair,
Leam cha 'n eibhneas ceòl nan àrd-chlag:
An crodh 's a' gheumnaich mach mu 'n àiridh,
'S a' ghrian a' tearnadh fo sgéith Beinn Eallair.

When I set out around the city streets,
the music of the bells is no joy to me:
[better] the lowing of the cattle on the shielings
as the sun sets over Ben Alder.[237]

The principal themes of this poetry – the intimacy of the landscape, the agricultural cycle, the emotions of love, the excitement of the hunt, the celebration of war – are portrayed with sensitivity, tenderness and humour, or with the driving rhythms of work and dance; while in more serious vein are the eulogies and sacred verse.[238] This appears a culturally confident, vibrant, and positive society, echoing the view that, in contrast to the stereotype of material impoverishment, Highlanders were 'in their own cultural expressions . . . intelligent, resourceful, confident, and resilient'.[239] Similarly, Marianne Maclean noted that the Glengarry community was 'not a defeated society with a morbid culture', but rather was, 'extraordinarily self-confident'.[240]

•   •   •

For many historians of the Highlands, rising population has been portrayed as 'probably the greatest single determinant of social and economic change', leading, particularly in the west, to a 'downward spiral' in living standards.[241] This, however, was not the case in Badenoch which experienced demographic stability and even decline towards the end of the eighteenth century. Between 1750 and 1800, Highland population grew by 20 per cent, Inverness-shire by 22 per cent and the western Highlands, in spite of emigration, by 34 per cent, whereas Badenoch experienced a decrease of 15 per cent (Table 6).[242] Even allowing for statistical inaccuracies – and in 1801 many Badenoch men were still on military service outwith the region, while many of the young may have been on seasonal migration to the Lowlands – the trend is still clear. Indeed, not one source ever suggested that the region suffered over-population: the Reverend John Anderson, intimate with every facet of the local economy, believed that 'the soil could be brought to maintain double the number of its present inhabitants'.[243] However, all the local *Statistical Accounts* indicate a consistently higher number of births than deaths, confirmed in Captain John's droll observation: 'The old trade is going on prosperously, for there are many coming into the World, and few leaving it'.[244] Population should therefore have been rising in line with the wider Highland trend, meaning the actual decrease was much greater than 15 per cent.

This pattern of rapid increase in the north and west Highlands with stable or falling numbers in the south and east has long been recognised, and in Badenoch's case it creates an apparent population paradox in that numbers were declining in the very decade that prosperity was rising – suggesting that depopulation was not simply driven by poverty.[245] Indeed, if rising population

Table 6
Population change in Badenoch 1750s–1801.

	1750s	1790s	1801
Laggan	1460	1512	1333
Kingussie	1900	1803	1306
Alvie	1021	1011	1058
Badenoch total	4381	4326	3697
Percentage change		-1.3	-15

Note: Though not precise, these early censuses are a useful general indicator. There is no obvious reason for Kingussie's substantial drop in 1801, but even if slightly inaccurate, Badenoch's population would still show a decline.
Sources: Kyd, *Scottish Population Statistics* (Edinburgh, 1975), 59–60; *OSA*, 13, 380; 3, 38–9, 148.

was causing a decline in living standards in the western Highlands, the corollary must be that a stable or declining population, as in Badenoch, could have contributed to improving standards by reducing the pressure on land and food, while forcing wages upwards.

Inevitably, demographic debate has been dominated by the emotive 'push' factor, but, as far as Badenoch is concerned, deliberate depopulation, even if economically beneficial, was contrary to the Duke's interests and wishes. In the 1770s, the estate had desperately sought ways to prevent depopulation and emigration, while in 1792, to facilitate the Duke's military ambitions, Tod was charged with the problematic task of getting 'a fair Value for the Lands, without Depopulating the Country'.[246] As late as 1811, Glenbanchor was described as the Duke's '*breeding* Colony of Highlanders', while half the land from Crathie to Balgowan was to be developed as small five-acre crofts which would provide 'an excellent Nursery for Men'.[247] Nor, until the late 1790s, were the gentry keen on depopulation, for a substantial labour force was needed for farms, services and improvements. In fact, any serious reduction in numbers, as in the 1772 famine, the recruitment shortages, or the seasonal migration crisis of 1795, threatened the region's economic viability.[248]

The reasons for Badenoch's gradual depopulation even in a time of comparative prosperity were actually simple enough. The famines of the early 1770s and 1780s had undoubtedly lowered the population base, and even at a time of rising birth rates, recovery by 1800 could only have been gradual, especially with wartime losses. At the same time, the slow but steady process of economic reconstruction and improvement reduced the numbers of communal farms and hence of tenant prospects. For the increasing number of families with little chance of land or permanent jobs, the Lowlands provided a vital safety valve, an easily accessible opportunity for a more secure future. In that sense Badenoch's population may already have been settling into a natural equilibrium before the end of the century, with its surplus numbers steadily drifting southwards. [249]

The late 1790s, however, brought an additional factor into the depopulation conundrum, a sudden upsurge of clearance in the wake of the new Laggan sheep farms. Mrs Grant indeed condemned the 'rage for sheep-farming', precisely because it ousted families with 'neither language, money, nor education, to push their way anywhere else'.[250] Though referring to the Ross-shire clearances, the sentiment was equally applicable to her Laggan home. Surveying the Gordon estates in 1803, Alexander Low put it equally bluntly: 'with Regard to the introduction of sheep farming Depopulating a Country, there is no effectual Remedy for it', though acknowledging that the Duke had tried unsuccessfully to do so.[251] Furthermore, Badenoch lacked the alternative economic system of the west coast where the cleared tenantry were deliberately resettled in crofting townships to supplement their incomes through industries like kelp and fishing. Without such options, Badenoch simply could not accommodate the many evicted families.

Clearances like these, where people were rendered both landless and homeless for sheep, cannot be measured purely in economic and social impact, but in what Devine calls the 'cultural trauma of dispossession'.[252] Betrayal features strongly not just in Gaelic poetry, with lines such as 'Who has destroyed the Gaelic people?/. . . English ways have destroyed us', or 'What have we done wrong to be banished', but also in the English poetry of the Gael: 'Shall men be banish'd from their native scenes/Whilst alien flocks roam o'er these vast demesnes'.[253] Only one such poem survives in Badenoch Gaelic, attacking the proposed clearance of Crathie during the French wars, but there is no doubting the sentiment:

> *Cha thill reitheachan tòir,*
> *'S cha dian cìobar le 'chleòc bonn stàth;*
> *Cha chum caoraich nan glean*
> *Na Frangaich thall; -*
> *'S och! 's mis' tha 's an àm-s' fo phràmh*

Rams will not turn the battle,
Nor will herdsmen with cloak be of use;
Sheep of the glens will not
Keep off the French; -
And alas at this time I'm in woe.[254]

The trauma, however, transcended betrayal and anger, for it encompassed the fears of a peasantry deprived of the means of subsistence – giving the term 'poverty' a stark new reality – and facing exile in an alien urban society.

It would be totally wrong, however, to see population decline purely in terms of estate management and evictions, for economic conditions, particularly in the early 1770s and 1780s, had undoubtedly been a huge factor in forcing many of the poorest to seek a future in the Lowlands. But nor should this southwards exodus be seen purely in negative terms, for years of seasonal migration had facilitated the road to permanent settlement. Many of Badenoch's departing citizens were undoubtedly willing migrants seduced by the lure of Lowland society – city life, better jobs and higher wages – a life with which they were already well acquainted, and for which they were already well equipped.[255]

Conclusion

In an unusually positive view of Highland history, T.C. Smout observed that 'optimism . . . was the keynote of those in command of Highland society in the last three or four decades of the eighteenth century . . . a hopefulness without parallel in Highland experience' – though contrasting this sombrely with 'the dark stagnation of the past and the darker disillusion that was to come'.[256] Optimism certainly captures the last decade of the century in Badenoch. The correspondence, particularly of Anderson and Captain John, resounds with energy and enthusiasm, confidence and hope. It was a decade of improvement schemes – draining Loch Insh, constructing floodbanks, reclaiming moorland and haughs, clearing and enclosing fields, liming, new crops, forestry, sawmills, and the founding of Kingussie – in which the entire social spectrum from the Duchess to the Invereshie boatman were participants. Wartime cattle prices, military incomes and the rapid expansion of sheep farming all fuelled an optimism undented even by increasing rentals – and not only those in 'command of society' enjoyed its fruits. Captain John's talk of 'peace and plenty' and 'easier circumstances', of people 'never more comfortable than they are at present', paints a remarkably positive view of the Highland peasantry, all the more significant in coming from the private correspondence of an insider with intimate knowledge of the area and its people.[257] It is in marked contrast to the stereotype of the impoverished Highland peasant.

Allan Macinnes, adopting a similar positive stance, recognised the 'improved bargaining position of the Gael' by 1800, and this was certainly true of Badenoch.[258] The terminology of the French Revolution – particularly liberty and equality – had insidiously invaded common parlance, fostering an ideological concept of rights among the commonalty. Years of seasonal labour had exposed the younger generation of Highlanders to the Lowland world, including the radicalised working class of Tayside, scene of violent food riots in the 1770s.[259] More significantly they had experienced southern wage levels, instilling a new sense of their own economic worth. That such influences combined to produce a more assertive and calculating populace is hardly surprising: common people stating terms to drovers, manipulating wage levels, legally challenging evictions, negotiating bounty payments, even demanding land in return for enlistment. The erstwhile clansman was learning to exploit market forces even in the remote mountains of Badenoch. Yet paradoxically, at the very time of this increasing empowerment, the peasantry were undergoing social dislocation resulting from agricultural improvement, particularly the rapid expansion of sheep, leaving no alternative for many but to abandon their Badenoch homeland – the Enlightenment concept of 'improvement' was not necessarily the reality experienced by the individual.

Even for the vast majority of Badenoch people, however, the prosperity of the 1790s, based on war and a fortuitous climatic upturn, had a sense of fragility – a fragility emphasised by over-confident tacksmen with over-extended credit lines. The decade was punctuated with warnings: the droving collapse, bankruptcies, even the black hole of Gordon debts. Indeed, Captain John's prophetic warning of 1798 that 'these good times cannot last long', came to fruition far quicker than he could have imagined.[260] Laird and minister catalogued the impending disaster: October 1799 – the very year the Duke yet again raised rents – 'looks very gloomy for the poor people indeed . . . when Meal sells at 26 shillings the Boll [a 63 per cent increase] . . . and neither Cow nor Sheep will be taken at any price – the condition of the Peasantry is really to be pitied'; December, 'reason to dread a very Severe Scarcity'; January 1800, 'We are buried in Snow; and we have a thousand Presentiments of *future*

Evil. In February 1800, Anderson succinctly captured the horror with reference to the 1782–3 famine: 'The Pease Year was but a Joke to this.' Smout's 'darker disillusion' was already pervading Badenoch.[261]

Conclusion:
A Society in Transition

'Who has destroyed the Gaelic people?', lamented an eighteenth-century Highland poet.[1] Historians today also see the destruction of traditional society within the *Gàidhealtachd* by the end of the century.[2] With Britain in the throes of a rapidly accelerating economic and social revolution accompanied by an all-consuming struggle for global power, it was little wonder that the Highlands, though a seemingly peripheral, backward and culturally distinct region, were steadily sucked into this maelstrom – and not necessarily reluctantly. The pace of change, which had begun in the previous century, accelerated dramatically after 1750, partly due to the government's post-Culloden policies, but more because of the willingness of Highlanders themselves to grasp the benefits of British imperialism. This transformation cannot, however, be viewed as a universal entity affecting the entirety of this vast and diverse region in the same ways and at the same time. Rather, it needs to be interpreted in terms of Michael Lynch's view of the Highlands as 'a collection of intensely local societies.'[3] In this context, Badenoch not only followed a rather different economic and social path from other regions, but even displayed a considerable internal divergence of response to the challenges facing the community. Indeed, the degree of social continuity within Badenoch begs the question of how far society had actually been destroyed by the end of the century.

This regional distinctiveness, however, cannot be divorced from the wider context of a shared geographical and cultural identity. Badenoch obviously experienced many of the same environmental and climatic problems, was subject to the same government policies and legislation, and developed within the same imperial framework as the rest of the Highlands. Furthermore, its historical evolution broadly falls into Allan Macinnes's 'first phase of clearance' – commercialisation of the economy, self-interest superseding clan and kinship ties, and the gradual clearance of the tenantry.[4]

It is precisely these common factors, however, that make Badenoch's pattern of conformity and divergence so significant, firstly through the specific constraints imposed by localised environmental factors, and secondly through the variation of individual response to the wider framework of change. Indeed, it is the interplay of the personal forces of human will and agency with the impersonal forces of geographic and environmental factors that shaped the destiny of this 'intensely local society'. The final analysis of the distinctive nature of change and continuity within Badenoch is best achieved through examining the three constituent classes in the social hierarchy as analysed in Chapter 1: landowners, tacksmen and peasantry.

The Landowners

Though never resident in Badenoch, the Gordons dominated the region. Nothing about their absenteeism, extravagance, or ambition is new to our understanding of aristocratic elitism, yet the intimacy of documentation does permit a more critical analysis. Recent historiography has been relatively sympathetic to aristocratic lifestyles, suggesting not only that 'increased consumption was synonymous with the very status of being a great landowner' but that they were subject to 'irresistible social pressures'.[5] The 4th Duke and Duchess were undoubtedly driven by such pressures, desperate to maintain their social and political status as leading lights in British society. Nor was this view contradictory to their estate responsibilities, for the greater the Duke's political influence, the greater his ability to help his tenantry, as Andrew Macpherson of Benchar had earlier acknowledged.[6] Alexander did indeed see himself as a paternalistic landowner, providing famine relief, opposing sheep farms to protect his tenantry, and providing employment opportunities within his own regiments.

Scrutiny of the Duke's policies, however, makes it hard to sustain this view. The 'irresistible social pressures' of life – gambling, political ambition, the opulence of Gordon Castle – resulted not so much in 'increased consumption' as in a reckless extravagance that pushed the estate to the verge of bankruptcy, with serious human consequences. Without any major industrial or colonial resources, this vast expenditure could only be financed through internal revenue, but even major assets like Glenmore Forest or the huge bonus of wartime cattle profits made little impression on the spiralling debts. The brunt thus fell on estate rentals, as James Ross's frantic letters of the 1770s revealed only too clearly. Indeed, six rent increases (a fivefold rise) between 1700 and 1800, sometimes coinciding with times of extreme hardship, placed a crippling burden on the tenantry (and, inevitably, high levels of rent arrears) while stifling those tacksmen who wished to improve their own lands.

It has also been argued that landowners themselves were 'victims of economic forces over which they had little control', but this again is debatable.[7] The Gordons were conscious and willing agents of their own expenditure – a point clearly understood by those beleaguered estate officials who not only warned them of the dangers of debt and bankruptcy, but desperately tried to curb expenditure, even restricting the personal allowances of both Duke and Duchess. Besides, had there been no adverse economic forces in the 1770s, and had the entire estate tenantry paid the full rental throughout that decade, the family's expenditure would still have outstripped total income by many thousands of pounds. If the Gordons were victims, then it was not of impersonal forces, but of self-inflicted wounds.

Yet ducal culpability goes beyond extravagance and rentals, for Alexander's *laissez-faire* estate management did little to help his people. The failure to invest in local improvements or estate reorganisation, even when capital was available, undoubtedly damaged the economic potential of the tenantry. Other problems, as identified by the Reverends Gordon of Alvie and Anderson of Kingussie, included 'the smallness of holdings', 'the shortness of the leases', or, indeed, their total absence, 'vexatious servitudes [and] feudal oppression', and the fear that any tenant-led improvements would bring increased rents, or worse, 'an overbidder [someone offering a higher rent] next lease'.[8] Such problems were neither the fault of the peasantry nor a consequence of impersonal forces, but were directly attributable to the landowner. Indeed, the Duke's failure to provide long leases for the common people denied them any opportunity for self-improvement.

Even Alexander's paternalistic credentials do not stand up to scrutiny. Famine relief, often belated and inadequate, was but a tiny fraction of the family's personal expenditure, and starving tenants were expected to pay, with interest. Nor was his resistance to sheep altruistic, but rather to service his own military, and hence political, ambitions by preventing clearances and depopulation. Regiment raising also had self-interest at its heart – both prestige and wealth – and undoubtedly facilitated his appointments as Knight of the Thistle, Lord Lieutenant of Aberdeenshire and Keeper of the Great Seal of Scotland – the last, which he held for thirty-one years, being worth £3,000 per annum. The paternalist image is further dented by the strained relations between estate and tacksmen, from the douchassers of the 1750s through to John Anderson's 'dirty mushrooms' comment in the 1790s, while the common tenantry's reluctance to support the Duke's regiments suggests a similar level of disenchantment.[9] Aristocratic landownership indeed had done little to improve the economic or social welfare of their Badenoch tenants by 1800.

In marked contrast to the Gordon estates, Invereshie, under the resident management of George Macpherson and Captain John, had undergone an extensive improvement process resulting in a remarkable degree of prosperity by the end of the century. That this was done without wild extravagance or bankruptcy – and even more so without the colonial wealth of men like Munro of Novar – illustrates the significance of personal responsibility.[10] Invereshie demonstrates what could be achieved in even the most inhospitable environment under enlightened management, wedding the best of Lowland improvements to the specific needs of a Highland economy – a distinctive Highland agricultural revolution achieved without mass depopulation. The only other sizeable local estate, Cluny, falls more into the Highland stereotype. Suffering years of stagnation under government administration, and then a brief interlude of relatively successful improvement under the Commissioners of Annexed Estates, the restoration of Colonel Duncan Macpherson in 1784 saw the focus shift towards sheep, bringing clearance and hardship in its wake.

Like most of the Highlands, the late eighteenth century proved a death warrant to the lesser lairds. Those small estates acquired as feus or wadsets in the previous century simply lacked the resources to compete in an increasingly commercial world – especially when petty laird met social ambition. Not one of Badenoch's small estates survived the century, though the land did not yet fall to outsiders, for the Duke and James Macpherson quickly snapped them up, the latter combining his purchases into the larger economic unit of Belleville. Macpherson, however, represents a huge watershed, for though of local pedigree, he was the first in the region to acquire his estate – and hence his social status – through external capital, though his local roots and enthusiasm for clanship at least ensured a degree of cultural and social continuity.

Though the proprietorial classes experienced hugely different fortunes in the late eighteenth century, all faced the same challenge of surviving in an increasingly commercial world. But while the basic economic structure of the estates remained broadly similar, the challenges were met in different ways. Traditional farming and cattle remained the norm for some, while others embraced new agricultural methods; timber and textiles marked the first tentative steps towards industry; sheep, and even grouse, were emerging as an alternative future by 1800. That there was as yet no commonly perceived route to prosperity demonstrates not just the uncertainties of the Highland economy but also the importance of the individual proprietor in determining his estate's future.

The Tacksmen

Tacksmen across the eighteenth-century Highlands have been broadly demonised as parasitic undesirables. Yet in Badenoch a very different picture emerges of a strong entrepreneurial class retaining considerable power into the next century, and enjoying the support, albeit strained, of the principal landowners. Accustomed to power within the clan, the tacksmen clung tenaciously to their status during the post-Culloden assault on clanship, provoking a power struggle with the Gordons, beginning with the successful defiance of the 'douchassers' to estate reorganisation in 1750.[11] When again challenging ducal policy in the 1770s, their united front was broken through the adroit manipulations of Tod and Ross, and the tacksmen were, at least temporarily, reined in. Unlike the western Highlands, however, the tacksman class was neither banished nor eradicated: indeed, the estate did everything possible to *avoid* losing its tacksmen – their importance defined in Tod's words, 'we cannot afford to lose them.'[12]

Throughout this confrontation, the Badenoch tacksmen never felt sufficiently threatened to follow their west-coast brethren to America, but remained firmly rooted in their *duthchas*. Indeed, their independent spirit resurfaced as they shunned the Duke's regimental plans in 1778, and again in the 1790s when some openly defied the Duke's anti-sheep policy. As late as 1811, when offering new leases, the estate worried that the tacksmen would 'enter into Combinations to depreciate the Value of their possessions, and to dissuade others . . . from coming among them' – a *déjà vu* from 1750.[13]

The estate's reluctance to eradicate the tacksmen, as Argyll had done in the 1730s, was purely pragmatic. Badenoch was a vast region, far from Gordon Castle, with only one factor covering both it and Lochaber. It also contained a large, scattered, peasant population too poor to afford economic rents, and certainly lacking the wherewithal for commercial enterprise. Somebody had to manage the domestic economy, organising townships, runrig lands, soumings, shielings, and, of course, setting and collecting rents; somebody with an innate understanding of a mountain economy; somebody with the education and cultural credibility to exercise authority over the native Gaelic populace. The tacksmen were simply indispensable, not just as economic managers but as community leaders, administrators and magistrates with responsibilities as diverse as law and order, roads, licensing and famine relief – a role not inconsistent with their traditional clan function, excepting, of course, the military aspects.[14]

Their importance, however, far outweighed mere middle management, for it was the tacksmen who filled the estate coffers. While earlier historiography generally saw commercial pastoralism as the preserve of landowners, incomers and southern capitalists, the lucrative Badenoch cattle trade was clearly driven by the entrepreneurial indigenous tacksman class. Recognising the insatiable demand arising from southern urbanisation, they successfully exploited it through a sophisticated use of their only significant natural resource, the vast hill grazings. That some went bankrupt was hardly surprising in the insecure world of eighteenth-century finance, but in this they were no different to the innumerable failed industrial enterprises of the south.[15] Many, however, proved themselves highly successful businessmen, managing substantial cattle and droving networks that involved major investments, financial transactions, credit facilities, and, if lucky, substantial rewards over several decades.

In spite of this success, the Highland economy has generally suffered a rather negative spin. Tom Devine, for instance, sees it as an 'economic satellite' – an understandable assessment, but one which essentially denies the Highland gentry's significance as proactive drivers of their own economy.[16] In a parallel scenario, Boyd Hilton inverted the satellite concept, arguing that without the produce of the Northumberland coalmines, 'a megalopolis such as London could not have operated'.[17] The same is true of Highland cattle. The wealthy business, professional and political classes of London did not – could not – function on bread alone, but were largely fuelled by a high-protein intake of meat. Equally dependent was the British navy, four pounds of salt beef per week being integral to sailor diet.[18] In that sense, not just the supremacy of the British capital, but the entire security of the Empire was dependent on the continuing supply of cattle from the Celtic fringes of Scotland, Wales and Ireland. It is, thus, more instructive to see the Highland economy – including those Badenoch tacksmen – not as a peripheral satellite gratefully touching its forelock to the London markets, but as a vital cog in an integrated national and global economy, forging a mutually beneficial partnership with the British state.

Though cattle predominated, the enterprising tacksmen had fingers in many economic pies, including some remarkable agricultural improvements, sheep farming, timber and textiles – albeit with varied degrees of success – in attempts to diversify their financial interests. Others used their education to forge careers outside the Highlands as lawyers, ministers, or merchants. The most lucrative economic return, however, came from service within the British Empire, largely through the patronage network of General Grant and James Macpherson. Indeed, the Badenoch evidence exemplifies the huge significance of military and imperial incomes to the Highlands – a lifetime subsidy for tacksman families – ensuring rental payments and hence security, compensating for agricultural depression, filling the industrial void, and providing essential investment capital. Scarce a gentleman's family in Badenoch between 1757 and 1800 did not have multiple army and Indian connections – another factor in the estate's desire to hold on to them.

Through this economic and managerial importance, the tacksmen remained an essential component in the Badenoch social hierarchy well into the nineteenth century. They were not immune to change, however, for the economic, social and cultural world of 1800 bore little relation to the pre-'45 clan into which the likes of John Dow had been born – and they, themselves, had been catalysts in that change. Fluent in English since the seventeenth century, the tacksman class were increasingly being driven by economic interests outside the *Gàidhealtachd*. Some had joined the British military establishment even before 1745, while during the rising many had remained loyal, even co-operating with the Hanoverians. The subsequent decades saw their commercial, military and imperial interests merge increasingly into the aspirations, culture and fashions of the British establishment. Some of their new-found wealth (at least, what the Duke did not cream off in rents) enabled modestly improved lifestyles, emulating their southern counterparts – though, unlike the Duke, largely financed out of their own endeavours. While their identity remained Highland, it increasingly became a British Highlandism. Captain John, Invereshie, might banter about 'our auld enemies the English', but when in America he fought for 'my friend John Bull'.[19]

This new mindset rose in tandem with the decline of traditional notions of clanship. In truth, clanship across the Highlands had long been undermined by commercial and social aspirations, and Allan Macinnes regards post-Culloden repression as no more than the 'final convulsion' of the clan.[20] Yet the tenacity of Clan Macpherson is a significant feature of eighteenth-century Badenoch: dismantling the trappings of clanship proved easier than erasing an identity forged over centuries, and the Macpherson tacksmen harnessed that collective identity in the post-Culloden world to defy both the Duke and the Barons of Exchequer. But theirs was a very different notion of clanship – a clan run by tacksmen, a brotherhood of Macpherson gentry empowered by the absence of a chief, an institution for furthering their own economic, social, political and military aspirations.

Though the restoration of 1784 brought a flickering hope for past ideals, it was no more than a transitory illusion, for the bonds of communality had been irrevocably broken. The return of a chief, a professional army officer with no concept of traditional clanship, did little to further notions of resurrection, while for the new generation of tacksmen an imperial future proved more enticing than the preservation of archaic ideals. As the elite commandeered the clan, the lower ranks found themselves increasingly alienated, appealing to higher (and external) authorities like the Duke, and even the government agencies, against oppression by the clan hierarchy. This fracturing was further highlighted by their reluctance to enlist with the clan gentry, forcing Colonel Duncan to acknowledge that former clansmen would no longer follow their chief. 'The Spirit of Clanship' had indeed been broken, its apparent tenacity simply due to its reinvention by the tacksmen as an 'old-boy' network.

The traditional role of tacksmanship, too, was changing, gradually metamorphosing into that of principal tenant, a gentleman farmer managing his affairs on a commercial basis, dutifully paying rent to his landlord. Some even abandoned the traditional economy, clearing their tenantry in search of profit. Yet the essential element of tacksmanship endured: the right to sublet, which, with its associated control over land, people and rent, was still universal on Gordon lands in 1800. Subliminal ties also lingered, for these tacksmen were bound to the remnants of clanship by generations of familial interrelationships, bound to the past through associations with ancestral lands, bound to a cultural heritage in which Gaelic tradition still resonated. If the tacksman's demise in the Highlands was 'one of the clearest demonstrations of the death of the old Gaelic society', then traditional society in Badenoch, though in a transitional phase, had clearly not succumbed by 1800.[21]

The Peasantry

Though aristocracy and gentry are abundantly documented, the peasantry remains largely anonymous. No contemporary biographical account exists of any of Badenoch's lower classes, scarce a document addressed to or written by them, their only surviving voice being those colourful testimonies over boundary disputes. Ironically, it is through the writings of their social superiors that the people emerge from the shadows, but even from this potentially unsympathetic source emerges a society far removed from the stereotype of early travellers like James Robertson, who saw the Badenoch people as 'poor, ignorant, unskillful', suffering 'abject idleness', and with a 'veneration for old customs which impels the Highlanders like all Savages, to oppose all innovations' – criticisms echoed in early historiography with Henry Gray Graham's patronising references to 'rags, dirt and squalor', 'hopeless, continual poverty', and 'uncouth pleasures'.[22]

While life at the lower end of the hierarchy was undoubtedly hard, and at times desperate, it was not, however, one of perpetual misery. Indeed, the peasant economy of Badenoch, with its heavy pastoral transhumance element, was more sophisticated than generally recognised, while the extensive reliance on dairy helped counter the annual crop deficiencies and even provided some security in times of total crop failure. But, with most families still eking out a meagre subsistence in small individual farms and communal townships, or as the even lower strata of cottars and labourers, little appeared to have improved in Badenoch by 1800. Indeed, the Alvie minister's condemnation of the 'absurd and unproductive' runrig system as late as 1835 reveals that traditional economic and social structures, including transhumance, continued well into the nineteenth century, particularly on the Gordon estates.[23] Nor had the appalling hardship of famine, as witnessed in the early 1770s and 1780s, been completely eradicated as the impending crisis of 1800 demonstrated. Such crises, however, were not a unique product of Highland life, but were universal to peasant communities across Britain and Europe.

For most of the Badenoch tenantry, however, conditions were improving. Potatoes, land reclamation, new crops and the extensive use of lime in some areas all boosted arable and pasture yields. Some runrig farmers even initiated their own improvements. The Cluny tenantry benefited from the enclosure and drainage schemes of the Commissioners, while those on Invereshie enjoyed the small self-sufficient farms established by their resident laird. Most significant, however, was the security derived from long leases and moderate rents which facilitated self-improvement amongst the Cluny and Invereshie (but not Gordon) tenants – a far cry from the emerging crofting system of the western Highlands. Equally crucial, however, was the increased earning potential. Textiles and timber created some new employment opportunities.

Military recruitment provided a vital bonus of short-term injections of cash, though, being limited to the duration of war or period of service, this was not the permanent panacea it was for the tacksmen. By far the most important supplementary income came from seasonal labour which by the end of the century was not only bringing substantial annual earnings, but was forcing local wages upwards, thereby benefiting the entire lower end of the social spectrum – a point clearly demonstrated by the antagonism of the gentry towards the seasonal exodus.

Recent research into the concept of agency amongst the common people is substantiated by the growing sense of independence in Badenoch. Collective opposition appeared as early as the rent strikes of the 1720s, followed in the 1750s with the successful protests against Uvie. Later, the physical resistance to the Aberarder evictions, the reluctance over enlistment, and the use of law to counter eviction, all suggest an increasing assertiveness.[24] Military service and seasonal migration brought a greater awareness of the world and of their worth within it, encouraging bargaining over wages, bounties and land. Evidence of commercial opportunism appears in the renting of shielings to drovers, the grazing of *gall* cattle, the attendance of local women at the spinning schools, and the desire to initiate improvements.[25] This enthusiasm for self-improvement might have had even greater impact but for the obstructive practices of their social superiors – failing to grant leases, rack-renting, labour services, appropriating common grazings, trying to prevent seasonal migration and imposing wage controls. Mr Kemp, secretary of the SSPCK, recognised this problem while touring the Highlands in 1791, observing that, while the Highlander was 'excelled by none' in diligence and initiative, he was stifled by 'oppression and forced labour'.[26] In spite of tacksman repression, however, the Badenoch peasantry was clearly evolving into an increasingly confident and assertive class, ready to exploit opportunities for self-improvement, but also ready to defend its rights – 'aspiring at Independence' as Parson Robert had put it in the 1770s, sentiments reiterated by Captain John two decades later.[27]

There remained, however, the negative associations of eviction. For those relocated during internal estate reorganisation as at Invereshie there was an inevitable drop in status to cottar and labourer, and though in economic terms they might 'scarcely have noticed the change', there was the 'stigma of being landless', and the clamour for crofts in return for enlistment does indeed suggest that possession of land remained important to economic and social status.[28] Mass clearances, however, were a different matter. Allan Macinnes believes that such traumatic events, in tandem with alienation from the clan elite and creeping Anglicisation, left Highlanders 'perplexed, demoralised and disoriented', and for those Laggan families removed for sheep in the 1790s and facing homelessness, poverty, and a Lowland future, these words would have undoubted resonance.[29] But across Badenoch as a whole, such an image contradicts the notion of a more assertive and confident peasantry, and clearly those with their own independent farms, reaping the benefits of higher prices and living standards as on Invereshie, were in no way 'demoralised'. Even cultural disorientation was less significant here, for generations of seasonal migration had brought an assimilation of southern values and culture that was simply not possible in more remote regions of the *Gàidhealtachd*.

•   •   •

The poet's question regarding the destruction of the Gaelic people requires a rather ambivalent answer for Badenoch. That the region was in the throes of a turbulent and traumatic upheaval is self-evident, but much of the economic and social structure clearly survived into the next century – pastoralism, transhumance, cattle-based commercialism, runrig townships, native propri-etorship, indigenous tacksmen, peasant subtenantry all suggesting a continuity beyond the Highland norm. Yet beneath the surface, the transition was accel-erating dramatically: more importantly, it was irreversible. The clan, whose practices and hierarchy had for centuries dominated local society, was dead in its traditional form, gradually yielding to the social and cultural values of the south. Communality surrendered to capitalism, driven largely by the indigenous gentry whose self-interest undermined the cohesion of traditional society, driving a wedge between the old clan elite and their erstwhile clansmen. But even the latter were embracing change, seeking to improve their own status, challenging the old social order, and in the process absorbing southern values and culture. Traditional society in Badenoch might still persist in 1800, but its roots had been destroyed, its future aspirations moulded by a progressively Anglocentric world.

It was a process that inevitably gathered pace in the early nineteenth century. Further climatic troughs weakened the regional economy; peace in 1815 saw cattle prices drop by two-thirds while the grossly inflated wartime rentals remained; the sheep revolution swept through the region, while sporting estates became the new panacea, destroying the pastoral economy. Depopulation increased, not just by the continuing Lowland exodus, but also through extensive clearances and the first waves of mass emigration from Badenoch in the 1830s, to both Canada and Australia. Even the traditional tacksmen, broken by post-war depression, deprived of their subtenantry, or themselves removed for sheep and deer, either abandoned their ancestral lands or merged into gentleman sheep farmers.

Nor did the estates escape the transition. Invereshie, absorbed into the far wealthier Ballindalloch estate which Captain John's son (later, Sir George Macpherson-Grant) had inherited, suffered under its new, ambitious absentee laird; Cluny continued expanding his domain and his sheep farms; Belleville remained with 'Fingal's' various offspring who also initiated substantial sheep clearances. Most significant, however, was the disappearance of the Gordons from Badenoch after 400 years, the debt mountain finally forcing the sale of their Highland estates in the 1830s. So overwhelming and comprehensive, indeed, was the nature of change, that the Badenoch of 1850 would scarcely have been recognisable to those old clan stalwarts who have featured so heavily in this study – Donald Macpherson of Breakachy, Andrew Macpherson of Benchar, Parson Robert, Captain John Macpherson of Invereshie, and, of course, the inimitable John Dow.

•   •   •

On the penultimate day of the eighteenth century, John Dow, at the age of seventy-six, headed into the remote wilds of the forest of Gaick with four companions for what would be his last hunting expedition. The new year dawned with a storm of intense ferocity, triggering an avalanche that obliterated the bothy in which he and his companions slept, their firearms 'bent, broken and twisted in every possible shape' by the sheer force of snow. Such was the devastation, and the character of the man himself, that mutterings about pacts with the devil soon arose, and the legend of *An t-Othaichear Dubh*, 'The Black Officer', was born – John Dow forever enshrined in his own Faustian legend.[30]

Nobody embodies the eighteenth-century Badenoch tacksman more than Captain John Dow Macpherson of Ballachroan – the young Iain Dubh mac Alasdair from Phones who had watched General Wade's soldiers building the road past his house when but a child: officer with both Charles Edward Stuart and King George, half-pay captain, successful recruiter; tacksman of three large farms, cattle farmer, sheep farmer, agricultural improver, flax grower; wealthy drover, opportunistic entrepreneur, estate factor; poacher and deer stalker *par excellence*; all combined with his social functions as member of the clan elite, Justice of the Peace and magistrate in Ruthven Quarter-Session Court; valued by estate officials and entertained by Duke and Duchess. But he also embodied the negatives: ruthless, aggressive, fraudulent, litigious; brutal pressgang officer, tyrannical towards the peasantry, evicting his own subtenantry; ultimately, a bankrupt.[31]

This enigmatic old man truly was the last of his kind, one of the last of the old Macpherson tacksmen born into pre-Culloden clan society. It is tempting (if rather unhistorical) to see a certain symbolism in the nature and timing of his death, meeting his fate in such dramatic circumstances at the very birth of the new century, a century that would render the old-style tacksman an anachronism in his own land. There is, too, in light of the arguments presented in this narrative, a certain irony that the man who had so forcefully implanted his personality on the region should have perished in one of the most powerful of impersonal forces. Lachlan Macpherson of Biallid, one of his younger contemporaries, wrote of him, 'if we lived a hundred years, we should not see his like again' – a fitting epitaph not just for John Dow, but for the entire Badenoch tacksman class he so epitomised.[32]

Glossary

Anker:	Old liquid measure of roughly 10 gallons.
Annexed estates:	Estates forfeited after the 1745 Jacobite rising and annexed by the Crown in 1752.
Aughtens:	Measure of land within the runrig farms based on extent (one-eighth, or aughten, of the farm arable) rather than monetary value.
Baile:	Farming township.
Baron Court:	Responsible for regulation and administration of estate affairs.
Barons of Exchequer:	Scottish court initially responsible for administering the forfeited estates.
Board of Commissioners:	Responsible for administering the annexed estates after 1752, though not till 1770 on Cluny estate.
Bothy:	Shieling hut.
Commissioners:	Management team responsible for the Gordon estates.
Controverted:	Land under ownership dispute.
Cottar:	Lowest level of agricultural subtenant, possessing house, garden and a cow's grass, in return for labour.
Customs:	Rents paid in kind (produce).
Davoch:	Ancient administrative division of land, also referred to as daugh. Badenoch traditionally possessed sixty davochs.
Deer forest:	Mountain reserves for deer hunting, generally with few trees.
Douchasser:	Wealthy tacksman holding his land as a *duthchas*.
Duthchas:	Traditional right to land within the clan system.
Enlightenment:	Eighteenth-century intellectual movement advancing science, improvement, and rationality of thought.
Feu:	Portion of land or estate bought from a superior for which an annual feu duty is paid.
Fire house:	Dwelling with fireplace.
Forfeited Estates:	Estates confiscated by the Crown after the 1745 Jacobite rising.

Garth:	Garden.
Gentleman volunteer:	Gentry joining the army without a commission, but hoping to acquire one during the campaign.
Haughs:	Rich, low-lying riverside lands prone to regular flooding.
Head dyke:	Boundary separating the arable from the hill ground.
Heritable jurisdictions:	The powers of landowners and clan chiefs abolished in 1747.
Heritors:	Landowners.
Horning:	Declaring bankrupt.
King's lands:	Lands confiscated after the 1745 Jacobite rising (also referred to as His Majesty's lands).
Lb	Pounds weight. There were 14lb (sometimes 28lb) in 1 stone.
Mealander/mailander/mailer:	Roughly synonymous with cottar.
Meliorations:	Improvements made to farm or buildings for which compensation was due when tenant left.
Merk:	Two-thirds of £1 Scots.
Nabob:	British gentry returning with large fortunes from India.
Nawab:	Wealthy Indian prince.
Poinding:	Confiscating straying livestock and extracting fine from the owner.
Rack-rent:	Rent well above market value.
Reek-hen:	Hen paid as rent from every house with a hearth.
Regality:	Estate owned by aristocrat with heritable jurisdictions.
Roup:	Public sale of stock and gear by outgoing farmer.
Runrig:	System of communal landholding with intermixed arable rigs (ridges/strips).
Services:	Labour required of tenants as part of rent.
Servitude:	Traditional right of tenantry, for example, to timber or peat.
Sett:	Formal letting of estate by landowner to tenants.
Shielings:	Residential hill grazings, used between spring and autumn.
Souming:	Allowance of animals for each tenant on farm/estate.
SSPCK	Scottish Society for the Propagation of Christian Knowledge, responsible for establishing schools in large Highland parishes.
Superior:	The feudal superior was the principal landowner who had sold or granted feus of land to lesser proprietors (known as vassals), while retaining certain rights of superiority over the land.

Superiority:	Superiority was the rights retained by the principal landowner over land sold to lesser proprietors. The principal landowner could sell these superiorities to the proprietors, relinquishing his remaining rights over the land.
Tacksman:	Gentry holding land from landowner as principal tenant and subletting it to peasant farmers.
Tathing:	Systematic manuring of pasture ground prior to sowing with crops.
Township:	Communal runrig farming settlement.
Tryst:	Cattle market.
Wadset, proper:	Land held by tenant in return for a loan to the landowner, where interest on the loan and the rent due for the land are equal, so cancel each other out.
Wadset, improper:	As above, but where the rent is higher than the interest, and the tenant pays a 'superplus' duty as balance.
Wedder:	Castrated young male sheep.
Whig	One of two British political parties, the other being the Tories.
Yeld:	In eighteenth-century terms, a non-breeding beast whether male or female.

Notes

Abbreviations

AUL	Aberdeen University Library (Sir Duncan Rice Library)
Craigdhu	Sir Thomas Macpherson Archive, Craigdhu House
EUL	Edinburgh University Library
HAC	Highland Archive Centre, Inverness
HFM	Highland Folk Museum Archive
HL	Huntington Library, California, Loudoun Scottish Collection.
NLS	National Library of Scotland
NRS	National Records of Scotland
NRAS	National Register of Archives for Scotland
NSA	*New Statistical Account*
OSA	*Old Statistical Account*
PP	Parliamentary Papers
RCAHMS	Royal Commission on the Ancient and Historical Monuments of Scotland
SHR	*Scottish Historical Review*
TGSI	*Transactions of the Gaelic Society of Inverness*
WSRO	West Sussex Record Office, Goodwood Archive

Introduction

1 Pho-ness: almost equal emphasis on both syllables. Alan G. Macpherson, *A Day's March to Ruin* (Clan Macpherson Association, 1996), 27–8. Thanks to local farmer and historian, Graham Grant, for pointing out 'Cope's Turn'.

2 William Taylor, *The Military Roads in Scotland* (London, 1976), 16, 48–52, 138; Alexander Macpherson, *Glimpses of Church and Social Life in the Highlands in Olden Times* (Edinburgh, 1893), 144–9; Edmund Burt, *Letters from a Gentleman in the North of Scotland to his Friend in London*, vols 1 and 2 (London, 1754).

3 Macpherson, *Day's March*, 3, 10; John Macpherson of Strathmashie, in *Lyon in Mourning*, vol. 2 (Edinburgh, 1895), 93; NRS, E745/19/3, Petition, Major John Macpherson (Cluny), 1766; Huntington Library, Loudoun Scottish Collection, HL, LO12193, Cluny, 13 July 1745.

4 John Dow (pronounced as in *dubh*, Gaelic for black) is the name used throughout this book to distinguish him from the many other John Macphersons. 'An t-Othaic-hear Dubh' is the correct Badenoch Gaelic spelling of 'The Black Officer'. See also Macpherson, *Glimpses*, 144–9. For the legend of the Black Officer see Affleck Gray, *Legends of the Cairngorms* (Edinburgh, 1987), 68–79.

5 Badenoch is perhaps the most neglected area in Highland historiography. Other regions have been far better served: *inter alia*, Malcolm Bangor-Jones, *The Assynt Clearances* (Dundee, 1998); Eric Cregeen, *Argyll Estate Instructions 1771–1805* (Edinburgh, 1964); Robert McGeachy, *Argyll 1730–1850* (Edinburgh, 2005); Victor Gaffney, *The Lordship of Strathavon* (Aberdeen, 1960); Leah Leneman, *Living in Atholl* (Edinburgh, 1986); Iain Macdonald, *Glencoe and Beyond: The Sheep Farming Years – 1780–1830* (Edinburgh, 2005); Marianne MacLean, *The People of Glengarry: Highlanders in Transition, 1745–1820* (Montreal, 1991); Eric Richards and Monica Clough, *Cromartie: Highland Life 1650–1914* (Aberdeen, 1989); John Barrett, *The Making of a Scottish Landscape: Moray's Regular Revolution* (Croydon, 2015); not including the heavy emphasis on Sutherland, Skye and the west coast in many general Highland studies.
There are, however, a number of good local studies of Badenoch including Charles Fraser-Mackintosh, *Antiquarian Notes* (Inverness, 1897), *Dunachton Past and Present* (Inverness, 1866); Macpherson, *Glimpses*; Macpherson, *Day's March*; George Dixon, 'The Founding of Kingussie', I–XVII, *Strathspey and Badenoch Herald*, 13 June–17 December 1971; I.F. Grant, *Every-day Life on an Old Highland Farm* (London, 1981); Anne Glen, *The Cairngorm Gateway* (Dalkeith, 2002); Meryl Marshall, *Glen Feshie: The History and Archaeology of a Highland Glen* (Fort William, 2005); Earl John Chapman (ed.), *Letters from North America 1758–1761: The Private Correspondence of Parson Robert Macpherson* (Montreal, 2013); R. Ross Noble, 'Turf-walled houses in the central Highlands', in *Folk Life* 22 (1983–4).

6 T.M. Devine, *Scotland's Empire: The Origins of the Global Diaspora* (London 2004), 120.

7 *OSA* 3, 147.

8 George Dixon, 'The Founding of Kingussie', I, *Strathspey and Badenoch Herald*, 13 June 1971; Barry Robertson, 'Continuity and Change in the Scottish Nobility: The House of Huntly, 1603–1690', unpublished PhD thesis, University of Aberdeen, 2007, 16 n.29. The earldom became a dukedom in 1684.

9 Malcolm Gray, *The Highland Economy 1750–1850* (Edinburgh, 1957), 9–10; Charles Withers, *Gaelic Scotland: The Transformation of a Culture Region* (London, 1988), 3, 82 – a distinction more appropriate for the nineteenth century than the eighteenth.

10 Michael Lynch, *Scotland: A New History* (London, 1992), 369. See also Withers, *Gaelic Scotland*, 9–10.

11 John Leyden, *Tour in the Highlands and Western Islands* (Edinburgh, 1903), 197.

12 James Hogg, *The Shepherd's Guide: Being a Practical Treatise of the Diseases of Sheep* (Edinburgh, 1807), 282.

13 *An Account of the Principal Pleasure Tours in Scotland* (2nd edition, Edinburgh, 1819), 93; NLS, MS29491, 'Tour in Scotland, 1794', 43–4.

14 NLS, MS2509, John Anderson, 'Sketch of a Ramble through the Highlands of Scotland, the Summer of 1818', 131; Henry Skrine, *Three Successive Tours in the North Part of England and Great Part of Scotland* (London, 1795), 141; NLS, MS29492, Anon, 'Tour Through England and Scotland in 1790', 72; Colonel Thornton, *A Sporting Tour Through the Northern Parts of England, and Great Part of the Highlands of Scotland* (London, 1804), 116.

15 Eric Richards, *The Highland Clearances*, vol. 1 (London, 1982), 1, 7; Gaskell, *Morvern Transformed* (Cambridge, 1980), 26; Withers, *Gaelic Scotland*, 10.

16 Richards, *The Highland Clearances*, vol. 2 (London, 1985), 154–5.

17 T.M. Devine, *Clearance and Improvement: Land, Power and People in Scotland 1700–1900* (Edinburgh, 2006), 14; Matthew P. Dziennik, 'The Fatal Land: War, Empire, and the Highland Soldier in British America, 1756–1783', unpublished PhD thesis, University of Edinburgh, 2011, 5, 12. Andrew Mackillop, *More Fruitful than the Soil: Army, Empire and the Scottish Highlands 1715–1815* (East Linton, 2000), also presents the identity of the Highlander in a very positive light.

18 James Hunter, *The Making of the Crofting Community* (Edinburgh, 1995), 5.

19 Robert Dodgshon, *From Chiefs to Landlords: Social and Economic Change in the Western Highlands and Islands 1493–1820* (Edinburgh, 1998), 7–121; T.M. Devine, *Clanship to Crofters' War: The Social Transformation of the Scottish Highlands* (Manchester, 1994), 11–17; Allan Macinnes, *Clanship, Commerce and the House of Stuart 1603–1788* (East Linton, 1996), 1–190; Stana Nenadic, *Lairds and Luxury: The Highland Gentry in Eighteenth Century Scotland* (Edinburgh, 2007).

20 Macinnes, *Clanship, Commerce*, 211–21; Devine, *Clanship to Crofters' War*, 32–4.

21 NRS, GD44/28/31/8, James Stewart, 23 October 1732; Dixon, *Kingussie*, I.

22 NRS, GD44/27/3/75, 79, Malcolm Clark, 1735.

23 Macpherson, *Glimpses*, 31–2.

24 NRS, GD44/27/13/10, Killiehuntly, 1727.

25 HL, LO12193, Cluny, 13 July 1745; HL, LO12194, Cluny, 3 August 1745.

26 HL, LO12203, Killiehuntly to Loudoun, 31 October 1745.

27 Macpherson, *Day's March*, 272–99; NRS, GD128/50/3, papers relating to Cluny, 1745.

28 Macpherson, *Day's March*, 262.

29 Ibid., 269.

30 Macinnes, *Clanship, Commerce*, 211; pp. 211–17 provide an excellent discussion of post-Culloden policy.

31 NRS, GD248/48/4/30, Archibald Grant [Monymusk?] to Ludovick Grant [son of clan chief, Sir James], 23 April 1746.

32 Macpherson, *Day's March*, 169.

33 NRS, GD248/48/5/16, James Lawtie to Sir James Grant, 28 February 1747.

34 NLS, MS305, 106, Bland to Captain Troughear, 3 July 1755.

35 New Spalding Club, *Historical Papers 1699–1750* (Aberdeen, 1896), 538; HL, LO10576, Ruthven, 1 September 1746.

36 Macpherson, *Day's March*, 201.

37 Bland to Lord Barrington, 22 January 1756, in Provost Macpherson, 'Gleanings from the Cluny Charter Chest III', *TGSI* 21 (1896–7), 439.

38 NLS, MS305, 115, Bland to Lord George Beauclerck, 24 July 1755.

39 NLS, MS305, 106, Bland to Captain Troughear, 3 July 1755.

40 Macpherson, *Glimpses*, 452.

41 Quoted in Allan Burnett and Linda Andersson Burnett (eds), *Blind Ossian's Fingal* (Edinburgh, 2011), 54.

42 NRS, GD44/14/15/33, Abstract of Damages, 1 August 1746, 10 September 1746; NRS, GD44/27/54, NRS, GD44/51/732/9.

43 Anon., *c.*1760, quoted in Macpherson, *Glimpses*, 455.

44 Journal of an English Medical Officer, *The Contrast: or Scotland as it was in the Year 1745 and Scotland in the Year 1819* (London, 1825), 156.

45 NRS, GD248/48/4/32, Patrick Grant to James Lawtie, 30 April 1746.

46 Strathmashie, in *Lyon in Mourning*, 93.

47 Quoted in Macpherson, *Day's March*, 189.

48 NRS, GD44/14/15/33, Precognition anent Damages, 10 September 1746.

49 NRS, E745/38/4, Ramsay's Accounts, 1752.

50 Medical Officer, *The Contrast*, 157. Bad though it was, Cluny himself acknowledged that his lands had escaped relatively lightly compared to Lochaber (Macpherson, *Day's March*, 188).

51 NRS, GD44/27/4/54, Report and Sett of Badenoch, 1751, 6.

52 NRS, GD44/28/23, Replies for Cullinlean, 11 August 1768.

53 NRS, GD44/51/405, Alexander Farquharson, 20 May 1769.

54 NRS, GD44/27/18, Duke to Captain Duncan Macpherson, 1790, marginal note.

55 HL, LO12191, Bessie Macpherson, 2 December 1746.

56 NRS, GD44/41/28/2/27, Petition, 1749.

57 NRS, GD44/39/3/12, Depositions, Dalnashalg, 1782.

58 HL, LO10840, Kenneth Bethune, schoolmaster.

59 Estimates from Macpherson, *Day's March*, 260–99.

60 Ibid.; HL, LO10840, Kenneth Bethune, schoolmaster.

61 HL, LO12203, Killiehuntly to Loudoun, 31 October 1745; HL, LO12192, Macpherson to Grant, 6 February 1746.

62 NRS, GD248/48/4/30, Macpherson to Grant, 18 April 1746.

63 HL, LO12195, 10576, 1 September 1746.

64 Macpherson, *Day's March*, 204.

65 Quoted in Andrew Lang (ed.), *The Highlands of Scotland in 1750* (Edinburgh, 1898), 143–5.

66 New Spalding Club, *Historical Papers*, 550.

67 See James Hunter, *Last of the Free: A Millennial History of the Highlands and Islands of Scotland* (Edinburgh, 1999), 210.

1. The Social Hierarchy

1. NRS, GD44/34/38, Memorial, 1792. Superiorities were rights to land retained by the principal landowner even after sale.
2. NRAS, 771/581, Killiehuntly Rental, 1752.
3. James Robertson, *General View of the Agriculture of the County of Inverness* (London, 1813), 226.
4. Devine, *Clearance*, 195–7; Dodgshon, *Chiefs*, 236–8.
5. Robertson, 'Continuity and Change', 214.
6. Thornton, *Sporting Tour*, 104.
7. NRAS, 771/131, William to John Macpherson, 1779.
8. Annette Smith, *Jacobite Estates of the Forty-Five* (Edinburgh, 1982), 23; Macinnes, *Clanship, Commerce*, 217.
9. NRS, E745/1/3, Cluny Rentroll, 1748.
10. Nenadic, *Lairds*, 62, refers to the habits of the gentry filtering down to the tacksmen, but in Badenoch many were equal to or wealthier than the lairds.
11. Macinnes, *Clanship, Commerce*, 222; T.M. Devine, *The Scottish Nation* (London, 1999), 174.
12. Macinnes, *Clanship, Commerce*, 16; Devine, *Clanship to Crofters' War*, 11. For the Lowland equivalent, Kindly Tenancy, see Margaret Sanderson, *Scottish Rural Society in the Sixteenth Century* (Edinburgh, 1982), 58–62.
13. NRS, GD44/27/17, Memorial of Hugh Macpherson, 26 April 1773.
14. NRS, GD44/27/4/23, Duncan Macpherson, 29 September 1784.
15. NRS, GD44/27/11/20x, Tod to Ross, 19 March 1772.
16. NRS, GD44/27/11/134, Shaw to Ross, April 1776.
17. NRS, GD44/27/11/99x, Shaw to Tod, 30 March 1776, Tod's addendum.
18. Macpherson, *Day's March*, 299.
19. Macinnes, *Clanship, Commerce*, 170.
20. NRS, CR8/195, George Brown, Contents, Measures and Estimates of the Lordship of Badenoch, 1771, 13–18 (hereafter Brown, survey).
21. Dodgshon, *Chiefs*, 127; Macinnes, *Clanship, Commerce*, 16.
22. RCAHMS, SC1082428, George Taylor, A Plan of Part of the Lordship of Badenoch, 1773 (hereafter Taylor, Plan); NRS, E745/60, Tennoch, Report of the Contents, Measures and estimated rents of Cluny estate, 1771–2 (hereafter, Tennoch, survey), 20; NRS, CR8/195, Brown, survey, 1771, 1.
23. NRAS, 771/581, Killiehuntly Rental, 1752.
24. NRS, CR8/194, Taylor, Contents and Estimates of the Lordship of Badenoch, 1770–2 (hereafter Taylor, survey), 65–9.
25. NRS, GD44/27/18, Captain Duncan Macpherson and the Duke of Gordon, 1790.
26. NRS, CR8/195, Brown, survey, 1771, 7, 11; HAC, GB0232/D307/1/6, 7, Hamilton to Macdonell, 1750; Macdonald, *Glencoe*, 21.
27. NRS, GD44/27/54, Sett of Badenoch, 1751, 8–12.

28 NRS, CR8/194, Taylor, survey, 31, 35, 37; NRS, GD44/43/177/10, Tod to Ross, 21 March 1777; NRS, CS236/M/10/7, Sequestration of John Macpherson; Macdonald, *Glencoe*, 24.

29 NRS, GD44/27/19/2, Duke to John Macpherson, 1744.

30 NRS, GD44/28/32/9, Tack of Sherrabeg, Sherramore, Garvabeg, Garvamore, Turfadown, Druminard and Blargiebeg, 1751.

31 NRS, CR8/194, Taylor, survey, 7–10, 13–16, 31–6, 45–6; NRS, CR8/195, Brown, survey, 41–6. Where ground was common figures have been estimated. Benchar and Clune estimates were based on averages for surrounding davochs.

32 NRS, E745/60, Tennoch, survey, tables.

33 Alexander Wight, *An Enquiry into the Rise and Progress of Parliament Chiefly in Scotland* (Edinburgh, 1794), 240.

34 HAC, GB0232/CH2/437/1, Abernethy Presbytery Records, 24 June 1755, 483.

35 NRS, GD44/27/18, Duke of Gordon & Capt. Duncan McPherson, 1790.

36 NRS, GD44/27/54, Sett of Badenoch, 1751, 8–12.

37 Wight, *Enquiry*, 243. In an 'improper wadset' (where rent exceeded interest payments) the landowner still received a reduced rent to cover the balance.

38 NRS, GD44/27/19/3, John Macpherson to Duke, *c.*1740s.

39 NRS, GD44/27/11/25x, Tod to Ross, 15 April 1772.

40 William Ramsay, 'Bad Times Within the Bounds of Badenoch', *TGSI* (1996); NRS, GD44/27/19/6, Charter of Sale, 1787; NRS, GD176/907, Sasine, John Macpherson, 15 October 1787.

41 NRS, CR8/195, Brown, survey, 7, 11.

42 NRS, GD44/27/10/5, Donald Grant, 23 October 1770.

43 NRS, GD44/27/11/1/20x, Tod to Ross, 19 March 1772.

44 NRS, CR8/195, Brown, survey, 47.

45 Mrs Grant of Laggan, *Letters from the Mountains*, 2 vols (London, 1845), vol. 2, 13, 4 June 1791.

46 Smith, *Jacobite Estates*, 59.

47 NRS, GD44/27/10/197x, Tod to Ross, 20 November 1771.

48 NRS, GD44/51/732/9, Rental, 1770–1.

49 NRS, GD44/27/21, Abstract of Sale, 2 July 1784.

50 NRS, GD1/141/2, Balnespick Tutory, 19 June 1786 (incorrectly dated 1785 in document), 18 November 1791, 5 February 1792, 28 November 1793.

51 NRS, GD128/22/10, Helen Mackintosh to Campbell Mackintosh, 26 January 1789.

52 NRS, GD44/27/18, Duke of Gordon & Capt. Duncan McPherson, 1790; Rev. Campbell, 1743, quoted in Macpherson, *Glimpses*, 340; NRS, GD44/27/10/33x, Tod to Ross, 19 July 1770; NRS, GD44/27/11/16x, Tod to Ross, 23 March 1772.

53 Hunter, *Last of the Free*, 210.

54 Fraser-Mackintosh, *Antiquarian Notes*, 357.

55 NRS, GD44/27/18, Duke of Gordon & Capt. Duncan Macpherson, 1790.

56 Dr. Archibald Cameron's Memorial Concerning the Locharkaig Treasure *c.*1750, in http://www.lochiel.net/archives/arch189.html

57 NRS, E702/2/132, James Small, 1753.

58 NRS, E745/2/3, NRS, E745, 2/4/1, Affidavits, 1764. Killiehuntly was a Hanoverian loyalist.

59 NRS, E745/9/11/2, James Small's report on Killiehuntly; NRS, E745/12/3, Killiehuntly to James Smollet, 10 November 1764. Fraser-Mackintosh, 'The Boycotting of Killlihuntly', TGSI 24 (1904), gives an entertaining account of this incident. For the testimonies of the lynch mob see NRS, E745/9/11. Macpherson, *Day's March*, 183–200, offers a strong defence of Cluny's handling of this money, but these documents leave little doubt that some of the French gold had, rightly or wrongly, found its way into the hands of the Macpherson gentry.

60 NRS, E745/10/2/2, LG (an estate creditor), 22 December 1761.

61 NRS, GD44/28/20, Instrument of Protest, 3, 1770.

62 Macdonald, *Glencoe*, 229; NRS, GD44/43/117/13, John Macpherson to Ross, 21 March 1777.

63 Macdonald, *Glencoe*, 31; NRS, GD128/30/4, Ranald Macdonald to Alexander Macdonald, 12 February 1806; NRS, GD44/52/38, Ross to Tod, 10 April 1772, 20.

64 Rosalind Mitchison, 'The Highland Clearances', *Scottish Economic & Social History* 1 (1981), 16, sees it not as a right of individual *duthchas*, but one 'of the society'.

65 Alan Macpherson, 'An Old Highland Parish Register: Survivals of Clanship and Social Change in Laggan, Inverness-shire, 1773–1854', *Scottish Studies* 11 (1967), 189.

66 NRS, GD44/51/732/1, Gordon Rental, 1729, 31; NRS, GD44/51/732/30, Glenbanchor, 1804.

67 John Barrett, 'A Regular Revolution: cooperation, change and classification in the Moray Landscape, 1760–1840', unpublished PhD thesis, University of Aberdeen, 2013, 84. See also Eric Richards, *The Highland Clearances* (Cambridge, 2000), 39–40; Devine, *Scottish Nation*, 175; Leneman, *Atholl*, 51.

68 NRS, GD128/50/3/A, Proof, 1793, Alexander Kennedy, Malcolm Macpherson; NRS, GD44/39/3/12, James Macpherson.

69 See Dodgshon, 'Everyday Structures, Rhythms and Spaces of the Scottish Countryside', in Elizabeth Foyster and Christopher Whatley, *A History of Everyday Life in Scotland, 1600–1800* (Edinburgh, 2010), 33.

70 Dodgshon, *Chiefs*, 123–225, provides a thorough analysis of the evolution and function of communal townships.

71 NRS, GD44/28/12/10, Tack, 14 April 1726. Place-names in the eighteenth-century estate records are almost exclusively Gaelic, so the use of English suggests these were not traditional names.

72 NRS, CH2/1419/1, Kingussie Parish Records, 162.

73 NRS, GD44/27/21, Memorial & Abstract of Sale, 2 July 1784; NRS, E745/1/3, Cluny Rentroll, 1748; NRS, GD44/51/732/1, Gordon Rental, 1729, 21–2.

74 NRS, E745/1/3, Cluny Rentroll, 1748; NRS, E745/42/1, 4, Cluny Rentals, 1770, 1784.

75 NRAS, 771/1268, Sett of Invereshie, 1813.

76 NRS, GD44/43/17/2, Rental of Strathmashie, 1728; NRS, GD44/732/50, Rental, 1729, 21–2.

77 John Walker, *An Economical History of the Hebrides and Highlands of Scotland*, vol. 1 (Edinburgh, 1812), 64; McGeachy, *Argyll*, 25.

78 NRS, GD214/353/2, Tack, Robertson and Macdonald, 1769; NRS, GD44/27/11/145, Presmuchrach Petition, 1776; NRS,GD44/28/12/10, Tack, 14 April 1726.

79 NRS, GD44/27/21, Memorial, 2 July 1784.

80 For analysis of Badenoch rentals, see Alan G. Macpherson, 'Tenure, Social Structure, Land Use: Scottish Highlands 1747–1784', unpublished PhD thesis, McGill University, 1969, 12–130.

81 See Dodgshon, 'Everyday Structures', 32.

82 NRS, GD44/51/732/49, Gordon Rental, 1730; NRS,GD44/51/732/54, Gordon Rental, 1595.

83 NRAS, 771/581, Killiehuntly Rental, 1752.

84 Hunter, *Crofting Community*, gives the best account of nineteenth-century crofting.

85 NRS, GD44/51/732/54, Gordon Rental, 1595; NRS, GD44/51/732/49, Gordon Rental, 1730.

86 NRS, CR8/194, Taylor, survey, 45, 111.

87 Ibid., 45; Peter May to Barclay, 26 January 1780, in Ian Adams (ed.), *Peter May, Land Surveyor* (Edinburgh, 1979), 217.

88 NRS, GD44/51/732/1, Gordon Rental, 1729, 31.

89 NRS, GD44/51/732/9, Badenoch Rental, 1770–71.

90 NRS, CR8/194, Taylor, survey, 51, 59.

91 NRS, GD44/27/3/83, Gordon Papers, 1735.

92 NRS, CR8/195, Brown, survey, 2.

93 NRS, CS25/1787/7/19, Sale of Raitts, 1787; NRS, GD44/27/54, Sett of Badenoch, 1751, 8–12.

94 NRS, GD44/27/21, Memorial & Abstract of Sale, 2 July 1784; NRS, CR8/194, Taylor, survey, 25, 107.

95 NRS, GD44/27/54, Sett of Badenoch, 1751, 8–12.

96 NRS, CS25/1787/7/19, Sale of Raitts, 1787; NRS, GD214/353/2, Tack, Robertsons and Macdonald, 1769.

97 NRS, GD214/353/2, Tack, Robertsons and Macdonald, 1769; NRS, CR8/194, Taylor, survey, 1770–2, 25.

98 Eric Richards, *Debating the Highland Clearances* (Edinburgh, 2007), 29.

99 NRAS, 771/94, John Macpherson to Invereshie, 22 November 1805.

100 NRS, GD44/51/732/1, Gordon Rental, 1729, 21–2.

101 NRAS, 771/1304, Lachlan Maclean to Macpherson-Grant, 30/6/1830.

102 NRS, E745/22/9/1, John Macpherson, 29 June 1773.

103 NRS, E745/24/4/1, Alexander Macdonell, 1766. Devine, *Clearance*, 126, argues that cottars, unlike subtenants, could be removed without legal notice, seemingly confirmed by this source.

104 NRAS, 771/684, Agreement Regarding Servants Absconding, 1769.

105 NRAS, 771/684, Answer to Claim Before Baillie of Ruthven, 1766.

106 NRAS, 771/581, Killiehuntly Rental, 1752; NRS, GD44/27/3/50, Strone Rental, 1725; NRS, GD44/27/3/48, Presmuchrach, Judicial Rental, 1725. A wedder was a castrated male sheep; a reek-hen was one paid in rent from every house with a hearth; the weight of a 'head' of cheese was not defined.

107 NRS, GD44/27/16, Ardbryllach Rental, 1712.

108 NRS, GD44/27/22/2/11, Breakachy Rental, 1725.

109 NRS, GD44/27/17/49, Tack of Uvie, 1744; NRS, GD44/27/54, Sett of Badenoch, 1751, 8–12.

110 NRS, GD44/27/22/2/12, Breakachy Rental, 1725.

111 NRS, GD44/27/4/54, Report & Sett of Badenoch, 1751, 2; NRS, GD44/52/37/156, Ross to Tod, 29 May 1771.

112 NRS, GD44/27/3/50, Strone Rental, 1725.

113 McGeachy, *Argyll*, 67–9, discusses similar peasant protest.

114 NRAS, 771/209, Notebook, 28 June 1769.

115 NRAS, 771/668, Anderson to William Macpherson, 10 June 1800.

116 NRAS, 771/50, Conditions of Lease, 1840; Craigdhu, Lease, James Stewart, 1843.

117 A Lover of His Country, *An Essay on Ways and Means for Inclosing, Fallowing, Planting, etc. Scotland* (Edinburgh, 1729), 60, 61, 66.

118 NRS, GD44/27/10/20x, Tod to Ross, 5 July 1770.

119 Grant, *Every-day Life*, 73.

120 NRAS, 771/697, Mackintosh to George Macpherson, 19 July 1768.

121 NRAS, 771/362, Rental, Phones & Etterish, 1783, 3; NRAS, 771/581, Killiehuntly Rental, 1752; NRS, GD44/27/3/48, Judicial Rental, 1725; NRAS, 771/665, Tack, Donald Gollonach, 1767; NRS, GD44/27/17, Tack, Hugh Macpherson, 1767.

122 NRAS, 771/665, Tacks, 11 February 1767, 1, 4, 6.

123 Mrs Grant, *Letters*, vol. 1, 230, 27 August, 1788.

124 I.F. Grant, *Highland Folk Ways* (London, 1961), 201.

125 NRS, GD214/353/1, Tack, Alexander Macpherson, 1768.

126 NRAS, 771/1268, Sett of Invereshie, 1812.

127 Thornton, *Sporting Tour*, 156.

128 NRAS, 771/665, Tacks, Alexander Shaw, Donald Gollonach, 1, 4; NRS, GD214/353/2, Tack, Robertsons and Macdonald, 1769.

129 Grant, *Every-day Life*, 159.

130 NRS, GD176/880, Tack, Dalnavert, 19 May 1797.

131 NRS, GD176/1566, Tack, Alexander Meldrum, 24 January 1804.

132 NRS, GD44/27/3/49, Judicial Rental, 1725.

133 NRS, GD44/27/11/57, Tod to Ross, 23 June 1772.

134 NRS, GD44/52/37, Ross to John Stewart, 27 June 1771, 169.

135 NRS, GD44/52/37, Ross to Tod, 19 April 1771, 125.

136 NRS, GD44/52/35, Ross to Tod, 16 July 1770, 166; NRS, GD44/27/7/80x, Anderson to Fyter, 5 April 1820.

137 NRAS, 771/1268, Sett of Invereshie, 1812.

138 NRS, GD44/52/35, Ross to Tod, 16 July 1770, 165.

139 NRS, GD44/28/35/13, Anderson to Mitchell, 14 February 1807.

140 NRAS, 771/677 Tack, Lubenreoch, 15 January 1734; NRAS, 771/1268, Sett of Invereshie, 1812.

141 NRAS, 771/131, Statute Labour, 30 June 1770 – a legal requirement for road maintenance.

142 NRS, GD128/12/4, Mackintosh to Campbell Mackintosh, 23 March 1792.
143 NRS, GD44/27/7/122, 126, Tenants of Drumgellovie, Brae Ruthven, 1819.
144 NRS, GD44/27/7/84, Allan Macpherson to Anderson, 14 March 1820.
145 NRS, GD44/28/35/18, Agreement with Strone, 25 May 1808.
146 DMR, 'Highland Notes & Queries', *Northern Chronicle*, 17 November 1909.
147 NRAS, 771/665, Baron Court Book, 1766.
148 NRS, GD44/27/3/74, Long carriages, 1735.
149 NRS, GD44/27/10/12, Biallidmore, 5 July 1769.
150 NRS, GD44/27/10/21x, Tod, 10 July 1770.
151 NRAS, 771/362, Rental, Phones & Etterish, 1783.
152 NRAS, 771/665, Tack, Alexander Gordon, 11 February 1767; NRS, GD214/353/2, Tack Robertsons and Macdonald, 1769.
153 NRAS, 771/668, Anderson to William Macpherson, 18 May 1800.
154 NRAS, 771/466, McInnes to Macpherson-Grant, 28 March 1837.
155 Craigdhu, Lease, James Stewart, 1843; Belleville rental, 1872, in author's possession.
156 Allan Macinnes, 'Scottish Gaeldom: The First Phase of Clearance', in T.M. Devine and R. Mitchison (eds), *People and Society in Scotland* (Edinburgh, 1988), 79.
157 *OSA* 3, 37.
158 Gray, *Highland Economy*, 25, recognises this 'tiny element of mobility'.

2. The Subsistence Economy

1 *OSA* 3, 36.
2 Withers, *Gaelic Scotland*, 218.
3 NLS, MS2508, James Robertson, Journal, 1771, 48.
4 W.G. Stewart, *Lectures on the Mountains*, Series 1 (London, 1860) 4, 5; Henry Gray Graham, *Social Life in the Eighteenth Century* (Edinburgh, 1964, first published 1899), 222.
5 Gaskell, *Morvern*, 9.
6 Peter Womack, *Improvement and Romance: Constructing the Myth of the Highlands* (London 1989), 167.
7 See Devine, *Scotland's Empire*, 213.
8 Grant, *Every-day Life*, 123.
9 T.M. Devine, *The Scottish Nation 1700–2000* (London, 1999) 187.
10 *Spalding Club Miscellany*, vol. 2 (Aberdeen, 1842), 5.
11 Robertson, *Inverness*, 30; Elizabeth Grant of Rothiemurchus, *Memoirs of a Highland Lady* (Canongate, 1992), 24.
12 NRAS, 771/564, Grant to William Macpherson, 6 October 1795; James Robertson, *General View of the Agriculture in the County of Perth* (Perth, 1799), 463.
13 Leneman, *Atholl*, 210. The Atholl linen industry was successful because of proximity to Lowland markets.
14 NRS, GD44/27/4/17, 1735.
15 NRS, GD44/41/28/35, Petition to Duke, 1748.

16 Ibid.

17 Taylor, *Military Roads*, 50. The bridge was built by local contractor John Scot, NRS, GD248/37/4, Lorimer, Notebook 3, 70.

18 NRS, GD44/43/85/47, John Clerk, 23 February 1773.

19 NRS, GD44/28/20, Tod to Ross, 24 July 1770.

20 *OSA* 3, 38.

21 Mrs Grant, *Letters*, vol. 2, 6, 27 March 1791.

22 Margaret Adam, 'The Causes of the Highland Emigrations of 1783–1803', *SHR*, vol. 17 (1920), 81; Gray, *Highland Economy*, 99–100; Grant, *Every-day Life*, 33–4; Walker, *Hebrides*, vol. 1, 314.

23 NRS, GD44/27/11, John Macpherson to James Ross, 24 June 1775; NRS, E745/20/11/1, Tenants of Biallidbeg, 1763; NRS, GD128/12/4, Cluny to Mackintosh, 26 July 1786; NRS, GD80/384/18x, William Cattanach, 1769.

24 Dodgshon, *Chiefs*, 203.

25 NRS, E745/59, Tennoch, survey, tables.

26 Smith, *Jacobite Estates*, 88; NRAS, 771/197, Teind Cause, 12 February 1799.

27 NRS, GD44/51/747/1, 3; NRS, GD44/51/732/51, 52.

28 NRS, CR8/194, Taylor, survey, 119; NRS, CR8/195, Brown, survey 51–2; NRS, E745/60, Tennoch, survey, tables.

29 Dodgshon, *Land*, 288.

30 NRS, CR8/195, Brown, survey, 38, 40.

31 Dodgshon, *Chiefs*, 290.

32 NRS, E745/59, Tennoch, survey, tables; NRS, CR8/195, Brown, survey, 45–6, 1–2, 7–8.

33 NRS, E745/59, Tennoch, survey, tables; Gray, *Highland Economy*, 6.

34 Hall, *Travels*, 391, 418.

35 NRS, E745/60, Tennoch, survey, 1; CR8/195, Brown, survey, 3.

36 NRS, E745/60, Tennoch, survey, 9.

37 Dodgshon, *Chiefs*, 224.

38 *OSA* 3, 36.

39 *The Climate of Scotland* (HMSO, 1989), 14 (Glenmore figures); http://www.metoffice.gov.uk/climate/uk/averages/ (accessed 21 November 2012).

40 NRS, GD44/43/71/13, Tod to Ross, 4 August 1772; *Climate*, 4, 6; NRS, E745/60, Tennoch, survey, 20; http://www.metoffice.gov.uk/hadobs/hadukp/data/download.html (accessed 21 November 2012).

41 Thornton, *Sporting Tour*, 95.

42 NRS, GD44/28/34/49, Journal, 1769, 7.

43 NRS, GD44/27/11/74, Tod to Ross, 10 September 1772.

44 NRS, GD44/43/129/29, Tod to Ross, 29 September 1774; NRAS, 771/574, John Macpherson, 6 June 1793.

45 Hall, *Travels*, 418; Smith, *Jacobite Estates*, 88.

46 Grant, *Every-day Life*, 179, 220, 255, 260.

47 NRS, E788/20/3/1, Notes on Souming, 4.

48 NRS, GD128/22/9, William Mackintosh, 9 November 1787; NRS, GD128/22/10, Mackintosh, 24 November 1789.

49 Grant, *Every-day Life*, 54.

50 McLean, *Glengarry*, 50, 65.

51 Robert Clyde, *From Rebel to Hero* (East Linton, 1995), 110; Adams, *Peter May*, 13, May to Commissioners, 2 November 1756.

52 Hunter, *Last of the Free*, 222. For a very positive analysis of the communal township, see John Barrett, 'Shaping a Scottish Landscape: Moray's Cooperative Countryside', in *History Scotland* 15:4 (2015), 40–5.

53 NRS, CR8/195, Brown, survey 41, 45, 13. Robertson, *Perthshire*, 62, defines Kavells as in the text; Walker, *Hebrides*, 176, defines it as the division of infield for crop rotation, but that seems unlikely for Badenoch.

54 NRAS, 771/556, Anderson, 15 December 1800; *NSA* 14, 91–2.

55 NRS, GD44/27/11/145, Tenants, Presmuchrach, 1776.

56 NRS, CR8/195, Brown, survey, 6, 8; NRS, CR8/194, Taylor, survey, 3.

57 James Maclean, 'A Dissertation Relative to the Agriculture of Badenoch and Strath-spey', in Robertson, *Inverness*, Appendix III, 407 [son of John Maclean of Pitmain].

58 NRS, CR8/194, Taylor, survey, 1, 51; NRS, CR8/195, Brown, survey, 3.

59 NRS, CR8/195, Brown, survey, 3, 13, 33.

60 Grant, *Folk Ways*, 72; *Every-day Life*, 278–89.

61 Hall, *Travels*, 424.

62 Gray, *Highland Economy*, 37.

63 Mary Mackellar, 'The Sheiling: Its Traditions and Songs', *TGSI* 14 (1887–8), 149.

64 Richards, *Clearances* (2000), 44.

65 Dodgshon, *Chiefs*, 225; Dodgshon, 'Strategies of Farming in the Western Highlands and Islands of Scotland Prior to Crofting and the Clearances', *Economic History Review* 46:4 (1993), 680, 700.

66 Hall, *Travels*, 424.

67 NRS, GD 248/37/4, Lorimer, notebook 3, 1762, 13; Robertson, *Inverness*, 197.

68 Samuel Johnson, *A Journey to the Western Isles of Scotland* (London, 1984), 55, 72, 73, 92; James Boswell, *The Journal of a Tour to the Hebrides* (London, 1984), 231–2.

69 Mackellar, 'Sheiling', 147; also David Stewart of Garth, *Sketches of the Highlanders of Scotland* (Edinburgh, 1825), vol. 1, 90; Sir Aeneas Mackintosh of Mackintosh, *Notes Descriptive and Historical* (Inverness, 1892 – written 1774–83), 13; Walker, *Hebrides*, vol. 2, 62; Grant, *Folk Ways*, 72.

70 Smout, *Exploring Environmental History* (Edinburgh, 2011), 118.

71 NRS, GD44/27/11/70, Macdonell to Tod, 28 July 1772.

72 NRAS, 771/1172, Grant to General Grant, 16 May 1800.

73 *OSA* 8, 501.

74 Robert Mathieson, *The Survival of the Unfittest: The Highland Clearances and the End of Isolation* (Edinburgh, 2000), 98–106; Elizabeth Whatley, 'Work, Time and Pastimes', in Foyster and Whatley, *A History of Everyday Life*, 289.

75 McLean, 'Dissertation', *Inverness*, 405. Grant, *Every-day Life*, 108, refers to ox-ploughing in Badenoch, but all the evidence points to native Highland ponies: Henry Butter, NRS, E745/53/3/2, 23 July 1774; *OSA* 3, 148; *OSA* 3, 377–8; Robertson, *Inverness*, 262; Marshall, *General View of the Agriculture of the Central*

Highlands of Scotland (London, 1794), 34; Alexander Fenton, *Scottish Country Life* (East Linton, 1999), 37.

76 NRS, GD44/28/34/53, Tod, 28 January 1770; NRS, GD44/28/4, Rental, Crubenbeg, 1727.

77 NRS, CR8/194, Taylor, survey, 119; NRS, CR8/195, Brown, survey, 51–2; NRS, E745/60, Tennoch, survey, tables.

78 Dodgshon, 'Traditional Highland Field Systems: Their Constraints and Thresholds', in John A. Atkinson, Ian Banks and Ian McGregor (eds) *Townships to Farmsteads* (Glasgow, 2000), 111.

79 NRS, CR8/194, Taylor, survey, 7, 13.

80 Andrew Wight, *Present State of the Husbandry in Scotland*, vol. 4, Part 1 (Edinburgh, 1784), 145.

81 NRS, E745/59, Tennoch, survey, tables.

82 Based on Cluny acreage compared to other areas. Another calculation based on cattle per head of population reached a similar total of 5,000. Totals include only domestic, not commercial, stock.

83 NRS, E745/42/1; NRS, E745/59, Rental, 1770, Tennoch, survey, tables.

84 NLS, MS2508, James Robertson, Journal, 1771, 45–6.

85 Walker, *Hebrides*, vol. 2, 57; McLean, *Glengarry*, 30.

86 NRS, CR8/194, Brown, survey, 11.

87 NRS, GD44/28/36, Lease, 1777.

88 NRS, GD44/28/2/2 Duke against Killiehuntly, 1727.

89 Bishop Forbes, *Journals of Episcopal Visitations* (London, 1886), 146; NRS, GD44/28/30, Notes upon Raitts, 2.

90 Marshall, *Central Highlands*, 37–8.

91 NRS, E745/24/10/2, Report of Henry Butter, 1768; NRS, GD44/27/11/16x, Tod to Ross, 23 March 1772; NRAS, 771/276, John to William Macpherson, 1 January 1789.

92 NRAS, 771/564, General Grant to William Macpherson, 29 March 1795.

93 NRAS, 771/574, John to William, 3 October 1798.

94 NRS, E728/34/17, Peter Robertson, 23 February 1784; NRAS, 771/574, John Macpherson to William, 13 July 1793.

95 NRS, GD44/43/215/37, Ballachroan to Tod, 14 January 1779.

96 NRS, CR8/195, Brown, survey, 3.

97 NRAS, 771/987, Article of Charges, 1800.

98 Robertson, *Inverness*, 78.

99 'Survey of the Province of Moray', in Lachlan Shaw, *History of the Province of Moray*, 3 vols, vol. 1 (Glasgow, 1882), 290; NRS, CR8/194, Taylor, survey, 118; NRS, CR8/195, Brown, survey, 51–2.

100 NRS, E745/53/4, Ralia to Commissioners, 1774.

101 See for instance, James Handley, *Scottish Farming in the 18th Century* (London, 1953), 101; Leneman, *Atholl*, 176. The only serious study of shielings is Albert Bil, *The Shieling, 1600–1840* (East Linton, 1990). Swedish scholars have similarly been criticised for not relating 'the summer farm to the household's main farm and

economy': Jesper Larsson, 'The Expansion and Decline of a Transhumance System in Sweden, 1550–1920', *Historia Agraria* 56 (April 2012), 13.

102 Grant, *Folk Ways*, 74, 128.

103 Hall, *Travels*, 409.

104 NRS, GD248/37/4/3, Notebook 3, 13.

105 William Ferguson, *The Identity of the Scottish Nation* (Edinburgh, 1998), 227–42; James Hunter, *On the Other Side of Sorrow: Nature and People in the Scottish Highlands* (Edinburgh, 2014), 105–14.

106 Charles Withers, 'The Historical Creation of the Scottish Highlands', in Ian Donnachie and Christopher A. Whatley (eds), *The Manufacture of Scottish History* (Edinburgh, 1992), 147.

107 Mrs Grant, *Letters*, vol. 2, 136, 15 July 1797; Mrs Grant, quoted in Thomas Sinton, *By Loch and River* (Inverness, 1910), 188.

108 Mrs Grant, quoted in Sinton, *Loch and River*, 188. Luckily her letters are somewhat superior to her poetry.

109 CH2/1172/1/158, John Macpherson, Alvie Kirk Session, 1749.

110 NRS, E745/53/3/1, Duncan Macpherson, 25 July 1774.

111 NRS, E745/53/4, Ralia, 1774.

112 NRS, E745/53/3/2, Butter, Report, 23 July 1774.

113 NRS, GD44/27/17, Macpherson to Duke, 19 September 1784.

114 NRS, GD44/27/17, Tod to Duke, 13 July 1785.

115 NRS, GD44/27/13/1, Macpherson to Forest Court, 18 November, 1682.

116 NRAS, 771/581, Killiehuntly rental, 1752.

117 NRS, GD44/27/10/89, Instructions to Taylor, 1770.

118 Gaffney, *Strathavon*, 34.

119 Alasdair Ross, 'Improvement on the Grant estates in Strathspey in the Later Eighteenth Century: Theory, Practice, and Failure?', in Richard Hoyle (ed.), *Custom, Improvement and the Landscape in Early Modern Britain* (Farnham, 2011), 289–311. Malcolm Bangor-Jones, 'From Clanship to Crofting: Landownership, Economy and the Church in the Province of Strathnaver', in John Baldwin (ed.), *The Province of Strathnaver* (Edinburgh, 2000), 72, describes the colonisation of shielings there. Garth, *Sketches*, vol. 1, 181, criticises this policy.

120 NRS, CR8/183, Low, Report & Valuation, 1803, 61.

121 Robertson, *Inverness*, 198–9.

122 Ibid., 250.

123 Mrs Grant, *Letters*, vol. 1, 229–31, 27 August 1788.

124 NRS, E745/53/4, Ralia, 1774; Robertson, *Perth*, 335.

125 NRS, CR8/194, Taylor, survey, 7, 27.

126 NRS, GD44/39/3/12, Christian Macpherson, 1782.

127 Mrs Grant, *Letters*, vol. 2, 202, 10 September 1802.

128 NRS, RHP 1835, Badenoch, George Brown, 1771.

129 NRS, CR8/194, Taylor, survey, 8, 3.

130 NRS, E745/53/3/1, Macpherson, 25 July 1774; NRS, GD44/27/17, Macpherson, 19 September 1784.

131 NRS, E745/53/3/2, Butter, report, 23 July 1774.
132 Quoted in Michael Newton (ed.), *Duthchus nan Gaidheal: Collected Essays of John MacInnes* (Edinburgh, 2010), 151.
133 NRS GD44/28/2, Agreement, Huntly & Cluny, 1728; NRS, GD44/51/732/29, Brown, Valuation of the Forrest of Feshie, 1804.
134 Mrs Grant, *Letters*, vol. 2, 135–6, 15 July 1797; vol. 1, 231, 27 August 1788.
135 Ibid., vol. 2, 202.
136 NRS, GD128/50/3/A, Proof, 1793.
137 NRS, E745/53/4, Ralia; Atholl Papers, Box33/XI/25.
138 NRS, GD44/27/13, Proof, Dalnacardoch, 4 September 1767, John Macpherson, 13.
139 Ibid., James Macpherson; GD44/39/3/12, James Macpherson, 1782; NRS, GD44/39/3/15, Feshie-Gaick March, 1783.
140 NRS, GD128/50/3/A, Proof, 1793.
141 NRS, E788/20/3/3, Lochgarry, 1771, 9. The document specifies the number of days/weeks at each site; the dates have been calculated from this to give a clearer indication of the grazing calendar.
142 For other timetables see NRS, E788/20/1; Bil, *Shielings*, 175–8.
143 NRS, GD44/28/34/102x, John Williams to Duke of Gordon, 31 July 1769; NRS, GD44/28/36, Lease conditions XI, 1777; Robertson, *Perth*, 339.
144 NRS, GD44/27/17, Macpherson, 19 September 1784; NRS, GD128/31/11, Ralia, 6 January 1793.
145 NRS, GD44/27/13, Duncan Robertson, 1727, 26.
146 NRS, GD44/39/3/12, James Macpherson, 1782.
147 NRS, GD44/27/13/34 Proof, Dalnacardoch, 4 September 1767, Finlay Macpherson, 50.
148 NRS, GD44/27/13/16, Alexander Macintyre, John Macpherson, 1727, 3.
149 Atholl Papers, Box33/XI/26, Robertson, 1793.
150 NRAS, 771/574, John Macpherson, 15 February 1785.
151 NRS, GD44/52/37, Ross to Tod, 26 August 1771, 217.
152 NRS, GD44/39/3/12, Christian Macpherson, 1782.
153 NRS, GD44/27/13/35, Proof, Dalnacardoch, 3 September 1767, Angus Macdonald, 69.
154 NRS, GD44/27/13, Gordon against John Shaw, 1727.
155 NRS, E745/60, Tennoch, survey, 4.
156 Walker, *Hebrides*, vol. 2, 61. Swiss research proves slower-growing mountain pasture contains more protein and oil than lowland grass, giving dairy produce a 15–30 per cent higher fat and natural-oil content: Alice Feng, 'Holy Cow! Cheese and Cultural Identity in the Swiss Alps', http://alicefeng.net/?p=438 (accessed 27 June 2012).
157 Forbes, *Journals*, 144.
158 NRS, GD44/43/186, Tod to Ross, 3 August 1777; NRAS771/131, 30 June 1770.
159 Mrs Grant, *Letters*, vol. 2, 136, 15 July 1797.
160 T.M. Devine, 'The Rise and Fall of Illicit Whisky-Making in Northern Scotland, c.1780–1840', *SHR* 54:2 (1975), 160.
161 NRS, GD44/27/13/34, Proof, Dalnacardoch, 4 September 1767, Donald Macpherson, 42.

162 Bishop Geddes, '*Ambula Coram Deo*', 2, *Innes Review* 6 (1955), 136–7.

163 Robertson, *Perth*, 336.

164 NLS, MS2509, John Anderson, 'Sketch of a Ramble through the Highlands of Scotland'; Forbes, *Journals*, 143–4.

165 Macinnes, 'Scottish Gaeldom', 75.

166 Larsson, 'Expansion and Decline', 20; Feng, 'Holy Cow!'

167 J.M. Bumsted, *The People's Clearance, 1770–1815* (Edinburgh, 1982), 40; Macinnes, 'Scottish Gaeldom', 75, agrees that Highlanders were 'less vulnerable' to harvest fluctuation.

168 Grant, *Every-day Life*, 153, 155.

3. The Commercial Economy

1 NRS, GD44/27/13/34, Proof, Dalnacardoch, 4 September 1767, 46–7.

2 NLS, Adv. Ms. 28/1/6/1, James Small to Moncrieffe, 25 July 1757, 497.

3 Dodgshon, *Chiefs*, 239; Devine, *Scottish Nation*, 185; T.C. Smout, *A History of the Scottish People, 1560–1830* (London, 1970), 348; Richards, *Clearances* (2000), 42.

4 Devine, *Clearance*, 178; Richards, *Clearances* (2000), 43. Macinnes, 'Scottish Gaeldom', 76, and Richards, *Clearances* (2000), 40–2, both acknowledge the rise of indigenous capitalism in the Highlands, though the latter attributes this more to landowners than tacksmen.

5 NRS, CR8/195, Brown, survey, 37.

6 Atholl Papers, Box 43/IV/A28/2, The Ruine of the Duke of Gordon's fforest of Gaick, 1709.

7 Dixon, *Mar Lodge Estate, Grampian: An Archaeological Survey* (Edinburgh, 1995), 9, table 1.

8 NRS, E745/59, Tennoch, survey, tables.

9 Grant, *Every-day Life*, 162; NRAS, 771/197, Inventory, 9 November 1770; NRAS, 771/129, Invereshie livestock, 1786.

10 NRS, GD128/53/5, Macpherson against McDonell, 1773; NRAS, 771/574, John Macpherson to William Macpherson, 1 January 1792.

11 NRAS, 771/177, Andrew Macpherson to William Macpherson, 13 October 1784.

12 *Spalding Club Miscellany*, vol. 2 (Aberdeen, 1842), 87–9.

13 NRS, GD44/41/28/2/15, J.G. to Duke, September 1749.

14 NRS, GD44/25/37, James Ross to Tod, 17 February 1772, 315.

15 NRS, SC29/57/5, Petition, Benchar, 31 July 1756.

16 NRS, CR8/183, Low, Report & Valuation, 1803, 61.

17 Grant, *Every-day Life*, 201.

18 NRS, GD128/53/5, Macpherson against McDonell, 1773; NRAS, 771/574, John Macpherson, 29 January 1799; NRS, GD44/27/11/11x, Tod to Ross, 10 March 1772.

19 NRS, GD44/43/85/12, Tod to Ross, 18 February 1773.

20 NRS, GD44/43/177/10, Tod to Ross, 21 March 1777.

21 Robertson, *Inverness*, 261.

22 Manuscript c.1760, quoted in Macpherson, *Glimpses*, 455.

23 Forbes, *Journals*, 144.

24 Virginia Wills (ed.) *Reports on the Annexed Estates 1755–1769* (Edinburgh, 1973), 32; NRS, GD44/27/17, Macpherson to Duke, 19 September 1784.

25 NRS, GD44/27/11/112, John McHardy, 29 December 1777.

26 Robertson, *Inverness*, 261; James Small, in Wills, *Reports*, 32.

27 NRS, E745/53/8/1, Duncan Macpherson, 1760s.

28 NRS, CR8/195, Brown, survey, 33, 41; NRAS, 771/209, Notebook, 28 June 1769.

29 NRS, GD44/27/13, Proof, Dalnacardoch, 4 September 1767, 50.

30 Wight, *Husbandry*, vol. 4, Part 1, 145.

31 NRS, GD44/27/13/21, Declaration of March 1735, 3, Deposition, Ewen Macpherson; NRS, GD44/39/3/12, Dalnashalg Marches, 1782; NRAS, 771/209, Notebook, 28 June 1769.

32 Grant, *Every-day Life*, 62.

33 Ibid., 63.

34 NRS, GD128/22/10, Helen Mackintosh to Campbell Mackintosh, 26 January 1789. The standard stone for cheese was 28lb, so the amount sold was 560lb; 3 ankers was approximately 30 gallons.

35 NRS, GD128/22/9, Helen Mackintosh to Campbell Mackintosh, 16 June 1788.

36 NRS, GD128/22/10, Helen Mackintosh to Campbell Mackintosh, 19 January 1789.

37 Hall, *Travels*, 424; NRS, GD44/28/34/40, John Williams, Report on Lochaber, 1769, 2.

38 Bangor-Jones, 'Clanship to Crofting', 67; Cregeen, *Argyll*, xx.

39 Barrett, 'Regular Revolution', 62, confirms that lowland Morayshire was virtually uninterrupted arable.

40 NRS, CR8/195, Brown, survey, 1.

41 NRS, GD44/27/13/35, Proof, Dalnacardoch, 3 September 1767, 18, 38. The 'Account of the Duke of Atholl's Forests', in Leneman, *Atholl*, 195, mentions Lowland oxen being grazed in Drumochter, 1712.

42 NRS, GD44/39/3, Thomas Macpherson, 1782. Tullichierro and Dalnashalg are Glen Banchor townships.

43 NRS, GD44/28/2/2, Agreement, Huntly & Cluny, 1728.

44 NRS, GD44/27/13/35, Proof, Dalnacardoch, 3 September 1767, 75.

45 Ibid., 63. Corrydoan (Coire Dhomhain) lies west of Drumochter summit.

46 NRS, E745/24/4/9, Testimonial, 1766.

47 NRS, SC29/57/1, Bundle 4, Defender's Proof, 1765.

48 Wight, *Husbandry*, vol. 1, 4; James Donaldson, *General View of the Agriculture of the County of Nairn* (London, 1794), 21.

49 Gaffney, *Strathavon*, 14, 81.

50 NRS, GD44/27/13/35, Proof, Dalnacardoch, 3 September 1767, 33, 41, 45, 52.

51 NRAS, 771/664, Stolen Cattle, 11 November, 1772; NRS, GD44/27/13/35, Proof, Dalnacardoch, 3 September 1767, 60.

52 NRS, CR8/195, Brown survey, 1, 3, 33; NRS, GD44/27/11/145, Presmuchrach, 1776; NRAS, 771/665, Baron Court, c.1782.

53 NRS, GD44/51/732/29, Brown, Valuation of the Forrest of Feshie, 1804.

54 NRS, GD44/27/13/28, Loch Ericht March, 1773.
55 NRS, GD44/25/5/41, McDonald to Tod, 13 December 1771.
56 Atholl Papers, Box 33, Parcel XI/2, 21, John Welsh, 31 January 1793.
57 Walker, *Hebrides*, vol. 2, 403; Devine, *Clanship to Crofters' War*, 35; McGeachy, *Argyll*, 245.
58 NRS, GD44/43/171/35, Tod to Ross, 26 October 1776.
59 NRS, GD44/27/17, Hugh Macpherson, 26 April 1773.
60 NRS, GD44/27/13/35, Proof, Dalnacardoch, 3 September 1767, 28, 34, 66, 68. Both these mountains are Munros, and Flichity's cattle were grazing on the summits.
61 NRS, E728/34/3, Alexander Macdonell, 14 February 1774.
62 NRS, E767/46, Report, Loch Gary and Arnprior, 1772, 2–3.
63 NRS, GD128/50/3/A, Malcolm Macpherson, 1793; NRS, GD44/27/11/145, Presmuchrach tenants, 1776; Atholl Papers, Box 33, Parcel XI/2, 23, John Welsh, 31 January, 1793.
64 NRS, E728/59, Petition of dealers, 1773.
65 NRS, SC29/57/5, Strathmashie to Donald Macpherson, 1757; NRS, GD44/27/13/28, Drumochter/Loch Ericht March, 1773.
66 NRS, CR8/195, Brown, survey, 1, 11.
67 Ibid., 15; NRAS, 771/665, Invereshie Baron Court, *c.*1782.
68 A Lover of His Country, *Ways and Means*, x; Lachlan Shaw, *The History of the Province of Moray* (Edinburgh, 1775), 154.
69 NRS, GD44/27/13/34, Proof, Dalnacardoch, 4 September 1767, 39; NRS, GD44/28/3, Memorial for Cluny, 1788; NRS, GD44/28/15/2, Tack, Invereshie, 1752.
70 NRS, CR8/194, Taylor, survey, 115; NRS, GD44/27/11/112, John McHardy, 29 December 1777.
71 NRAS, 771/665, Baron Court, 31 January 1782.
72 NRS, GD44/27/13/34, Proof, Dalnacardoch, 4 September 1767, 34.
73 NRS, GD44/27/11/112, John McHardy, 29 December 1777.
74 NRS, GD44/27/10/185, 186x, 190x, 193, Tod to Ross, 14, 22, 27 August 1771.
75 NRS, CR8/194, Taylor, survey, 93.
76 NRS, GD44/27/13/42, Account of Expense, 18 January 1771; NRS, CR8/194, Taylor, survey, 93.
77 NRS, GD44/28/20, Tod to Ross, 3 August 1770.
78 NRS, GD44/27/14, Memorial for Duke, 1819, 126.
79 NRS, GD248/37/4, William Lorimer, 1762, notebook 3, 165.
80 NRS, GD128/31/10, Andrew and Angus Macpherson, 8 September 1769; NRS, GD44/28/34/58, Tod to Duke, 21 June 1771.
81 NRS, CR8/194, Taylor, survey, 91–3.
82 DMR, *Northern Chronicle*, 3 November 1909; Ruthven Baron Court, 9 August 1734.
83 NRS, GD128/50/3/A, Alexander Kennedy, 1793.
84 Ibid., Donald Macpherson.
85 See McLean, *Glengarry*, 25, for 'individualistic goals' undermining clan ethos.
86 NRS, CR8/182, Marches of Badenoch and Strathspey, 1765.
87 NRS, GD128/50/3/A, John Macpherson, 1793.

88 NRS, GD44/27/13/21/23x, Declaration of March 1735, Donald McIllespick; NRS, GD44/27/13/35, Proof, Dalnacardoch, 3 September 1767, Duncan Robertson, 79, Patrick Robertson, 46; NRS, GD44/39/3/12, Mary Fraser, 1782; NRS, GD44/28/3, Letter of Forrestry, 1752.

89 NRS, GD44/39/3/12, Donald Kennedy, 1782; NRS, GD128/50/3/A, John Macdonald, 1793; NRS, GD44/27/13/21, John Macpherson, 1735, 1.

90 NRS, GD44/27/13/21, Donald Macpherson, 2; NRS, GD44/27/13/34, Proof, Dalnacardoch, 4 September 1767 – Depositions at Ruthven, John Macpherson, 1735, 5 (at end of document); NRS, GD44/27/13/35, Proof, Dalnacardoch, 3 September 1767, 18, 38.

91 Atholl Papers, Box 8, parcel 1, Drumochter, 1767.

92 This commercial element of transhumance is quite different from the Scandinavian experience, where peasant proprietorship prevented capitalist exploitation of the land by the gentry.

93 NRS, GD44/43/215/28, Gordon to James Ross, 13 January 1779.

94 NRS, GD44/27/13/34, Proof, Dalnacardoch, 4 September 1767, Ruthven Depositions, John Macpherson, 1735, 5 (at end of document).

95 NRS, GD44/43/171/6, Tod to Ross, 4 October 1776.

96 NRS, CS229/Mc/5/12, McDonald v. Macpherson, 1788, Answers for Alexander Macpherson.

97 NRAS, 771/574, John Macpherson to William Macpherson, 3 October 1798; NRAS, 771/194, Duncan McEdward, 1783.

98 NRS, GD44/28/24, John Anderson to James Robertson, n.d.

99 NRAS, 771/669, Anderson to William Macpherson, 8 July 1796.

100 NRS, GD128/22/9, Nelly Mackintosh to Campbell Mackintosh, 16 June 1788.

101 A.R.B. Haldane, *Drove Roads* (Plymouth, 1973), 47–8.

102 NRAS, 771/706, Tod to Invereshie, 18 December 1776.

103 Robertson, *Inverness*, 250.

104 NRS, GD44/43/106/34, Tod to Ross, 11 November 1773.

105 NRS, GD44/28/34/64x, Tod to Ross, 15 October 1772.

106 NRAS, 771/209, Notebook, 18 October 1780.

107 NRAS, 771/126, John Macpherson to William, 30 August 1787.

108 NRS, DI8/209, John Macpherson's Creditors, 21 July 1794, 861.

109 Newton, *Duthchus nan Gaidheal*, 150.

110 NRS, GD128/31/10, John Macpherson, February 1776.

111 NRS, DI8/209, 786, 481, 817.

112 NRS, CS239/M/28/13, Kennedy and Cullachy, 29 November 1794.

113 Macpherson, 'Parish Register, II', *Scottish Studies* 12 (1968), 84.

114 NRS, CS236/M/10/8, Allan Macpherson's Examination, 9 February, 14 March 1795.

115 Ibid.

116 NRS, CS236/M/10/7, Meeting of creditors, 11 September 1794.

117 NRS, GD80/695, Evan Macpherson, Bond, 5 April 1790; NRS, DI8/209, Kennedy agt Macpherson, 22 April 1794, 485; NRS, CS177/851, Liberating Evan Macpherson, 15 December 1795.

118 NRS, DI8/209/857, Hugh Macpherson agt Aeneas Macpherson, 1794.
119 Macdonald, *Glencoe*, 215–17.
120 NRS, GD80/919, Ralia to Allan Macpherson, 27 April 1794.
121 NRS, GD128/58/12, Macdonell to Campbell Mackintosh, 23 June 1792, 7 June 1796, 4 July 1796.
122 NRS, GD248/201/2/1, Ralia to Sir James Grant, 25 August 1772.
123 Ibid., 28 August 1772; Hunter, *Last of the Free*, 218–19 – drovers had 'entrepreneurial abilities of an extremely high order'.
124 NRS, GD128/58/12, Macdonell to Campbell Mackintosh, 13 August 1798.
125 *St James's Chronicle*, 21 October 1788; *Star*, 24 February 1792; Alexander Irvine, *An Inquiry into the Causes and Effects of Emigration from the Highlands and Western Islands of Scotland, with Observations on the Means to be Employed for Preventing It* (Edinburgh, 1802), 117.
126 NRS, GD44/28/15/5, Advertisement, Glen Feshie, 1806.
127 NRS, GD128/46/12, Evidence Respecting Drove Roads, 1827; Brown, Badenoch, 1771, RHP1835.
128 Forbes, *Journals*, 235–7; NRS GD128/31/10, John Macpherson, 2 June 1775.
129 NRS, CS236/M/10/8, Allan Macpherson's Examination, 9 February, 14 March 1795.
130 NRS, GD44/43/140, William Bell to Frederick Crerar, 19 May 1775.
131 Robertson, *Inverness*, 249.
132 NRS, GD44/28/34/53, Tod, 28 January 1770, 2.
133 NRS, GD128/58/12, Macdonell to Mackintosh, 30 August 1787, 17 November 1796; NRS, GD80/919, Ralia to Allan Macpherson, 24 December 1787; NRS, GD128/30/4, Angus Macdonald, 1 November 1788.
134 NRS, GD128/31/9/28, John Macpherson, Benchar, to John Anderson, 14 December 1788.
135 NRAS, 771/574, John to William Macpherson, 25 November 1795.
136 *Caledonian Mercury*, 26 June 1775.
137 *St James's Chronicle*, 22 October 1795.
138 Ibid., 21 October 1788.
139 NRS, GD128/31/10, Petition, John Macpherson, February 1776.
140 NRS, CS229/Mc/5/12, McDonald v. Macpherson, 1788, Petition of Donald Macdonald.
141 NRS, GD44/52/42, Ross to Tod, 10 October 1781, 416.
142 NRS, GD128/31/10, Replies, John Macpherson, 2 June 1775.
143 Ibid.
144 NRS, GD128/46/12, Evidence Respecting Drove Roads, 1827 (referring to the 1760s–1790s).
145 NRS, GD44/43/106/34, Tod to Ross, 11 November 1773.
146 NRS, GD44/43/243/40, Ralia to Tod, 20 September 1780.
147 NRS, GD44/43/243/39, Tod to Ross, 30 September 1780.
148 NRS, GD44/43/210/70, Tod to Ross, 17 October 1778.
149 NRS, GD128/30/4, Angus Macdonald, 1 November 1788.
150 NRS, GD128/58/12, Macdonell to Mackintosh, 7 March 1795.

151 NRAS, 771/574, John to William, 17 February 1798.

152 Catlag, Flichity, Bleaton, Wester Gask, Moniack.

153 NRS, GD44/51/405/1, Legal Processes, 9 March 1771, 13.

154 NRAS, 771/574, John to William, 6 February 1797; NRS, GD44/51/405/20x, Gordon Accounts; NRS, CS236/M/10/8, Bankruptcy papers.

155 NRS, CS229/Mc/5/12, Macdonald v. Macpherson, 1788, Condescendence for Poor Macdonald.

156 NRAS, 771/198, Alexander Clark to William Macpherson, 11 April 1785.

157 NRAS, 771/138, Bankruptcy papers, 1784.

158 NRS, GD44/28/24, Anderson to James Robertson, nd.

159 NRAS, 771/574, John to William, 22 December 1793.

160 Ibid., 14 July 1794.

161 NRS, CS236/M/10/7, Sequestration, John Macpherson, 1794.

162 NRS, CS236/M/10/8, Allan Macpherson, Bankruptcy papers, 1794; NRAS, 771/667, Anderson to William Macpherson, 1 February 1794.

163 NRAS, 771/574, John to William, 14 July 1794; NRS, CS236/M/10/7, Sequestration, John Macpherson, 1794; NRAS, 771/203, Charles Macpherson to John Macpherson, 8 December 1797.

164 NRAS, 771/667, Anderson to William Macpherson, 1 February 1794.

165 NRAS, 771/1235, Anderson, 16 February 1808.

166 NRAS, 771/667, Anderson to William Macpherson, 1 February 1794.

167 NRS, GD128/46/3, John Stewart, John Macpherson to Campbell Mackintosh, 11 January 1794, 4 January 1794.

168 NRS, CS236/M/10/8, Division among Creditors, 23 September 1797.

169 NRAS, 771/667, Anderson to William Macpherson, 1 February 1794; NRS, GD44/28/24, Anderson to James Robertson, n.d.

170 NRAS, 771/200, John to William, 24 December 1781; NRAS, 771/154, John to William, 10 November 1785.

171 NRS, GD44/52/40, Ross, 21 March 1777, 272.

172 NRS, GD44/52/39, to Tod, 24 June 1774, 158; NRS, GD44/52/37, to Baxter, 1 February 1771, 62; NRS, GD44/52/39, to Gordon, 23 November 1774, 223.

173 NRS, GD44/52/39, to Duke, 5 March 1775, 260.

174 NRS, GD44/52/41, to Gordon, 18 December 1778, 314.

175 NRS, GD44/52/39, to Tod, 29 November 1773, 24.

176 NRS, GD44/43/171/6, Tod to Ross, 4 October 1776; NRS, GD44/43/245/27, Tod to Ross, 25 November 1780.

177 NRS, GD44/43/249/15, Tod to Ross, 25 January 1781.

178 Newton, *Duthchas nan Gaidheal*, 150.

179 NRS, GD494/1/47, Robert Macpherson to William Macpherson, 18 November 1758.

180 Robertson, *Inverness*, 279.

181 Malcolm Gray, quoted in Richards, *The Highland Clearances* (1985), 129.

182 Nenadic, *Lairds and Luxury*, 6, suggests cattle 'no longer made a profit' by the late eighteenth century, but this seems highly unlikely considering 100,000 cattle a year passed through Falkirk, with prices reaching their peak during the 1790s.

183 Forbes, *Journals*, 145, quoting Psalm 50.

4. 1750–70: Reorganisation and Improvement

1 A Lover of His Country (Borlum), *An Essay on Ways and Means for Inclosing, Fallowing, Planting, etc.* (Edinburgh, 1729), 109, 14.
2 Frederick Albritton Jonsson, *Enlightenment's Frontier* (New Haven, 2013), 11–48; Devine, *Scottish Nation*, 66–7, 81–2.
3 Lythe and Butt, *An Economic History of Scotland 1100–1939* (Glasgow, 1975), 118.
4 Barrett, 'Regular Revolution', 129.
5 Kames, quoted in Jonsson, *Enlightenment*, 29; Withers, *Gaelic Scotland*, 58–64.
6 Macinnes, *Clanship, Commerce*, 211, 217.
7 Clyde, *Rebel to Hero*, 1.
8 Cregeen, *Argyll*, xii-xv; Ross, 'Grant estates', 289–311; Devine, *Scottish Nation*, 114, 175, 185–6.
9 Borlum, *Essay*, xliii, xliv.
10 NRS, GD44/14/15/33, Memorial for Duke, 1746.
11 Cregeen, *Argyll*, xii–xv.
12 NRS, GD44/28/34/28, Plan for Badenoch, 9 June 1750.
13 NRS, GD44/27/4/54, Sett of Badenoch, 1751.
14 NRS, GD44/28/34/28, Plan for Badenoch, 9 June 1750.
15 NRS, GD44/27/10, Thomas Fraser of Gortuleg, 1757.
16 NRS, GD44/27/4/54, Sett of Badenoch, 1751.
17 AUL, MS1062, Gordon Badenoch correspondence, Tod to Duke, 16 February 1789.
18 NRS, GD44/27/4/54, Sett of Badenoch, 1751.
19 Ibid.
20 NRS, GD44/27/4/54, Abstract, Sett of Badenoch, 1751, 8–12.
21 NRS, GD44/27/11/3/147,148x, Bids, 1776.
22 NRS, GD44/27/11/119, Macpherson to Tod, 1773.
23 NRS, GD44/27/4/54, Sett of Badenoch, 1751.
24 NRS, GD44/27/4/51, Tack, 1752.
25 NRS, GD44/27/4/54, Abstract, Sett of Badenoch 1751.
26 NRS, GD44/28/34, Plan for Badenoch, 1750.
27 NRS, GD44/14/15/33, Memorial for Duke, 1746.
28 NRS, GD44/28/34, Plan for Badenoch, 1750.
29 AUL, MS1062, Tod to Duke, 16 February 1789.
30 NRS, GD44/28/34, Plan for Badenoch, 1750.
31 NRS, GD44/27/4/54, Sett of Badenoch, 1751.
32 NRS, GD44/27/4/51, Tack, Pitchurn, 1752.
33 NRS, GD44/27/4/54, Sett of Badenoch, 1751.
34 Mackillop, *More Fruitful*, 81–2.
35 NRS, CR8/195, Brown, survey, 7, 23, 27, 37.
36 NRS GD44/27/11/146, Macpherson to Ross, 1776.

37 NRS, CR8/194, Taylor, survey, ii.
38 NRS, GD44/27/10/60, Macpherson to Ross, 1770.
39 NRS, GD44/27/17, Memorial, 26 April 1773.
40 NRS, GD44/28/29/2, Memorial, 1766; NRS, GD44/28/29/3, Memorial and claim.
41 Jonsson, *Enlightenment's Frontier*, 45, discusses the impact of 'ideology and intellectual fashions' on Highland agriculture; Mackillop, *More Fruitful*, 77–82.
42 NRS, CR8/195, Brown, survey, 31.
43 Ibid.; Grant, *Every-day Life*, 182; NRS, CR8/195, Brown, survey, 31.
44 NRS, GD44/28/29/2, Memorial, 1766; NRS, CR8/195, Brown, survey, 36.
45 NRS, GD44/28/29/1, Tack, Pitmean, 1726; NRS, GD44/51/732/1, Rental, Glengynack, 1729, 21–2.
46 NRS, RHP1859, William Taylor, Pitmain, 1771.
47 Wight, *Husbandry*, vol. 4, Part 1, 207.
48 NRS, GD44/43/218/84; 44/52/35/249; NRS, GD44/52/37/53; NRS, GD44/27/11/53; NRS, GD44/28/34/53.
49 NRS, GD44/52/38/361, Ross to Tod, 23 May 1773.
50 NRS, GD44/43/71/37, Tod to Ross, 13 August 1772; NRS, GD44/27/11/112, John McHardy, 29 December 1777. Gaffney, *Strathavon*, 86–9, describes similar 'commercial' poinding there.
51 NRS, GD44/43/218/84, Mchardy, 26 February 1779.
52 NRS, GD44/27/12, Allan Maclean, c1779 (no relation).
53 NLS, MS2508, Journal, 1771.
54 NRAS, 771/197, Anderson to John Macpherson, 29 November 1795.
55 NRS, RHP1859, William Taylor, Pitmain, 1771; NRS, GD44/51/386/4/32, Inventory, 1787.
56 NRS, GD44/28/34/28, Duke of Gordon's Estate, 9 June 1750.
57 See Ross, 'Grant estates', 289–311. Barrett, 'Regular Revolution', 129 – agricultural ideas in Morayshire were spread more by local network than the 'evangelical writings of remote theoreticians'.
58 NRAS, 771/679.
59 NRAS, 771/677, Tack, 15 January 1734.
60 Jonsson, *Enlightenment's Frontier*, 119, 213; Richards, 'Agrarian Change, Modernisation and the Clearances', in Donald Omand (ed.), *The Ross and Cromarty Book* (Golspie, 1984), 161.
61 NRS, RD14/83, 21 February 1743. Thanks to Malcolm Bangor-Jones for this source.
62 Walker, *Economical History*, 90–5. Leneman, *Atholl*, 32–3, places this kind of lease in the 1760s–1770s.
63 NRAS, 771/665, Invereshie Tacks, 1767. £1 Scots was one-twelfth £1 sterling.
64 NRAS, 771/581, Rental, 1752; NRAS, 771/693, Killiehuntly Lets, 1753.
65 NRAS, 771/129, Rental, 1796.
66 NRS, GD44/27/15/7, James Gordon to Duke, 23 September 1769.
67 NRAS, 771/665, Invereshie Tacks, 1767. A firehouse was a dwelling; a sheep-cot a building for housing sheep.
68 NRAS, 771/684, Tack, 1767.

69 The fore-mentioned lease at Invernahavon also had shared responsibility.

70 NRAS, 771/665, Baron Court Book, 1766.

71 NRS, GD44/28/15/2, Tack, 1752; NRAS, 771/665, Invereshie tacks, 1767. Invereshie leased Glen Feshie until buying it in 1816.

72 NRAS, 771/665, Baron Court Book, 1766. Leneman, *Atholl*, 35, regards the Atholl date of 1776 as a 'very early date for the widespread use of potatoes', an interesting perspective on Invereshie's improvements.

73 Hunter, *Crofting Community* (1995), 3.

74 *Report from the Commissioners appointed for inquiring into the Administration and Practical Operation of the Poor Laws in Scotland:* Appendix, Part 2, vol. 21, 1844.

75 NRAS, 771/42, Census, 1817.

76 NRS, E745/54, His Majestie's Advocate against Cluny Wadsetters, 1770; Mackillop, *More Fruitful*, 78–82; Smith, *Jacobite Estates*, 21–6.

77 Quoted in Macpherson, *Day's March*, 195.

78 NRS, E745/38/1, Ramsay's Accounts, 1752; NRS, E745/1/3, Francis Grant, Rent-roll, 1748.

79 NRS, E745/38/2/10, Sheriff Officer, 1752.

80 NRS, E700/2, Minutes, 6 August 1756, 22 June 1757, 198, 229.

81 NRS, E745/9/3, Small, December 1758.

82 NRS, E745/20/5/1, Petition, 16 December 1758; NRS, E745/20/5/2, Petition, 21 February 1757.

83 NRS, E745/20/5/1, Petition, 16 December 1758.

84 NRS, E745/20/5/2, Petition, 21 February 1757.

85 NRS, E745/17/10/1, Small, 3 February 1764.

86 NRS, E745/53/1/1, Petition, Macpherson, 1773.

87 NRS, E745/60, Tennoch, survey, 1771, 10.

88 NRS, E745/53/8/2, Factor's response, c.1766.

89 NRS, E745/20/17/1, 2, Petition, Macdonald, April 1766; Smith, *Jacobite Estates*, 15.

90 NRS, E745/20/22/2, Petition, Nuidebeg, c.1760s.

91 NRS, E745/20/14/1, Gaskinloan, Petition, 2 February 1764.

92 NRS, E745/60, Tennoch, survey, 20.

93 NRS, GD80/666, Petition, Macpherson.

94 NRS, E745/20/19, Petition, Macpherson, 1766.

95 NRS, E745/20/22/2, Petition, Nuidebeg; NRS, E745/3/16, Removal, Tenants of Nuidebeg, 1769.

96 NRS, E745/39/2/6, Accounts, James Small.

97 NRS, E745/39/6/2/5, Petition, 24 January 1759.

98 NRS, E745/20/12, Petition, Tenants of Noidbeg & Beladbeg, 1764.

99 Smith, *Jacobite Estates*, 34.

100 NRS, E745/20/2, Petition, Mackay, 24 June 1757.

101 NRS, E745/17/7/1, Small, 9 February 1762.

102 NRS, E745/9/10/2, Lachlan Macpherson to Small, 8 July 1763.

103 NRS, E745/20/11/1, Petition, Ballidbeg, n.d. His Majesty's lands were the Annexed Estates.

104 NRS, E745/17/12/1, Small, 17 July 1766.

105 NRS, E745/20/15/1, Petition, 1767.

106 NRS, E745/17/12/1, Small, 17 July 1766.

107 Ibid.

108 NRS, E745/20/13/1, Duncan Macpherson, 24 July 1764.

109 NRS, E745/20/16, Memorial, Donald Macpherson, 1765.

110 NRS, GD44/27/10/103, Petition, Strone tenants, 1770; NRS, GD44/25/5/8, Tullochroam to Tod, 4 April 1771.

111 NRS, GD128/31/10, Angus Macpherson, 8 September 1769; NRS, GD44/27/10/34, Letter to Duke, 1770.

112 NRS, GD44/27/11/25x, Tod to Ross, 15 April 1772.

113 McGeachy, *Argyll*, 67–91, discusses tenant opposition in Argyllshire.

114 NRS, GD44/27/10/14, petition, Andrew and Angus Macpherson, 1769.

115 Charles Fraser-Mackintosh, 'The Depopulation of Aberarder in Badenoch', *Celtic Magazine* 2 (1877), 418–26; William Ramsay, 'Construction, Contention and Clearance: Life in Badenoch in the Eighteenth Century', *TGSI* (2004), 339; Chapman, *Letters*, 14–18. Michael Fry, *Wild Scots* (London, 2005), 158–9, states that no Highland estate was cleared pre-1800 – Aberarder proves this incorrect.

116 According to James Boswell, Ranald was 'quite an untamed Highlander', Boswell, 13 May 1761, quoted in Richard Cole, 'Young Boswell defends the Highlanders', *Studies in Scottish Literature* 20:1 (1985), 2.

117 Smith, *Jacobite Estates*, 60.

118 Fraser-Mackintosh, 'Aberarder', 420; NRS, E745/24/5, Petition, MacDonells, 25 July 1766.

119 NRS, GD80/676, Cluny's claim, n.d.; NRS, GD44/28/20/2, Tod to Ross, 25 July 1770.

120 NRS, E745/24/9, NRS, E745/24/5, Petitions, Macdonells, 25 July 1766, 16 December 1766.

121 Smith, *Jacobite Estates*, 58–65.

122 Ibid., 86; NRS, E745/24/9, Petition, Macdonells, February 1767.

123 NRS, GD44/41/28/2/15, J.G. to Duke, September 1749 (name withheld through fear).

124 NRS, E745/9/7, Small to Moncrieffe, 22 November 1759.

125 NRS, E745/48, Memorial, Macpherson, 12 March 1766; NRS, E745/24/1/1, Petition, Macpherson, 20 June 1766.

126 NRS, E74524/1/2, Report, 1766.

127 NRS, E745/24/1, 2, 3, Petition, 1 July 1766.

128 NRS, E745/24/4/1, Petition, 1766.

129 NRS, E745/24/4/2, Certificates.

130 NRS, CS21/1769/8/1, Memorial, Aberarder, 1769; Cole, *Young Boswell*, 3, 6.

131 See Smith, *Jacobite Estates*, 86.

132 NRS, E745/24/10/1, Petition, Macpherson, 4 August 1768.

133 NRS, GD44/27/10/20x, Tod to Ross, 5 July 1770.

134 NRS, GD44/27/11, Tod to Ross, 9 July 1772; NRS, GD44/27/10/197, John Garden for the Duke and Duchess of Norfolk to the Duke of Gordon, 29 August 1771.

135 James to John Macpherson, 1770, quoted in James Maclean of Glensanda, 'The Early
Political Careers of James "Fingal" Macpherson and Sir John Macpherson',
unpublished PhD thesis, University of Edinburgh, 1967, 212, 224.
136 Ibid.
137 NRS, GD44/27/11, Tod to Ross, 9 July 1772.
138 Fraser-Mackintosh, 'Aberarder', 418; Smith, *Jacobite Estates*, 86.
139 NRS, E745/24/10/1, NRS, E745/24/13, Petitions, 4 August 1768, 8 December 1769.
140 NRS, GD44/27/10/197, John Garden.
141 NRS, GD248/346/3/18/2, Observations on the Woollen Industry.
142 See Maureen Hammond, 'Textile Manufacturing in Badenoch', unpublished MLitt
Thesis, UHI, 2014.
143 NRS, GD248/346/3/63, Duncan Grant, Notes on Weaving, n.d.
144 NRS, E728/16/1, Grant petition, 1758.
145 NRS, GD248/346/3/32/2, Spinning-school, Badenoch, 1761.
146 NRS, NG1/1/16, Linen Committee, 9 January 1761, 16; NRS, GD248/37/4, Lorimer,
Notebook 3, 1762, 67.
147 NRS, E727/26/6/3, List of wheels and reels, 1764.
148 NRS, NG1/1/16, vol. 17, Petition for Angus Macpherson, 25 November 1763, 204;
NRS, E728/16/5, Memorial, Duncan Grant, 1763.
149 NRS, E727/26/1/1, Lintseed distributed in Badenoch, April 1764.
150 NRS, NG1/1/16, Linen Committee, 9 January 1761, 16; NRS, NG1/1/16, vol. 17, 114.
151 NRS, NG1/1/16, Vol. 17, 115, 118.
152 NRS, E728/16/4, Memorial anent the petition of Duncan Grant, 6 August 1759.
153 NRS, E727/26/6/1, Grant to Board, 4 July, 1765; NRS, GD248/363/3/68, Grant to
SSPCK, n.d.
154 NRS, E728/19/8, Memorial of JPs and Gentlemen of Badenoch, 1 July 1765;
E728/16/6/5, Note of flax sent to . . . Badenoch, 1759–63.
155 NRS, GD248/346/3/64, Grant, Notes on Weaving, n.d.; NRS, E727/26/6/2, Grant to
Board, 4 July 1765.
156 NRS, NG1/1/16, Linen Committee, 9 January 1761, 17.
157 NRS, E727/26/11/1, Grant, 12 March, 1767.
158 NRS, GD248/346/3/31, Grant, 9 October 1761.
158 Smith, *Jacobite Estates*, 116.
160 NRS, E727/26/5/1, reports of Embezzlement of premiums in Badenoch, April 1765;
NRS, E727/26/7/11, Letter in support of Duncan Grant, 13 May 1765.
161 NRS, E728/19/8, Memorial of JPs and Gentlemen of Badenoch, 1 July 1765.
162 NRS, GD44/28/34/50, Williams, Journal, 1770, 11.
163 NRS, GD44/28/34/49 and 50, Williams' Journals, 1769–70; Devine, *Scottish Nation*, 66.
164 See Withers, *Urban Highlanders*, 62. Discussion on seasonal migration is generally
based on nineteenth-century examples when circumstances were rather different.
165 NRAS 771/ 700, Chisholm to George Macpherson, 29 April 1783.
166 Devine, *Clanship to Crofters' War*, 136. Christopher Whatley, *Scottish Society
1707–1830* (Manchester 2000), 250, argues that seasonal labour was mainly female,
but there is nothing in the Badenoch evidence to suggest this.

167 NRAS, 771/684, Agreement Regarding Servants Absconding, 1769.

168 Historiography has largely ignored this aspect of seasonal migration, but see Mackillop, *More Fruitful*, 155.

169 NRS, GD128/29/2/15, Strathdearn, 1786; thanks to Malcolm Bangor-Jones for the Lairg example (1771).

170 NRAS, 771/684, Will of Alexander Campbell, 1757.

171 Gordon, *Last Dukes*, 26.

172 NRS, GD80/892, General Graeme to Cluny, 15 October 1761.

173 Stewart, *Sketches*, vol. 2, 89; Chapman, *Letters*, 2–7.

174 NRS, GD494/1/47, Robert to William Macpherson, 28 August 1758.

175 NRAS, 771/697, John Macpherson to John Mackenzie, 12 December 1769.

176 Matthew Dziennik, 'Whig Tartan: Material Culture and its use in the Scottish Highlands, 1746–1815', *Past & Present* 217 (November 2012), 120–2.

177 WO24/326, Establishment Papers, 78th Foot, 1757.

178 NRS, GD44/51/732/9, Rental of Badenoch 1770–1.

179 NRS, E745/53/8/1, Duncan Macpherson, c.1760s; NRS, GD44/27/10/60, Lachlan Macpherson, 1770.

180 Mackillop, *More Fruitful*, 11, 148.

181 Calculated from rentals, NRS, GD44/51/732/9; NRS, GD44/27/12/11; NRS, GD44/27/4/18.

182 Nenadic, *Lairds and Luxury*, 91; NRS GD44/27/54, Sett of Badenoch, 1751, 8–12.

183 NRAS, 771/697, Alexander Brodie to George Macpherson, 5 February 1763; NRAS, 771/697, John Macpherson to William Macpherson, 7 August 1774.

184 NRAS, 771/130, John Macpherson's Accounts, 16 July 1767.

185 NRAS, 771/697, Mackenzie to George Macpherson, September 1767.

186 Ibid., John Macpherson to William, 7 August 1774.

187 Stana Nenadic, 'The Impact of the Military Profession on Highland Gentry Families, c1730–1830', *SHR* 85:1 (2006), 90; *Lairds and Luxury*, 89–109.

188 NRS, E700/2, Barons of Exchequer, 8 February 1757, 216.

189 Stewart, *Sketches*, vol. 1, 406; Ian Macpherson McCulloch, *Sons of the Mountains*, vol. 2 (New York, 2006), 105.

190 NRS, E745/20/5/2, Cluny Tenants, 21 February 1757.

191 Gordon, *Last Dukes*, 27.

192 NRS, E745/19/3, John Macpherson, 1766.

193 Mackillop, *More Fruitful*, 143.

194 NRS, E745/20/5/2, Petition, 21 February 1757; NRS, E745/20/5/1, Petition, 16 December 1758; NRS, NG1/1/16, Linen Committee, 9 January 1761, 17.

195 NRS, GD494/1/47, Robert Macpherson to William Macpherson, 24 December 1761.

196 NRS, GD80/898, Fraser to Colonel Graeme (catalogue date 1765, but must be 1761).

197 Mackillop, *More Fruitful*, 152.

198 NRS, GD494/1/47, Robert to William, 24 December 1761.

199 WO, 120–5, Regimental Registers of Pensioners, 78th Regiment of Foot, Chelsea Royal Hospital. Thanks to Earl Chapman for these lists. Mackillop, *More Fruitful*, 150.

200 NRS, GD494/1/47, Robert to William, 28 August 1758, 24 August 1760.

201 NRS, GD494/1/47, Robert to William, 24 December 1761.

202 Ibid.

203 Dziennik, 'Fatal Land', 181; J.R. Harper, *The Fraser Highlanders* (Montreal, 1979), 122, 128.

204 Mackillop, *More Fruitful*, 186; NRS, E745/20, Petition, Phones, 10 December 1766; Adams, *Peter May*, 38.

205 Dziennik, 'Fatal Land', 5, 116, 149, 265.

206 Quoted in Mackillop, *More Fruitful*, 89–90.

207 Paraphrasing Lord Kames (Jonsson, *Enlightenment*, 29).

208 Cregeen, *Argyll*, xxii, claims that 'clan sentiment remained extremely strong among the small tenants', but there is no evidence of this in Badenoch.

209 Macinnes, 'Scottish Gaeldom', 71, *Clanship*, 215, 233; Richards, *Clearances* (2000), 38–9; Devine, *Clearance*, 164, *Clanship*, 33.

5. The 1770s: A Turbulent Decade

1 Maclean, *Glengarry*, Chapter 6; Bumsted, *People's Clearance*, Chapter 3; James Hunter, *A Dance Called America: The Scottish Highlands, the United States and Canada* (Edinburgh, 1994), Chapter 4; Marjory Harper, *Adventurers and Exiles: The Great Scottish Exodus* (London, 2004), 21, 71, 73; Richards, *Clearances*, vol. 2 (1985), 353.

2 Also true of Sutherland: Bangor-Jones, 'Clanship to Crofting', 72.

3 NRS, GD44/52/37, Ross to Benchar, 19 April 1771, 128.

4 NRS, GD44/27/11/9x, Tod to Ross, 20 February 1772.

5 NRS, GD44/28/34/53, Tod, Report, 28 January 1770.

6 NRS, GD44/25/5/20, Tod to Ross, 14 June 1771; *Westminster Journal*, 19 October 1771; NRS, GD44/25/5/41, McDonald to Tod, 13 December 1771.

7 NRS, GD44/25/5/20, Tod to Ross, 14 June 1771; NRS, GD44/52/37, Ross to Duke, 24 January 1772, 296.

8 NRS, GD44/28/34, Tod to Ross, 15 October 1772; NRS, GD44/43/84/44, Tod to Ross, 11 February 1773.

9 NRS, GD44/52/39, Ross to Tod, 28 November 1774, 225; *Morning Chronicle and London Advertiser*, 25 October 1774; NRS, GD44/43/149/8, Tod to Ross, 2 September 1775; NRS, GD44/43/171/6, Tod to Ross, 4 October 1776; NRS, GD44/43/171/25, Tod to Ross, 20 October 1776; *General Evening Post*, 22 October 1776.

10 NRS, GD44/43/210/69, Ralia to Tod, 17 October 1778; NRS, GD44/43/210/70, Tod to Ross, 30 October 1778; NRS, E767/31/16, Macpherson to Butter, 19 April 1779.

11 NRS, GD44/43/84/44, Tod to Ross, 11 February 1773.

12 Helmut Landsberg, quoted in George Dixon, 'The Highland "Clearances"?' (unpublished manuscript, October, 1983), 12, and Brian Fagan, 'The Little Ice Age: The Big Chill', http://www.youtube.com/watch?v=QFQHTdn8egw (accessed 21

January 2013); Graeme Whittington, 'The Little Ice Age and Scotland's Weather', *Scottish Geographical Magazine*, 101, 3, 1985, 174.

13 Personal communication, Dr Rob Wilson, Director of the Scottish Pine Project, St Andrews University, http://www.st-Andrews.ac.uk/~rjsw/ScottishPine/ (accessed 22 January 2013).

14 *Westminster Journal*, 19 May 1770.

15 NRS, GD44/52/35, 84, 107, 128–9, 130, 138, Ross to various correspondents. Famine seems to have hit Lochaber before Badenoch, though the documents do not distinguish clearly between the two districts.

16 NRS, GD44/52/37, 38, 62; NRS, GD44/52/38, 28, 53, 82, Ross to various correspondents.

17 NRS, GD44/27/10/134, Tod to Ross, 3 May 1771; Mackintosh, *Notes Descriptive*, 2.

18 NRS, GD44/27/10/96, Brown to Ross, 15 June 1771.

19 NRS, GD44/25/5/43, Tod to Ross, 25/12/1771.

20 NRS, GD44/52/37, Ross to Duke, 24 January 1772, 296.

21 NRS, GD44/27/11/11x, Tod to Ross, 10 March 1772.

22 NRS, GD44/27/11/38x, Tod to Ross, nd.

23 NRS, GD44/27/11/16x, Tod to Ross, 23 March 1772.

24 NRS, GD44/43/71/13, Tod to Ross 4 August 1772; NRS, GD44/27/11/74, Tod to Ross, 10 September 1772; NRS, GD44/43/85/11, John Macpherson, miller, Kingussie, 1773; NRS, GD44/43/85/44, Alexander Mackintosh, miller, Crathiemore, 1773; NRS, GD44/43/84/42, Angus Macpherson, Phones to Tod, 10 February 1773.

25 NRS, GD44/43/84/44, Tod to Ross, 11 February 1773.

26 *London Evening Post*, 21 September 1773. Though hardship was felt in the Lowlands as well (Devine, *Scotland's Empire*, 116), this famine is often neglected by historians – for instance, M. Flinn (ed.), *Scottish Population History* (Cambridge, 1977), 232, 246, makes only a brief reference.

27 NRS, GD44/43/127/2, Tod to Ross, 17 August 1774; NRS, GD44/43/129/29, Tod to Ross, 29 September 1774; NRS, GD44/25/7/7, Tod to Ross, 9 November 1777.

28 NRS, GD44/27/12/13/4, Ralia to Tod, 26 June 1778.

29 NRS, E745/53/6/1, Petition, William Macpherson, read 12 February 1781 – destruction verified by Tod (NRS, GD44/27/12/13/1) and Parson Robert (NRS, E745/47/2).

30 NRS, GD44/52/41, Ross to Baxter, 8 January 1779, 323; NRS, GD44/43/215/37, John Dow to Tod, 14 January 1779.

31 NRS, GD44/27/11/43, Tod to Ross, 22 May 1772.

32 NRS, GD44/52/38, Ross to Tod, 10 June 1772, 106.

33 Ibid., 15 July 1772, 148; NRS, E786/37/11/2, Butter's Memorials, 1772; NRS, GD44/52/37, Ross to Charles Gordon, 19 April 1771, 129.

34 NRS, GD44/52/35, Ross to Macpherson, 11, 22 June 1770, 128–9, 138.

35 NRS, GD44/52/38, Ross to Tod, 8 August 1772, 165; Ross to Butter, 25 May 1772, 82; Ross to Macpherson, 1 May 1772, 53.

36 NRS, GD44/43/71/13, Tod to Ross, 4 August 1772. 7.5 per cent was the usual rate.

37 NRS, GD44/52/38, Ross to Tod, 3 July 1772, 131 – distances from Kingussie.

38 NRS, GD44/27/11/48, Tod to Ross, 6 June 1772.

39 NRS, GD44/52/38, Ross to Tod, 24 May 1772, 79.

40 NRS/GD44/27/11/62, Tod to Ross, 9 July 1772.

41 NRS, GD44/52/38, Ross to John Dow, 7 June 1772, 102.

42 NRS, GD44/27/11/71, 72, Ann Clark to Ross, Tod to Ross, 30 July 1772.

43 NRS, GD44/52/138, Ross to Tod, 15 July 1772, 148.

44 Ibid., Ross to Butter, 25 May 1772, 82; NRS, GD44/27/11/62, Tod to Ross, 9 July 1772.

45 NRS, GD44/27/11/62, Tod to Ross, 9 July 1772.

46 NRS, GD44/27/11/25x, Tod to Ross, 15 April 1772; NRS, GD128/30/4, Allan Macdonald, Gallovie, to James Grant, 8 September 1777.

47 NRS, GD44/25/5/61, Tod to Ross, 17 June 1772; NRS, GD44/52/38, Ross to Tod, 22 June 1772, 127.

48 NRS, GD44/43/84/44, Tod to Ross, 1773.

49 NRS, GD44/43/180/15, Tod to Ross, 4 May 1777. Not one Badenoch name appears in the emigration lists in Viola Cameron, *Emigrants from Scotland to America, 1774–5* (Baltimore, 1976).

50 NRS GD44/27/11/129, Mrs Macpherson to Tod, 1776; NRS, GD44/29/9/1/4/C, Patrick Grant to Ross, 13 February 1773; NRS, GD44/43/71, Memorial of Evan Macpherson, 1772; NRS, GD44/43/85/47, John Clerk, 23 February 1773; NRS, GD44/43/84/15, Lachlan Macpherson to Tod, 3 February 1773; NRS, GD44/43/85/52, Alex Macpherson, 28 January 1773.

51 NRS, GD44/52/37, Ross to Duke, 29 March 1772, 359.

52 NRS, GD44/52/38, Ross to Duke, 1 August 1773, 421.

53 Ibid., Ross to Charles Gordon, 25 July 1773, 416; 12 July 1772, 145.

54 A Highlander, *The Present Conduct of the Chieftains and Proprietors of Lands in the Highlands of Scotland* (1773), 13, 10.

55 Cregeen, *Argyll*, xxxiv; Lenman, *Integration*, 18.

56 NRS, GD44/27/4/54, Abstract, sett of Badenoch, 1751, 8–12; NRS, GD44/51/732/9, Rental, 1771.

57 NRS, GD44/52/37, Ross to Andrew Macpherson, 19 April 1771, 128; NRAS, 771/296, Atholl to Grant, 2 May 1772.

58 The 3rd Duke of Atholl apparently followed his own dictum and did not raise his rents (Leneman, *Athol*, 25).

59 NRS, GD44/43/84/15, Macpherson to Tod, 3 February 1773; NRS, GD44/27/11/139, Mrs Macpherson to Tod, 1776; NRS, GD44/43/85/47, Clerk to Tod, 23 February 1773; NRS, GD44/43/85/15, John Macpherson to Tod, 18 February 1773; NRS, GD44/27/10/5, Grant, 23 October 1770.

60 NRS, GD44/27/11/90x, Tod to Ross, 21 May 1775; NRS, GD44/27/11/82x, Instructions, Ross to Tod, 10 April 1773; NRS, GD44/43/71/37, Tod to Ross, 13 August 1772.

61 NRS, GD44/52/38, Ross to Tod, 5 June 1772, 96.

62 NRS, GD44/52/38, Ross to Tod, 24 April 1772, 42.

63 NRS, GD44/25/5/20, Tod to Ross, 14 June 1771; NRS, GD44/52/37, Ross to Tod, 17 February 1772, 315.

64 NRS, GD44/52/38, Ross to Tod, 20 July 1773, 411; NRS, GD44/27/11/87/1, Arrears, 1774. Economic conditions, of course, contributed to these arrears.

65 NRS, GD44/27/11/82x, Instructions, Ross to Tod, 10 April 1773.

66 NRS, 44/25/5/61, Tod to Ross, 17 June 1772; NRS, GD44/52/37, Ross to Tod, 17 February 1772, 364.

67 NRS, GD44/51/405/26, Accounts; NRS, GD44/27/12/11, Rental, 1773.

68 NRS, GD44/27/11/82x, Instructions, Ross to Tod, 10 April 1773.

69 NRS, GD44/27/10/132, Benchar to Tod, 1771.

70 NRS, GD44/27/11/131x, Benchar to Ross, 18 July 1774.

71 NRS, GD44/27/11/38x, Tod to Ross, April 1772; Smout, *Scottish People*, 348. Similarly, Withers, *Gaelic Scotland*, 213; Harper, *Adventurers*, 21.

72 NRS, GD44/28/20, Tod to Ross, 3 August 1770.

73 NRS, GD/44/52/35, Ross to Tod, 29 December 1769, 15; Ross to Charles Gordon, 1 March 1770, 68.

74 NRS, GD44/52/37, Ross to Tod, 23 May 1771, 152.

75 NRS, GD44/25/5/43, Tod to Ross, 25 December 1771.

76 NRS, GD44/52/37, Ross to Tod, 30 July 1771, 198.

77 NRS, GD44/52/35, Ross to Charles Gordon, 1 March 1770, 68; NRS, GD44/51/405/1, Legal Process, 9 March 1771, 11, 12; NRS, GD44/51/763/1, Cullinlean, 9 August 1770.

78 NRS, GD44/27/11/25x, Tod to Ross, 15 April 1772.

79 NRS, GD44/27/12/11, Rental, 1773.

80 NRS, GD44/28/20, Tod to Ross, 25 July 1770.

81 NRS, GD44/52/37, Ross to Tod, 19 April 1771, 125.

82 NRS, GD44/27/11/8, Tod to Ross, 20 February 1772.

83 NRS, GD44/27/11/48, Tod to Ross, 6 June 1772.

84 NRS, GD44/28/20, Tod to Ross, 25 July 1770.

85 NRS, GD44/52/38, Ross to Tod, 24 April 1772, 42.

86 NRS, GD44/25/2, Campbell to Charles Gordon, 23 January 1770.

87 NRS, GD44/27/11/82x, Instructions, Ross to Tod, 10 April 1773.

88 NRS, GD44/27/11/130, Benchar to Ross, 1776.

89 NRS, GD44/52/35, Ross to Charles Gordon, 20 July, 12 August 1770, 177, 221. Inverhall was also called Invertromie.

90 NRS, GD44/52/37, Ross to Tod, 3 May 1771, 134.

91 NRS, GD44/27/10/170x, Andrew Gallie to Ross, 1 November 1771; NRS, GD44/43/84/44, Tod to Ross, 11 February 1773; NRS, GD44/43/84/44, Lachlan Macpherson to Tod, 3 February 1773; NRS, GD44/43/85/52, Alex Macpherson, 28 January 1773; NRS, GD44/43/85/12, Tod to Ross, 18 February 1773; NRS, GD44/27/11/82x, Ross to Tod, 10 April 1773; NRS, GD44/27/11/85, Lt. Macpherson to Tod, 17 December 1773.

92 NRS, GD44/43/84/44, Tod to Ross, 11 February 1773.

93 NRS, GD44/27/11/16x, Tod to Ross, 23 March 1772.

94 Ibid. Tod echoed anti-emigration sentiments across the Highlands.

95 NRS, GD44/27/11/39, 42, Tod to Ross, 14 May 1772.

96 NRS, GD44/27/11/27, Campbell to Ross, 4 April 1772.

97 NRS, GD44/25/5/43, Tod to Ross, 25 December 1771.

98 NRS, GD44/27/11/38x, Tod to Ross, April 1772; NRS, GD44/43/71/13, Tod to Ross, 4 August 1772; NRS, GD44/27/11/19x, Tod to Ross, 19 March 1772.

99 NRS, GD44/43/84/44, Tod to Ross, 11 February 1773.

100 NRS, GD44/52/37, Ross to Tod, 3 May 1771, 134; 18 November 1771, 253; 30 March 1772, 364.

101 NRS, GD44/43/85/12, Tod to Ross, 18 February 1773.

102 NRS, GD44/27/11/2, Tod to Ross, 12 February 1772.

103 NRS, GD44/27/11/21, Tod to Ross, 1 April 1772.

104 Ibid.

105 NRS, GD44/27/11/25x, Tod to Ross, 15 April 1772.

106 NRS, GD44/27/11/40x, Tod to Ross, 14 May 1772.

107 NRS, GD44/27/11/25x, Tod to Ross, 15 April 1772; NRS, GD44/27/10/93, Taylor to Ross, 18 May 1771.

108 NRS, GD44/27/11/40x, Tod to Ross, 14 May 1772.

109 NRS, GD44/43/85/12, Tod to Ross, 18 February 1773.

110 NRS, GD44/27/11/82x, Instructions, Ross to Tod, 10 April 1773.

111 NRS, GD44/52/38, Ross to Tod, 7 May 1773, 347.

112 Ibid., Ross to Breakachy, 17 May 1773, 358.

113 NRS, GD44/43/127/14, Tod to Ross, 22 August 1774; Barrett, 'Regular Revolution', 222. Similarly the Duke of Argyll, McGeachy, *Argyll*, 55.

114 NRS, GD44/27/11/90x, Tod to Ross, 21 May 1775.

115 NRS, GD44/52/39, Ross to Duke, 24 July 1774, 174.

116 Ibid.

117 NRS, GD44/27/11/90x, Tod to Ross, 21 May 1775.

118 NRS, GD44/43/140, William Bell to Frederick Crerar, 19 May 1775; NRS, GD44/27/11/91x, Tod to Ross, 21 May 1775; *Aberdeen Journal*, 29 May 1775.

119 Richards, *Clearances* (2000), 24.

120 *Caledonian Mercury*, 28 February 1776.

121 NRS, GD44/43/157/18, Tod to Ross, 9 March 1776.

122 NRS, GD44/52/39, Ross to Duke, 15 March 1776, 446; NRS, GD44/52/40, Ross to Duke, 15 May 1776, 11.

123 NRS, GD44/52/39, Ross to Tod, 1 April 1776, 457.

124 NRS, GD44/27/11/85, Macpherson to Tod, 17 December 1773.

125 NRS, GD44/52/40, Ross to Tod, 8 March 1777, 259.

126 Ibid., Ross to Tod, 14 March 1777, 263.

127 NRS, GD44/43/85/52, Alex Macpherson to Tod, 28 January 1773.

128 NRS, GD44/27/11/11x, Tod to Ross, 10 March 1772.

129 NRS, GD44/25/5/61, Tod to Ross, 17 June 1772; NRS, GD44/27/11/25x, Tod to Ross, 15 April 1772.

130 NRS, GD44/52/40, Ross to Duke, 15 November 1776, 172.

131 NRS, GD44/43/177/11, Tod to Ross, 21 March 1777, 5.

132 NRS, GD44/27/11/90x, Tod to Ross, 21 May 1775 (primarily referring to tacksmen).

133 Maclean, *Glengarry*, provides an excellent account of west-coast emigration. James Hunter, *Scottish Exodus: Travels Among a Worldwide Clan* (Edinburgh, 2007), 85, cites a contemporary estimate that Hebridean emigrants alone took out £10,000 specie in just one decade, further highlighting the importance of Tod's achievement. Bangor-Jones, 'Clanship to Crofting', 72, describes an alternative scenario in Sutherland where the tacksmen organised emigrations for the tenantry for profit – another example of the divergence in regional responses.

134 NRS, E745/57/1/3; NRS, E745/57/2, 3, 4, 5, Leases, 1775–6.

135 NRS, E745/38/1, Ramsay's Accounts, 1752; NRS, E745/42/1, 2, Rentals, 1770, 1774.

136 NRS, E745/53/2, Duncan Macpherson, 10 July 1773.

137 NRS, E745/57/5, Lease, Macpherson, 1776.

138 NRS, E745/57/7, Lachlan Macpherson, 1777; NRS, E745/57/10, Macphersons, Biallidbeg, 1777; NRS, E745/57/6, Macdonalds, Tynrich, 1777.

139 NRS, E786/26/2, Dyking Vouchers.

140 NRS, E732/16, Accompts, Butter, 1775.

141 NRS, GD44/28/36, Conditions of Lease, 1777.

142 NRS, GD44/27/11/56, John Maclean to Ross, 26 June 1772; NRS, GD44/28/34/96, John Williams, 1770; NRS, GD44/28/34/93x, Badenoch, Sett, *c*.1769; NRS, SC29/57/8, Conditions for Leases, 1777.

143 NRS, GD128/50/3, Donald, Duncan and Hugh Macpherson to Duke, 3 June 1773.

144 NRS, GD44/27/11/48, Tod to Ross, 6 June 1772.

145 Wight, *Husbandry*, vol. 4, 151.

146 NRS, GD44/52/37, Ross to Tod, 19 April 1771, 126; NRS, GD44/28/34/56, Tod to Ross, 8 May 1771.

147 NRAS, 771/664, 11 November 1772.

148 NRS, GD128/31/10, Duplies for Lachlan MacIntosh, 4 June 1776, quoting letter of 3 July 1770.

149 NRS, GD44/52/35, Ross to Tod, 10 September 1770, 247.

150 NRS, GD44/52/41, Ross to Duke, 25 March 1778, 153; NRS, GD44/52/41, Ross to Charles Gordon, 5 February 1779, 348; NRS, GD44/52/38, Ross to Mansfield Hunter, 10 September 1773, 444.

151 NRS, GD44/52/38, Ross to Tod, 28 May 1773, 372.

152 NRS, GD44/27/18, Petition, MacIntyre, 29 May 1779.

153 Gray, *Legends*, 68–79; NRS, GD44/43/149/8, Tod to Ross, 2 September 1775.

154 NRS, RHP94411, Plan, Ballachroan, 1778.

155 NRS, GD44/27/11/89, Ballachroan to Ross, 24 June 1775; NRS, GD44/25/2/52, Principal Tacksmen, Lochaber, 1770.

156 NRS, RHP94411, Plan, Ballachroan, 1778.

157 NRS, GD44/43/127/15, Tod to Ross, 22 August 1774; NRS, GD44/43/215/33, Tod to Ross, 14 January 1779.

158 NRS, GD44/27/11/89, John Dow to Ross, 24 June 1775.

159 NRS, GD44/27/12/17/2, Tod to Ross, 3 August 1778.

160 NRS, GD44/52/40, Ross to Duke, 15 May 1776, 11.

161 NRS, GD44/27/11/89, John Dow to Ross, 24 June 1775; NRS, GD44/52/41, Ross to John Dow, 6 August 1778, 224; NRS, RHP94411, Plan, Ballachroan, 1778.

162 NRS, GD44/27/18, Tack, Ballachroan, 1779.

163 NRS, GD44/52/39, Ross to Rothiemurchus, 18 December 1775, 413; NRS, GD44/52/38, Ross to Tod, 24 April 1772, 42.

164 NRS, GD44/52/41, Ross to Charles Gordon, 5 February 1779, 348.

165 NRS, GD44/27/12/6, John Dow, 10 March 1778.

166 NRS, GD44/27/12, Petition, Macpherson, 2 May 1780.

167 NRS, GD44/43/177/30, John Dow, 26 March 1777; NRS, GD128/31/10, Accounts, 1763.

168 NRS, GD128/31/10, Phones, 31 March 1768; NRS, SC29/57/8, Factory, Flichity; NRS, GD44/43/129/30, John Dow to Tod, 17 September 1774; NRS, GD44/27/12/19, McHardy, 27 August 1778.

169 NRS, GD44/51/732/49, Rental, 1730; NRS, CR8/195 Brown, survey, 1771, 37; NRS, RHP94411, Plan, Ballachroan, 1778.

170 NRS, GD44/52/39, Ross to Tait, 24 March 1775, 265.

171 Piers Dixon, *Mar Lodge Estate* (Edinburgh, 1995), 9; Gaskell, *Morvern*, 16; Cameron, *Emigrants*, 91; Maclean, *Glengarry*, 8; Harper, *Adventurers*, 45.

172 NRS, GD44/52/39, Ross to Tod, 9 September 1775, 288.

173 NRS, GD44/43/142/5, William Fraser, 2 June 1775.

174 NRS, GD44/43/143/1, Fraser to Ross, 16 June 1775.

175 NRS, GD44/43/142/46, Tod to Ross, 12 June 1775.

176 NRS, GD44/52/39, Ross to Gillespie, 29 March 1776, 452; Ross to Hodge, 31 March 1776, 454.

177 NRS, GD44/52/40, Ross to Capt. Ross, 13 December 1776, 202.

178 Ibid., Ross to Cubison, 28 November 1777, 473; 17 December 1777, 499.

179 Ibid., Ross to Cubison, 17 December 1777, 499; Richards, *Debating*, 45, points out that sheep farmers often demanded removal of tenants before taking leases.

180 NRS, GD44/52/40, Ross to Cubison, 28 November 1777, 473.

181 NRS, GD44/43/180/15, Tod to Ross, 4 May 1777.

182 NRS, GD44/52/43, Ross to Cubison, 5 April 1782, 96.

183 Mackillop, *More Fruitful*, 191, 242, notes that 'clearance' landowners were regarded as unpatriotic, and that, as in Badenoch, recruiting delayed the spread of sheep farming.

184 NRS, GD44/43/157/18, Tod to Ross, 9 March 1776.

185 NRS, GD44/43/217/29, McHardy to Ross, 7 February 1779.

186 NRS, GD44/43/216/41, Robert Macpherson, 29 January 1779.

187 NRS, E745/1/4, Kinlochlaggan Rental, 1772; *OSA* 3, 149.

188 NRS, GD494/1/47, John Macpherson to George Macpherson, 2 September 1776.

189 NRS, GD44/52/41, Ross to Duke, 20 January 1778, 20.

190 NRS, GD494/1/47, John to William, 20 November 1776, John to George, 25 December 1776.

191 NRS; GD44/52/42, Ross to Biallidmore, 10 December 1781, 458.

192 NRS, GD44/43/218, Ranald Macdonell to Ross, 15 February 1779.

193 NRS, GD494/1/47, John to William, 20 November 1776.

194 Ibid.

195 NRS, GD44/43/198/22, Tod to Ross, 2 February 1778. Fingal was James Macpherson; the Nabob (Sir) John Macpherson of Skye.

196 NRS, GD44/43/157/1, Tod to Ross, 2 March 1776.

197 NRS, GD494/1/47, John to William, 20 November 1776.

198 NRS, GD44/43/157, Tod to Ross, 2 March 1776.

199 NRS, GD44/47/2/75, Robert Macpherson to Tod, 6 April 1778.

200 NRS, GD44/43/153/10, Tod to Ross, 11 December 1775.

201 NRS, GD44/52/41 p. 8, Ross to Duke, 9 January 1778; NRS, GD44/52/41, Ross to Duke, 20 January 1778, 20.

202 John Malcolm Bulloch, *Territorial Soldiering in the North-East of Scotland during 1759–1814* (Aberdeen, 1914), 88.

203 NRS, GD44/25/7/18, Tod to Shaw, 5 April 1778.

204 NRS, GD44/43/153/10, Tod to Ross, 11 December 1775.

205 NRS, GD44/43/215/37, John Dow to Tod, 14 January 1779; NRS, GD44/43/196/4, Bell to Ross, 14 January 1778; NRS, GD44/52/41, Ross to Duke, 22 January 1778, 32; NRS, GD44/47/2/75, Robert Macpherson to Tod, 6 April 1778.

206 NRS, GD44/47/9/7, Macintyre to Ross, 1778; NRS, GD44/47/2, Macdonell to Tod, 9 May 1778; NRS, GD44/43/205/6, Duke to Macqueen, 1778.

207 NRS, GD44/27/12/43, Tod to Ross, 21 January 1780.

208 NRS, GD44/52/38, Ross to Charles Gordon, 4 June 1773, 381.

209 NRS, GD44/52/41, Ross to Duke, 14 and 22 January 1778, 18, 32.

210 NRAS, 771/166, Duke to George Macpherson, 8 April 1778.

211 NRS, GD44/47/5, Benchar to Ross, 12 September 1778.

212 NRS, GD44/52/41, Ross to Duke, 15 and 19 April 1778, 172, 177.

213 NRS, GD44/52/41, Ross to Charles Gordon, 15 July 1778, 215.

214 NRS, GD44/52/41, Ross to Alexander Duthie, 30 April 1778, 186.

215 NRS, GD44/52/41, Ross to Tod, 18 July 1778, 216.

216 NRS, GD44/52/41, Ross to Charles Gordon, 14 August 1778, 229; NRS, GD44/25/7/18, Tod to Shaw, 5 April 1778; Carron to Sir James Grant, 9 July 1779, quoted in William Fraser (ed.), *The Chiefs of Grant* (Edinburgh, 1883), vol. 2, 467.

217 NRS, GD44/52/41, Ross to William Bell, 30 April 1778, 187.

218 NRS, GD44/51/476/1/25, Estimate of Sundries, 1778.

219 Bulloch, *Territorial Soldiering*, 112; NRS, GD44/47/6/30, Clothing account, 15 February 1780.

220 Gordon to Duke, 11 July 1778, quoted in Bulloch, *Territorial Soldiering*, 95.

221 For the Scottish elite and Highland dress, see Dziennik, 'Whig Tartan', 117–47.

222 Mackillop, *More Fruitful*, 155.

223 NRS, GD44/47/2/75, Robert Macpherson to Tod, 6 April 1778.

224 Ibid., Tod to Ross, 10 May 1778.

225 Bulloch, *Territorial Soldiering*, 107.

226 NRS, GD44/47/2/75, Tod to Ross, 10 May 1778; Macpherson to Tod, 6 April 1778.

227 NRS, GD44/47/2/75, Macpherson to Tod, 6 April 1778; NRS, GD44/52/40, Ross to Cubison, 17 December 1777, 499.

228 NRS, GD44/47/2/75, Macpherson to Tod, 6 April 1778.

229 NRS, GD44/47/4, William Macpherson to Ross, 5 August 1778.

230 NRS, GD44/47/2/108, Tod to Ross, 25 May 1778.

231 NRS, GD44/47/2, George Macpherson to Ross, 27 April 1778; NRS, GD44/47/4, Andrew Macpherson to Ross, 31 August 1778.

232 NRS, GD44/43/206/24, Tod to Ross, 11 July 1778.

233 NRS, GD44/47/2/55, Tod to Ross, 3 May 1778.

234 NRS, GD44/43/218/84, McHardy to Ross, 26 February 1779.

235 Lt Shaw, in Bulloch, *Territorial Soldiering*, 106.

236 NRS, GD44/47/2/108, Tod to Ross, 25 May 1778; NRS, GD44/43/206/24, Tod to Ross, 11 July 1778.

237 NRS, GD44/47/2, George Macpherson to Ross, 27 April 1778.

238 NRS, GD44/47/2/75, Robert Macpherson to Tod, 6 April 1778. See John Prebble, *Mutiny* (Penguin, 1975) for an analysis of the troubled relationship between army and Highland recruits.

239 Quoted in Prebble, *Mutiny*, 126.

240 NRS, GD44/47/5, Andrew Macpherson to Ross, 12 September 1778; NRS, GD44/47/5, Murdoch Macpherson to Ross, 8 September 1778; NRS, GD44/47/2/55, Tod to Ross, 3 May 1778.

241 NRS, GD44/52/41, Ross to Charles Gordon, 22 February 1778, 101.

242 NRS, GD44/43/249/18, Ballachroan's Reply, 21 January 1781.

243 NRS, GD44/43/215/37, John Dow to Tod, 14 January 1779.

244 NRS, GD44/27/12/7, Shaw to Ross, 21 March 1778.

245 NRS, GD44/52/41, Ross to Tod, 6 April 1778, 163.

246 Ibid., 12 and 19 May 1779, 394, 405.

247 NRS, GD44/27/12/3, Gordon to Tod, 22 June 1778.

248 Bulloch, *Terrotorial Soldiering*, 104.

249 NRS, GD44/43/249/16, Petition, Macpherson, 1780.

250 NRS, E767/31/7, Barclay to Butter, 8 March 1779.

251 NRS, E767/31/9/2, Macpherson to Butter, 2 April 1779.

252 Ibid.

253 NRS, E767/31/11, Macpherson to Butter, 10 April 1779.

254 Maclean, *Glengarry*, 10; Macinnes, *Clanship, Commerce*, 232, also sees 1770s' emigration as self-improvement.

255 Devine, *Scotland's Empire*, 137.

256 NRS, GD44/47/2/75, Macpherson to Tod, 6 April 1778.

257 Hunter, *Dance Called America*, 40.

6. The 1780s: Continuity, Contrast and Seeds of Change

1 Womack, *Improvement and* Romance, 96, 78, 80; William Ferguson, *The Identity of the Scottish Nation* (Edinburgh, 1998), 241; 227–42 for wider discussion. See Allan and Linda Burnett, *Blind Ossian's Fingal* (Edinburgh, 2011) for the authenticity controversy. For its dramatic international impact, see Howard Gaskill (ed.), *The Reception of Ossian in Europe* (London, 2004). John MacQueen, *Progress and Poetry: The Enlightenment and Scottish Literature* (Edinburgh, 1982), 91, suggests that even *The Lord of the Rings* 'owes a good deal to Macpherson', while Hunter, *Sorrow*, 126–32, traces the evolution of ideas from Macpherson to the National Parks of Yellowstone and Yosemite.

2 Thornton, *Sporting Tour*, 95; Robert Burns, 'The Highland Journal, 1787', http://www.burnsmuseum.org.uk/collections/transcript/3373, 12 (accessed 23 June 2013); Mrs Grant, *Letters*, vol. 1, 214, 7 August 1785; Womack, *Improvement and Romance*, 78, 80, 96.

3 PP 1846, XXXVII, *Documents relative to the Distress and Famine in Scotland in the year 1783 in consequence of the late Harvest and Loss of the Potatoe Crop* (hereafter PP, *Distress*) 8, no. 10, Lachlan Macpherson to Colonel Macpherson [Cluny], 8 March 1783; NRS, E730/30/1/1, Henry Butter, March 1783; Alastair Dawson, *So Foul and Fair a Day: A History of Scotland's Weather and Climate* (Edinburgh, 2009), 141–8.

4 PP, *Distress* 8, no. 9, [John/William] Macpherson to Kenneth Macpherson, 27 April 1783. The letter's content and reply (NRAS, 771/145, May 1783) show its author to be either Captain John Macpherson, Invereshie, or his brother William. Kenneth was a London relative. For the 1690s famine see Karen Cullen, *Famine in Scotland: The 'Ill Years' of the 1690s* (Edinburgh, 2010).

5 NRAS, 771/166, Benchar to William Macpherson, 24 March 1782.

6 NRS, GD44/52/43, Ross to Duke, 10 April 1782; Ross to Angus Macdonell, 5 May 1782, 100, 125.

7 Mrs Grant, *Letters*, vol. 1, 201, 8 March 1782.

8 NRS, GD44/43/271/8, McHardy to Ross, 4 May 1782.

9 *OSA* 3, 507; *OSA* 4, 474.

10 *OSA* 3, 147; PP, *Distress* 8, no. 10, 8 March 1783.

11 NRS, GD128/22/9, Tod to Balnespick, 6 January 1783.

12 PP, *Distress* 8, no. 9, Macpherson, 27 April 1783.

13 NRAS, 771/145, Kenneth to John Macpherson, May 1783, referring to Scotland's propensity for oatcakes.

14 NRAS, 771/198, Grant to William Macpherson, 25 April 1783.

15 NRS, E730/30/3.

16 NRS, GD44//52/44, John Menzies to Charles Gordon, 28 March and 4 June 1783, 54, 81.

17 NRS, GD44/51/405/20x, Gordon Accounts, 1783; Richards and Clough, *Cromarty*, 115.

18 NRS, GD44/52/43, Ross to Duke, 10 April 1782, 100; NRS, GD44/52/44, Menzies to Charles Gordon, 28 March 1783, 54.

19 NRS, GD44/52/44, Menzies to James Gordon (merchant, Portsoy), 15 August 1783, 104.
20 PP, *Distress* 1–4, 9–11; Michael Flinn (ed.), *Scottish Population History* (Cambridge, 1977), 235; NRS, GD44/43/285/5, Charles Gordon, 7 July 1783.
21 'Famine and Famine-relief in Scotland', in L.M. Cullen and T.C. Smout (eds), *Comparative Aspects of Scottish and Irish Economic and Social History 1600–1900* (Edinburgh, 1977), 27.
22 NRS, GD44/43/284/29, Charles Gordon, 25 June 1783.
23 Quoted in Charles Fraser-Mackintosh, *Letters of Two Centuries* (Inverness, 1890), 303–5.
24 Sabina Michnowicz, 'The Laki Fissure Eruption and UK Mortality Crises of 1783–1784', unpublished MPhil thesis, University of Aberystwyth, 2011, 3, 7.
25 Grant, *Folk Ways*, 95; Dawson, *Foul and Fair*, 143, 148.
26 NRAS, 771/145, Donald Gordon to John Macpherson, 28 August 1784.
27 NRAS, 771/126, John to William Macpherson, 30 August 1787, 5 June 1787.
28 NRS, GD128/22/9, Balnespick to Campbell Mackintosh, 9 November 1787.
29 NRAS, 771/205, John Anderson to William Macpherson, 10 October 1789.
30 NRS, GD128/22/10, Balnespick to Campbell Mackintosh, 24 November 1789.
31 NRS, GD44/43/243/39, Tod to Ross, 30 September 1780; NRS, GD44/43/243/40, Ralia to Tod, 20 September 1780; NRS, GD44/52/42, Ross to Charles Gordon, 7 June 1780, 137.
32 NRS, GD44/43/260/59, Tod to Ross, 30 September 1781; NRS, CS229/Mc/5/12, Poor Macdonald v Macpherson, 4 August 1787; NRAS, 771/145, Donald Gordon to John Macpherson, 28 August 1784.
33 Richards, 'Agrarian Change', 159.
34 Devine, *Scottish Nation*, 176; NRS, GD44/43/284/16, John Gordon, 15 June 1783.
35 NRAS, 771/154, John to William, 10 November, 25 December 1785.
36 *World and Fashionable Advertiser*, 3 November 1787; NRAS, 771/126, John to William, 30 August 1787; *St James's Chronicle*, 21 October 1788, 20 October 1789.
37 NRAS, 771/154, John to William, 10 November 1785; NRAS, 771/126, John to William, 30 August 1787.
38 Thornton, *Sporting Tour*, 76.
39 NRS, CH2/1419/1, 41–3, 47.
40 *OSA* 4, 310; *OSA* 8, 501.
41 NRS, GD44/43/215/28, Gordon to Ross, 13 January 1779.
42 NRS, GD44/43/215/30, Charlotte to Charles Gordon, 5 January 1779. Charlotte became Duchess of Richmond, famed hostess of the eve of Waterloo ball.
43 NRS, GD44/51/405/9, 10, 33x, Accounts; NRS, GD44/52/38, Ross to Charles Gordon, 4 June 1773, 381. For rough modern equivalency multiply by at least sixty.
44 NRS, GD44/52/38, Ross to Duke, 1 August 1773, 420; NRS, GD44/52/35, Ross to Charles Gordon, 5 August 1770, 202; NRS, GD44/52/39, Ross to Duke, 15 April 1774, 115.
45 NRS, GD44/52/39, Ross to Duke, 20 April 1774, 152.
46 NRS, GD44/51/405/25, Accounts.

47 NRS, GD44/52/42, Ross to Baxter, 20 February 1780, 30; WSRO, Goodwood, MS1171, J. Beattie to Ross, 2 December 1779.
48 NRS, GD44/52/41, Ross to Charles Gordon, 1 December 1779, 519.
49 NRS, GD44/51/405/17, Accounts.
50 Claude Nattes, *Scotia Depicta* (London, 1819), Notes on Plate VI; Thornton, *Sporting Tour*, 194; NLS, MS29492, Anon, 'Tour through England and Scotland in 1790', 81; NRS, GD44/43/245/46, Window Tax.
51 NRS, GD44/52/37, Ross to Baxter, 1 February 1770, 62; NRS, GD44/51/385/112, Accounts, 1774; NRS, GD44/52/35, Ross to Alexander Shaw, 24 May 1770, 116–7; Smout, MacDonald and Watson, *A History of the Native Woodlands of Scotland 1500–1920* (Edinburgh, 2005), 129; Alan Thomson, 'The Scottish Timber Trade, 1680–1800', unpublished PhD thesis, University of St Andrews, 1990, 148.
52 NRS, GD44/52/35, Ross to Baxter, 3 April 1770, 88–9.
53 NRS, GD44/51/405/44, Abstract, 1 January 1771 to 1 January 1774.
54 NRS, GD44/52/35, to Tod, 16 May 1770, 108–9; NRS, GD44/52/37, to Baxter, 1 February 1771, 62; NRS, GD44/52/39, to Alexander Tait, 5 September 1774, 204; NRS, GD44/52/39, to Charles Gordon, 23 November 1774, 223; NRS, GD44/52/40, to Charles Gordon, 11 May 1777, 316; NRS, GD44/52/41, to Charles Gordon, 17 October 1779, 491.
55 NRS, GD44/52/35, Ross to Baxter, 9 February 1770, 54–5; NRS, GD44/52/35, Ross to Hugh Gordon, 12 May 1770, 105; NRS,GD44/52/37, Ross to Baxter, 13 February 1771, 69.
56 NRS, GD44/52/35, Ross to Charles Gordon, 1 March 1770, 68. For example of floating disputes see NRS,GD44/51/392/29.
57 NRS, GD44/52/38, Ross to George Bean, 8 November 1773, 464; NRS, GD44/52/39, Ross to Charles Gordon, 6 April 1774 and 21 August 1774, 110, 186; Lenman, *Integration*, 78.
58 NRS, GD44/51/405/17, Gordon Debts, 1792; NRS, GD44/51/405/44, Abstract, 1 January 1771 to 1 January 1774.
59 NRS, GD44/51/405/54, Farquharson (accountant), 6 February 1775.
60 NRS, GD44/51/405/7x, Expenditure Review, 11 October 1780.
61 NRS, GD44/51/405/44, Abstract, 1 January 1771 to 1 January 1774.
62 NRS, GD44/51/405/21, Annuities, 1780.
63 NRAS, 771/154, Hart to William Macpherson, 28 December 1784.
64 NRAS, 771/131, Kenneth Mackenzie to William Macpherson, 6 April 1786; NLS, MS3288, Drummond to Patricia Blair, 21 February 1786.
65 NRS, GD44/51/405/6, Expenditure, 11 October 1780.
66 NRS, GD44/52/42, Ross to Charles Gordon, 6 May 1781, 335.
67 Amanda Foreman, *Georgiana, Duchess of Devonshire* (London, 1999), 296.
68 Quoted in Foreman, *Georgiana*, 219.
69 Ibid., 220.
70 Lewis Duff, quoted in Fraser, *Chiefs of Grant*, vol. 2, 494–5.
71 WSRO, Goodwood, MS1171, Beattie to Ross, 2 December 1779.
72 NRS, GD44/52/46, Menzies to Charles Gordon, 5 December 1791, 39.

73 NRS, GD44/51/405/2, Duchess's expenditure, 15 November 1793.

74 NRS, GD44/34/38, Housekeeping necessaries, 1794; Debts, 26 May 1796; Cash disbursed, Sundries, November 1794–5.

75 NRS, GD44/51/405/4x, Accounts, 25 June 1796; NRS, GD44/34/38, Sederunt, 25 June 1796.

76 NRS, GD44/51/405/62, Accounts, 1791–1809.

77 Nenadic, *Lairds and Luxury*, gives an insight into this phenomenon at a lower social level.

78 Richards, *The Leviathan of Wealth* (London, 1973), 153.

79 NRS, GD44/51/732/33, Rental, 1786.

80 NRS, GD44/34/38, Minutes, Sederunt, 2 October 1784.

81 NRAS, 771/177, Benchar to William Macpherson, 13 October 1784.

82 NRAS, 771/154, Robert to William Macpherson, 15 November 1784.

83 NRS, GD44/43/217/20, Uvie to Ross, 6 February 1779; NRS, GD44/52/41, Ross to John Macpherson, 29 November 1778, 292; Ross to Tod, 10 May 1779, 389.

84 NRS, GD44/274/23, Duncan Macpherson, 29 September 1784 (parenthesis original); NRS, GD44/51/732/33, Rental, Badenoch, 1786.

85 NRS, GD80/903/2, Lt. Macpherson to Capt. Allan Macpherson, 6 March 1780.

86 Mrs Grant, *Letters*, vol. 2, 61, 8 April 1793; NRS, GD128/58/12, Macdonell to Campbell Mackintosh, 1 March 1793.

87 Ruthven was correctly designated a grammar school in the Presbytery records (George Dixon, 'Kingussie School, 1770–1825', Part 1, *Strathspey and Badenoch Herald*, 9 June 1972), contrary to biographies of James Macpherson which refer to it as a parish, SSPCK, or charity school.

88 NRS, GD1/141/2, Balnespick Tutory, 4 November 1792, 7 November 1794.

89 Mrs Grant, 'Letters Concerning Highland Affairs in the 18th Century', *SHS* 26 (1896), 278.

90 NRAS, 771/345, John to General Grant, 12 January 1795; Mrs Grant, *Letters*, vol. 2, 61, 8 April 1793.

91 NRS, GD44/27/10/9, Benchar, 10 December 1768; NRS, GD44/27/11/130, Benchar to Tod, 1776.

92 NRS, E745/21/1/2, Memorial; NRS, GD128/22/10, Accounts, 3 June 1789; NRS, GD1/141/2, Balnespick Tutory, 4 November 1792; NRS, GD128/44/5, Charles Macpherson, Memorandum, 1789; Mrs Grant, *Letters*, vol. 2, 253, 17 May 1803.

93 NLS, MS.1384, Lady Cluny to Delvine, 26 May 1750; Alec Macpherson to Tod, 30 January 1802, in Charles Rampini, 'The Correspondence of an Old Scotch Factor', *Scottish Review*, xvii, 121–2.

94 NRAS, 771/556, Insurance Bill, 29 December 1800; NRAS, 771/706, Tod to George Macpherson 1774; NRS, GD128/31/10, John Macpherson, 1792.

95 NRS, GD494/1/47, Robert to William, 27 February 1759. Butler lampoons Taliacotius, an Italian surgeon interested in transplanting body parts, as cutting noses from Porter's buttocks. Basically Robert is saying that he and William are as similar as two noses cut from the same buttocks (as two peas in a pod). See Chapman, *Letters*, 38–9.

96 Mrs Grant, *Letters*, vol. 1, 198–9, 6 November 1781.

97 NRS, GD494/1/47, John to William, 20 November 1776, referring to the city coffee-house culture of political debate.

98 HFM, Ruthven Quarter-Session Book.

99 NRS, GD128/58/12, Macdonell to Campbell Mackintosh, 4 March 1789, 20 June 1789.

100 Ibid., 4 July 1796, 15 March 1796, 23 April 1791, 12 May 1793.

101 Ibid., 23 June 1792.

102 Grant, *Every-day Life*, 134–49.

103 Mrs Grant, *Letters*, vol. 1, 226, 30 July 1786; See Nenadic, *Lairds and Luxury.*

104 John Macpherson, in *Lyon in Mourning*, 93; NRS, E745/14, Cluny to Barons, 9 August 1784; NRS, E745/20/5/2 Petition, 21 February 1757; NRS, E745/42/3, Butter's Report, 1774; NRS, E745/15/6, Colonel Macpherson to John Russell, 6 August 1784.

105 NRAS, 771/714, John Scott's accounts, 1760.

106 NRS, CS177/471, Ralia v Creditors of Raitts, 18 July 1779; Capt. John Macintyre to Col. Allan Macpherson, 5 January 1787, in *Strathspey and Badenoch Herald*, n.d.

107 NRS, RHP1859, William Taylor, Pitmain, 1771; Grant, *Every-day Life*, 90; NRS, CR8/195, Brown, survey, 37.

108 The new church was built in 1792, so John Dow's house dates from then.

109 HAC, GB0232/D351/2/21, Helen Mackintosh, 18 August 1787.

110 NRS, GD128/22/11, Inventory, 20 June 1786.

111 Mrs Grant, *Letters*, vol. 1, 197, 219, 221, 6 November 1781, 5 July 1786.

112 NRAS, 771/197, Inventory, Inverhall, 9 November 1770; NRAS, 771/209, Inventory, Invereshie, 1789.

113 NRS, GD128/31/10, Account, 1763.

114 HAC, GB0232/D351/2/34, Jessy Mackintosh to Campbell Mackintosh, 13/10/1795.

115 NRAS, 771/198, Mrs Macpherson to William, 29 May 1780.

116 Ibid., Robert to William, 2 April 1783.

117 Grant, *Every-day Life*, 171, 173.

118 NRAS, 771/205, John to William, 29 August 1789; NRAS, 771/198, John Macpherson (Benchar) to William, 28 April 1783.

119 NRS, GD494/1/47, Robert to William, 24 December 1761; *Ranger's Impartial List of the Ladies of Pleasure in Edinburgh* (Edinburgh, 1775).

120 Thornton, *Sporting Tour*, 112; NRS, GD248/192/3/49, John to Sir James Grant, 18 August 1797; NRAS, 771/667, Anderson to William, 28 October 1792; NRAS, 771/631, Elphinstone to General Grant; NRAS, 771/564, General Grant to William, 29 March and 21 October 1795.

121 Thornton, *Sporting Tour*, 180.

122 Macinnes, 'Scottish Gaeldom', 82, *Clanship*, 219. Smith, *Jacobite Estates*, 224–36, provides a more sympathetic evaluation.

123 Smith, *Jacobite Estates*, 76; NRS, E745/38/1, Ramsay's Accounts, 1752; NRS, E745/42/1, 2, Rentals, 1770, 1774.

124 NRS, E745/57/2, 3, 4, 5, Leases, 1775–6.

125 Ibid.; NRS, GD44/52/39, Ross to Duke, 24 July 1774, 174; NRS, GD44/28/36, Leases, 1777.
126 NRS, E702/3/92, Moncrieffe to Small, 7 December 1758.
127 NRS, E732/16, Potato premiums, 1775; NRS, E786/28, Accounts, 1768–71; NRS, E745/62, Account, 1779; NRS, E702/2/158, Ramsay to Barons, 1754.
128 Wight, *Husbandry*, vol. 4, Part 1, 151–2.
129 NRS, E745/42/3, Report, Rental, 1774; NRS, E745/53/2/2, 1773.
130 NRS, E732/16, Improvements.
131 Smith, 'The Work of the Forfeited Estates', 62.
132 NRS, E745/26/1, Memorandum, June 1784.
133 NRS, GD80/996/5, Tack, Gallovie, 1787.
134 NRS, SC29/7/1, Inverness Sheriff Court Decreets, 10 April 1788; NRS, GD80/694, Sale of Laggan Lands, 17 February 1790, confirms it had become a sheep farm.
135 Fraser-Mackintosh, *Antiquarian Notes*, 363, though the author admits to being openly hostile to all things Macpherson.
136 NRAS, 771/198, Grant to William Macpherson, 25 July 1783.
137 NRAS, 771/127, Fraser, 13 January 1774.
138 NRAS, 771/177, John Macpherson to William Macpherson, 1784; NRS, GD80/971, Pitmain Ball Guest List, 3 September 1784.
139 Thornton, *Sporting Tour*, 171–3.
140 Quoted in Nenadic, 'Necessities: Food and Clothing in the Long Eighteenth Century', in Foyster and Whatley, *History of Everyday Life*, 154.
141 Mrs Grant, *Letters*, vol. 1, 222, 5 July 1786.
142 NRAS, 771/131, Colonel Duncan to William Macpherson, 29 May 1786.
143 NRAS, 771/286, Rothiemurchus, 4 March 1782.
144 NRAS, 771/383, Duchess to Rothiemurchus, 12 January 1782.
145 NRS, CS29/1794/1/21, Delfour.
146 NRAS, 771/362, Rents and Arrears, Phones & Etterish, 1784; Sale of Phones, 2 July 1783.
147 *Public Advertiser*, 29 April 1773; *London Gazette*, 8 June 1773; NRS, GD44/28/30/1/12, Memorial, Ross, 1775; Ramsay, 'Bad Times', 129–45.
148 Grant, *Highland Lady*, 343–4.
149 NRAS, 771/196, James Macpherson to William Macpherson, 9 August 1787; NRAS, 771/126, Charles Gordon to William, 16 June 1787; John Macpherson to William, 5 June 1787. Stephen Foster, *A Private Empire* (Sydney, 2011), 84–102, believes James acquired these estates by cheating his cousin, Colonel Allan Macpherson. There is, however, considerable confusion over who bought what and with whose money.
150 Craigdhu, E1, J.E. Macpherson, 'The Vindication of James Macpherson'; Glensanda, 'Early Political Careers', 179.
151 Glensanda, 'Early Political Careers', 235, 305.
152 Ibid., 23.
153 NRAS, 771/205, James Macpherson to William, 26 October 1788, 30 July 1789.

154 Ibid., Anderson to William, 28 October, 1788, 10 October 1789. Ossian's father, Fingal, King of Selma, was famous for hosting banquets where the drinking shells were never dry.

155 Mrs Grant, *Letters*, vol. 1, 236, 10 October 1788.

156 NRAS, 771/196, James to William, 17 November 1788, spells the name 'Belleville'; Macpherson, *Glimpses*, 327.

157 Mrs Grant, *Letters* vol. 1, 286, 10 October 1790.

158 NRAS, 771/196, James to William, 9 August 1787.

159 Richards, *Leviathan*, 154, discusses the importance of outside capital to the Highlands.

160 David Young, *Agriculture, the Primary Interest of Great Britain* (Edinburgh, 1788), 266–71.

161 Wight, *Husbandry*, 207–9.

162 Young, *Agriculture*, 266–71; Brian Bonnyman, *The Third Duke of Buccleuch and Adam Smith: Estate Management and Improvement in Enlightenment Scotland* (Edinburgh, 2014), 118.

163 Ibid., 268.

164 Gray, *Highland Economy*, 26.

165 Thornton, *Sporting Tour*, 104.

166 NRAS, 771/200, John to William, 24 December 1781; NRAS, 771/209, George Macpherson's Notebook, 5 June 1781; NRAS, 771/196, James Macpherson, 17 November 1788.

167 NRAS, 771/196, William Macpherson to John, January 1789; NRAS, 771/205, John Anderson to William, 20 April 1789.

168 NRAS, 771/556, Let of Killiehuntly, December 1788.

169 NRAS, 771/205, John to William, 20 July 1789.

170 NRAS, 771/154, Aeneas Mackintosh to William, 5 July 1785.

171 NRAS, 771/145, Donald Gordon to John, 28 August 1784.

172 NRAS, 771/205, John to William, 8 March 1789.

173 NRAS, 771/129, Ballintua Resignation, 3 March 1787.

174 NRAS, 771/154, John to William, 10 November 1785.

175 NRAS, 771/126, John to William, 5 June 1787.

176 Richards, *Debating*, 238; NRAS, 771/362, Rental, Phones and Etterish, 1783, 8; NRS, GD128/30/4, Allan Macdonald, Strathmashie, 19 March 1788; NRS, GD80/996/5, Tack, Gallovie, 1787.

177 NRS, GD128/43/7, Phones, 19 July 1788.

178 Ibid., Shaw, 4 May 1789.

179 NRS, SC29/7/1, Inverness Sheriff Court, Decreets Extracted, 7April 1789.

180 NRAS, 2614/158, James to Allan Macpherson and John Macintyre, 29 October 1783.

181 NRS, GD44/52/43, Ross to Buchanan and Robert Stewart, 22 March 1782, 90, 91.

182 NRS, GD44/43/256/41, John Dow to Ross, 17 June 1781; Mrs Grant, *Letters*, vol. 1, 197, 6 November 1781.

183 NRS, GD128/22/10, Mackintosh to Tod, 18 April 1789.

184 NRAS, 771/126, Charles Gordon to William, 16 June 1787.
185 AUL, MS1062, 43, George Gordon to Tod, 11 September 1790; NRS, GD4/51/268/4, Thornton to Duke, 7 August 1791; AUL, MS1062, 24, Tod to Duke, 16 February 1789.
186 Alastair Durie, '"Unconscious benefactors": grouse-shooting in Scotland, 1780–1914', *The International Journal of the History of Sport* 15:3 (1998), 59.
187 NRS, GD44/27/17, Colt to Duke, 8 September 1784; Tod to Duke, 13 July 1785.
188 NRS, GD44/27/10/114, Maclean to John McHardy, 14 January 1771. Dixon 'Kingussie', gives an excellent account of the tortuous development of Badenoch's linen industry.
189 NRS, GD44/27/11/18x, Tod to Ross, 23 March 1772.
190 NRS, GD44/27/10/132, Benchar to Duke, 9 May 1772; NRS, GD44/27/10/114, Maclean to McHardy, 14 January 1771.
191 NRS, GD44/27/11/18x, Tod to Ross, 23/3/1772; NRS, GD44/27/10/132, Benchar to Duke, 9 May 1772.
192 NRS, GD44/27/10/115x, 116, James McHardy to Tod, John McHardy to Duke, 1771.
193 NRS, GD44/27/10/89, Instructions to Alexander Taylor, 1770; NRS, CR8/195, Brown, survey, 29.
194 NRS, GD44/27/11/18x, Tod to Ross, 23 March 1772.
195 NRS, GD44/27/11/83x, Tod to Trustees, 1776.
196 NRS, GD44/52/40, Ross to James Guthrie, 5 December 1777, 484.
197 NRS, GD44/52/43, Ross to Trustees, 8 February 1782, 41–2.
198 Ibid., Ross to Robert Davidson, 25 March 1782, 94; NRS, GD44/52/165/66, Duke's Affairs, 1782–5, Tod's Accounts.
199 NRAS, 771/198, John Macpherson to William, 28 April 1783.
200 NRS, GD44/51/14/2/1, Discharged Acct, Alex Moubray, 14 August 1783; NRAS, 771/131, Trustees to George Macpherson, 23 February 1786.
201 Kames to Duchess, August 1770, in *The Lady's Magazine* 38 (1807), 590; NRAS, 771/697, Tod to George Macpherson, 2 August 1782.
202 NRS, GD44/14/2/5, Estimate of Lint Mill, 1782; NRAS, 771/697, Tod to George Macpherson, 2 August 1782; NRAS, 771/198, McHardy to William, 5 May 1785.
203 NRS, GD44/51/732/33, Rental, 1786; NRS, GD44/51/732/35, Arrears, 1789; AUL, MS1062, Tod to Duke, 16 February, 1789.
204 Mrs Grant, *Letters*, vol. 1, 196, 6 November 1781; 206, 7 August 1784.
205 NRS, E745/42/1,2,3,4, Forfeited Estate Rentals 1784.
206 NRAS, 771/154, William to John, 5 March 1786.
207 T.C. Smout, 'The History of Rothiemurchus Woods in the Eighteenth Century', *Northern Scotland* 15 (1995), 24–5.
208 Wight, *Husbandry*, 210.
209 Barrett, 'Regular Revolution', 254–5; Smout, 'Rothiemurchus Woods', 24–5; T.C. Smout, A.R. MacDonald, Fiona Watson, *A History of the Native Woodlands of Scotland, 1500–1920* (Edinburgh, 2007), 298–9.
210 NRS, GD176/1582/1, 19, Glenfeshie Wood Company, 1785–7.

211 J. Skelton, *Speybuilt: The Story of a Forgotten Industry* (Garmouth, 1994), 22.

212 NRS, GD44/52/44, Menzies to Charles Gordon, 3 March 1784, 174; NRS, GD44/51/405/5, Servants, 1780.

213 NRS, GD44/51/392/14, 21, 26, 27, 35, 41, 42, accounts, Glenmore, 1784–8; NRS, GD44/52/43/167, Ross to Lancelot Harrison, 12 June 1782.

214 Quoted in T.C. Smout (ed.), *People and Woods in Scotland: A History* (Edinburgh, 2003), 119.

215 Skelton, *Speybuilt*, 25; quoted in R. Carruthers, *Highland Note-Book* (Edinburgh, 1843), 189.

216 NRAS, 771/154, Anne Mackenzie to William, 11 June 1783; NRAS, 771/198, John Macpherson to William, 18 April 1783.

217 Obituary, James Macpherson, *Colonial Patriot*, 16 July 1831.

218 NRAS, 771/126, John Dow to William, 4 November 1787; NRAS, 771/200, John to William, 24 December 1781.

219 Douglas Hamilton, *Scotland, the Caribbean and the Atlantic World, 1750–1820* (Manchester, 2005). The Bristol Baillies were Dochfour's sons and grandsons.

220 Macpherson, *Glimpses*, 497.

221 NRAS, 771/166, Donald Macpherson to William, 3 May 1774; NRAS, 771/700, Dugall Macpherson to George Macpherson, 3 November 1780.

222 Andrew Mackillop, 'The Highlands and the Returning Nabob: Sir Hector Munro of Novar, 1760–1807', in Marjory Harper (ed.), *Emigrant Homecomings: The Return Movement of Emigrants 1600–2000* (Manchester, 2005), 255.

223 Quoted in George McGilvray, *East India Patronage and the British State* (London, 2008), 180.

224 Devine, *Scotland's Empire*, 251–70.

225 John Macpherson to Rev. Martin Macpherson, 20 October 1769, quoted in Glensanda, 'Political Careers', 130.

226 Ibid., John to Martin Macpherson, 174.

227 William Charles Macpherson, *Soldiering in India* (Edinburgh, 1928) outlines Allan's career in India.

228 John to James, in Glensanda, 'Political Careers', 217, 219, 276.

229 Ibid., 358; NRS, GD80/900, Charles Macpherson to Allan, 5 July 1776. Many of these Macphersons were also part of the old Ruthven grammar school network.

230 NRAS, 2614/156, James to Allan, 4 June 1779, as quoted in NRAS catalogue.

231 NRS, GD80/907/7, James to Macintyre, 27 June 1782 (erroneously dated 1781).

232 NRS, GD80/902, James to Capt. John Macpherson, 15 June 1778.

233 NRS, GD248/462/4/35x, William Taylor to Sir James Grant, 2 August 1774.

234 NRS, GD80/903/6, Alex Macpherson to Captain Macintyre, 20 May 1785.

235 NRS, GD80/900, Capt. John Macpherson to Allan, 20 October 1787.

236 James to John, 12 July 1783, 30 July 1784, in Glensanda, 'Political Careers', 510, 512.

237 Hastings to James, 14 March 1780, in Macpherson, *Soldiering*, 322–4.

238 Lenman, *Integration*, 81; Philip Lawson, *The East India Company* (London, 1993), 116.

239 Mackillop, 'The Returning Nabob', discusses the importance of sojourners to the Highland economy.

240 Foster, *Private Empire*, 83.

241 Ibid., 88, 95.

242 Macpherson, *Soldiering*, 316. NRS, GD80/907/8, James to Macintyre, 28 December 1786.

243 Glensanda, 'Political Careers', 502.

244 NRS, GD80/907/9, Macintyre to Allan, 12 February 1787.

245 NRS, GD80/917/10x, Macintyre to Allan, 22 July 1789.

246 NRS, GD80/919, Allan to Ralia, 4 January 1804.

247 NRS, GD80/907/12, Allan Macpherson Account, 7 January 1788; NRAS, 2614/122, Allan to Colonel Kyd, 24 February 1789.

248 NRAS, 771/145, Kenneth Macpherson to Invereshie, May 1783; Macpherson, *Soldiering*, 387.

249 NRS, GD80/903/4, John Macpherson to Colonel Allan Macpherson, 22 March 1783.

250 NRS, GD80/913/2, Andrew Macpherson to Allan, 27 August 1801; NRS, GD44/51/732/33, Rental, Badenoch, 1786.

251 Macpherson, *Soldiering*, 503–4, 516; Glensanda, 'Political Careers', 503–4. Nabobs were gentry returning from India with fortunes.

252 NRAS, 771/198, John to William, 28 April 1780. See Lenman, *Integration*, 120–1, for a savage, subjective, and inaccurate character assassination.

253 NRS, GD44/51/732/33, Rental, 1786.

7. The 1790s: Years of Optimism

1 NRAS, 771/574, John to William, 22 November 1793.

2 See Henry Meikle, *Scotland and the French Revolution* (Glasgow, 1912); William Ferguson, *Scotland 1689 to the Present* (Edinburgh, 1968), 234–65; J.E. Cookson, *The British Armed Nation 1793–1815* (Oxford, 1997).

3 Richards, 'Agrarian Change', 160; *Clearances* (2000), 77–111.

4 NRS, GD44/52/43, James Ross to Synod of Moray, 9 April 1782, 98.

5 NRAS, 771/126, Robert Macpherson to William Macpherson, 13 February 1791.

6 NRAS, 771/565, Anderson to John Macpherson, 13 February 1797.

7 Ibid., 26 February 1797.

8 NRAS, 771/574, John to William, 1 January 1792.

9 Ibid., 3 April 1793, 13 July 1793.

10 NRAS, 771/667, Anderson to William, 3 May 1795; Dawson, *So Foul and Fair*, 150; NRAS, 771/574, John to William, 22 March 1798, 1 March 1799.

11 *OSA* 13, 376.

12 NRAS, 771/574, John to William, 13 July 1793, 14 November 1794, 30 July 1795, 27 August 1796, 21 October 1797.

13 NRAS, 771/667, Anderson to William, 30 August 1795.

14 Mrs Grant, *Letters*, vol. 2, 101, 15 August 1795; 136, 15 July 1797; 141, 4 July 1798.

15 NRAS, 771/574, John to William, 18 February 1796.

16 NRAS, 771/580, John to William, 17 November 1794; NRAS, 771/574, John to William, 7 August 1795.
17 NRAS, 771/574, John to William, 25 November 1795.
18 NRAS, 771/667, Anderson to William, 8 July 1796.
19 NRAS, 771/574, John to William, 28 July 1797; NRAS, 771/978, John Grant to General Grant, 7 February 1797; *Whitehall Evening Post*, December 1797.
20 NRAS, 771/574, John to William, 24 February 1798.
21 Cattle prices based on newspaper and estate records, wool from Richards, *Debating*, 238.
22 NRAS, 771/129, Rental, 1796.
23 NRAS, 771/42, Census, April 1817.
24 NRAS, 771/667, Anderson to William, 25 July 1792.
25 NRAS, 771/574, John to William, 22 December 1793.
26 Ibid., 14 November 1794.
27 Ibid., 27 August 1796.
28 Ibid., 6 February 1797.
29 Ibid., 6 February 1797.
30 NRAS, 771/126, John to William, 28 January 1797; NRAS, 771/574, John to William, late 1795.
31 NRS, 248/453/7, John to James Grant, 1 February 1797.
32 NRAS, 771/574, John to William, 14 November 1794 – the earliest identified reference to turnips in Badenoch.
33 Ibid., 6 June 1793, 13 July 1793.
34 NRAS, 771/667, Anderson to William, 25 August 1793.
35 NRAS, 771/574, John to William, 27 March 1796.
36 Ibid., 22 November 1793.
37 Ibid., 6 July 1796, 4 February 1796.
38 Ibid., 3 January 1796; NRAS, 771/1618, Sheep farm of Rysauntick, 1790–2.
39 NRAS, 771/574, John to William, 22 December 1793.
40 Andrew Ker, *Report to Sir John Sinclair of the State of Sheep Farming* (Edinburgh, 1791), 26.
41 Hall, *Travels*, 444.
42 NRAS, 771/574, John to William, 9 May 1792, 3 April 1793.
43 Ibid., 6 June 1793, 22 November 1793.
44 Ibid., 14 July 1794.
45 NRAS, 771/667, Anderson to William, 3 May 1795, 12 February 1792.
46 NRAS, 771/574, John to William, 3 April 1793.
47 Ibid., 27 July 1792, 3 April 1793.
48 Ibid., November[?] 1795, 27 July 1792; NRAS, 771/126, John to William, 28 January, 1797.
49 NRAS, 771/203, John to Tod, 9 June 1796; NRS, GD128/19/9/59, John to Campbell McIntosh, 31 March 1795.
50 NRAS, 771/574, John to William, 3 April 1793, 22 November 1793.
51 Ibid., 22 March 1798.

52 NRS, GD128/19/9/44, Memorial, n.d.

53 NRS, GD128/19/9/57, John to Campbell Mackintosh, 3 December 1794; NRS, GD128/19/9/41, Alex Clark to Robert Ross, 3 June 1789.

54 NRAS, 771/574, John to William, 27 February 1792, 2 May 1796. The SSPCK set up schools in remote communities, initially with the aim of spreading English language and civilisation (see Devine, *Scottish Nation*, 95).

55 Ibid., 17 February 1798.

56 Ibid., November 1795.

57 NRAS, 771/667, Anderson to William, 3 May 1795.

58 NRS, GD128/19/9/67, John to Campbell Mackintosh, 18 April 1796; NRAS, 771/345, John to General Grant, 12 January 1795; NRAS, 771/124, Accounts; Isabel Anderson, *An Inverness Lawyer and His Sons, 1796–1878* (Aberdeen, 1900), 3.

59 NRAS, 771/574, John to William, 14 November 1794, 25 November 1795, 6 February 1797.

60 Ibid., 6 February 1797.

61 Ibid., 28 July 1797; NRAS, 771/565, George Cumming to John, 7 December 1796.

62 NRAS, 771/574, John to William, 25 November 1795.

63 Smout, *Scottish People*, 346.

64 NRAS, 771/574, John to William, 27 July 1792.

65 NRAS, 771/565, Anderson to John, 26 February 1797.

66 NRS, GD44/51/732/33, Rental, 1786; NRS, GD44/51/732/36, Sett of Badenoch, 1796; NRS, GD44/51/732/32/2, Rental, 1799.

67 NRS, GD44/51/732/16, Rental, 1808; NRS, GD44/27/6/103, Rental, Badenoch, 1812.

68 NRAS, 771/580, John to William, 28 December 1798; NRAS, 771/197, Teind Cause, 12 February 1799; NRAS, 771/668, Anderson to William, 29 October 1799.

69 Campbell, *Scotland*, 131.

70 Quoted in Gordon, *Last Dukes*, 77, 113; Smout, *Environmental History*, 22. Hunter, *Other Side of Sorrow*, provides a fascinating account of the Gael's historic appreciation of the environment.

71 NRAS, 771/574, John to William, 10 October 1795.

72 Grant, *Highland Lady*, 45–6.

73 NRAS, 771/94, Anderson to George Macpherson, 11 May 1804.

74 John Stoddart, *Local Scenery and Manners in Scotland 1799–1800* (London, n.d.), 155–8.

75 Sir Uvedale Price, *An Essay on the Picturesque, as Compared with the Sublime and the Beautiful; And on the Use of Studying Pictures, for the Purpose of Improving Real Landscape* (London, 1796). Price's designs emphasised natural beauty – old trees, ruins, winding paths and natural slopes – rather than the earlier formal gardens of 'Capability' Brown. A.A. Tait, *The Landscape Garden in Scotland 1735–1835* (Edinburgh, 1980), 120–2, discusses Kinrara.

76 Stoddart, *Local Scenery*, 157.

77 Ibid., 158.

78 Mrs Grant, *Letters*, vol. 2, 142, 4 July 1798.

79 Duchess to Henry Erskine, 1806, quoted in Gordon, *Last Dukes*, 148–9.

80 Ibid.

81 Dixon, 'Kingussie', XI and XII, *Herald*, 10 and 24 September 1971.

82 Stoddart, *Local Scenery*, 156.

83 *Aberdeen Journal*, 21 January 1799; NRAS, 771/574, John to William, 29 January 1799.

84 Smout, 'The landowner and the planned village in Scotland, 1730–1830', in Phillipson and Mitchison (eds), *Scotland in the Age of Improvement* (Edinburgh, 1970), 77–8; Withers, *Gaelic Scotland*, 87; Womack, *Improvement and Romance*, 174.

85 Robertson, *Inverness*, 314.

86 George and Peter Anderson, *Guide to the Highlands and Islands of Scotland* (London, 1834), 86.

87 Irvine, *An Inquiry*, 108; Smout, 'The landowner and the planned village', 78.

88 Duchess to Francis Farquharson, 7 May 1805, quoted in, *An Autobiographical Chapter in the Life of Jane, Duchess of Gordon* (Glasgow, 1864), 11; Duchess to Erskine, 1806, quoted in Gordon, *Last Dukes*, 148–9.

89 Duchess to Farquharson, 7 May 1805, *Autobiographical Chapter*, 9. These letters are particularly bitter, for instance, referring to herself as 'a prisoner, and really upon bread and water', 6.

90 Stoddart, *Local Scenery*, 158.

91 Duchess to Erskine, 1806, Gordon, *Last Dukes*, 148–9.

92 Duchess to Farquharson, 7 May 1805, *Autobiographical Chapter*, 9.

93 Stoddart, *Local Scenery*, 156; Horace Walpole, 1791, quoted in Lady Russell, *Three Generations of Fascinating Women* (London, 1905), 218; NRAS, 771/565, Tod to Captain John, 5 March 1799; Duchess, quoted in Gordon, *Last Dukes*, 120.

94 NRS, GD176/1424, Tack, 1792.

95 NRS, GD176/1285, William Cumming, survey, 1803.

96 NRS, GD1/141/2, Balnespick Tutory, 18 November 1791, 5 February 1792.

97 NRAS, 771/574, John to William, 3 April 1793, 25 November 1795.

98 NRAS, 771/667, Anderson to William, 6 November 1795; R. Carruthers, *Highland Note-book* (Edinburgh, 1843), 311.

99 NRS, GD128/41/10, Alex Clark (factor) to Campbell Mackintosh, 20 May 1792, 15 March 1796; NRS, CS29/7/3, Decreet of Removals, Lt James Macpherson, 12 April 1796.

100 NRS, GD44/37/15/25, Belleville Rental, 1796.

101 NRAS, 771/574, John to William, 14 November 1794; NRAS, 771/565, Tod to Duke, 21 September 1796; NRAS, 771/564, General Grant to William, 23 April 1795.

102 Mrs Grant, *Letters*, vol. 2, 103–4, 20 February 1796.

103 NRAS, 771/126, Charles Gordon to William, 16 June 1787.

104 NRAS, 771/564, General Grant to William, 29 March 1795.

105 NRAS, 771/574, John to William, 3 April 1793, 29 March 1795.

106 NRAS, 771/667, Anderson to William, 1 February 1792, 25 July 1792, 27 July 1792, 3 May 1795.

107 NRAS, 771/565, Carmichael to John, 30 January 1797; NRAS, 771/203, Mackintosh to Ballindalloch, 8 December 1790; Robertson, *Inverness*, 314.

108 NRAS, 771/667, Anderson to William, 8 July 1796.

109 NRS, GD128/31/10, Bankruptcy proceedings, 16 May 1795.

110 NRS, CS236/M/10/7, Minutes of Creditors; NRS, CS236/M/9/9, John Macfarlane.

111 NRAS, 771/574, John to William, 27 March 1796; NRAS, 771/667, Anderson to William, 6 November 1795.

112 NRAS, 771/574, John to William, 3 October 1798; NRAS, 771/667, Anderson to William, 6 November 1795.

113 Cregeen, 'Argyll', 14.

114 Figures compiled primarily from rentals, but numbers cannot be 100 per cent certain because relationships between succeeding Macpherson tacksmen are difficult to prove, though many can be verified from other sources. The broad trend remains a valid indicator.

115 Macpherson, 'Parish Register', 2, 97.

116 Devine, *Scotland's Empire*, 126.

117 The Hon. Mrs Murray of Kensington, *A Companion and Useful Guide to the Beauties of Scotland* (London, 1799), 276; Ker, *Report*, 26.

118 NRAS, 771/206, John to William, 20 February 1790; Atholl Muniments, Box 33/XI/2, Answers for Duke of Atholl, 19 December 1792; Atholl Muniments, Box 59/1/7, Tod to Garth, 24 December 1793.

119 Atholl Muniments, Box 65/9/43, James Stobie to Atholl, 25 January 1791.

120 NRS, GD128/31/10, 1792.

121 NRAS, 771/574, John to William, 11 May 1793.

122 Atholl Muniments, Box 59/1/7, Tod to Garth, 24 December 1793.

123 *OSA* 13, 376; NRS, GD44/51/732/25, Sett of Badenoch, c.1803; *OSA* 3, 37.

124 NRS, GD44/51/732/32/2, Rental, Badenoch, 1799.

125 *OSA* 3, 147, 150.

126 Ibid., 150; James Logan, *The Scottish Gael or Celtic Manners*, vol. 2 (London, 1831), 75.

127 NRS, CS29/7/3, Decreet of Removing, 23 April 1796; Murray, *Companion*, 295.

128 NRS, GD44/34/38, Memorial for Duke, 1792.

129 Macdonald, *Glencoe*, 4, believes most commercial sheep farming was 'undertaken by Highlanders'; Bangor-Jones, 'Clanship to Crofting', 72, similarly for the Sutherland tacksmen; Richards, *Clearances* (2000), 81, also notes that recent research has shown that Highlanders were more 'heavily implicated' in sheep farming and clearance than previously recognised.

130 Mrs Grant, *Letters*, vol. 1, 264, 13 August 1789.

131 *OSA* 3, 36; Murray, *Companion*, 284, 13 August 1799; Mrs Grant, *Letters*, vol. 2, 195, 17 August 1802.

132 Quoted in Durie, 'Unconscious benefactors', 58; *OSA* 13, 376; NRAS, 771/574, John to William, 27 July 1792.

133 NRS, GD44/27/17, Macpherson to Duke, 19 September 1784; Macpherson, 'Tenure, Social Structure, Land Use', 322.

134 Smout, *Environmental History*, 27, 'the full-blown sporting estate was on the market before mid-[nineteenth] century'.

135 NRS, GD128/46/9/1, Invertromie sale, 1793.

136 Smout, *Environmental History*, 23, argues that there was a clash between commercial and aesthetic interests in the Highlands, but this does not actually appear to be the case.

137 *OSA* 13, 378–9.

138 *OSA* 3, 38.

139 Ibid.; *OSA* 13, 376–7.

140 Hall, *Travels*, 435–6.

141 NRS, GD176/1582/2, Cameron to Campbell Mackintosh, 10 March 1792; NRAS, 771/574, John to William, 3 April 1793; NRAS, 771/126, John to William, 16 May 1791.

142 NRAS, 771/574, John to William, 9 May, 27 July 1792.

143 Ibid., 22 December 1793, 14 November 1794.

144 Smout, *Environmental History*, 78, emphasises the role of lairds rather than tacksmen in the 1790s.

145 *OSA* 13, 378.

146 PP, *Report from the Committee upon Illicit Practices used in Defrauding the Revenue* (June 1798), John Young, 176, 404.

147 Cookson, *Armed Nation*, 21; Bulloch, *Territorial Soldiering*, 70.

148 NRS, GD44/47/23, Recruits, Badenoch, November 1790.

149 NRS, GD44/47/12/1, Forsyth to Menzies, 29 October 1790.

150 NRS, GD44/47/23/1, Petition, 1790.

151 NRS, GD44/47/13/3, Amherst to Duke, 24 January 1794; Cookson, *Armed Nation*, 130. Mackillop, *More Fruitful*, 133.

152 NRS, GD44/47/13/16, Captain Finlayson to Menzies, 19 February 1794.

153 NRS, GD44/47/22, Book of Expenditure, 1794.

154 NRS, GD44/47/13/63, Finlayson to Menzies, 7 March 1794.

155 NRS, GD44/47/13/46, Cox and Greenwood, 1794.

156 NRAS, 771/568, Tod to John, 9 June 1795.

157 HFM, Quarter-Session Book, 18 June 1795.

158 AUL, MS1062, Recruitment notice, 22 January 1797.

159 Ibid., Duncan Macpherson of Cluny to Tod, 22 February 1797.

160 NRS, GD44/28/35/28, Petition, McDonald of Crathymore, 1806; NRS, GD44/27/7/52, Petition, Donald Robertson, 1819.

161 Mackillop, *More Fruitful*, 116.

162 NRS, GD44/47/23/1/4, Clothing Estimate; NRS, GD44/47/12/68x, Finlayson to Menzies, 15 August 1793; Prebble, *Mutiny*, 279.

163 NRS, GD44/47/23/2, Roll of men; NRS, GD44/47/12/72, Account of recruiting, June 1793; Bulloch, *Territorial Soldiering*, 146.

164 NRAS, 771/574, John to William, 3 April 1793.

165 NRAS, 771/203, List of Persons, 7 August 1794.

166 Cookson, *Armed Nation*, 24; NRAS, 771/345, John to General Grant, 12 January 1795.

167 NRAS, 771/574, John to William, 21 October 1797. See Prebble, *Mutiny*, and

Kenneth Logue, *Popular Disturbances in Scotland 1780–1815* (Edinburgh, 1979), Chapter 3, for militia riots.

168 *Lloyd's Evening Post*, 29 September 1797.

169 NRS, GD248/129/3/76, Cluny to Sir James Grant, 23 September 1797.

170 AUL, MS1062, Tod to Capt. Cameron, 3 March 1797.

171 NRS, GD44/47/24/2/1, Regimenting the Highland Clans, February 1797.

172 NLS, MS.14838, Private Hints submitted to Mr Dundas, 2 May 1797, 182. Cookson, *Armed Nation*, 35, appears to accept this dubious notion of a society 'impregnable to radical subversion where traditional loyalties continued to be taken seriously'.

173 A. Fairrie, 'The Militia, Fencibles and Non-Regular Forces of Inverness-shire, from the Napoleonic War to 1914', *Loch Ness and Thereabouts* (Inverness, 1991), 76; Mackillop, *More Fruitful*, 65; Cookson, *Armed Nation*, 127. Bulloch, *Territorial Soldiering*, xxxix–xliv, discusses the Clan Levy.

174 NRS, GD44/47/24/2/5, 6, Cluny to Duke, 6 March 1797; Mackintosh to Duke, 16 March 1797.

175 Duke of Portland to Sir James Grant, 9 September 1794, quoted in Fraser, *Chiefs of Grant*, vol. 2, 560–1.

176 NRS, GD248/462/4, John to Sir James Grant, 1 February 1799.

177 *OSA* 13, 382.

178 *OSA* 4, 315.

179 NRS, GD248/451/2, John to James Grant, November 1794.

180 NRAS, 771/574, John to William, 21 October 1792.

181 Ibid., 21 October 1792, 11 May 1793; NRS, GD44/47/23/1/4, Men discharged, 1793.

182 NRAS, 771/574, John to William, 14 November 1794, 30 July 1795, 3 October 1798.

183 NRAS, 771/462, William to General Grant, 23 June 1795.

184 Though doing well, no Badenoch sojourner seems to have made the vast profits of nabobs like Munro of Novar (Mackillop, 'The Returning Nabob', 246–8).

185 Nenadic, 'Military Profession', 76–7.

186 Clements Library, Michigan, Melville papers, Box 9, Gordon to Dundas, 27 February 1795 – thanks to Matthew Dziennik for this source; Cookson, *Armed Nation*, 131, 142.

187 NRS, GD44/47/13/61, Cluny to Duke, 7 March 1794.

188 Mrs Grant, *Letters*, vol. 2, 100, 138. Nenadic, 'Military Profession', 84, explains it was cheaper to send boys to regiments than to boarding schools.

189 NRAS, 771/574, John to William, 17 February 1798; NRAS, 771/668, Will, Captain Evan Macpherson, 13 June 1800.

190 NRS, GD44/47/24/1, Losses, 2 October 1799.

191 NRS, GD44/47/23/2, Petition, December 1799.

192 NRAS, 771/697, John to William, 22 June 1777.

193 Nenadic, 'Military Profession', 90–2; but see Mackillop, *More Fruitful*, 148–50.

194 Calculations are based on previously cited rental and military sources.

195 NRAS, 771/198, John to William, 26 June 1780; NRS, E745/19/3, Petition, John Macpherson, 1766; NRAS, 771/661, Captain Robert Grant to General Grant, 9 December 1771; HAC, GB0232/D351/2/8, Lachlan Mackintosh to William Mackintosh, 15 January 1783.

196 Mackillop, *More Fruitful*, 243.

197 Campbell, *Scotland*, 128, talks of 'grinding poverty'; Cregeen, *Argyll*, xxviii–xxix, of 'progressive poverty'; Gaskell, *Morvern*, 9, of 'penury and squalor'; Mitchison, 'Highland Clearances', 14, even condemned nostalgic memories of life in the Highlands as 'clearly rubbish'.

198 Alexander Fenton, 'Agricultural Change around Loch Ness, Post Culloden', in *Loch Ness*, 39.

199 Thomas Sinton, *The Poetry of Badenoch* (Inverness, 1906), 344; Ronald Black (ed.), *An Laisir* (Edinburgh, 2001), 311–15, 503–5.

200 Campbell, *A Journey from Edinburgh through Parts of North Britain* (London, 1802), 199.

201 NRAS, 771/669, Anderson to William, 8 July 1796.

202 NRAS, 771/574, John to William, 14 November 1794; Stewart, *Sketches*, vol. 1, 365. Sir John Sinclair mentioned men who 'almost starved themselves, in order to send money home' (1795), quoted in Philip Haythornthwaite, *The Armies of Wellington* (London, 1996), 62.

203 NRS, GD44/47/22, Book of Expenditure; Bulloch, *Territorial Soldiering*, 209.

204 Mackillop, *More Fruitful*, 152–3, 231, suggests that in other areas the percentage was lower; see also, Cookson, *Armed Nation*, 142.

205 NRS, GD494/1/23, Robert Grant, 14 March 1795; Whatley, 'Work, Time and Pastimes', 276.

206 Robertson, *Perth*, 343.

207 HFM, Ruthven Quarter-Session Book, 17 July 1795.

208 *OSA* 3, 39.

209 *OSA* 4, 312.

210 Robertson, *Inverness*, 271.

211 NRAS, 771/1036, Wage books.

212 NRAS, 771/574, John to William, 6 February 1797, 17 February 1798.

213 Hall, *Travels*, 417, 439; Irvine, *An Inquiry*, 23, 25.

214 NRAS, 771/334, Mackenzie to Sir James Grant, 1 July 1793; NRAS, 771/574, John to William, 22 November 1793.

215 *OSA* 4, 316.

216 NRAS, 771/344, Ross to General Grant, 29 March 1794; Ross to Sir James Grant, 10 September 1794.

217 NRAS, 771/565, Anderson to John, 26 February 1797.

218 NRAS, 771/574, John to William, 17 February, 23 March 1798.

219 NRS, GD128/41/10, Clark to Campbell Mackintosh, 15 March 1796.

220 Logue, *Disturbances*, Chapters 3, 4; Prebble, *Mutiny*, 279–87, 291–7; Richards, *Clearances* (2000), 86–102. Fencible mutinies were primarily over the fear of being sent overseas. Similarly McGeachy, *Argyll*, 83–5; Bonnyman, *Buccleuch*, 170–1.

221 NRS, GD44/37/15/25, Rental, Belleville, 1796; NRAS, 771/129, Rental, Invereshie, 1796; NRS, CR8/183, Low, Reprt & Valuation', 1803, 61.

222 *OSA* 3, 40; IV, 312; Logue, *Disturbances*, 24, 25, 30; Foyster and Whatley,

'Recovering the Everyday in Early Modern Scotland', in Foyster and Whatley, *A History of Everyday Life*, 12.

223 *OSA* 3, 40; *OSA* 13, 379.

224 Peter Barker (ed.), 'Journal of a Traveller in Scotland 1795–6', *SHR* 36 (1957), 49; NRAS, 2614/233, Harriot Macpherson to Eliza Macpherson, 2 August 1801.

225 Highland Folk Museum, http://www.highlandfolk.com/newtonmore-township.php (accessed 26 January 2014); Lelong and Wood, 'A township through time', in Atkinson, *Townships*, 41–8. Though both sources identify this site as Easter Raitts, it is more likely Mid Raitts.

226 Grant, *Highland Lady*, 208.

227 *OSA* 3, 40–2, 150; *OSA* 4, 39; *OSA* 13, 379–81.

228 Mrs Grant, *Letters*, vol. 1, 221, 5 July 1786; vol. 2, 136, 15 July 1797; Robertson, *Inverness*, 198–9.

229 Sinton, *Poetry*, 13, also 364–70. See also Michael Newton, *Bho Chluaidh gu Calasraid* (Stornoway, 1999), 257–9.

230 Macpherson, *Glimpses*, 236; Rosemary Gibson, *The Boys of the Eilan: Shinty in Newtonmore 1820–1945* (Newtonmore, 2015), 2.

231 Grant, *Letters*, vol. 2, 124, 19 October 1796.

232 Ibid., 115–17, 9 August 1796.

233 NRAS, 771/124, Account, 1795.

234 Grant, *Highland Lady*, 261–3, 267–8. The Floaters' Ball was like a harvest home for the foresters.

235 Hall, *Travels*, 387.

236 Mrs Grant, *Letters*, vol. 2, 117–8, 9 August 1796; 81, 9 September 1794.

237 Sinton, *Poetry*, xxxvi, 11–12, 365; Newton, *Warriors of the World* (Edinburgh, 2009), 312.

238 Sinton, *Poetry*.

239 Newton, *Warriors*, 329.

240 MacLean, *Glengarry*, 82, 10.

241 Richards, 'Agrarian Change', 166; Macinnes, 'Scottish Gaeldom', 80.

242 Devine, *Clearance*, 176; Flinn, *Scottish Population*, 305.

243 *OSA* 3, 37.

244 NRAS, 771/574, John Macpherson to William Macpherson, 13 March 1797.

245 Campbell, *Scotland*, 14.

246 NRS, GD44/34/38, Memorial for Duke, 1792.

247 NRS, GD44/27/5/155x, Anderson to Belleville, 1811; NRS, GD44/27/15/54, View of the Duke of Gordon's Lands, 1811.

248 Mackillop, *More Fruitful*, 155.

249 Macinnes, 'Scottish Gaeldom', 85, argues that eighteenth-century clearances were often spread over several generations.

250 Mrs Grant, *Letters*, vol. 2, 47, 1 December 1792.

251 NRS, CR8/183, Low, Report & Valuation, 1803, 88.

252 Devine, *Clanship to Crofters' War*, 41.

253 Michael Newton, Blog, 'Highland Clearances 3', 25 November 2013, http://virtualgael.wordpress.com/2013/11/25/highland-clearances-3/ (accessed 10 January 2014); Newton, *Bho Chluaidh*, 247–53, 257; Alexander Campbell, *Grampians Desolate* (Edinburgh, 1804), 37.

254 Sinton, *Poetry*, 376.

255 See Christopher Whatley, *Scottish Society 1707–1830* (Manchester, 2000), 244, for out-migration and population.

256 Smout, *Scottish People*, 346.

257 NRAS, 771/574, John to William, 25 November 1795, 6 February 1797, 28 July 1797.

258 Macinnes, 'Scottish Gaeldom', 79.

259 S.G.E Lythe, 'The Tayside Meal Mobs 1772–3', *SHR* 46 (1967), 32.

260 NRAS, 771/574, John to William, 6 February 1797.

261 NRAS, 771/668, Anderson to William, 29 October 1799; NRAS, 771/580, John to William, 12 December 1799; NRAS, 771/558, Anderson to William, 20 January 1800; NRAS, 771/668, Anderson to William, 1 February 1800.

Conclusion

1 Newton, Blog, 'Clearances 3', 25 November 2013.

2 Devine, *Scottish Nation*, 172; MacLean, *Glengarry*, 76.

3 Lynch, *Scotland*, 369.

4 Macinnes, 'Scottish Gaeldom', 70–87.

5 Devine, *Clearance*, 196.

6 NRS, GD44/47/5, Benchar to Ross, 12 September 1778.

7 Campbell, *Scotland*, 14.

8 *OSA* 13, 377, 383; *OSA* 3, 37; Macinnes, 'Scottish Gaeldom', 75.

9 NRAS, 771/565, Anderson to John, 26 February 1797.

10 Mackillop, 'The Returning Nabob', 246–8.

11 NRS, GF44/28/34/28, Duke's estate, 9 June 1750.

12 NRS, GD44/27/11/38x, Tod to Ross, April 1772.

13 NRS, GD44/27/4/31, Arrangement of Lands, *c.*1811.

14 See Macinnes, *Clanship, Commerce*, 170.

15 Boyd Hilton, *A Mad, Bad & Dangerous People: England 1783–1846* (Oxford, 2006), 23.

16 Devine, *Clanship to Crofters' War*, 32.

17 Hilton, *Mad, Bad & Dangerous*, 2.

18 Purser's Instructions, *c.*1785, quoted in Meryl Rutz, 'Salt Horse and Ship's Biscuit', http://www.navyandmarine.org/ondeck/1776salthorse.htm (accessed 24 January 2014), required for approximately 100,000 sailors by 1800.

19 NRAS, 771/580, 11 May 1792; NRS, GD494/1/47, John to George Macpherson, 25 December 1776.

20 Macinnes, *Clanship, Commerce*, 210.

21 Devine, *Clanship to Crofters' War*, 34.

22 NLS, MS2508, Robertson, Journal, 1771, 48; Graham, *Social Life*, 223–4.

23 *NSA* 14, 91.

24 McGeachy, *Argyll*, 67–84, discusses peasant opposition in Argyllshire.

25 See Devine, *Clearance*, 164–5. Macinnes, 'Scottish Gaeldom', 71, agrees that the Gael was 'neither unprepared nor unreceptive to change'. For the 'conservative' view, see Smith, *Jacobite Estates*, 88.

26 'Mr. Kemp's Tour of the Highlands', *Scots Magazine* (Edinburgh), February 1792, 58.

27 NRS, GD44/47/2/75, Macpherson to Tod, 6 April 1778; NRAS, 771/574, John to William, 22 November 1793, 17 February 1798, 23 March 1798.

28 Barrett, 'Regular Revolution', 24; Smout, *Scottish People*, 348; Macinnes, 'Scottish Gaeldom', 79, also discusses enforced downward mobility.

29 Macinnes, *Clanship, Commerce*, 233.

30 See Macpherson, *Glimpses*, 149–51, for a factual account of the incident; Gray, *Legends of the Cairngorms*, 68–79, for the actual legend; and Andrew Wiseman, 'The Black Captain and the Catastrophe of Gaick', in *History Scotland* 14:4 (2014), 30–34, and 14, 5, 30–4, for the origins and spread of the legend.

31 Clan historians, as in Macpherson, *Glimpses*, 152–5, vigorously dispute negative interpretations of his character, though the evidence to the contrary is indisputable.

32 Quoted in Macpherson, *Glimpses*, 155.

Bibliography

PRIMARY SOURCES

ARCHIVES

University of Aberdeen Archive

MS1062   The Badenoch Gordon Family Correspondence.

Highland Archive Centre

GB0232/D351	Balnespick Papers.
GB0232/CH2/1172	Kirk Session, Alvie.
GB0232/CH2/1419	Kirk Session, Kingussie.
GB0232/CH2/437	Presbytery of Abernethy.
GB0232/CH2/271	Synod of Moray.

Highland Folk Museum

Ruthven Quarter Session Book.

Huntingdon Library, San Marino

LO   Loudoun Papers.

National Library of Scotland

MS305	General Bland's Letter Book 1754–6.
MS10691/20	Reports of Captain Teesdale's men, 15 September 1753.
MS1384	Delvine Papers, Lady Cluny.
MS2507	Journal of James Robertson 1767.
MS2508	Journal of James Robertson 1771.
MS2509	James Anderson: Sketch of a ramble through the Highlands of Scotland in the summer of 1818.
MS3271	Journal of George Brown, 1799–1815.

MS3288(iii) f31   Letters of the Blairs of Balthayock.
MS3529   Journal of a tour through some parts of Scotland 1819.
MS14838 f182   Melville Papers, Private hints submitted to Mr Dundas, 2 May
                  1797.
MS29491   Tour in Scotland 1794.
MS29492   Tour through England and Scotland in 1790.

Private Archives

Atholl Estate Papers, Blair Castle.
Sir Thomas Macpherson Archive, Craigdhu House.
Belleville Estate Papers, author's possession.

The National Archives of Scotland

GD1/141   Balnespick Papers.
GD44   Gordon Muniments.
GD80   Macpherson of Cluny Papers.
GD176   Mackintosh Muniments.
GD248   Seafield Papers.
GD128   Fraser-Mackintosh Collection.
E   Forfeited Estate Papers.
E745   Annexed Estate of Cluny.
NG   Board of Trustees for Fisheries, Manufactures and Improvements in
                  Scotland.
CS   Court of Session Papers.
SC29   Inverness Sheriff Court Records.

The National Register of Archives for Scotland

NRAS, 771   Macpherson-Grant of Ballindalloch Papers.

MAPS AND PLANS

Atholl Papers

Map of Perthshire from Mr Stobie's map 1784, copied 1819.

National Library of Scotland

Roy, Military Survey of Scotland, 1747–55.

RCAHMS

SC1082428   George Taylor, Plan of Badenoch.

The National Archives of Scotland

RHP60	The high hill grazings of Lochgarry, *c.*1790.
RHP673	Controverted ground between Cluny and Rannoch, 1767.
RHP1307	Cluny-Belleville march, 1805.
RHP13927	Plan of Bullarden, Aviemore and Grenish, 1809.
RHP1835	George Brown, Badenoch, 1771.
RHP1836	Kinrara, 1771.
RHP1856	Hill grazings of Glen Markie, 1771.
RHP1859	William Taylor, Pitmain, 1771.
RHP2018	Allt an t-Sluie marches, Dalwhinnie, 1770.
RHP2496	Controverted ground in Drumochter, 1770.
RHP2497	Kinrara, 1771.
RHP31711	Controverted ground between Breakachy and Dalwhinnie, 1806.
RHP3398	William Tennoch, The annexed estate of Lochgarry, 1771.
RHP3489	William Tennoch, The annexed estate of Cluny, 1771.
RHP3890	Controverted ground between Banchor and Crathy.
RHP4064	Controverted marches between Lochgarry and Badenoch.
RHP4065	Strone and Banchor, marches, 1767.
RHP4151	Controverted grounds between Raitts and Kerrowmeanach, 1771.
RHP4153	Badenoch–Strathspey march, 1766.
RHP4157	Wester Lynwilg, early 19th century.
RHP9411,	Ballachroan, 1778.
RHP11595	George Brown, Road from Fort William to Pitmain, 1792.
RHP11632	Road from Fort William to Pitmain, 1805.
RHP31702	Controverted ground between Banchor and Strone.
RHP31768	Lochan Uvie, 1765.

PRINTED PRIMARY SOURCES

'A Brieff Account of the Watch Undertaken by Cluny Macpherson MDCCXLIV', *Spalding Club Miscellany*, vol. 2 (Aberdeen, 1842).

Anderson, George and Peter, *Guide to the Highlands and Islands of Scotland* (London, 1834).

An Account of the Principal Pleasures in Scotland (2nd edn, Edinburgh, 1819).

Autobiography of the Rev. Dr Carlyle (Edinburgh, 1860).

Annals of Agriculture and Other useful Arts, vol. 41(London, 1804).

Barker, Peter (ed.), 'Journal of a Traveller in Scotland', *SHR* 36 (1957).

Bell, William, *Dictionary and Digest of the Law of Scotland* (Edinburgh, 1838).

Burt, Edmund, *Letters from a Gentleman in the North of Scotland to his Friend in London*, 2 vols (London, 1754).

Campbell, Alexander, *The Grampians Desolate* (Edinburgh, 1804).

—, *A Journey from Edinburgh through Parts of North Britain* (London, 1802).

Correspondence of the Right Honourable Sir John Sinclair, Bart., vol. 1 (London, 1831).

Defoe, Daniel, *A Tour Through the Island of Great Britain*, vol. 1 (London, 1778).

Documents Relative to the Distress and Famine in Scotland in the Year 1783 in Consequence of the late Harvest and Loss of the Potatoe Crop, Parliamentary Papers, 1846, 37.

Donaldson, James, *General View of the Agriculture of the County of Nairn* (London, 1794).

Forbes, Reverend Robert, *Journals of Episcopal Visitations* (London, 1886).

—, *Lyon in Mourning* (Edinburgh, 1895).

Garnett, Thomas, *Observations on a Tour through the Highlands and Part of the Western Islands of Scotland* (London, 1811).

Geddes, Bishop John, 'Ambula Coram Deo', *Innes Review* 6 (1955).

Grant, Anne, of Laggan, *Letters From The Mountains*, vols 1 and 2 (London, 1845). This edition has been used because it corrects some erroneous dates in earlier editions.

Grant, Elizabeth of Rothiemurchus, *Memoirs of a Highland Lady* (Edinburgh, 1992).

JWG (ed.), *An Autobiographical Chapter in the Life of Jane, Duchess of Gordon* (Glasgow, 1864).

Hall, Reverend James, *Travels in Scotland by an Unusual Route* (London, 1807).

Hanway, Mary Ann, *A Journey to the Highlands of Scotland* (London, 1777).

Hogg, James, *The Shepherd's Guide: Being a Practical Treatise of the Diseases of Sheep* (Edinburgh, 1807).

Irvine, Alexander, *An Inquiry into the Causes and Effects of Emigration from the Highlands and Western Islands of Scotland, with Observations on the Means to be Employed for Preventing it* (Edinburgh, 1802).

Johnson, Samuel, and Boswell, James, *A Journey to the Western Islands of Scotland: The Journal of a Tour to the Hebrides* (London, 1984).

Ker, Andrew, *Report to Sir John Sinclair of the State of Sheep Farming* (Edinburgh, 1791).

Knox, John, *A Tour through the Highlands of Scotland and the Hebride Isles in 1786* (Edinburgh, 1975).

Lang, Andrew (ed.), *The Highlands of Scotland in 1750* (Edinburgh, 1898).

Leyden, John, *Tour in the Highlands and Western Islands, 1800* (Edinburgh, 1903).

Logan, James, *The Scottish Gael or Celtic Manners*, vol. 2 (London, 1831).

Maclean, Reverend Donald, *The Effect of the 1745 Rising on the Social and Economic Conditions of the Highlands* (Edinburgh, n.d.).

Mackintosh of Borlum, William, A Lover of his Country, *An Essay on Ways and Means for Inclosing, Fallowing, Planting, etc.* (Edinburgh, 1729).

Mackintosh of Mackintosh, Aeneas, *Notes Descriptive and Historical* (privately printed, 1892, but written c.1774–1783).

McWilliam, H.D., *The Black Watch Mutiny Records* (London, 1910).

Marshall, William, *General View of the Agriculture of the Central Highlands of Scotland* (London, 1794).

'Mr Kemp's Tour of the Highlands', *Scots Magazine*, February 1792.

Murray, The Hon. Mrs of Kensington, *A Companion and Useful Guide to the Beauties of Scotland* (London, 1799).

—, *A Companion and Useful Guide to the Beauties in the Western Highlands of Scotland, and in the Hebrides*(London, 1805).

Nattes, Claudes, *Scotia Depicta* (London, 1819).

New Statistical Account, vol. 14, http://stat-acc-scot.edina.ac.uk/sas/sas.asp?action=public.

Old Statistical Account, vols 3, 4, 13, http://stat-acc-scot.edina.ac.uk/sas/sas.asp?action=public

Price, Uvedale, *An Essay on the Picturesque, as Compared with the Sublime and the Beautiful; And on the Use of Studying Pictures, for the Purpose of Improving Real Landscape* (London, 1796).

Report from the Commissioners Appointed for Inquiring into the Administration and Practical Operation of the Poor Laws in Scotland: Appendix, Part 2, vol. 21, 1844.

Report of the Committee of the Highland Society of Scotland appointed to Enquire into the Nature and Authenticity of the Poems of Ossian (Edinburgh, 1805).

Robertson, James, *General View of the Agriculture of the County of Inverness* (London, 1813).

—, *General View of the Agriculture in the County of Perth* (Perth, 1799).

Robertson, Reverend Joseph, *The Traveller's Guide: or a Topographical Description of Scotland* (Edinburgh, 1998).

Shaw, Lachlan, *History of the Province of Moray* (Edinburgh, 1775).

—, *The History of the Province of Moray* (new edn in 3 vols, Glasgow, 1882).

Sinclair, Sir John, *General Report of the Agricultural State, and Political Circumstances, of Scotland* (Edinburgh, 1814).

Sinton, Thomas, *By Loch and River* (Inverness, 1910).

—, *The Poetry of Badenoch* (Inverness, 1906).

Skrine, Henry, *Three Successive Tours in the North Part of England and Great Part of Scotland* (London, 1795).

Spalding Club Miscellany Miscellany, vol. 2 (Aberdeen 1842).

Stewart, David, of Garth, *Sketches of the Highlanders of Scotland*, vols 1 and 2 (Edinburgh, 1825).

Stoddart, John, *Local Scenery and Manners in Scotland 1799–1800* (London, n.d.).

'The Journal of an English Medical Officer who attended the Duke of Cumberland's Army', *The Contrast: or Scotland as it was in the Year 1745 and Scotland in the Year 1819* (London, 1825).

The Present Conduct of the Chieftains and Proprietors of Lands in the Highlands of Scotland, By a Highlander (1773).

The Lady's Magazine: or Entertaining Companion for the Fair Sex, vol. 38 (London, November 1807).

Thornton, Colonel Thomas, *A Sporting Tour through the Northern Parts of England and Great Parts of the Highlands of Scotland* (London, 1804).

Walker, John, *An Economical History of the Hebrides and Highlands of Scotland*, vols 1 and 2 (Edinburgh, 1812).

Wight, Alexander, *An Enquiry into the Rise and Progress of Parliament Chiefly in Scotland* (Edinburgh, 1794).

Wight, Andrew, *Present State of Husbandry in Scotland*, vol. 1 (Edinburgh, 1778); vol. 4, part 1 (Edinburgh, 1784).
Young, David, *Agriculture, the Primary Interest of Great Britain* (Edinburgh, 1788).

NEWSPAPERS AND PERIODICALS

Aberdeen Journal.
Caledonian Mercury.
Colonial Patriot.
General Evening Post.
Lady's Magazine.
Lloyd's Evening Post.
London Evening Post.
London Gazette.
Morning Chronicle and London Advertiser.
Public Advertiser.
Scots Magazine.
St James's Chronicle.
Strathspey and Badenoch Herald.
Westminster Journal and London Political Miscellany.
Whitehall Evening Post.
World and Fashionable Advertiser.

SECONDARY SOURCES

ARTICLES AND CHAPTERS

Adam, Margaret, 'The Causes of the Highland Emigrations of 1783–1803', *SHR* 17 (1920), 73–89.
Barrow, G.W.S., 'Badenoch and Strathspey, 1130–1312, Part 1: Secular and Political'; 'Part 2: The Church', *Northern Scotland* 8 (1988), 1–17; *Northern Scotland* 9 (1989), 1–16.
Malcolm Bangor-Jones, 'From Clanship to Crofting: Landownership, Economy and the Church in the Province of Strathnaver', in Baldwin, John (ed.), *The Province of Strathnaver* (Edinburgh, 2000), 35–99.
—, 'Sheep farming in Sutherland in the Eighteenth Century', *The Agricultural History Review* 50:2 (2002), 181–202.
Barrett, John, 'Shaping a Scottish Landscape: Moray's Cooperative Countryside', *History Scotland* 15:4 (2015), 40–5.
Barton, John, 'Cousins at War', *Creag Dhubh* 66 (2014), 71–4.
Boyle, Steve, 'Ben Lawers: An Improvement-Period Landscape on Loch Tayside', in Govan, Sarah (ed), *Medieval or Later Rural Settlement in Scotland: 10 Years On* (Edinburgh, 2003), 17–30.

Busteed, Mervyn, 'The Practice of Improvement in the Irish Context – The Castle Caldwell Estate in County Fermanagh in the Second Half of the Eighteenth Century', *Irish Geography* 33:1 (2000), 15–36.

Campbell, RH, 'The Landed Classes', in Devine, T.M. and Mitchison, R. (eds), *People and Society in Scotland*, vol. 1 (Edinburgh, 1988), 91–108.

Chapman, Earl John, "There Goes the Brave Old Highlander': Malcolm Macpherson of Phones', *Journal of the Society for Army Historical Research* 90 (2012), 1–10.

Clough, Monica, 'The Cromartie Estate, 1660–1784: Aspects of Trade and Organisation', in Baldwin, John (ed.), *Firthlands of Ross and Sutherland* (Edinburgh, 1986), 89–97.

Cole, Richard, 'Young Boswell defends the Highlanders', *Studies in Scottish Literature* 20:1 (1985), 1–10.

Devine, T.M., 'The Rise and Fall of the Illicit Whisky-Making Industry in Northern Scotland, c. 1780–1840', *SHR* 54:2 (1975), 155–77.

Dixon, George, 'The Founding of Kingussie', *Strathspey and Badenoch Herald*, 13 June–17 December 1971.

—, 'Kingussie School, 1770–1820', *Strathspey and Badenoch Herald*, 9 June 1972–11 August 1972.

Dixon, Piers and Fraser, Iain, 'The Medieval and Later Landscape', in *In the Shadow of Bennachie* (Edinburgh, 2007), 137–214.

DMR, 'Highland Notes & Queries', *Northern Chronicle*, 3 November 1909.

Dodgshon, Robert, 'Everyday Structures, Rhythms and Spaces of the Scottish Country-side', in Foyster, Elizabeth, and Whatley, Christopher, *A History of Everyday Life in Scotland, 1600–1800* (Edinburgh, 2010), 27–50.

—, 'Strategies of Farming in the Western Highlands and Islands of Scotland Prior to Crofting and the Clearances', *Economic History Review* 46:4 (1993), 679–701.

—, 'Traditional Field Systems: Their Constraints and Threshholds', in Atkinson, *et al.* (eds), *Townships to Farmsteads* (Glasgow, 2000), 109–16.

Durie, Alastair, '"Unconscious benefactors": Grouse-shooting in Scotland, 1780–1914', *The International Journal of the History of Sport* 15:3 (1998), 57–73.

Dziennik, Matthew P., 'Through an Imperial Prism: Land, Liberty and Highland Loyalism in the War of American Independence', *Journal of British Studies* 50:3 (2011), 332–58.

—, 'Whig Tartan: Material Culture and its Use in the Scottish Highlands, 1746–1815', *Past & Present* 217 (2012), 117–47.

Epperson, Amanda, '"It would be my earnest desire that you all would come": Networks, the Migration Process and Highland Emigration', *SHR* 88:2 (2009), 313–31.

Fairrie, A.A., 'The Militia, Fencibles and Non-Regular Forces of Inverness-shire, from the Napoleonic War to 1914', in *Loch Ness and Thereabouts* (Inverness, 1991), 74–80.

Fenton, Alexander, 'Agricultural Change Around Loch Ness, Post Culloden', in *Loch Ness and Thereabouts* (Inverness, 1991), 32–41.

Finlay, Richard, 'Caledonia or North Britain? Scottish Identity in the Eighteenth Century', in Broun *et al.* (eds), *Image & Identity: The Making and Remaking of Scotland Through the Ages* (Edinburgh, 1998), 143–56.

Fraser-Mackintosh, Charles, 'The Depopulation of Aberarder in Badenoch', *Celtic Magazine* 2 (1877), 418–43.

—, 'The Boycotting of Killihuntly', *TGSI* 24 (1904), 100–19.

Gaffney, Victor, 'Summer Shielings', *SHR* 38:1 (1959), 20–35.

—, 'Shielings of Drumochter', *Scottish Studies* 11:1 (1967), 91–9.

Honeyman, Val, 'A Very Dangerous Place', *SHR* 87:2 (October 2008), 278–305.

Hug & Baccini, 'Physiological Interactions between Highland and Lowland Regions in the Context of Long-Term Resource Management', *Mountain Research and Development* 22:2 (2002), 168–76.

Larsson, Jesper, 'The Expansion and Decline of a Transhumance System in Sweden, 1550–1920', *Historia Agraria* 56 (2012), 11–39.

Lelong, Olivia, and Wood, John, 'A Township Through Time', in Atkinson *et al.* (eds), *Townships to Farmsteads: Rural Settlement Studies in Scotland, England, Wales* (Glasgow, 2000), 40–9.

Lockhart, Douglas, 'Lotted Lands and Planned Villages in North-East Scotland', *The Agricultural History Review* 49:1 (2001), 17–40.

Lythe, 'The Tayside Meal Mobs 1772–73', *SHR* 46:1 (1967), 26–36.

Macinnes, Allan, 'Scottish Gaeldom: The First Phase of Clearance', in Devine, T.M. and Mitchison, R. (eds), *People and Society in Scotland*, vol. 1 (Edinburgh, 1988), 70–90.

Mackellar, Mary Cameron, 'The Sheiling: Its Traditions and Songs', *TGSI* 14 (1887–8), 135–52.

McKichan, Finlay, 'Lord Seaforth and Highland Estate Management in the First Phase of Clearance (1783–1815)', *SHR* 86:1 (2007), 50–68.

Mackillop, Andrew, 'The Highlands and the Returning Nabob: Sir Hector Munro of Novar, 1760–1807', in Marjory Harper (ed.), *Emigrant Homecomings: The Return Movement of Emigrants 1600–2000* (Manchester, 2005), 233–61.

—, 'Highland Estate Change and Tenant Emigration', in Devine, T.M. and Young, J.R. (eds) *Eighteenth Century Scotland: New Perspectives* (East Linton, 1999), 237–58.

MacPhail, J.R.N. (ed.), 'Letters by Mrs Grant of Laggan Concerning Highland Affairs in the Eighteenth Century', in *Scottish History Society* 26 (Edinburgh, 1896), 249–330.

Macpherson, Alan G., 'An Old Highland Parish Register: Survivals of Clanship and Social Change in Laggan, Inverness-shire, 1775–1854', Part 1, *Scottish Studies* 11 (1967), 149–92; Part 2, *Scottish Studies* 12 (1968), 81–111.

—, 'Migration Fields in a Traditional Highland Community, 1350–1850', *Journal of Historical Geography* 10:1 (1984), 1–14.

—, 'Daniel Macpherson: Highland Emigrant, Loyalist Soldier, Gasperisan Merchant-settler and Canadian Seigneur', *Canadian Genealogist* 6:2 (1984), 105–7.

—, and MacIntyre, Alistair K., 'Lieut-Gen John Macintyre: The Laird of Balavil that never was', *Creag Dhubh* (2007), 71–7.

Macpherson, Alexander, 'Gleanings from the Cluny Charter Chest III', *TGSI* 21 (1896–7), 391–452.

Milburn, Paula (ed.), *Discovery and Excavation in Scotland* 13 (2012).

Miller, Donald, 'Land Use by Summer Shielings', *Scottish Studies* 11 (1967), 193–221.

Mitchison, Rosalind, 'The Highland Clearances', *Scottish Economic & Social History* 1 (1981), 4–24.

Morton, Graeme, 'What if? The Significance of Scotland's Missing Nationalism in the Nineteenth Century', in Broun, D. *et al.* (eds), *Image & Identity: The Making and Remaking of Scotland Through the Ages* (Edinburgh, 1998), 157–76.

Nenadic Stana, 'The Impact of the Military Profession on Highland Gentry Families 1730–1830', *SHR* 85:1 (April 2006), 75–99.

—, 'Necessities: Food and Clothing in the Long Eighteenth Century', in Foyster, E., and Whatley, C., *A History of Everyday Life in Scotland, 1600–1800*, 137–63.

Noble, Ross, 'Turf-walled Houses in the Central Highlands', *Folk Life* 22 (1983–4), 68–83.

Ramsay, William, 'Construction, Contention and Clearance: Life in Badenoch in the Eighteenth Century', *TGSI* 63 (2004), 337–57.

—, 'Bad Times within the Bounds of Badenoch: The Trial of Edward Shaw MacIntosh of Borlum, 1773', *TGSI* 59 (1996), 129–47.

Rampini, Charles, 'The Correspondence of an Old Scotch Factor', *The Scottish Review* 17 (1891), 114–39.

Richards, Eric, 'Agrarian Changes, Modernisation and the Clearances', in Omand, Donald (ed.), *The Ross and Cromarty Book* (Golspie, 1984), 159–82.

Ross, Alasdair, 'Improvement on the Grant Estates in Strathspey in the Later Eighteenth Century: Theory, Practice, and Failure?', in Hoyle, Richard W. (ed.), *Custom, Improvement and the Landscape in Early Modern Britain* (Farnham, 2011), 289–311.

—, 'Two Surveys of Vernacular Buildings and Tree Usage in the Lordship of Strathavon, Banffshire, 1585x1612', *Miscellany of the Scottish History Society* 14 (2010), 1–60.

Shaw, Alexander Mackintosh, 'Brigadier Mackintosh of Borlum', *Celtic Magazine* 2 (1877), 250–95.

Smith, Annette, 'Two Highland Inns', *SHR* 56:2 (1977), 184–8.

—, 'The Work of the Forfeited Estates Board Around Loch Ness', *Loch Ness and Thereabouts* (Inverness, 1991), 56–73.

Smout, T.C., 'Famine and Famine Relief in Scotland', in Cullen, L., and Smout, T.C. *Comparative Aspects of Scottish and Irish Economic and Social History 1600–1900* (Edinburgh, 1977), 21–31.

—, 'The History of the Rothiemurchus Woods in the Eighteenth Century', *Northern Scotland* 15 (1995), 19–31.

Walton, Kenneth, 'Climate and Famines in North East Scotland', *Scottish Geographical Magazine* 68:1 (1952), 13–21.

Whatley, Christopher, 'Work, Time and Pastimes', in Foyster, Elizabeth, and Whatley, Christopher, *A History of Everyday Life in Scotland, 1600–1800* (Edinburgh, 2010), 273–303.

Whittington, Graeme, 'The Little Ice Age and Scotland's Weather', *Scottish Geographical Magazine* 101:3 (1985), 174–8.

Withers, Charles, 'The Historical Creation of the Scottish Highlands', in Donnachie, I. and Whatley, C. (eds), *The Manufacture of Scottish History* (Edinburgh, 1992), 143–56.

Wilson, Rob, *et al.*, 'Reconstructing Holocene Climate from Tree Rings: The Potential for a Long Chronology from the Scottish Highlands', *The Holocene* 22:1 (2012), 3–11.

BIBLIOGRAPHY

BOOKS

Adams, Ian (ed.), *Peter May Land Surveyor 1749–1793* (Edinburgh, 1979).

Anderson, Isabel, *An Inverness Lawyer and His Sons, 1796–1878* (Aberdeen, 1900).

Anderson, R.D., *Education and the Scottish People 1750–1918* (Oxford, 1995).

Arnold, Denis, *Scottish Cattle Droving and the Hambleton Drove Road* (Osmotherley, 1982).

Atkinson, John, Banks, Iain, MacGregor, Gavin (eds), *Townships to Farmsteads* (Glasgow, 2000).

Bailyn, Bernard, *Voyagers to the West: A Passage in the Peopling of America on the Eve of the Revolution* (New York, 1986).

Bangor-Jones, Malcolm, *The Assynt Clearances* (Dundee, 1998).

Barrett, John, *The Making of a Scottish Landscape – Moray's Regular Revolution* (Croydon, 2015).

Basu, Paul, *Highland Homecomings* (New York, 2007).

Bennett, Margaret, *Oatmeal and the Catechism* (Edinburgh, 1998).

Bil, Albert, *The Shieling 1600–1840* (Edinburgh, 1990).

Bingham, Caroline, *Behind the Highland Line* (London, 1991).

Bishop, Bruce, *Lost Badenoch and Strathspey* (Edinburgh, 2011).

Black, Ronald (ed.), *An Laisir* (Edinburgh, 2001).

Blundel, Odo, *The Catholic Highlands of Scotland* (Edinburgh, 1917).

Bonnyman, Brian, *The Third Duke of Buccleuch and Adam Smith: Estate Management and Improvement in Enlightenment Scotland* (Edinburgh, 2014).

Broun, Dauvit, Finlay, R.J. and Lynch, Michael (eds), *Image and Identity: The Making and Re-making of Scotland Through the Ages* (Edinburgh, 1998).

Buchan, James, *Crowded with Genius: The Scottish Enlightenment: Edinburgh's Moment of the Mind* (New York, 2003).

Bulloch, John Malcolm, *The House of Gordon* (Aberdeen, 1903).

—, *Territorial Soldiering in the North-East of Scotland during 1759–1814* (Aberdeen, 1914).

Bumsted, J.M., *The People's Clearance: Highland Emigration to British North America, 1770–1815* (Edinburgh, 1982).

Burnett, John, *The Making of the Modern Scottish Highlands 1939–1965* (Dublin, 2011).

Burnett, Allan and Linda (eds), *Blind Ossian's Fingal* (Edinburgh, 2011).

Cameron, Viola, *Emigrants from Scotland to America 1774–75* (Baltimore, 1976).

Campbell, Roy, *Scotland since 1707* (Glasgow, 1985).

Campey, Lucille H., *An Unstoppable Force: The Scottish Exodus to Canada* (Edinburgh, 2008).

—, *The Scottish Pioneers of Upper Canada, 1784–1855* (Toronto, 2005).

Carrurthers, Robert, *The Highland Notebook* (Edinburgh, 1843).

Chapman, Earl John (ed.), *Letters from North America 1758–1761: The Private Correspondence of Parson Robert Macpherson* (Montreal, 2013).

— and McCulloch, Ian, *A Bard of Wolfe's Army: James Thompson, Gentleman Volunteer 1733–1830* (Montreal, 2010).

Clyde, Robert, *From Rebel to Hero* (East Linton, 1995).

Craik, Henry, *A Century of Scottish History* (Edinburgh, 1901).

Cregeen, Eric, *Argyll Estate Instructions 1771–1805* (Edinburgh, 1964).

Cullen, Karen, *Famine in Scotland: The 'Ill Years' of the 1690s* (Edinburgh, 2010).

Cullen, L.M. and Smout, T.C., *Comparative Aspects of Scottish and Irish Economic and Social History 1600–1900* (Edinburgh, 1977).

Dawson, A.G., *So Foul and Fair a Day: A History of Scotland's Weather and Climate* (Edinburgh, 2009).

Devine, T.M., *Clanship to Crofters' War: The Social Transformation of the Scottish Highlands* (Manchester, 1994).

—, *Clearance and Improvement: Land, Power and People in Scotland 1700–1900* (Edinburgh, 2006).

—, *Scotland's Empire: The Origins of the Global Diaspora* (London, 2004).

—, *Scottish Emigration and Scottish Society* (Edinburgh, 1992).

—, *The Great Highland Famine* (Edinburgh, 1988)

—, *The Scottish Nation* (London, 1999).

— and Mitchison R. (eds), *People and Society in Scotland, 1760–1830* (Edinburgh, 1988).

— and Young, J.R. (eds), *Eighteenth Century Scotland: New Perspectives* (East Linton, 1999).

Dixon, Piers, *Mar Lodge Estate, Grampian: An Archaeological Survey* (Edinburgh, 1995).

Dobson, David, *The People of Inverness-shire: Scottish Emigration to Colonial America 1607–1785* (Georgia, 1994).

Dodgshon, Robert, *From Chiefs to Landlords* (Edinburgh, 1998).

—, *Land and Society in Early Scotland* (Oxford, 1981).

—, *The Age of the Clans* (Edinburgh, 2002).

Donnachie, Ian, *The Seventeenth Century in the Highlands* (Inverness, 1986).

Donnachie, Ian and Whatley, Christopher (eds), *The Manufacture of Scottish History* (Edinburgh, 1992).

Durie, Alastair, *Scotland for the Holidays: Tourism in Scotland c1780–1939* (East Linton, 2003).

Dyer, Michael, *Men of Property and Intelligence: The Scottish Electoral System prior to 1884* (Aberdeen, 1996).

Fagan, Brian, *The Little Ice Age: How Climate made History* (New York, 2002).

Fenton, Alexander, *Scottish Country Life* (Edinburgh, 1976).

Ferguson, William, *The Identity of the Scottish Nation* (Edinburgh, 1998).

—, *Scotland 1689 to the Present* (Edinburgh, 1968).

Fergusson, Alexander, *Henry Erskine: His Kinsfolk and Times* (Edinburgh, 1882).

Flinn, M., *Scottish Population History* (Cambridge, 1977).

Foreman, Amanda, *Georgiana, Duchess of Devonshire* (London, 1999).

Foster, Stephen, *A Private Empire* (Sydney, 2011).

Forsyth, William, *In the Shadow of the Cairngorms* (Lynwilg, 1999).

Foyster, Elizabeth and Whatley, Christopher (eds), *A History of Everyday Life in Scotland, 1600–1800* (Edinburgh, 2010).

Franklin, T. Bedford, *A History of Scottish Farming* (Edinburgh, 1952).

Fraser, G.M., *The Strathspey Mutineers* (Kinloss, 2003).

Fraser, William, *The Chiefs of Grant*, vol. 2 (Edinburgh, 1883).

Fraser-Mackintosh, Charles, *Antiquarian Notes* (Inverness, 1897).

—, *Dunachton Past and Present* (Inverness, 1866).

—, *Letters of Two Centuries* (Inverness, 1890).

Fry, Michael, *Wild Scots* (London, 2005).

Gaffney, Victor, *The Lordship of Strathavon* (Aberdeen, 1960).

Gardyne, Lt-Col C. Greenhill, *The Life of a Regiment: The History of the Gordon Highlanders* (Edinburgh, 1901).

Gaskill, Philip, *Morvern Transformed: A Highland Parish in the Nineteenth Century* (Cambridge, 1980).

Gaskill, Howard (ed.), *The Poems of Ossian* (Edinburgh, 1996).

—, *The Reception of Ossian in Europe* (London, 2004).

Gibson, Robert, *Highland Cowboys* (Edinburgh, 2010).

Gibson, Rosemary, *The Boys of the Eilan: Shinty in Newtonmore 1820–1945* (Newtonmore, 2015).

Glen, Anne, *The Cairngorm Gateway* (Dalkeith, 2002).

Gordon, George, *The Last Dukes of Gordon and their Consorts, 1753–1864* (Aberdeen, 1980).

Graham, Henry Grey, *Social Life in the Eighteenth Century* (Edinburgh, 1964).

Graham, Ian, *Colonists from Scotland to North America 1707–1783* (New York, 1956).

Grant, I.F., *Along a Highland Road* (London, 1980).

—, *An Economic History of Scotland* (London, 1934).

—, *Every-day Life on an Old Highland Farm* (London, 1924).

—, *Highland Folk Ways* (London, 1997).

— and Cheape, Hugh, *Periods in Highland History* (London, 1987).

Gray, Affleck, *Legends of the Cairngorms* (Edinburgh, 1987).

Gray, Malcolm, *The Highland Economy 1750–1850* (Edinburgh, 1957).

—, *The Statistical Account of Scotland*, vol. 18, Introduction (Wakefield, 1981).

Haldane, A.R.B., *The Drove Roads of Scotland* (Plymouth, 1973).

Hamilton, Douglas, *Scotland, the Caribbean and the Atlantic World, 1750–1820* (Manchester, 2005).

Handley, James, *Scottish Farming in the 18th Century* (London, 1953).

Harper, J.R., *The Fraser Highlanders* (Montreal, 1979).

Harper, Marjory, *Adventurers and Exiles: The Great Scottish Exodus* (London, 2004).

— (ed.), *Emigrant Homecomings* (Manchester, 2005).

— and Vance, Michael, *Myth, Migration and the Making of Memory: Scotia and Novia Scotia, c1700–1900* (Edinburgh, 2000).

Haythornthwaite, Philip, *The Armies of Wellington* (London, 1996).

Hilton, Boyd, *A Mad, Bad, & Dangerous People: England 1783–1846.* (Oxford, 2006).

HMSO, *The Climate of Scotland* (Edinburgh, 1989).

Holden, Timothy, *The Archaeology of Scottish Thatch* (Edinburgh, 1998).

Holmes, Richard, *Redcoat: The British Soldier in the Age of Horse and Musket* (London, 2002).

Hunter, James, *Dance Called America* (Edinburgh, 1994).

—, *On the Other Side of Sorrow: Nature and People in the Scottish Highlands* (Edinburgh, 2014).

—, *Scottish Exodus: Travels Among a Worldwide Clan* (Edinburgh, 2007).

—, *The Last of the Free: A Millennial History of the Highlands and Islands of Scotland* (Edinburgh, 1999).

—, *The Making of the Crofting Community* (Edinburgh, 1995, first published 1976, and 2nd edn, 2000).

Jonsonn, Frederick Albritton, *Enlightenment's Frontier: The Scottish Highlands and the Origins of Environmentalism* (New Haven, 2013).

Kyd, James Grey, *Scottish Population Statistics* (Edinburgh, 1975).

Lawson, Philip, *The East India Company* (London, 1993).

Lelong, Olivia, *Excavations at the Deserted Settlement of Easter Raitts, Badenoch, 1997: Interim Report* (Aberdeen, 1997).

—, *Excavations at the Deserted Settlement of Easter Raitts, Badenoch, 1998: Interim Report* (Aberdeen, 1998).

Leneman, Leah, *Living in Atholl* (Edinburgh, 1986).

Lenman, Bruce, *Integration, Enlightenment, and Industrialisation. Scotland 1746–1832* (London, 1981).

Lewis, Judith, *Sacred to Female Patriotism: Gender, Class and Politics in Late Georgian Britain* (London, 2003).

Livingstone, Alastair, Aikman, Christian, Hart, Betty, *No Quarter Given: The Muster Roll of Prince Charles Edward Stuart's Army, 1745–46* (Aberdeen, 1984).

Logue, Kenneth, *Popular Disturbances in Scotland, 1780–1815* (Edinburgh, 1979).

Lynch, Michael, *Scotland: A New History* (London, 1992).

Lythe, S.G.E. and Butt, John, *An Economic History of Scotland 1100–1939* (Glasgow, 1975).

McCulloch, Ian Macpherson, *Highlanders in the French-Indian War* (Oxford, 2008).

—, *Sons of the Mountains: The Highland Regiments in the French & Indian War, 1756–1767* (New York 2006).

Macdonald, Iain S., *Glencoe and Beyond: The Sheep Farming Years 1780–1830* (Edinburgh, 2005).

McGeachy, Robert, *Argyll, 1730–1850* (Edinburgh, 2005).

McGilvary, George, *East India Patronage and the British State* (London, 2008).

Macinnes, Allan, *Clanship, Commerce and the House of Stuart 1603–1788* (East Linton, 1996).

Mackenzie, Alexander, *The History of the Highland Clearances* (Glasgow, 1883).

MacKillop, Andrew, *More Fruitful than the Soil: Army, Empire and the Scottish Highlands 1715–1815* (East Linton, 2000).

Mackintosh, A.M., *The Mackintoshes and Clan Chattan* (Edinburgh 1903).

Mackintosh, H.B., *The Northern or Gordon Fencibles 1778–1787* (privately printed, 1929).

MacLean, Marianne, *The People of Glengarry: Highlanders in Transition, 1745–1820* (Montreal, 1991).

Macpherson, Alan G., *A Day's March to Ruin* (Clan Macpherson Association, 1996).

Macpherson, Alexander, *Captain John Macpherson of Ballachroan and the Gaick Catastrophe of the Christmas of 1799 (OS): A Counterblast* (Kingussie, 1900).

—, *Glimpses of Church and Social Life in the Highlands in Olden Times* (Edinburgh, 1893).

Macpherson, William Charles, *Soldiering in India, 1764–1787* (Edinburgh, 1928).

MacQueen, John, *Progress and Poetry: The Enlightenment and Scottish Literature* (Edinburgh, 1982).

Marshall, Meryl, *Glen Feshie: The History and Archaeology of a Highland Glen* (Fort William, 2005, 2nd edition 2013).

Mathieson, Robert, *The Survival of the Unfittest: The Highland Clearances and the End of Isolation* (Edinburgh, 2000).

Meikle, Henry, *Scotland and the French Revolution* (Glasgow, 1912).

Mitchell, Alison, *Pre-1855 Gravestone Inscriptions from Speyside* (Scottish Genealogy Society, 1977).

Mitchison, Rosalind, *A History of Scotland* (London, 1982).

Murray, D., *The York Buildings Company* (Edinburgh, 1973).

Nenadic, Stana, *Lairds and Luxury: The Highland Gentry in Eighteenth-century Scotland* (Edinburgh, 2007).

Newton, Michael, *Bho Chluaidh gu Calasraid: From the Clyde to Callander* (Stornoway, 1999).

— (ed.), *Duthchas nan Gaidheal: Collected Essays of John Macinnes* (Edinburgh, 2010).

—, *The Warriors of the World* (Edinburgh, 2009).

Omand, Donald (ed.), *The Ross and Cromarty Book* (Golspie, 1984).

Ormond, Richard, *The Monarch of the Glen: Landseer in the Highlands* (Edinburgh, 2005).

Paton, Henry, *The Mackintosh Muniments, 1442–1820* (privately printed, 1903).

Philipson, N. and Mitchison, R. (eds), *Scotland in the Age of Improvement* (Edinburgh, 1970).

Prebble, John, *Mutiny: Highland Regiments in Revolt, 1743–1804* (London, 1977).

—, *The Highland Clearances* (London, 1969).

Rackwitz, Martin, *Travels to Terra Incognita: The Scottish Highlands and Hebrides in Early Modern Travellers'Accounts c.1600–1800* (Berlin, 2007).

Richards, Eric, *A History of the Highland Clearances*, vol.1 (London, 1982); vol. 2 (London, 1985).

—, *A History of the Highland Clearances* (Cambridge, 2000).

—, *Debating the Highland Clearances* (Edinburgh, 2007).

—, *Patrick Sellar* (Edinburgh, 1999).

—, *The Leviathan of Wealth* (London, 1973).

— and Clough, Monica, *Cromartie: Highland Life 1650–1914* (Aberdeen, 1989).

Richardson, Ian, *Laggan: Past and Present* (Laggan, 1990).

Russell, Helen, *The Past Around Us: History and the Parish of Alvie and Insh* (Nairn, 1995).

Russell, Lady, *Three Generations of Fascinating Women* (London, 1905).

Sanderson, Margaret, *Scottish Rural Society in the Sixteenth Century* (Edinburgh, 1982).

Saunders, Bailey, *The Life and Letters of James Macpherson* (London, 1894).
Sawyers, June Skinner, *Bearing the People Away: The Portable Highland Clearances Companion* (Cape Breton, 2013).
Scarlett, Meta, *In the Glens Where I was Young* (Inverness, 1988).
Skelton, J. *Speybuilt: The Story of a Forgotten Industry* (Garmouth, 1994).
Slimon, Campbell, *Stells Stools Strupag* (Laggan Heritage, 2007).
Smith, Annette, *Jacobite Estates of the Forty-five* (Edinburgh, 1982).
Smout, T.C., *A History of the Scottish People 1560–1830* (London, 1970).
—, *Exploring Environmental History* (Edinburgh, 2011).
— (ed.), *People and Woods in Scotland* (Edinburgh, 2003).
— (ed.), *Scottish Woodland History* (Dalkeith, 1997).
— (ed.), *Understanding the Historical Landscape in its Environmental Setting* (Dalkeith, 2002).
— and Lambert, R.A., *Rothiemurchus: Nature and People on a Highland Estate 1500–2000* (Dalkeith, 1999).
—, MacDonald, A.R., Watson, Fiona, *A History of the Native Woodlands of Scotland, 1500–1920* (Edinburgh, 2007).
Stell, Geoffrey, Shaw, John, Storrier, Susan (eds), *Scotland's Buildings* (East Linton, 2003).
Stewart, W.G., *Lectures on the Mountains or Highlands and Highlanders*, series 1 and 2 (London, 1860).
Stewart, Katherine, *Women of the Highlands* (Edinburgh, 2006).
Storrier, Susan (ed.), *Scotland's Domestic Life* (Edinburgh, 2003).
Symon, J.A., *Scottish Farming Past and Present* (Edinburgh, 1959).
Tait, A.A., *The Landscape Garden in Scotland 1735–1835* (Edinburgh, 1980).
Taylor, William, *The Military Roads of Scotland* (London, 1976).
Walker, Bruce, *Earth Structures and Construction in Scotland* (Edinburgh, 1996).
—, *Scottish Turf Construction* (Edinburgh, 2006).
Wharton, Grace, *The Queens of Society* (London, 1861).
Whatley, Christopher, *Scottish Society 1707–1830: Beyond Jacobitism, towards Industrialisation* (Manchester, 2000).
Whyte, Ian, *Agriculture and Society in 17th Century Scotland* (John Donald, 1979).
Whyte, Donald: *Scottish Emigration to Canada*, 4 vols (Ontario, 1986).
Wills, Virginia (ed.), *Reports on the Annexed Estates 1755–1769* (Edinburgh, 1973).
Withers, Charles W.J., *Gaelic Scotland: The Transformation of a Culture Region* (London, 1988).
—, *Urban Highlanders* (East Linton, 1998).
Withrington, Donald J., *Going to School* (Edinburgh, 1997).
Womack,Peter, *Improvement and Romance: Constructing the Myth of the Highlands* (London, 1989).
Youngson, A.J., *After the '45* (Edinburgh, 1973).
—, *Beyond the Highland Line* (London, 1974).

BIBLIOGRAPHY

UNPUBLISHED SOURCES

M Litt

Hammond, Maureen, 'Textile Manufacturing in Badenoch', University of the Highlands and Islands, 2014.

M Phil

Michnowicz, Sabina, 'The Laki Fissure Eruption and UK Mortality Crises of 1783–1784', University of Aberystwyth, 2011.

PhD

Barrett, John, 'A Regular Revolution: Cooperation, Change and Classification in the Moray Landscape 1760–1840', University of Aberdeen, 2013.

Dziennik, Matthew P., 'The Fatal Land: War, Empire, and the Highland Soldier in British America, 1756–1783', University of Edinburgh, 2011.

Lindfield-Ott, Kristin, 'See Scot and Saxon Coalesc'd in One': James Macpherson's *The Highlander* in its Intellectual and Cultural Contexts, with an Annotated Text of the Poem, University of St. Andrews, 2011.

Maclean of Glensanda, James, 'The Early Political Careers of James "Fingal" Macpherson and Sir John Macpherson', University of Edinburgh, 1967.

Macpherson, Alan G., 'Tenure, Social Structure, Land Use: Scottish Highlands 1747–1784', McGill University, 1969.

Robertson, Barry, 'Continuity and Change in the Scottish Nobility: The House of Huntly, 1603–1690', University of Aberdeen, 2007.

Alan Thomson, 'The Scottish Timber Trade, 1680–1800', University of St Andrews, 1990.

PAPERS

George Dixon, 'The Highland "Clearances"?', paper read to Stirling University History Society, 17 October 1983.

WEBSITES

Buntgen, *et al.*, 'Filling the Eastern European Gap in Millennium-long Temperature Reconstructions', www.pnas.org/cgi/doi/10.1073/pnas.1211485110 (accessed 18 January 2013).

Burns, Robert, 'The Highland Journal, 1787', http://www.burnsmuseum.org.uk/ collections/transcript/3373, 12 (accessed 23 June 2013).

Fagan, Brian, 'The Little Ice Age: The Big Chill', www.youtube.com/watch?v=QFQHTdn8egw (accessed 21 January 2013).

Feng, Alice, 'Holy Cow! Cheese and Cultural Identity in the Swiss Alps', http://alicefeng.net/?p=438 (accessed 27 June 2012).

Morrison, Arnold, 'Some Scottish Sources on Militias, Fencibles and Volunteer Corps.
1793–1800', www.scribd.com/doc/68100606/The-Defence-of-Scotland-Militias-
Fencibles-and-Volunteer-Corps1793–1820 (accessed 23 September 2013).

Newton, Michael, http://virtualgael.wordpress.com/2013/11/25/highland-clearances-3/
(accessed 10 January 2014).

Rutz, Meryl, 'Salt Horse and Ship's Biscuit', http://www.navyandmarine.org/ondeck/
1776salthorse.htm (accessed 24 January 2014),

Thomson, Derick, *Oxford Dictionary of National Biography*, 'James Macpherson',
www.oxforddnb.com/view/article/17728?docPos=3 (accessed 5 December 2013).

Wilson, Rob, 'The Scottish Pine Project', www.st-
andrews.ac.uk/~rjsw/ScottishPine(accessed 22 January 2013).

www.metoffice.gov.uk (accessed 21 November 2012).

www.highlandfolk.com/newtonmore-township.php (accessed 26 January 2014).

www.lochiel.net/archives/arch189.html (accessed 29 September 2015).

Index